Midlife Crisis

Midlife Crisis

The Feminist Origins of a Chauvinist Cliché

Susanne Schmidt

THE UNIVERSITY OF CHICAGO PRESS

CHICAGO AND LONDON

The University of Chicago Press, Chicago 60637
The University of Chicago Press, Ltd., London
© 2020 by The University of Chicago

Published 2020

29 28 27 26 25 24 23 22 21 20   1 2 3 4 5

ISBN-13: 978-0-226-68685-1 (cloth)
ISBN-13: 978-0-226-63714-3 (paper)
ISBN-13: 978-0-226-68699-8 (e-book)
DOI: https://doi.org/10.7208/chicago/9780226686998.001.0001

Library of Congress Cataloging-in-Publication Data

Names: Schmidt, Susanne (Historian), author.
Title: Midlife crisis : the feminist origins of a chauvinist cliché / Susanne
    Schmidt.
Description: Chicago ; London : University of Chicago Press, 2020. |
    Includes bibliographical references and index.
Identifiers: LCCN 2019034291 | ISBN 9780226686851 (cloth) | ISBN
    9780226637143 (paperback) | ISBN 9780226686998 (ebook)
Subjects: LCSH: Sheehy, Gail. Passages. | Midlife crisis. | Midlife
    crisis—History. | Feminist psychology—United States—History. |
    Psychology—United States—History—20th century.
Classification: LCC BF724.65.M53 S35 2020 | DDC 155.6/6—dc23
LC record available at https://lccn.loc.gov/2019034291

For FL

Contents

1

Introduction

One might not have expected the history of the midlife crisis to begin with a shocking scene from a notorious massacre, and still less that a woman would tell the tale. "I was talking to a young boy in Northern Ireland where I was on assignment for a magazine when a bullet blew his face off. British armored cars began to plow into the crowd. Paratroopers jackknifed out of the tanks with high-velocity rifles. They sprayed us with steel. The boy without a face fell on top of me."[1] On Bloody Sunday, January 30, 1972, British soldiers killed and wounded civilians protesting against internment. Gail Sheehy, a journalist for *New York* magazine, was in Derry to report on the role of women in the IRA and the movement for Irish Home Rule.[2] Four years later, a large international audience came to know Sheehy as the author of *Passages: Predictable Crises of Adult Life* (1976), the best-seller with which, I shall argue, the "midlife crisis" entered popular culture and the social sciences in the United States and abroad. The book opens with a description of Sheehy's own breakdown after Bloody Sunday. She attributed her condition in part to the trauma of Northern Ireland and in part to the imperative to reassess and change one's life when approaching the age of forty. Sheehy decided, she tells us, "to find out everything I could about this thing called *midlife crisis*."[3]

A favorite gendered cliché, the idea of midlife crisis conjures up images of male indulgence and irresponsibility—an affluent, middle-aged man speeding off in a red Corvette with a woman half his age—but it was first successfully presented as a concept about women's rights. Sheehy's own "midlife crisis" was expressed in a nervous breakdown that stretched over six months and ten pages in her book. This was tied to her observation of two political events, the traumatizing Bloody Sunday and the disastrous Democratic National Convention of July 10–13, 1972, at which tensions in

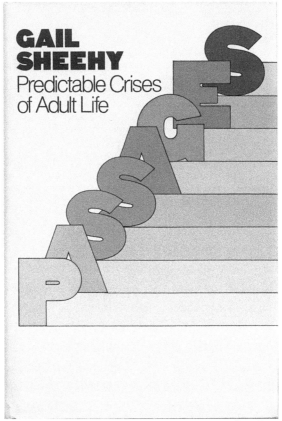

FIG. 1.1. Gail Sheehy's *Passages: Predictable Crises of Adult Life* (1976), front cover. Sheehy's best-seller is remembered for its Milton Glaser cover: a rainbow-colored flight of stairs. Bold colors and jumbo letters marked its publication as an event while also signifying seriousness.

the women's movement paralyzed the National Women's Political Caucus (NWPC) at its first national convention.[4] Sheehy did not refer again to that experience in *Passages*, which sought to establish the midlife crisis as a more universal phenomenon. As a literary device, autobiographical references were supposed to make the author relatable, but the danger Sheehy described would have been foreign to most of her readers. While depicting herself as a war correspondent and political commentator may have established her credibility and standing as a writer, the detailed rendering of her collapse potentially risked producing the opposite effect: "They'll think you're crazy," her copy editor warned.[5]

Above all, there was a certain uneasiness to the analogy between the deadly conflict in Northern Ireland and the midlife crisis of a jet-setting journalist. It recalled descriptions, by Ernest Hemingway and others, of war as a rite of passage of male personality development—only that Sheehy spoke of women. And that was the point. By situating the midlife crisis in the context of Bloody Sunday and the NWPC, Sheehy introduced it as a matter of women gaining consciousness and fighting for their rights—be it with arms, like in the IRA, or by the long march through the institutions begun at the Democratic convention. "The personal is political."[6]

Sheehy used the term "midlife crisis"—coined by the Canadian psychoanalyst and management consultant Elliott Jaques in the 1950s but not well-known in psychology or among a broader public—to describe how women reappraised their lives around the age of thirty-five, when, in a typical middle-class setting, the last child was sent off to school. They asked: "What am I giving up for this marriage?" "Why did I have all these children?" "Why didn't I finish my education?" "What good will my degree do me now after years out of circulation?" "Shall I take a job?" or "Why didn't anyone tell me I would *have* to go back to work?"[7]

Sheehy's men went through a midlife crisis, too, yet in a different way. While women negotiated trading the roles of at-home wife and mother for a career, men were disillusioned with the world of work. Turning forty, they experienced a period of dissatisfaction. Sometimes their careers stagnated or they even lost their jobs—this was the period right after the oil crisis and the stock market crash of 1973. But success was no safeguard. Sheehy's prime example of a male midlife crisis was an established and internationally successful New York professional—probably the graphic designer Milton Glaser, known for the I ♥ NY logo. At the height of his career, he felt forced to stop and scrutinize what his life was all about, and he realized that his achievements had been at the expense of his wife's happiness and self-fulfillment. As she returned to university, he went to cooking school.[8]

Passages wed Betty Friedan's *The Feminine Mystique* (1963) to David Riesman's *The Lonely Crowd* (1950), giving a new name to women's discontent with the domestic ideal and men's alienation from the world of work.[9] Critically acclaimed and very widely read, it made the midlife crisis broadly popular. It remained on American best-seller lists for two years, longer than any other book published the same year. By a rough estimate, at least 8 million Americans read Sheehy's book; even more knew it from reviews, excerpts, and author interviews, which were printed in major newspapers and in many academic journals, or from the bookshelves of friends and relatives. In Library of Congress surveys in the 1980s and '90s, readers voted *Passages* among the ten books that influenced their lives most—following the Bible and *The Feminine Mystique*.[10] The midlife crisis also circulated internationally. Translated into twenty-eight languages, Sheehy's message reached readers throughout North America and Western Europe, as well as audiences in Asian, African, and Latin-American countries and the South Pacific. Commentators spoke of a "global best-seller."[11]

*

The history of the midlife crisis has never been told. To be sure, most writing on the topic includes a brief origin story. Often presented in introductory remarks or brief asides, these mini-histories are characterized by a tacit consensus. One professor of psychology writes: "The midlife crisis started out very innocently with the less hyped-up name of 'midlife transition.' A Yale psychologist named Daniel Levinson published a book . . . called [*The*] *Seasons of a Man's Life.* . . . The midlife crisis got its punchy name with the aid of journalist Gail Sheehy, who published her own book (*Passages*), based heavily on Levinson's own work."[12] Whether a text is journalistic or academic, approving or dismissive, this historical précis is typical. Other authors attribute "midlife crisis" to psychiatrist George Vaillant, therapist Roger Gould, or psychoanalyst Jaques, all otherwise largely unknown.[13] (Alexander Mitscherlich, the German psychoanalyst, used to be a candidate but has fallen off the list.) Regardless of who precisely is given priority, there is general agreement, first, that "midlife crisis" emerged as an idea within psychology and, second, that Sheehy's *Passages* is the definitive "popularization."

This standard historical narrative is misleading—and significantly so, because it turns the true publishing chronology upside down. In this book, I will show that, thanks to *Passages*, the idea of midlife crisis was popular before the science of psychology claimed it, and that Sheehy's book was no "popularization" but a journalist's independent and critical publication. By citing Jaques, she invented a precursor to back up her own ideas. Levinson, Vaillant, Gould, and other scientific and medical experts authored their own books on midlife crisis in the wake of Sheehy's success.[14]

This book reverses histories of "popularization" by tracing how an idea moved from popular culture into academia and demonstrates how it matters to set this trajectory right. Contrary to the assumption that knowledge is created or discovered in libraries, surveys, and intellectual traditions, then trickles down to the public, the history of the midlife crisis illustrates how academics, writers, and activists swapped ideas back and forth and argued over issues of gender and the life course. Journalists not only "popularized" and "disseminated" scientific research; they also drew on it to advance their own arguments and frequently challenged academic findings and expertise. Moreover, popular wisdom informed social scientists who responded to magazine articles and borrowed or refuted ideas propagated in best-selling books, often utilizing their professional authority to delegitimize diverging views and criticism.[15]

The psychoanalyst and developmental theorist Erik Erikson, for example, was not amused when his former student Betty Friedan used his theory of "identity crisis" to bolster the case for women's right to work. Women's problems, Friedan claimed to broad attention, were not attributable to a "role crisis"—difficulties in adapting to the "feminine mystique"—but indicated a collective "identity crisis": an ideological reorientation such as Erikson had described for the young Martin Luther and the Protestant Reformation.[16] Erikson responded by clarifying, in a controversial paper about women's "inner space," that "biology *is* destiny": a woman's place was in the home.[17] The psychoanalyst did not counter Sheehy, whose concept of midlife crisis pushed Friedan's point further by redefining standards of maturity for men and women. But with Levinson, Vaillant, and Gould, some of Erikson's followers were central among those who disputed her alternative model of the life course.

Contrary to the received narrative, these three experts did not invent or discover the midlife crisis but reversed its meaning. They advanced a male-centered concept, which described midlife as the end of a man's family obligations and the moment when he would abandon his family to reinvent himself. This "crisis of masculinity" upended visions of the nuclear family but bolstered gender hierarchies. Categorically exempting women from midlife reinvention, Vaillant, Levinson, and Gould banned them from reimagining their family and work lives. The experts weaponized the notion of popularization to dodge and disparage Sheehy's critique of psychoanalytic models of identity and assert their own scientific respectability. Presented and read as more original and exact, the antifeminist definition of midlife crisis became dominant. Yet this was not a simple tale of conquest.

The received account of the midlife crisis misses not only the origins but also the tail end of the story. In the 1980s, the male midlife crisis was broadly refuted by feminist social scientists, most prominently the psychologist and ethicist Carol Gilligan, in her Harvard University Press best-seller *In a Different Voice* (1982), and Wellesley psychologists Grace Baruch and Rosalind Barnett, with a large-scale study on women who combined careers and family.[18] These psychologists represented different feminist visions of selfhood: Gilligan reclaimed the relevance of values and venues traditionally associated with femininity—care, human interconnectedness, and the ability to empathize—while Baruch and Barnett foregrounded women's autonomy, choice, and control over their lives. Yet they agreed on one point: midlife crisis was a social pathology.

Finding no "second adolescence" in women's lives, Gilligan, Baruch, and Barnett challenged the midlife crisis as a universal developmental stage and redefined its meaning for both genders. A midlife crisis resulted from adherence to traditional gender roles; it was a sign of regression and rigidity, not growth. Levinson, Vaillant, and Gould had merely chronicled some men's refusal to change.

The feminist critique circulated widely throughout the 1980s, with Gilligan's *In a Different Voice* the most-cited book of feminist theory for a decade.[19] In the early 2000s, when the authoritative Midlife in the United States (MIDUS) survey put the critique in quantitative terms, the results showed that personal and emotional turmoil in midlife occurred among less than 10 percent of the American population. This confirmed the received understanding of many Americans, for whom the midlife crisis had turned into a lame excuse and chauvinist cliché.[20]

*

Today, the question of what the midlife crisis is and how to deal with it, or whether it even exists, is the subject of a vast literature ranging from psychology, philosophy, and self-help literature to journalism, sociology, and social policy. There is "no handier excuse for human misbehavior than the midlife crisis," writes the psychiatrist and columnist Richard Friedman in the *New York Times*. (The remainder of the text makes clear that "human" misbehavior means "male.") "But you have to admit that 'I'm having a midlife crisis' sounds much better than 'I'm a narcissistic jerk.'"[21]

Others continue to insist that the midlife crisis exists. Economists and primatologists discuss the "U-shape" of satisfaction over the life course, which they observe in men and women (and chimpanzees), all over the world and irrespective of social and economic differences: starting at a high level in early life, well-being is supposed to reach a nadir in the forties, then rise again.[22] Fundamental questions about the meaning of life crystallize around the notion of middle age—or, as people assert, *in* middle age. For the MIT philosopher Kieran Setiya, the accumulation of biography

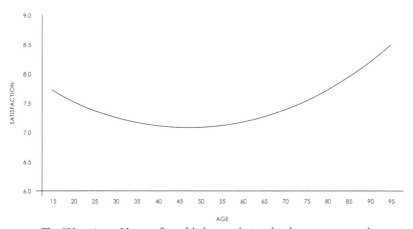

FIG. 1.2. The "Happiness U-curve" establishes a relationship between age and subjective well-being, with the low point in life satisfaction in the forties, around the world. Based on calculations from the economists Carol Graham and Milena Nikolova.

turns on the temporal features of human life: the progressive reduction of possibilities and regret about lost alternatives, the completion or failure of projects, and a sense of futility or constraint. He attributes the midlife crisis to an excessive focus on "telic activities," those oriented toward a terminal point, after which they will be finished and exhausted. Drawing on Aristotle and Schopenhauer, Setiya advises: "You can resolve the midlife crisis, or prevent it, by investing more deeply in atelic ends. Among the activities that matter most to you, the ones that give meaning to your life, must be activities that have no terminal point." Buying a sports car thus makes sense philosophically: "One does not buy a fast car in order to arrive at one's destination more rapidly. It's about the journey."[23]

Claims to universality notwithstanding, most contemporary tales of midlife crisis are about men. Judging from the major studies on midlife, the psychologist Mary Gergen observes, "one would think only men survived the third decade of life."[24] In the 1970s, the philosopher Bernard Williams celebrated the midlife "moral luck" of the banker-turned-painter Paul Gauguin (whose artistic achievement justified the "inconsiderate" act of abandoning his wife and children) yet called Anna Karenina a "failure" and exempted a woman's decision to change her life from his vindication of social transgression.[25] A good forty years later, Setiya's autobiographical exploration of midlife focuses on the male quest for self-knowledge, from the author himself and the great men of philosophy to fictional cases such as Leo Tolstoy's Count Vronsky—Anna Karenina's lover—and the Greek writer Paniotis, a character in Rachel Cusk's novel *Outline* (2014).[26] In choosing his examples, the philosopher seems unaware that both Tolstoy and Cusk told stories about women, with the men as supporting actors.

Here, I suggest that a sense of confinement in one's own life, regret about options missed, and the question "Is this all?" have importantly been linked to women's experiences and feminist agendas. I look at the midlife crisis not as a question of age or biological fact. Instead of asking how to cope with midlife crisis or whether there is such a thing, I explain the interest in the midlife crisis, its uses and applications, and the social and political sources, functions, and effects of conflicts over its nature and legitimacy. I show that the concept of midlife crisis has historical roots in debates about identity, work, and gender and in the shape these took in the United States in the last third of the twentieth century. The idea of having to change one's life halfway through became popular in a period when economic crisis and shifting social norms destabilized the model of the nuclear family with a male breadwinner and an at-home wife and mother. The rise of female breadwinners and two-earner families transformed men's and women's biographies.[27] As earlier, continuous models of the life course—notably Erikson's "Eight Stages of Man" from 1950— were found wanting, Sheehy's and others' definitions of the midlife crisis lent sense to the changes in the working world, family values, and patterns of life. Thus, the midlife crisis turns from an anthropological constant or excuse and fabrication into a historically, culturally, and socially specific construct for negotiating changing gender relations and life patterns.

*

This book tells the story of how the "change of life" and social change interacted. Historians, historical anthropologists, and literary scholars have pointed out the social, economic, and cultural functions of concepts of development and the life course and their important roles in making and changing social structures. The medievalist Philippe Ariès's revolutionary study of young people suggested that the modern European distinction between children and adults was closely linked to the construction of the bourgeois family as a private institution as well as to emerging concerns about education.[28] Social and legal historians and scholars of old age have explored how "stages of life" images, which became a dominant representation of the life course in Europe and North America in the nineteenth century, were used for navigating generational relations and conflicts over inheritance.[29] In the United States, postwar debates about the "generation gap" and "baby boom" illustrate how theories about youth, adolescence, and generational differences were used to understand change and control "unrest."[30] To date, however, little work has addressed the social functions of the modern notion of middle age; the productive and reproductive phase of modern life receives less attention than childhood, youth, and old age.

As the apex of development, conceptions of maturity structure the definition of earlier and later phases of life. Turning upside down the assumption that a model of development is built "like a pyramid from its

FIG. 1.3 *The various ages and degrees of human life.* Depicting middle age as the high-point of life, the "Stages of Life" were the most widespread image of aging and the life course in nineteenth-century Europe and North America. Etching, 1811. British Museum, London.

base in infancy," Gilligan suggested instead that it "hangs from its vertex of maturity, the point toward which progress is traced."[31] What midlife means and meant—even in terms of age—differs according to gender and social background. In her now-classic analysis of the "double standard of aging," Susan Sontag pointed out that middle age is bound up with gender: "Growing older is mainly an ordeal of the imagination—a moral disease, a social pathology—intrinsic to which is the fact that it afflicts women much more than men."[32]

A woman's middle age has been described as the end of her reproductive life, a process that is not tied to any specific age in adulthood, stretching from the weaning and growing up of children and the moment when they leave the home to the transition into menopause. It includes, too, Honoré de Balzac's "woman of a certain age," who was thirty and unmarried.[33] Always at stake is the question of female identity beyond reproduction. This has often been framed as a threat to a woman's well-being—

a "disease" and "pathology," yet there was also another option: like Sontag, many other women rejected the double standard of aging, taking the limits of reproductive capacity as proof that biology was not destiny. The end of problems of motherhood was the beginning of liberation into public and professional lives.

In their historical, sociological, and anthropological work on the menopause, the topic of most previous research on midlife, Carroll Smith-Rosenberg, Susan Bell, Margaret Lock, and others have drawn crucial attention to the ways in which medical, psychiatric, and psychoanalytic definitions of middle age discriminated against women and limited their rights and possibilities.[34] This research has contributed to a vast and important body of scholarship on masculine bias in science, technology, and medicine.[35] More recently, other scholars have pointed out the limits of expert authority and emphasized women's interests and investments in traditional gender ideologies. In their histories of menopause and its treatments, Judith Houck and Elizabeth Watkins highlight nuances and tensions within medical communities, differentiate between advice texts and physicians' actual practice, and make visible the hopes and expectations female patients attached to expertise.[36]

While I share an interest with many other scholars in uncovering women's agency and going beyond the equation of social science with social control, I do not rebut the analysis of the gendered double standard. Instead, I aim to highlight the centrality of feminist critiques and contributions as an important part of the history of identity and life planning. It is not by chance that a classic text on midlife—Sontag's "Double Standard"—is a social critique. Here, I ask: In what ways did women (and some men) use middle age for feminist purposes?

The human and social sciences have long been linked to conformity and control. For the period after World War II, historical studies traced the impact of political and military institutions and corporate agendas; ideas about personality, subjectivity, and relationships were understood as means of regulating individuals.[37] Yet later research has drawn attention to the diversity of political registers and highlighted the fact that the sciences had no simple relationship to business or the state. In the latter half of the twentieth century, social scientists were involved in making liberal, pluralist "open-mindedness" a virtue and connecting consumption to a political discourse of rights. The case of Margaret Mead's Cold War political engagement illustrates that often the problem was not that social science was too influential but that it was not influential enough. In the 1960s and '70s, academic communities and concepts were prominently involved in challenging rather than supporting the status quo.[38] Even Michel Foucault, whose work provided the basis for some of the earlier studies, thought of the "care of the self" as a starting point for exposing and rejecting disciplinary power.[39]

The history of the midlife crisis points to the ways in which social science and conceptions of identity and the self were used within academia and beyond to redefine women's rights and roles in the last third of the twentieth century.[40] Historians have shown that feminism extended and persisted beyond movements, "waves," and intellectual traditions: women's rights have been promoted in many forms and various social, political, and cultural settings.[41] By studying feminist agendas in best-selling books and lifestyle magazines, I complicate dichotomous understandings of feminism and the media in the 1970s. I challenge the notion of an end of feminism in the 1980s, when scholarly attention has centered on antifeminist backlash, by demonstrating how feminist ideas continued to circulate.[42] Finally, I trace different and diverging feminist perspectives on the life course and the midlife crisis, thus illustrating that feminists did not always speak with one voice.

Paying attention to "feminist voices" (Alexandra Rutherford) changes our understanding of age and aging: this meant an opening up of opportunities; another beginning, not just termination. The notion of middle life as the moment of a woman's entry into the public sphere is central to the history of the midlife crisis. The case of the reformers Alva Myrdal and Viola Klein, one Swedish, one British, offers a good example of this idea. Writing after World War II, they defined middle age as the moment when a woman would reenter the world of work. Their call upon Western governments to facilitate a comeback at forty for educated women and mothers influenced administrative, academic, and activist agendas in the United States and Europe.[43] Twenty years later, Sheehy incorporated the feminist concept of the life course into the midlife crisis.

Feminist critique and empowering concepts of midlife and gender were integral to public debates about identity and the life course. By seiz-

ing the meaning of maturity and looking at women's lives beyond reproduction, social reformers and social scientists, policy-makers, and medical
experts—many of them women—challenged perceptions of a woman's
roles throughout the entire life span. Celebrations of women's aging sometimes explicitly opposed the double standard of middle age, as when Anna
Garlin Spencer and Clelia Duel Mosher, respectively a high-profile writer
and a physician-activist, derided outmoded "chivalrous type" theories of
aging, which said nothing about the advantages midlife held for women.[44]
Yet rosy constructions of midlife liberation were more than defensive critiques; they formed a diverse and stable system of thought that, throughout the twentieth century, elicited responses and backlashes that attested
to their currency and influence.

Today, the debate about age, gender, and careers continues, and so it
should. "The typical male midlife crisis tends to hit out of the blue and
take men by surprise, but for women it's been lingering there all along,"
remarks the journalist Hanna Rosin.[45] The balances between work and
(family) life are interrogated on a daily basis by working mothers and
dual-income families, and in light of newer reproductive technologies
and their ambivalent effects on men's and women's life courses. Public
debates about "leaning in" (Sheryl Sandberg), still-sticky floors, the benefits and downsides of egg freezing, and professional women's "midlife
crisis at thirty" highlight the hopes and fears attached to the redefinition
of production and reproduction.[46] In this book, I trace the beginnings of
this transformation by telling the biography of a book as much as the history of an idea, the story of a forgotten journalist and public intellectual
as well as of gender and American social science in the 1970s and after.

*

The following chapters are organized chronologically to illustrate the
shape of the controversy over the midlife crisis as it moved from popular
culture into academia. Chapter 2 considers the emergence and consolida-
tion of the modern double standard of middle age in medicine and social
science, business, politics, and journalism from the late nineteenth century to the 1960s. Drawing on medical literature, guidebooks for women,
and policy debates—including Myrdal and Klein's *Women's Two Roles*

(1956)—I analyze the norms of gender, class, and race attached to aging and discuss positive, celebratory definitions of midlife as the moment of women's liberation from domesticity and the beginning of a period of professional success and increased public status.

The next two chapters focus on the feminist definition of "midlife crisis" and its wide popularity. Chapter 3 introduces Gail Sheehy's concept of midlife degendering, which applied to women and men and challenged the double standard of aging. Participating in feminist critiques and redefinitions of psychology—among them Friedan's appropriation of Erikson's developmental theory—*Passages* contested the psychoanalysts' influential stage model of identity development. Sheehy's book was a great success. Looking at reviews and extracts in newspapers, magazines, and academic and professional journals, the fourth chapter shows that the idea of midlife crisis filled the void left behind by linear, progressive postwar theories of the life course, which were ill equipped to account for the social transformations of the 1970s. Primarily—but not exclusively— read by women, *Passages* offered readers of different generations advice for planning or changing their lives. For many experts, it provided a starting point for new research.

Chapters 5 and 6 study the psychological redefinition of the midlife crisis, then the feminist riposte. Sheehy's enemies—the Eriksonian psychologist Daniel Levinson and the psychiatrists George Vaillant and Roger Gould—advanced a male-centered definition of middle age, which normalized men's transformation from breadwinners into playboys and barred women from changing their lives. Using Sheehy's position on the fringes of academia to discredit *Passages*, the experts presented their backlash as a more exact and scientific account of midlife. Despite their success, this crisis of masculinity was not universally accepted. The sixth and final chapter shows that in the 1980s, the psychologists Carol Gilligan, Grace Baruch, and Rosalind Barnett and other social scientists contested the male midlife crisis. Circulating throughout the following decades, their refutation and critique succeeded in turning the midlife crisis into a stereotype of chauvinism, thus attesting to the continued impact of feminist tales of midlife.

2

Double Standard

Although the midlife crisis became popular only in the 1970s, the idea was not entirely new. It built on older understandings of middle age as a critical phase in the life course, the currency of which probably contributed to the widespread resonance of the midlife crisis. According to Susan Sontag's classic analysis, the modern notion of aging—a process she located in middle, not old, age—"denounces women with special severity. Society is much more permissive about aging in men, as it is more tolerant of the sexual infidelities of husbands. Men are 'allowed' to age, without penalty, in several ways that women are not."[1] Sontag's analysis of aging—unlike her influential work on illness—has not seemed to need criticism; her critique has crystallized into a commonplace, attesting to the persistence of the double standard. A substantial body of historical scholarship now documents the disadvantages that aging brings women and how the double standard of middle age discriminates against them.[2]

Yet the relation between age and gender is more complicated. The double standard of aging was primarily a white middle-class phenomenon, which did not apply in the same manner to black or working-class people. Moreover, white middle-class women used the notion of midlife change to undermine gender hierarchies. The double standard competed with positive and feminist definitions of middle age.

A main reason for the omission of empowering concepts in historical writing on gender and middle age is a focus on menopause and thus on the writings of medical and psychiatric experts. Reproductive and clinical frameworks center on women's bodies and motherhood and foreground the pathological aspects of middle age.[3] In contrast, sociological research, business and policy reports, and journalistic and political publications often focus on social and professional contexts and describe midlife as a time of success, progress, and new beginnings for women. These sources display middle age as a welcome "release" from motherhood and domesticity, inaugurating a period of professional achievement and increased public influence. Such positive notions of aging undermine traditional gender roles and challenge male privileges. They introduce evidence of ambiguity and suggest that conflicting constructions of middle age competed, some stabilizing and others subverting gender hierarchies. Though influential, the double standard was neither the sole nor a universal feature of concepts of aging.

1 *Critical Years*

Theories of the *climacterium virile* or "male menopause," although often understood as emerging in the twentieth century, go back much further. For a long time, men's lives dominated discussions of middle age. The idea of "climacteric" or "critical" years is found in the Roman grammarians Censorinus and Aulus Gellius and other ancient writers, who attributed it to even older, Egyptian or Chaldean roots. According to this concept, human life proceeded by steps of seven (or sometimes nine) years; every seventh (or ninth) year was an *annus climactericus*. These climacterics brought sudden shifts in constitution. They were periods of change and decision, comparable to a "crisis" in the Hippocratic sense, the critical days or hours when the fever breaks and a disease changes for the better or worse. (A crisis was thought to occur at specific hours, on specific days or during specific weeks, depending on the kind of illness.)[4]

In children and youths, the climacteric years were seen as steps toward maturity: in the seventh year, children grew permanent teeth; in the fourteenth, they entered puberty. But every change also implied danger, and among the elderly, the profound change their bodies underwent in climacteric years could pose lethal risks. Numerous works explained that people often died in a climacteric year. The deadliest of all was the sixty-third, the *annus climactericus maximus* or *androklas* (man-killing), with the forty-ninth the slightly less dangerous "small climacteric year."[5]

In the sixteenth and seventeenth centuries, climacteric years were described by many authors and discussed at length. Humanists like Giovanni Battista Codronchi and Henricus Ranzovius sought to corroborate the theory of climacterics by compiling long lists of well- and little-known figures who had died in a septennial year. Eulogies, birthday speeches, and funeral orations often mentioned the "climacteric year" that the addressee—most often a sovereign—was about to enter, had just survived, or had succumbed to. Although climacterics occurred in the lives of men and women, the concept was applied to men more frequently. The speeches, like Baptista Codronchi's and Ranzovius's lists of the dead, contained men almost exclusively.[6] (The women listed were elite or saints.) This was because men were the measure of humanity but also because they were more prominent: the "critical" years were biographical benchmarks as much as medical measuring points.

Men remained central in modern medical diagnoses of the climacteric well into the nineteenth century, when the climacteric was narrowed down to middle age. Linked to swollen legs and a flabby stomach, a higher pulse, and increased rates of disease, depression, and death, the "climacteric disease" referred to men primarily. In an influential paper, "On the Climacteric Disease," the physician Sir Henry Halford, a well-known figure in British medicine—a fellow and, later, president of the Royal College of Physicians and physician in ordinary to George III—told the college in 1813 that "though this climacteric disease is sometimes equally remarkable in women as in men, yet most certainly I have not noticed it so frequently, nor so well characterized in females." Reprinted on various occasions, translated, and included in standard medical dictionaries, Halford's paper was a key text on the climacteric, still cited well into the twentieth century.[7]

The idea of a "female" climacteric was contested, at least in the Anglophone world. The American physician and obstetrician William Dewees, in *A Treatise on the Diseases of Females*, first published in 1826 and republished repeatedly in the following three decades, refuted the diagnosis of a female climacteric as a "vulgar error." Indeed, Dewees asserted, "it would seem that this period of female life is freer from diseases causing death, than almost any other."[8] Most physicians, even gynecologists, were indifferent to this part of the female life cycle. Many gynecological texts had nothing to say about the climacteric in women, and others offered only a paragraph or two, usually to the effect that those who experienced an early onset of menstruation could expect a late cessation. Major textbooks rarely devoted more than a paragraph to menopause. The *Index Medicus*, one of the leading indices to medical literature, gave menopause its own subject heading only in 1921, and even then referred the reader only to "menstruation, cessation."[9]

The bulk of medical and moralistic writing was aimed at younger women, addressing declining birthrates in the middle class in particular, and physicians were preoccupied with accounting for menstruation and its disorders. Menstruation was depicted as a debilitating function— prominently invoked, like pregnancy and motherhood, as an argument against women's growing presence in higher education and the professions.[10] But this did not necessarily mean that the end of menstruation was viewed positively. When they mentioned it, many physicians resisted the interpretation of menopause as a merciful release, which implied, after all, that women might live an active life again. Sometimes they discussed menopause in light of menstrual complaints. When the British pediatrician and obstetrician Charles West, in his 1858 *Lectures on the Diseases of Women*, spoke about "disordered menstruation," he called menopause the "permanent" cessation of the menses, mentioning it (if only briefly) next to "premature" cessation, absence of the menses ("amenhorrea"), and menstrual cramps ("dysmenhorrea").[11]

Like menstrual disorders, menopause indicated nonreproductivity, but so did regular menstruation. When older ideas about menstruation's purgative, purifying benefits were revised in the later nineteenth century and menstrual flow was connected to the cyclical production of the ovum and thus directly linked to conception, many physicians depicted menstruation as an unfortunate failure in bodily processes designed to build up a fetus. The menopausal discourse mirrored the menstrual one: "What applies to menstruation once a month applies to menopause once in every lifetime."[12] In the mid-1960s, the psychoanalyst Erik Erikson would still depict menstruation and menopause in this light: "Each menstruation . . . is crying to heaven in the mourning over a child; and it becomes a permanent scar in the menopause."[13] (Calculating by rough computation that a woman menstruates 450 times in her life, the feminist scholar and activist Kate Millett spoke of "a demographer's nightmare.")[14]

Medicine's relative silence about women's "critical years" may attest to the fact that doctors did not consider menopause a discrete medical problem, but it also indicated ignorance of women's health issues beyond reproduction. Female physicians, receiving licenses in the United States since the mid-nineteenth century, bemoaned this neglect and demanded more attention for women's climacteric problems.[15] Yet emerging medical definitions were often ambivalent in their implications about women's rights.

2 *Emptiness and Obsolescence*

One of the first Anglophone books on the female climacteric was by Edward Tilt, an English physician, who—like many of his colleagues— had been trained and had practiced in France, in the late 1830s and the 1840s, and imported the idea from there.[16] Tilt described it first in the later chapters of *On the Preservation of the Health of Women at the Critical Periods of Life* (1851), a small guide for women, as well as in a series of articles. A subsequent, larger book, directed to the medical community, *The Change of Life in Health and Disease: A Practical Treatise on the Nervous and Other Affections Incidental to Women at the Decline of Life* (1857), was dedicated to the topic entirely.[17] Here, alongside terms such as "climacteric" and "change of life," Tilt introduced the French physicians' term *la ménopause* (from the Greek for "month" or "monthlies" and "cessation"), coined by Charles-Pierre-Louis de Gardanne some forty years earlier, originally as *ménespausie*, to replace the unwieldy expression *cessation des menstrues*.[18]

Unlike "climacteric," the reference to menstruation linked "menopause" firmly to the female body. Reversing Halford's findings, Tilt described a change of life that was "insensibly" worked out in men, but "in woman the passage is often perilous and the result is more marked." He argued that physicians needed to pay more attention to this "crisis," which he attributed to ovarian "involution" or shrinkage. Tilt's menopausal patients, presented in numerous case studies, suffered from headaches, felt "giddy and stupid," feared going mad or losing their memory, and were melancholy and bad-tempered. He compared their condition to hysteria and called it "pseudo-narcotism."[19]

Tilt was the leading authority on the topic in the English-speaking world. *The Change of Life* was published in several editions in Britain and

America. There were multiple printings of the fourth (and last) edition, from 1882, which was in especially high demand in the United States, and a number of his patients crossed the Atlantic to see him.[20] British literature increasingly used the expression "female climacteric" from about the mid-1860s, and "menopause" entered English-language dictionaries in the late 1880s, although it did not become current until the following decade.[21] The new standing of the female climacteric was epitomized in the New York physician Andrew Currier's *The Menopause* (1897); an explicit attempt to update Tilt's work, it was the first monograph by an American physician on the topic.[22]

The menopause diagnosis alleviated suffering and made middle-aged women clinically visible as individuals who deserved relief and support. But like many other medical concepts, it also served important social purposes. By linking women's bodily functions and social roles, reproductive capacity and domesticity, it naturalized a woman's role as a wife and mother and rationalized the idea that her place was in the home.

As part of the emergence of menopause as a medical category, physicians emphasized the problems accompanying it. Rather than depicting menopause as a normal transition, they described it as an illness in need of treatment or an indication of a body in disorder, a cause of cancer and mental disequilibrium and, not least, a site for expert intervention.[23] Clinicians were aware of their pathological focus and its limits. Before describing the complications of middle age, Currier, in *The Menopause*, cautioned that "the majority of women pass through [menopause] with as little incident or discomfort as they experience at puberty. It is only the exceptional woman who has a hard time, and comes to the doctor to tell him about it. Upon this exceptional experience the doctrine of the danger and serious character of the menopause has been built up."[24] In giving reasons for those problems and suggesting therapies, physicians made the normative and anti-feminist implications of menopause particularly clear: they attributed menopausal problems to women's violation of social laws.

If menstruation blocked women's education, then menopause could stymie their careers. Currier spoke for many other physicians when he claimed that menopausal disorders were more serious among those who pursued "unwomanly occupations," using the example of working-class women in paid work.[25] The menopausal discourse generally focused on the middle and upper classes; the New York gynecologist himself presented menopause as a phenomenon found typically among upper-middle-class women. But medical books sometimes used working-class women as negative examples, to illustrate, for instance, that it was inappropriate for women to take paid work.[26]

Akin to contemporary medical arguments against women's entry into college, pathological definitions of menopause prevented them from leaving the home, thus constituting a backlash against their advancement in politics and the professions. In typical fashion, Currier asserted that most of his patients experienced menopausal problems—which he displayed as a sign of civilization—but that the "change of life" was less troublesome for "quiet placid" women. Education and a career, attempts at birth control or abortion, failure to devote herself to the needs of her husband and children, advocacy of women's suffrage, and even a too fashionable, sociable lifestyle were all seen as leading a woman to a particularly difficult menopause.[27]

Correspondingly, middle-aged women—much like their pubescent daughters and granddaughters—were told to avoid mental activities, shun new projects, and commit to domesticity. The recommended regimen for menopausal problems—introspection and careful diet, rest, and plenty of baths—implied withdrawal from society, and confinement was often explicitly advised. Women who did not comply with these prescriptions were mocked for acting inappropriately youthful and warned of a more difficult old age. "We insist," a women's guidebook counseled, "that every woman who hopes for a healthy old age ought to commence her prudent cares as early as the fortieth year or sooner. . . . She should cease to endeavor to appear young when she is no longer so, and withdraw from the excitements and fatigues of the gay world in the midst of her legitimate successes, to enter upon that more tranquil era of her existence now at hand."[28] Aging was a prescription.

But even women who adhered to domestic roles could not avoid menopausal problems. In his 1901 *Text-book of Gynecology*, Charles Reed, the president of the American Medical Association, was one of the first to emphasize the "mental" aspects of this period of loss for a woman: "She is suddenly brought to perceive that her charms, her youth, her sex itself, are passing from her. She is invited, with cruel abruptness, to be to her husband merely an intellectual companion or a sexless helpmeet, when she had been of late the object of his embraces and the mother of his babes. One third of her adult life is still before her, full of promise of placid enjoyment and great usefulness, but to her, remembering the glory of conquest and surrender, the future stretches a dreary waste of empty years."[29] Such depictions of middle age as the onset of emptiness and obsolescence would become characteristic of the mid-twentieth century.

Through the lens of endocrinology, the study of hormones, the menopause came to be seen primarily as the effect of a loss of estrogen or a "deficiency disease."[30] By the mid-1930s, when sex endocrinology was established, doctors were prescribing estrogen as a panacea for menopausal ailments. In his work on menopause, Abner Weisman described establishing one of the first endocrine clinics in New York City, which almost immediately attracted for treatment fifty to a hundred middle-aged women a day.[31] After the synthesis of an inexpensive form of estrogen in 1938, estrogen replacement therapy took off in the 1940s and increased in popularity after the war.[32] In the 1960s, the Brooklyn gynecologist and nurse Robert and Thelma Wilson, authors of the best-selling *Feminine Forever* (1966), proposed long-term prescription of estrogen to keep women from turning into "castrates" who "exist rather than live," as the Wilsons put it.[33] Hormonal therapy alleviated discomfort but also implied a more pessimistic dimension, amplifying the perception that menopause was an illness. Lifelong treatment, as advocated by the Wilsons, equated health and reproductivity and labeled women's aging a disease. In addition, at a time when women widely practiced birth control, the stress on fertility loss told premenopausal women that they should have children before it was too late.[34]

Psychoanalytic and psychological explanations, which associated declining estrogen levels and negative emotional states, were pivotal for casting middle age as a period of "symbolic loss."[35] Freud had paid relatively little attention to menopause; he focused on children and adolescents and published only passing remarks on aging. In a 1933 lecture on femininity, he dated women's stagnation to age thirty: "I cannot help mentioning an impression that we are constantly receiving during analytic practice. A man of about thirty strikes us as a youthful, somewhat unformed individual, whom we expect to make powerful use of the possibilities of development opened up to him by analysis. A woman of the same age, however, often frightens us by her psychical rigidity and unchangeability. . . . There are no paths open for further development; it is as though . . . the difficult development to femininity had exhausted the possibilities of the person."[36]

The key Freudian analysis of menopause came from the Austrian-Polish psychoanalyst Helene Deutsch, whose two-volume *Psychology of Women* (1944–45) included an epilogue on "the climacterium." Deutsch foregrounded the meaning of middle age as a period of "partial death," loss, and mourning. She described menopause as the moment when "woman has ended her existence as bearer of a future life, and has reached her natural end—her partial death—as servant of the species. She is now engaged in an active struggle against her decline. . . . Little by little the whole female genital apparatus is transformed into a number of inactive and superfluous structures." Instead of offering therapy, the theorist of "feminine masochism" prescribed suffering. Women should accept their fate, Deutsch sternly noted, forbidding the use of cosmetics, "narcissistic" reminiscence, and other "oddities of conduct."[37]

Not only about loss and mourning, such accounts implied the use-lessness and undesirability of midlife women. Experts and social critics depicted middle-aged women as superfluous and "obsolescent." Philip Wylie's infamous *Generation of Vipers* (1942), an assault on women's public and political efforts in the vein of late-nineteenth-century critiques of "maternalist" social reformers, stigmatized middle-aged women as "idle" and parasitical "moms."[38] In his 1969 best-seller *Everything You Always Wanted to Know about Sex (But Were Afraid to Ask)*, the psychiatrist David Reuben declared: "Once the ovaries stop, the very essence of being a woman stops. . . . Having outlived their ovaries, [women] have outlived their usefulness as human beings. The remaining years may be just mark-ing time until they follow their glands into oblivion."[39]

The anthropologist of science Emily Martin showed that in using eco-nomic and industrial metaphors for women's bodies, medical texts often cast menopause as a stopping or breakdown of technological systems that expressed the ultimate horror of idle workers or machines, disused factories, and failed businesses.[40] A similar *horror vacui* was conveyed by the quintessential postwar image for women's middle age, borrowed from ornithology: the "empty nest," an extended metaphor used as early as the 1880s, which became dominant in the 1950s to describe midlife changes in the nuclear family. The "empty nest syndrome," attributed to women whose children had grown and left the home, denoted a loss of purpose and identity.[41] It typified an understanding of middle age as the moment when women lost their presumed raison d'être, namely motherhood, in both nurturing and reproductive senses, along with the beauty ascribed to youth and denied to age in women. Many but not all men were exempt from this experience.

3 *Prime of Life*

As the notion of a physical change in middle age became essentially feminine, the earlier concept of a climacteric in men lost relevance. Concepts such as the *climacterium virile*, the "male" climacteric, or the "male" menopause now cast the male as a variation of the female condition, thus confirming women's bodies as the reference point. Physicians, psychiatrists, and, later, pharmacists attempted to ride the waves of mass-market books about and medication for the female climacteric by reapplying the concept to men, often under the pretext of drawing attention to a neglected phenomenon. Yet patients rejected the diagnosis as effeminizing and indicating failure to measure up to standards of masculinity. The debate about the "male menopause" continued, especially in the media, but as an expression of the fact that the diagnosis was not accepted.[42]

Physicians mostly mentioned a male climacteric to emphasize its irrelevance and accentuate the feminine character of climacteric problems. In this sense, the American obstetrician James Scott explained in 1898 that "the effects [of the climacteric] are by no means so clearly appreciable in men as in women. . . . Exceptionally virile power remains with men even to the most advanced age; but women, almost without exception, are sterile before they have reached the fiftieth year."[43] The gynecologist Reed explicitly contrasted the menopause with men's experience: "A man grows old by merciful and gentle gradations, and so he slides, half willingly, and half unconsciously, into the afternoon of life, with regrets so soft that they can scarce provoke a sigh. But for a woman, man's twenty years of change are compressed into two; she is rudely compelled to make an abrupt change. . . . It is evolution for him; it is revolution for her."[44] "A man," echoed Robert and Thelma Wilson in the 1960s, "remains a man until the end," whereas a woman bereaved of the "female hormone" became "only the 'part woman.'"[45]

Middle age was not only less harmful to men; it could even improve their lives. In his best-selling *Life Begins at Forty* (1932), the psychologist and journalist Walter Pitkin claimed that the brain improves (almost) as long as a man lives: "As the brain grows only with use, by developing proper insulation of nerve fibers under stimulation, this fact means that nobody under forty works his mind sufficiently to mature it." Pitkin, who had previously studied the psychology of achievement and would soon produce the self-help manual *Careers after Forty* (1937), was reflecting on careers as much as on the human mind.[46] The early twentieth century had seen the development of a professional class, whose members enjoyed a career during which income and status continually rose. Corporations such as Ford and DuPont transformed American business by replacing small-scale family firms with large companies and constructed the managerial career ladder with its regular salary scales and fixed promotion breaks.[47] Pitkin linked planned employment and identity development: "The more stages involved in a given accomplishment, the longer one must work; hence the later one arrives, as a rule. Careers support this unmistakably. Complexity, depth, and breadth postpone achievement."[48]

Success, the psychologist continued, might set in before the age of forty in some "mediocre" lines—light fiction, lyric music—but "by far the greater number of highly significant and constructive acts will be found on the shady side of that milestone. . . . The larger and the richer triumphs begin with graying hair." Pitkin cited artist biographies to substantiate this line of thought: Handel wrote *Messiah* when fifty-six and Bach the *St. Matthew Passion* at forty-four. In painting, Leonardo did the *Mona Lisa* at fifty-four, while Goya "painted nothing of consequence" up to his thirty-seventh year, then experienced "a prodigious outburst of creative genius which steadily improved throughout his forties, then through his fifties," and indeed almost until his death.[49]

Men who benefited from the value ascribed to skill and experience typically entered their peak earning years at age forty. The psychologist Bernice Neugarten, in interviews with businessmen in the 1960s, noted that they associated the onset of middle age with "deferential behavior accorded to them in the work setting." Asked how they became aware of middle age, one man spoke about "the first time a younger associate helped open a door for him; another, being called by his official title by a newcomer in the company; another, the first time he was ceremoniously asked for advice by a younger man."[50] With aspiration of success came "status panic" and fear of failure. Neugarten described how middle-class men felt diminished by aging, even while still young, if they had not shown distinction in their careers or made a lot of money. Men's aging crisis, Sontag noted similarly, was linked to "that terrible pressure on men to be 'successful' that defines their membership in the middle class." Taking stock in middle age, even successful professionals and businessmen experienced a "dreary panic"; achievements seemed paltry; they felt stuck on the job ladder or feared being pushed off by someone younger. Being denied careers and professional achievement in the first place, few women felt this age anxiety.[51]

A key life-course concept for men was adolescence, with their middle age rendered as a "second adolescence": a period of self-realization and rejuvenation seen to manifest itself in outbursts of genius and sexual escapades with young women. Biographies and autobiographies deployed this idea. The psychologist G. Stanley Hall, inventor of the idea of adolescence, sketched the life of Auguste Comte to illustrate what he called "the youth of old age": "Comte, born 1798, married at the age of twenty-seven and was divorced at forty-four. He . . . had his first crisis when he was forty. He met Clotilde de Vaux when he was forty-seven but she died a year later. He then became the high priest of humanity, developing his *Politique Positive* and a new religion."[52] A man, then, not only "remained a man" but only really became a man in middle age.

Such depictions of male middle age were often directed at women. Edmund Bergler, known as "the most punitively normative" psychoanalyst of his era, and one of the key interpreters of men's middle age in the 1950s, spoke of a "revolt" of middle-aged men, expressed in sudden discontent with "everything," and especially marriage (on which he was a published expert, author of titles such as *Unhappy Marriage and Divorce* and *Divorce Won't Help*).[53] Bergler's patients, successful businessmen, were "bored" and "annoyed" by their wives and acted on their "changed feelings" by replacing them with "young and beautiful creatures."[54] The psychoanalyst held that the main trouble was not men's behavior but "widespread ignorance" of their "suffering" and of the psychological implications and import of this "emotional second adolescence." He advised married women to be understanding and not punish their "revolting" husbands (for example, by filing for divorce) but rather to comply and conform to the changes the men were undergoing. Bergler painted a picture of what he saw as a better, though distant, future: when "women have been made familiar with . . . man's middle-age revolt, they will be prepared for it, take it for granted."[55]

The end of life for women, a second youth for men: the discourse about menopause and middle age exemplified what Sontag criticized as the "double standard about aging." She attributed this to overarching gender hierarchies: "The prejudices that mount against women as they grow older are an important arm of male privilege. It is that present unequal distribution of adult roles between the two sexes that gives men a freedom to age that women are denied."[56]

Middle age was not good for all men, however. Explicitly or implicitly, black men were exempt from growth in middle age. This was linked to a wider, normative exclusion of people of color from narratives of maturity. As the women's and civil rights activist Tish Sommers, writing at the same time as Sontag, summarized the diverging double standards of maturity: "The difference between the term 'boy' as used derogatorily against blacks and 'girl' against women is that a black wants to become a man—that is where the rewards are—while a woman secretly wants to stay a girl."[57] There is little research on race and midlife, yet in an ethnographic study conducted in the 1990s, informants from poor Harlem communities never mentioned "middle age" as a period in the life cycle; rather, they saw a long period of undifferentiated adulthood, ending in a clearly defined segment called "old age" or, sometimes, "going back to childhood."[58]

Aging cut along the lines of class as much as gender. In the forties, when the careers of middle-class men took off, the earning power of working-class men—which peaked in their thirties—was falling. Friedrich Engels, in his report on the condition of the English working class at the end of the first industrial revolution, reported: "The men wear out very early in consequence of the conditions under which they live and work. Most of them are unfit for work at forty years, a few hold out to forty-five, almost none to fifty years of age." The onset of old age was even earlier for miners, who became unfit for work when they were thirty-five. Engels made clear that "premature aging" was a question of class: "In Manchester, this premature old age among the operatives is so universal that almost every man of forty would be taken for ten or fifteen years older, while the prosperous classes, men as well as women, preserve their appearance exceedingly well if they do not drink too heavily."[59] But bad working conditions were not the only problem; employment patterns were another.

Working-class men did not have careers. Their jobs were generally unstable; contract work, cyclical unemployment, factory shutdowns, and layoffs were recurrent phenomena. Workers in their midthirties and older were particularly vulnerable to these insecurities. In the 1920s, Stuart Chase, the social commentator who would spell out the agenda for President Roosevelt's "New Deal," observed "the apparent increasing difficulty with which men over forty retain their jobs, and the even greater difficulty with which they find a new job once they have lost an old one."[60] Hence, working-class men worried about job stability before payment, as the social investigator Whiting Williams noted in his 1920 undercover labor reportage *What's on the Worker's Mind*: "Wages are interesting, but the *job* is the axis on which the whole world turns for the working man. If he has a job—even a poor one—he is at least established on a platform where he can stand for the present and plan for a better future."[61] Keeping a working-class job, however, was seldom related to promotion and improvement. While experience led to substantially higher earnings in education-based jobs, seniority and wage increases were not part of the secondary, low-skilled, or unskilled sectors, which offered little to no possibility of advancement. On the contrary, working-class men who kept a job often earned less as they grew older.[62]

Mechanization devalued the skills and experiences working-class men acquired over the life course. The results of this process, which set in particularly forcefully in the second industrial revolution, were documented by the sociologists Helen and Robert Lynd in their 1929 study of Muncie, Indiana, an "average" city—the Lynds called it "Middletown"—in which seven out of ten of those gainfully employed belonged to the working class. The Lynds purposefully limited their study to the white native-born residents, whom they defined as representative of the "average American." They sought out Muncie as their field site for what they believed to be its insignificant African American and immigrant population—although they were aware that such homogeneity was unusual. This illustrates another reason for the focus of middle-age discourses on white people, namely the scientific preoccupation with white study groups as the norm.[63]

Muncie's working-class population went to school—in the 1920s, attendance until fourteen was compulsory—and started to work from two to five years later than in the nineteenth century. Still, the pattern had changed little: "Male members from the working class start to work from fourteen to eighteen, reach their prime in their twenties, and begin to fail in their late forties." Asked about the future of her husband's job, the wife of a forty-year-old laborer told the Lynds: "When you get old they are done with you. The only thing a man can do is to keep as young as he can." Another woman, married to a patternmaker, replied: "He is forty and in about ten years now he will be on the shelf. A pattern maker really isn't much wanted after forty-five. They always put in the young men."[64]

Most factory representatives downplayed this effect, but the personnel manager of a prominent Middletown machine shop explained: "In production work forty to forty-five is the age limit because of the speed needed in the work. Men over forty are hired as sweepers and for similar jobs." The superintendent of another major plant admitted that "the age dead line is creeping down on those men—I'd say that by forty-five they are through."[65] Working-class men sometimes attempted to disguise their age by darkening their hair or abandoning their spectacles, yet these (by later standards) stereotypical midlife crisis behaviors resulted from the detrimental effect of age on employability.[66]

In the late 1920s, when the Lynds published their study, the problem of age discrimination in employment exploded in the American media, and it continued to be an important public and social policy issue throughout the rest of the century. After intense debates in the 1930s, middle-aged workers had a much easier time finding a job during World War II. Studies showed they performed as well as young workers, often in jobs they had not usually been granted prior to the war. But when younger GIs returned home and competed for jobs, the problem resurfaced. In the 1950s, a federal Labor Department study showed that job seekers began to encounter significant difficulty in seeking employment between the ages of thirty-five and forty-four. In a one-year period, workers age forty-five and older made up 40 percent of the job seekers at local employment offices in seven major cities but only 22 percent of all people hired. The study found that age limits, which applied to men and women, varied greatly from occupation to occupation. The white-collar worker and the blue-collar employee over forty-five without a specific skill faced the most difficult situations.[67]

Middle age, then, was the "prime of life" for only some men. It was a marker of race and class as well as gender. On the one hand, the exemption of white middle-class men from narratives of decline contributed to the privileged status of "hegemonic masculinity," constructed "in relation to various subordinated masculinities as well as in relation to women."[68] On the other hand, it indicates that the gendered double standard of aging applied primarily to the white middle class.

Sontag suggested that poor and working-class women felt aging earlier and more forcefully without having the resources to agonize about it.[69] But the difference was not simply a matter of degree. The Muncie women who worried about their husbands' jobs were in another situation entirely than middle-class mothers whose children were leaving the home. When working-class husbands were discharged, fell ill, or didn't earn enough, their wives stepped in. (The unwritten prewar rule in certain local plants against employing married women was disappearing.)[70] The Lynds described a typical setting in which a forty-five-year-old mother of four had worked recurrently during the previous five years to pay her husband's doctors' bills and replace lost income while he was sick and laid off.[71] Nor did black women in poor inner-city households in the 1990s experience an "empty nest," most having, at the minimum, adolescent children still in the home and many raising their grandchildren as primary caregivers.[72] The double standard of middle age was linked to work and family arrangements prevalent in the white middle class. But even white middle-class norms about gender and aging were contested.

4 A New Deal

Not all definitions of middle age cast women as obsolescent. Many portrayed it as the welcome end of a woman's childbearing years and the moment when she would receive a "new deal." This was how the journalist, educator, and independent minister Anna Garlin Spencer, a leader in the women's suffrage movement, put it in her treatise on women's equality, *Woman's Share in Social Culture*, published in 1913 and reissued in 1925. Using a metaphor of social and economic reform, Spencer offered an understanding of middle age diametrically opposed to the notion that aging meant decline: "When, however, the climacteric of middle life is reached, nature gives a new deal and starts a fresh balance of power between men and women." She agreed that the climacteric distinguished a woman's from a man's life course, but to her advantage. Men proceeded along a "long, straight path of progress, passing [from boyhood] on into youth, and later manhood, up to the point where senile decay threatens." By contrast, women experienced a period of rejuvenation in midlife, a "*second youth*" when they redefined their lives, trading domesticity for public "achievement." Middle age meant the capacity to participate in the larger social culture: "At last she emerges . . . and becomes in a peculiar and a new sense a citizen of the world, a [civil] *Person*, whose relationship to the social whole may now of right become her main concern."[73]

Spencer's definition of women's "second youth" was typical of positive concepts of midlife change, put forward by social reformers and sociologists, activists, and journalists but also physicians and psychiatrists—many of them women—in political treatises, sociological studies, and self-help literature. They shared an emphasis on social contexts rather than bodily functions: even physicians often highlighted issues unrelated to medicine, stressing the social changes concurrent with menopause. In some of this literature, middle age or menopause was the main topic, but many authors, like Spencer, drew on notions of midlife in the context of broader debates about women's rights. Their constructions of women's aging sometimes explicitly challenged the double standard of middle age, as when Spencer sneered at "old theories" that ignored the "rich and large possibility of later life."[74] Yet concepts of midlife liberation were more than defensive contestations; they formed a stable and self-contained body of thought. Swipes at "old theory" were rare.

In focusing on medical texts and thus on pathological concepts of menopause, histories of middle age have obscured these alternative definitions or even dismissed them as reinforcing the notion that before middle age women were obligated to sacrifice personal ambitions to the needs of family and nation; at best, they have been read as evidence of what dominant discourses about aging lacked.[75] However, if, as the historians Carl Degler and Carroll Smith-Rosenberg observed, women often ignored oppressive medical advice and were inclined to view menopause as a "release from a 'world of troubles,'" celebrations of aging may have represented their experience more accurately than pathological depictions.[76] At the very least, they indicate that the modern understanding of middle age and gender was more complex than morbid and gloomy definitions suggest.

Praise of midlife renewal drew on the same imagery for women as for men, casting middle age as a "second youth" and celebrating the "larger grasp," experience, and wisdom at the high point of life. In the widely circulated guidebook *What a Woman of Forty-Five Ought to Know* (1902), the obstetrician and writer Emma Drake, from Denver, Colorado, praised the fifth decade of life as a period of increased social standing and involvement. Dividing the female life course into three stages—from childhood to puberty, from puberty to menopause, and from menopause to the end of life—Drake described the third phase as a period of overview, not decline, like a "great table-land, where all sorts and kinds of opportunities lie in waiting, and where women may roam at will."[77]

While pathologies of menopause relied on anonymous case studies, positive portrayals tended to include hagiographical lists of accomplished women exemplifying that, for women as much as for men, public influence increased in middle age. Typical inspiring examples, catalogued by Drake and others, were the suffragist and educator Frances Willard, the journalist and women's rights advocate Mary Livermore ("has done the best work of her life since she passed forty-five"), and the poet, author, and social activist Julia Ward Howe.[78] Clara Steeholm and Ruth Freeman Fisher's *Women over Forty* (1934) included an entire chapter on great women. "It causes one to pause and think, this list of names," they wrote, and continued, echoing Spencer's notion of self-fulfillment at last, "to stop and then to realize that only *after* a woman has left her forties and her fruitfulness behind her, can she become of highest use to her fellow creatures in her own person."[79]

Pathologies and celebrations agreed that in middle age, women's role as mothers came to an end. Yet what morbid explanations depicted as a deficiency, liberating accounts pictured as increasing gender equality. In

"Health and the Woman Movement," a speech given before a national convention of the Young Women's Christian Association in 1915, the well-known physician, Stanford professor, and women's health advocate Clelia Duel Mosher depathologized menstruation, the main argument against women's paid work, and with it menopause.[80]

Mosher argued that menopause should be "welcomed" as a "release" from menstruation and pregnancy. Although a medical scientist, she insisted on understanding middle age and menopause as social and psychological more than physical events, defined as the time when a woman retired from her familial tasks: "Her condition is almost analogous to that of an active man who stops business in middle life." Framing worry about physical changes as hypochondriac, Mosher recommended escaping from disturbances of the climacteric by delving into "salaried positions," further education, or, most of all, political action.[81]

Making a medical case for women's legal equality, Mosher argued that suffrage would help to cope with the potential complications of middle age. During the years of homemaking and the bearing and rearing of children, many a woman laid aside intellectual occupations and interests outside the home, and this made the change of life more difficult. Women's suffrage would bring civic concerns into the home for discussion by "mothers and daughters as well as fathers and sons," thus creating a "passive interest in politics" among women that would continue until their family responsibilities subsided. Mosher argued that "Votes for Women" (the suffrage slogan) was "not only a safeguard to the woman of middle age, a help in preserving the integrity of the family, but . . . economically an asset in the productive use of the force and intelligence otherwise wasted in doctor's bills, sanatorium treatment, or too often expended in dangerous fads."[82]

Such associations between middle age and public and political engagement were frequently made. Many commentators described middle age as the period when women became politically active. They encouraged the menopausal woman to join women's clubs and see the world through her "universal motherhood." By promoting community housekeeping for postmenopausal women, they supported women's participation in public life. The language of community housekeeping might not have challenged the primacy of motherhood and domesticity for younger women. Yet

community housekeeping was not just a task assigned to women to maintain the social order. "Maternalist politics" was a strategy women used
to claim increased access to life outside the home. A particularly effective feminist approach in the late nineteenth and early twentieth centuries, maternalism extolled the private virtues of domesticity to legitimate
women's public relationships to politics and the state, community, workplace, and market.[83]

Throughout the twentieth century, midlife was also linked to the quest
for women's economic equality, and this became central after 1920, when
the ratification of the Nineteenth Amendment granted women the right
to vote. Commentators—often professionals themselves—encouraged
middle-aged women to acquire jobs, and when careers were discussed,
midlife often came up. On the pages of the *Independent Woman* (later
renamed *National Business Woman*), the official journal of the National
Federation of Business and Professional Women's Clubs (founded in
1919), stories about successful women emphatically refuted the idea that
"forty is the limit."[84] When the federation asked the economist and social
worker Grace Coyle to prepare a discussion guideline on married women
in business in 1928, the "older" woman—ten to fifteen years into marriage
and motherhood—was given special consideration; the piece opened
with a full-length quotation of Spencer's description of women's "second
youth."[85]

Emphasizing the new opportunities of middle age could be a way of
reinforcing women's domestic duties during their fertile years: women
could pursue their own dreams and interests outside the home, but only
after they had fulfilled their domestic obligations. In this sense, narratives
about a "new deal" in middle age provided an escape route: middle-class
women did not need to choose between work and home. But often the
reverse was true. Writers not only suggested acquiring a job in middle
age but, like Mosher—who used middle age as an argument for women's
continued political interests—often drew on the notion of midlife change
to argue for women's lifetime employment. Staying on was particularly
important, as most authors discussed and spoke to educated, middle-class
women for whom paid work, in particular at age forty, was described as
a career, linked to self-fulfillment and sharply distinguished from jobs to
make ends meet; it was, as the physician Edith Lowry pointed out, diffi-

cult to cold-start a career in middle age.[86] The understanding of midlife reentry and its difficulties, then, often justified employment more generally and throughout the life course.

Many writers warned against dropping out and advised women to keep up and develop nondomestic activities throughout the years of motherhood. Spencer bemoaned the "fatal tendency among young married women" to give up vocational interests and "waste" their opportunities.[87] Almost a quarter century later, in a 1936 investigative report on medication, the journalist Rachel Palmer and the physician Sarah Koslow Greenberg reiterated this. Critiquing as "hoax" and quackery "glandular products" for menopausal women, they recommended careers instead: "The solution to the psychological difficulties which some women experience lies in a different orientation to life long before the advent of middle age. . . . A career—or just a plain job—offers for the majority of women the most positive insurance against complete absorption in family life."[88] This line of reasoning was further pursued in the latter half of the twentieth century.

The later 1940s and the 1950s, when the discourse around women's middle age crystallized in endocrinological and psychoanalytic frameworks, were a period in which bleak concepts of menopause abounded.[89] Yet celebrations of aging persisted even against the backdrop of hormonal therapies and Freudian perspectives, which confirms general findings about the postwar period as more fraught and contradictory than received descriptions of sharply separate spheres have suggested. Women's retreat to domestic roles was partial and differentially determined by age as much as class and race, with more older women in the workforce than ever before. Even in advice on motherhood, arguments for cultivating identities beyond the home remained common; psychological experts often recommended that women should cultivate identities beyond that of "mother," particularly full-time employment.[90]

In *The Menopause* (1952; reissued as *Women Needn't Worry*), a leading book on the topic in the 1950s to early '60s, the gynecologist, psychiatrist, and sex educator Lena Levine and her coauthor, the journalist Beka Doherty—renowned for writing "the first really accessible book" on cancer—debunked domestic ideals.[91] Levine, a close colleague of Margaret Sanger and cofounder of the International Planned Parenthood

Federation, attributed many medical problems to misinformation and ignorance. She tried to provide accessible information and called upon physicians to recognize their responsibility for educating their patients. In *The Doctor Talks with the Bride* (first distributed in 1938 and reprinted through the 1960s) and other pamphlets written for Planned Parenthood, Levine addressed physicians and patients at the same time.[92] *The Menopause* spoke to the same dual audience. The New York State Department of Mental Hygiene wanted it "in every public library and every doctor's waiting room."[93]

Criticizing negative Freudian interpretations—specifically Deutsch—and cautioning against hormonal therapy, Levine and Doherty held that menopause was "simply a time of passage from one [normal] period of life to another." Using "menopause" for the sake of convenience, the authors made a case for "climacteric" as the "more accurate word."[94] The older term expressed two central concerns they sought to convey: the normality of midlife change and its social implications.

Noting that at-home women often arrived at the climacteric with more complaints, Levine and Doherty attributed menopausal problems to domestic exhaustion and alienation, noting that in middle age, many housewives "look back on lives that have been fantastically empty, through no fault of their own. Millions of women discover, at the middle of their lives, that they have worn themselves out repeating dull and unrewarding activities, many of which are necessary to keep a normal life routine going." Only very recently had labor-saving devices like efficient automatic washing machines begun to redefine housework. Even with the best equipment, Levine and Doherty continued, comparing the homemaker to the assembly-line worker, there were "thousands of routine tasks that must be performed over and over again to the point of desperation—a problem of major concern to people who want to keep up the morale and efficiency of factory workers . . . , but seldom mentioned in connection with housekeeping."[95]

Discussions of work and middle life were closely intertwined. In a *Life* magazine profile, the anthropologist and public intellectual Margaret Mead bemoaned that "we've focused on wifehood and reproductivity with no clue about what to do with mother after the children have left the home." Coining a "Meadism" that soon percolated through everyday speech, she famously continued: "We've found no way of using resources of women in the 25 years of *postmenopausal zest*."[96] When the television talk show host David Frost later asked Mead how she managed to accomplish so much, keeping up a pace that would exhaust someone half her age, she retorted: "It might have killed me too at that age! I attribute my energy to my postmenopausal zest."[97]

Midlife was also central when reformist arguments for married women's employment gained strength in the 1950s, as illustrated by one of the most influential agendas advocating careers for women: Alva Myrdal and Viola Klein's *Women's Two Roles: Work and Home* (1956), which was all about middle age. *Women's Two Roles* dated back to the mid-1940s, when the International Federation of University Women commissioned from the Swedish sociologist and policy-maker Myrdal a social survey on the needs for the social reforms that would allow women to reconcile family and professional life. Myrdal, then transitioning from a position as the head of the UN's welfare policy section to chair of UNESCO's social science section, collaborated on the project with the Austrian-British sociologist Klein. An expert on feminist and anti-feminist thought and on women and work, Klein shared Myrdal's concern about the limited career opportunities for educated women at a time when—though the absolute number of women in the workforce was increasing—the percentages of professional women were dropping rapidly. In academia, the number of faculty women declined from 27.7 percent in 1940 to 24.5 in 1950 and no more than 22 percent in 1960.[98]

Myrdal and Klein demanded married women's reentry into the workforce in their thirties to forties. Echoing earlier stage concepts of the female life cycle, they promoted what came to be known as the "three-phase model" of women's employment biographies: between the end of education and before marriage and motherhood, most women earned their own living, for a period of five to seven years, the "first phase of adulthood." They might then either continue as wage-earners, without marrying, or, as most did, retire from the labor market to set up a family. Motherhood and, occasionally, part-time employment characterized the second phase. After a period of fifteen years or so, women "retired" from domestic responsibilities and active motherhood and entered the third phase, in which they returned to an occupation. To implement this pattern and facilitate a "fresh start at forty," Myrdal and Klein recommended adjustments to the labor market, notably more opportunities for women to keep up or improve vocational skills during the years at home, for example, through part-time work.[99]

The three-phase model resonated widely. It was embraced enthusiastically in Myrdal's and Klein's home countries of Sweden and Britain and beyond. Attending Lord Heyworth's 1963 committee on university appointments boards, which produced the authoritative report on career guidance services in British higher education, Klein noted that speakers quoted *Women's Two Roles* "over and over again"; the secretary of the University of Cambridge's appointments board called it her "bible."[100]

In the United States, Myrdal and Klein's message supported research commissioned by governmental initiatives about women and work at a time of Cold War anxieties about manpower and "womanpower." In 1953 reports to the American Council on Education's Commission on the Education of Women (CEW), for example, the social psychologist Marie Jahoda and the developmental psychologist Mary Cover Jones put into perspective women's midlife trouble by comparing it to (men's) retirement.[101] In a follow-up study of middle-aged women, Jahoda demanded more attention be paid to "the positive aspects of [women's] life patterns."[102] At the conference "Work in the Lives of Married Women," held in 1957 and sponsored by the National Manpower Council (NMC), the noted child psychologist Eleanor Maccoby explained that sporadic work, not maternal employment per se, posed a problem for their children's development—an endorsement of women's careers taken up as the official position of the NMC.[103]

In the 1960s, the Kennedy administration endorsed the three-phase model as social policy. When the president established the Commission on the Status of Women in 1961, he included "recommendations for services which will enable women to continue their roles as wives and mothers while making a maximum contribution to the world around them" and agreed with the Myrdal-Klein thesis that "women should be assured the opportunity to develop their capacities and fulfill their aspirations on a continuing basis."[104] A couple of years later, Betty Friedan cited Myrdal, Klein, and Jahoda as an inspiration for *The Feminine Mystique*.[105]

In the final paragraphs of her essay, Sontag noted that the double standard, although operated by men, "could not work if women themselves did not acquiesce in it. Women reinforce it powerfully with their complacency, with their anguish, with their lies [about their age]."[106] Historical accounts of midlife liberation, by contrast, put into perspective the double standard of aging by showing that it was not universally perpetuated. Aging was not always an oppressive tool: for many women, it meant a liberation from traditional gender roles.

5 *Confidence and Ambition*

"Concepts have memories," a way of carrying their history with them, and the definition—and redefinition—of the midlife crisis in the 1970s was based on earlier understandings of middle age.[107] The idea of a change of life at forty built on the early-modern notion of predictable climacteric years in the human life course, understood as periods of "crisis" in the Hippocratic sense: critical phases of development that led to improvement or decline. Formulated in the tradition of a white middle-class discourse about gender and aging, the midlife crisis became popular as a feminist concept of change in men's and women's life courses that drew strongly on definitions of middle age as a "new deal" for women, the end of motherhood and the beginning of a career.

In 1972, Sontag was neither the first nor the only one to speak of a "double standard of aging."[108] Her contribution to the history of middle age is remembered because she gave a powerful voice to a familiar idea shared by many. Sontag concluded her critique by invoking positive concepts of middle age. "Women," she wrote, "have another option. They can aspire to be wise, not merely nice; to be competent, not merely helpful; to be strong . . . ; to be ambitious."[109] Writing at the same time, the journalist Gail Sheehy deployed such notions of middle-life empowerment in her definition of the midlife crisis as a critical period of change and degendering in men's and women's lives.

3
Feminist Origins

Building on earlier conceptions of women's new lease on life in middle age, the reporter and writer Gail Sheehy made the midlife crisis known as a concept of social criticism. "Crisis" is typically understood as a diagnostic category, which originated in ancient medicine. However, as the historian Reinhart Koselleck pointed out, in classical Greek *krísis* was first and foremost a political term. Used in governmental, military, and juridical contexts, it implied a normative "critique" as much as a descriptive "crisis."[1] During the 1970s, the notion of a "midlife crisis" gained a similar critical quality.

Although the psychoanalyst Elliott Jaques coined the term in the 1950s, it only came into general use two decades later, with Sheehy's best-selling *Passages* (1976), as a feminist idea that challenged the double standard of aging. Based on the life histories of 115 women and men, Sheehy's book combined earlier notions of middle age as a period of self-fulfillment and success for women with accounts of male "gray flannel-suit" fatigue and discontent. By depicting the dissolution of male and female gender roles at the onset of middle age, *Passages* displayed the midlife crisis as a critique of the work-and-life styles of the nuclear family.

Existing accounts of the history of the midlife crisis, often presented as cursory introductions, consistently mention Sheehy but assign her a marginal role. There is general agreement, in journalistic and disciplinary texts, that "midlife crisis" emerged as an idea within psychology before Sheehy "popularized" it. Even the historian Steven Mintz, who briefly mentions the midlife crisis, speaks of "a phrase introduced . . . by the Canadian psychoanalyst Elliott Jaques and popularized by Gail Sheehy."[2] Yet the received understanding of "popularization" as translation and dissemination obstructs the inventive features of knowledge circulation, a process that involves application, reappraisal, and even feedback.[3]

Sheehy actively attributed ideas to experts and invented precursors to bolster her own respectability. Without her book, few would think that the psychoanalyst Jaques introduced the term "midlife crisis." Moreover, rather than praising and promoting academic research, Sheehy—like many contemporary feminist activists, writers, and academics—took a swipe at psychological and psychoanalytic concepts of the life course, to which the "midlife crisis" provided a counternarrative.[4] *Passages* was no "popularization" but a critique of psychology and an important starting point for the history of the midlife crisis.

Sheehy's best-known target was the psychoanalyst Erik Erikson, whose "Eight Stages of Man" epitomized linear models of the life course. A description of men's lives, Erikson's theory also entailed guidelines for mothers and wives. When women objected to Erikson's endorsement of full-time motherhood, the psychoanalyst insisted on his point, in a treatise on women's "inner space." Historians have misread Erikson's well-known praise of interiority as an endorsement of feminist care ethics.[5] Yet the psychoanalyst untiringly objected to feminist framings. He glamorized an identity rooted in maternity and interiority to limit, not further, women's rights. Putting together male and female life courses, Sheehy rotated the entire structure to make available to women identities, activities, and opportunities traditionally reserved for men, and to revalue empathy, attachment, and subjectivity for men.

1 *Investigating New York*

When Sheehy's book came out, she had been a journalist for over a decade and a half. Born Gail Henion in 1937, the daughter of a salesman and a homemaker, she grew up in Westchester County, New York. After graduating from the University of Vermont, she worked as a traveling representative for J. C. Penney, a large department store. She married in 1960, taking her husband's last name, Sheehy, and lived in Rochester, New York, before moving to New York City in 1963, where their daughter was born the following year. The couple divorced in 1968. The same

FIG. 3.1 Gail Sheehy, 1975. Black-and-white glossy photograph submitted to the Penney-Missouri Magazine Awards committee, who chose Sheehy's 1974 *New York* article "Catch-30" as a winner of their annual competition. Penney-Missouri Journalism Awards Records, collection 4050, folder 163, State Historical Society of Missouri, Photograph Collection.

year, Sheehy became a contributing editor at the newly founded *New York* magazine.[6]

Sheehy had written before—for a local newspaper in Rochester, then briefly for the *New York World-Telegram and Sun*, and for a while at Helen Gurley Brown's *Cosmopolitan* as well as for *Holiday*, *McCall's*, and other magazines, but first and foremost for the *New York Herald Tribune*. A feature writer under the *Trib*'s illustrious fashion editor Eugenia Sheppard, Sheehy took pride in her contempt for "fak[ing] passion in print for the latest collection of Junior League tea dresses" and relished blighting the style pages with articles about topics Sheppard considered "unsightly at best and radical at worst" (but agreed to include): anti-war protests, abortion, women doctors administering medical care to beaten-up civil rights activists in Selma, and Harlem women on rent strike.[7]

Newspapers' "women's pages," while often criticized as a "soft news ghetto" that institutionalized the restrictions placed on women, were also central for feminism in the press. They raised important women's issues early and discussed them at greater length and in more detail than other parts of the news. Moreover, the politicization of the women's pages also enlarged the options for women journalists—for whom breaking into the hard news sections was difficult—as emergent feminist politics allowed women reporters to cover news.[8] In 1964, an investigative series on the maternity clinics of New York, published at a time when the city was experiencing an upsurge in infant mortality, brought Sheehy some attention and a Newswomen's Club of New York Front Page Award.[9]

When the *Trib* faltered in the wake of strikes, the editor Clay Felker and the graphic designer Milton Glaser built *New York* magazine from its Sunday supplement—the first issue was published in April 1968—and Sheehy became a contributing editor there.[10] Distributed in the New York metropolitan area with a circulation of just over 330,000, *New York* was a cradle of New Journalism, a style of reportage that used literary techniques. The magazine integrated consumer-oriented lifestyle reporting, investigative journalism, and innovative political and social analyses, a concoction perfected by Tom Wolfe in a piece about "radical chic."[11] In the types of men and women featured, *New York* represented a progressive gender politics. An incubator for Gloria Steinem's *Ms.* magazine, which it helped to launch in 1971, *New York* was among the first mass-market outlets to deal explicitly with feminism, and feminist writers saw it as sympathetic.[12]

New York became Sheehy's main outlet until the media mogul Rupert Murdoch took it over in 1977.[13] The most prolific writer for the magazine during that period, she authored fifty articles in nine years on a variety of topics—counterculture, drug use, the Black Panthers, and local politics—and gender was a mainstay.[14] The semantic distinction between biological "sex" and the social and ideological features of "gender" began to spread in the 1970s, yet "gender" was not in common parlance. Instead, "sex" also entailed a broader, nondeterministic conceptualization of the historical and cultural attitudes toward women and men and their relationship to the larger social order. Sheehy occasionally used the term "gender," but typically, she spoke of "sex roles," "sex difference," or the "two sexes," noting, for example, that "young women have been expected to be content with, and adjust to, a sense of identity bootlegged from their sex role."[15]

Sheehy's writing—her focus on heterosexual relationships and the white, educated middle class, and on sexism, or "patriarchy," separate from race and class—was representative of feminist agendas that received broad media representation in the 1970s.[16] Early pieces reported on American masculinity, glimpsed in commuter-train culture, or male "Indian clubs," the latter done as a photo story with Diane Arbus.[17] Sheehy wrote guest commentaries for Gloria Steinem's feminist column "The City Politic," reported on the first public speak-out on rape, organized by Susan Brownmiller and others in a Manhattan church in 1971, described an installation of Niki de Saint Phalle's provocative Nana sculptures in Central Park, and penned a series on family arrangements beyond the nuclear constellation of male breadwinner, female homemaker, and resident children.[18] She covered the 1971 Town Hall "Dialogue on Women's Liberation," where Germaine Greer vivisected Norman Mailer and famously told the *New York Times* book critic Anatole Broyard, when he asked what it was that women wanted: "Whatever it is we're asking for, it isn't you, honey."[19] In reportage and essays, Sheehy reflected on the sexual revolution, radical feminism, and women activists more generally—in the IRA, with the Black Panthers—and on Lionel Tiger, sociobiology, and the first stirrings of the men's movement.[20]

By 1970, observers of the media knew Sheehy as "one of New York's, and *New York Magazine*'s, most talked-about young writers."[21] After a fellowship in "interracial reporting" at Columbia University in 1969–70, she published *Panthermania* (1971), about the Black Panther trials in New Haven.[22] She followed this with an investigative report about prostitution in New York's Times Square, in the reform-oriented "muckraking" tradition. Sheehy's research revealed the big-business structures behind local prostitution. The mayor cited for journalistic excellence her *New York* article "Landlords of Hell's Bedroom" (1972)—a play on the midtown neighborhood Hell's Kitchen—and it informed municipal politics; her advice was seen as largely responsible for ridding the Times Square area of prostitution. The reportage won a Front Page Award and a National Magazine Award but also got caught in the controversy about New Journalism's fusion of fact and fiction for its usage of composite characters.[23] Sheehy's book-length account *Hustling* (1973) was the basis for a television film of the same name (1975), in which Lee Remick played Gail Sheehy as—in one commentator's apt characterization—a "chic, investigative" reporter, and, later, for the HBO series *The Deuce* (2017).[24]

Tying into Sheehy's long-standing interest in gender politics, *Passages* was a work of social criticism befitting an experienced journalist. She embarked on it in 1973, armed with a one-year journalism fellowship from the Alicia Patterson Foundation to turn a book "about couples," under contract with the small but respected New York publishing house E. P. Dutton, into a project on "ages and stages of development in men and women."[25]

2 *Inventing a Precursor*

Sheehy's study of the adult life course takes off in the late teens, when children leave their parents' homes, then follows the chronology through the twenties, thirties, and forties, and tapers out in the fifties. The focus is on the thirties and forties, for which the earlier decades of life—in particular the twenties—provide the backdrop. Sheehy's notion of midlife self-discovery depends on early adulthood to make sense, for "'maturity' implies previous 'immaturity,' and being 'grown up' implies previously having been childish or juvenile."[26] *Passages* delineates a continuous buildup of problems from the beginning of careers and relationships in the early twenties that culminates in a decisive biographical change in the middle thirties to early forties—just before, not during, middle age, as Sheehy emphasized, marking the transition from young adulthood to middle age.[27] The midlife crisis then demolished gender roles established in the twenties to early thirties.

Sheehy invented a number of telling terms to describe this period of upheaval and change. *New York* magazine was known for an expressive, colloquial style and a knack for inventing catchwords. Most did not catch on, like "grup," for adults reluctant to grow up, or "bullcrit," denoting the casual judgment of books and movies based entirely on reviews.[28] But *New York* followed "radical chic," with the "me decade" (also Wolfe's), and later claimed "couch potato."[29] In this spirit, Sheehy—a self-described "metaphor maven" also known as the "Presiding Princess of Adroit Alliteration"—introduced several terms to denote the "passages" of life: the "Trying Twenties" (echoing child doctor Benjamin Spock's "Terrible Twos"), "Catch-30" and "Switch-40" (borrowing from Joseph Heller's anti-war novel *Catch-22*), the "release from the nest" (the opposite of the "empty-nest syndrome") and, to compare men's and women's sexual life cycles, the "Sexual Diamond."[30]

Throughout *Passages*, Sheehy also used the term "midlife crisis," which she attributed to Jaques, who had published a paper called "Death and the Mid-life Crisis" some ten years earlier. In a fairly late section of the book, concerned with male middle age, she ascribed "midlife crisis" to the psychoanalyst, summarized his paper, and called it a "classic."[31] For Sheehy, this acknowledgment elevated her status as a writer and fortified her argument. By doing so, however, she invented a precursor. Similar effects have been observed within academia. Speaking of scientists, Georges Canguilhem noted that "he who happens on a theoretical or experimental result which had been up to that time inconceivable, which is disconcerting to his contemporaries, . . . looks to see whether perchance his thought has not already been previously thought. It is in looking in the past for an accreditation of his discovery . . . that an inventor invents his predecessors."[32] Not occurring only among specialists, founding myths were a strategy of legitimation also used where science and journalism met.

Jaques's concept predated *Passages*, but it was in fact neither a classic nor closely related to Sheehy's definition. The psychoanalyst coined the term "mid-life crisis" in 1957, in a talk to the British Psychoanalytic Society, given as part of his qualifying to become a member.[33] Born in Toronto in 1917, he had been based in London since being garrisoned there with the Canadian Army Medical Corps during World War II. Trained in medicine, Jaques was a practicing psychoanalyst and organizational psychologist, who taught at various colleges and universities and also worked as a management consultant. An expert on corporate hierarchies, Jaques was known for the concept of the "time-span of discretion," the idea that the main criterion by which the importance of a job is implicitly evaluated is the length of time before decisions taken by an individual are reviewed: the more important, the longer the time.[34]

Jaques's paper on the midlife crisis combined psychoanalytic case studies with quantitative methods of life-course research such as used by the nineteenth-century neurologist George Miller Beard, who claimed to have been "the first to make the discovery of the Law of the Relation of Age to Work."[35] *American Nervousness* (1881) included a study linking men's age and productivity. Analyzing the lives of five hundred of "the greatest men of the world," Beard determined that they did their best work in their thirties and forties: Francis Bacon published his first book, *Essays* (1597), at thirty-six, and the encyclopedic *The Advancement of Learning* (1605) at forty-four; art critic John Ruskin worked on the five-volume *Modern Painters* (1843) throughout his late twenties to mid-forties. Admiral Nelson was knighted at thirty-nine (after the battle of Cape St. Vincent) and was forty-seven at Trafalgar (where he died). J. M. W. Turner painted his best-known sea pieces in his "middle period," between thirty-nine and forty-five.[36]

In similar vein, by "mid-life crisis," Jaques meant biographical change in the lives of a good three hundred male "geniuses," most of them artists and writers, some scientists, who had lived in Europe (mostly Italy, France, Germany, and England) between the Middle Ages and the mid-twentieth century. The central case was Dante Alighieri—the *Divine Comedy* is a classic in life-course literature—but Jaques also referred to Raphael, Bach, Gauguin, and Einstein, among others, as well as an anonymous patient, "Mr. N," a successful and active man, a "do-er," with a career, a wife, and three children. (In dreams of broken glass milk bottles, he literally cried over spilled milk.) The paper also contained a brief report on the Freudian notion of "death instinct" and its usage by Jaques's former teacher Melanie Klein.[37]

In the tradition of earlier authors such as G. Stanley Hall and Walter Pitkin, Jaques declared middle age the time of achievement and self-actualization. He argued that at around age thirty-five, the men in his survey had gone through a "critical phase" (which not all of them survived), the "mid-life crisis." Comparing work executed by artists before and after this crisis, Jaques diagnosed a shift toward more refined approaches and techniques. Dante began writing *The Divine Comedy* (1321) at the age of thirty-seven, and Jaques read its opening stanza as autobiography: "In the middle of the journey of our life, I came to myself within a dark wood where the straight way was lost." In music, Johann Sebastian Bach (1685–1750) "was mainly an organist until his cantorship at Leipzig at 38, at which time he began his colossal achievements as a composer." Similarly, "at 33 Gauguin (1848–1903) gave up his job in a bank, and by 39 had established himself in his creative career as a painter. The work of Donatello (1386–1466) after 39 is described by a critic as showing a marked change in style."[38]

The midlife crisis was an in-built opportunity for "creative enhancement," and Jaques argued that what held for Bach and Gauguin was true also for his patient Mr. N: "Although I have . . . taken my examples from the extreme of genius, my main theme is that the mid-life crisis is a reaction which . . . manifests itself in some form in everyone."[39] However, Jaques made a series of exclusions to the concept, some explicit (women, he held, went through menopause instead of midlife crisis, and several years later), others more implicit (his sample comprised elite white Europeans only).[40] The "mid-life crisis" thus exemplified the modern double standard of aging, an image of male middle-age rejuvenation that excluded women, working-class men, and people of color.

Jaques's paper on the midlife crisis is a citation classic today, and he is known as the "scientist who coined 'midlife crisis.'"[41] In the more than fifty years that have passed since its 1965 publication, over 1,000 papers and books have cited "Death and the Mid-life Crisis," an average of over fifteen citations annually.[42] And yet Jaques is marginal to the beginning of the history of the midlife crisis. The references to his work only confirm the pivotal role of Sheehy, who cited him first.

The "midlife crisis" was hardly taken up initially, probably because of Jaques's fraught relations with the British Psychoanalytic Society. Discussion usually followed talks at the society, but when his finished, there was silence. As Jaques recalled: "I read it, and there was absolutely no discussion, the meeting ended with about five minutes of discussion as compared to the usual forty-five minutes to an hour of discussion of papers. I was very disappointed."[43] The recollection is plausible. Psychoanalytic categories focused on childhood, and many of the society's members might thus have had limited interest in a concept based on the notion of adult-hood.[44] Furthermore, after Freud's death in 1939, the society was racked by methodological conflict. The "controversial discussions" between Anna Freud and Melanie Klein during the 1940s had split British psychoanal-ysis into three warring subschools: Freudians, Kleinians, and the so-called Middle Group.[45] As a Kleinian, Jaques might have expected silence from the opposing groups, but his relations with the Kleinians were also com-plicated.

In 1947, with Wilfred Bion, John Bowlby, and others, Jaques had founded in London the Tavistock Institute of Human Relations, which had close ties to the British Psychoanalytic Society. At the society, Jaques had trained as a psychoanalyst with Melanie Klein as his teacher-analyst from 1946 to 1950. However, just one year after qualifying, Jaques left the Tavistock as the result of disagreements over methods and funding that led to a "very very emotional discussion." All parties framed his depar-ture as a break with psychoanalysis as represented by the society. Of the Kleinian approach, Jaques now held that "its weaknesses glare at you."[46]

Possibly as a result of these difficulties, the society published Jaques's paper with a delay of eight years. Put out in 1965, the article circulated in the psychoanalytic community, where it was mentioned in a few papers on aging and death, as well as among some British organizational psychol-ogists working on career plateaus and retirement.[47] In the United States, Roger Gould, a psychiatrist at UCLA, referred to Jaques in a paper on age groups in group therapy, while the *Archives of General Psychiatry* refuted the "midlife crisis," along with the "empty nest."[48] At times, Jaques was cited but misinterpreted. *Work in America* (1973), a government report, used the term "midlife crisis" to express managerial alienation and fear of failure, noting that "a general feeling of obsolescence appears to overtake middle managers when they reach their late 30's. Their careers appear to have reached a plateau, and they realize that life from here on will be along an inevitable decline. There is a marked increase in the death rate between the ages of 35 and 40 for employed men, apparently as a result of this so-called 'mid-life crisis.'"[49] This was closer to the white-collar woes of Wil-liam H. Whyte's "organization man" and David Riesman's "lonely crowd" than the creative renewal described by Jaques. When he reprinted "Death and the Mid-life Crisis" in his essay collection *Work, Creativity, and Social Justice* (1970), the paper was ignored by most reviewers or dismissed as unimaginative and old hat.[50]

Key publications on middle age, such as the World Federation for Mental Health's *Men in Middle Life* (1967), published two years after his paper, did not refer to Jaques.[51] Bernice Neugarten's reader *Middle Age and Aging* (1968), an often-referenced tome of almost six hundred pages, reprinted texts touching on middle age by eminent scholars from various disciplines—Erik Erikson, Else Frenkel-Brunswik, Robert Havighurst, and William Masters and Virginia Johnson, alongside previously unpublished papers, notably Neugarten's own programmatic "Adult Personality: Toward a Psychology of the Life Cycle."[52] Jaques's paper was not included; nor did the volume anywhere mention "mid-life crisis." Nobody defended Jaques's claim when the social psychologist Daniel Levinson, from Yale University, recoined the term in a talk at the Society for Life History Research annual meeting in 1972.[53] In the mid-1970s, a Social Science Research Council committee on middle age did not include Jaques's paper in its comprehensive bibliographies.[54]

Most people learned about Jaques from Sheehy. Narratives of affiliation do not merely strengthen the position of those laying claim to a purported legacy; they also bolster that of the "founder."[55] By calling his 1965 paper a "classic," she in fact conferred that status. Social scientists seldom referred to her book, but journalistic or not, enough of them seem to have read it to make Jaques's paper the "classic" Sheehy had claimed it to be. After the publication of *Passages*, citation rates for "Death and the Midlife Crisis" rose sharply, from an average of twice a year before Sheehy's book to more than ten times after it.[56] Crucially, Jaques was now cited by experts on middle age who had previously ignored him, including Bernice Neugarten and reinventor Daniel Levinson.[57]

This subsequent emergence, however, was not a "revival" of Jaques's concept; nor did Sheehy "popularize" his idea. If *Passages* drew attention to Jaques's "mid-life crisis," this was not central in the book. Sheehy interviewed several social scientists, but not him—although he was still alive. Moreover, her concept of midlife crisis had little in common with his. Sheehy challenged the very double standard that Jaques had corroborated.

Passages was closer to Betty Friedan's *The Feminine Mystique* than to his psychoanalytic insistence on male ingenuity.

3 *Critical Stories of Men and Women*

Indignation marked the starting point of *Passages* and drove Sheehy's engagement with much theory and research. In her memoirs, she remembers that she enjoyed a "shrug of insubordination" by dismissing canonical works of psychoanalysis that she saw as addressing "only one-third of a much bigger picture," while two further questions needed to be asked: "What are women doing and feeling as they negotiate that tricky passage [into middle age]? And how is the transition played out in the double-message dialogue of the couple?"[58]

To answer, Sheehy interviewed 115 men and women between eighteen and fifty-five years old. Most, but not all, were couples with children— and, as Sheehy highlighted, over half were divorced; many were based in New York and Washington, DC, and some on the coast of California; all but a few were anonymized.[59] (The journalist Carol Tavris remembers that New Yorkers enjoyed playing Guess the Pseudonym as they read Sheehy's portraits.)[60] One exception was a long section on the anthropologist Margaret Mead, drawn from an earlier *New York* magazine portrait. Sheehy linked Mead's midlife crisis to her decision to split up with Gregory Bateson—a resolution that, although it would not take effect until several years later, Mead described as propelled by the explosion of the atomic bombs over Japan in August 1945, when she was forty-three.[61]

Some of Sheehy's interviewees were friends and friends of friends, colleagues, or acquaintances.[62] Others responded to an early *New York* magazine article on the midlife crisis, "Catch-30," put out two years before *Passages*.[63] Shortly after this was published, Sheehy received a call from the former wife of one of her interviewees: she wanted to give her side of the story.[64] Another reader, a twenty-four-year-old woman whom Sheehy called "Serena Carter"—the "devoted carrier" of her husband's ambitions—wrote to complain. A college graduate working in low-level administration to support her husband through law school, Carter neither sympathized nor identified: "Your men are childish, unrealistic, insecure people who blame everything bad that happens to them on their wives, and everything good that happens on their own superior judgment." Sheehy wrote back: "My hunch is that you and your husband would be the ideal representatives of the twenties point of view. Can I persuade you both to be part of the book?" They consented "with enthusiasm."[65]

The vast majority of Sheehy's interviewees were from the white, educated middle class. The men were lawyers, doctors, chief executives, and middle managers, professors, politicians, and students, or worked in the arts, the media, and the sciences. Some of the women were high-achieving professionals in the same fields, but many were at-home mothers or worked part-time. Sheehy presented this group as most typical of American society at large, very selectively employing the experiences of working-class women and black men to generalize her theory. In her analysis of women's lives, she painted a bleak picture of working-class jobs to make a case for education and a continuous career.[66] Similarly, Sheehy drew on interviews with two exceptionally successful black men to illustrate that the crises she depicted applied to them, too: Dennis Watlington, a graduate from Hotchkiss (a leading prep school) and part-time student at a West Harlem acting school, and Arthur Mitchell, the first black dancer with the New York City Ballet and founder of the Dance Theatre of Harlem, known as the first black classical ballet company (both permitted the use of their real names). Referring to Watlington, who had grown up in East Harlem, Sheehy admitted that "things are quite different in families handicapped by class or color or both" but concluded: "Though [his] experiences . . . were offbeat, his *reactions* are typical."[67] (Brief mentions of Watlington's mother aside, black women did not figure in *Passages*; nor did working-class men, whether black or white.)

Sheehy's description of her sample as America's "pacesetter group," the beacon of social progress, made manifest this normative understanding of the white middle class, while also indicating her programmatic approach and reformist agenda.[68] What made her interviews "life histories" rather than memoirs, case studies, or simply people telling or writing their stories was the choice of subject. As the historian Rebecca Lemov points out, life histories gave voices to people who had been unheard and generally ignored, and their significance lay not so much in their individual particulars as in broader social insights.[69] Classic life histories or "own stories," such as the reporter Hutchins Hapgood's *Autobiography of a Thief* (1903) and *An Anarchist Woman* (1909), depicted the emerging political consciousness of their subjects.[70] Similarly, in describing crises, complications, and transformations, Sheehy argued for social change.

In the 1960s and '70s, biographical approaches were an important part of the women's movement. Women shared their "own stories" and experiences in consciousness-raising groups.[71] Often discredited as navel-gazing and ersatz therapy, "CR" was an important building block of movement organization, supposed to lead to thinking and acting: "Don't agonize, organize!" as the activist Tish Sommers famously proclaimed.[72]

Starting in the mid-1970s, women's stories increasingly went public as feminist writers and social scientists began to use life histories, personal documents, and other biographical approaches to illustrate and commend women's involvement in work and social institutions.[73] Evelyn Fox Keller's 1978 and 1979 interviews with the plant geneticist Barbara McClintock formed the basis for a profile in the popular science magazine *Science '81*, followed by an acclaimed biography, *A Feeling for the Organism* (1983), which proposed that McClintock's work expressed a neglected, intuitive scientific style. Five months after the book appeared, McClintock was awarded the Nobel Prize in Physiology or Medicine for her discerning of mobile genetic elements. She became a symbol for the struggles of women in academia, and Keller's brief book a founding text of the feminist critique of science.[74]

Sheehy's memories of a conversation with her *New York* colleague Gloria Steinem highlight the hopes attached to publicizing women's experiences. In the 1970s, the two journalists "began to grasp the concept that [author and activist] Robin Morgan was popularizing: the personal is political. As women dared to tell our real-life stories in public, it would expose gender inequality in every aspect of life."[75]

To this end, in addition to the life histories, Sheehy drew on biographies, autobiographies, and novels, some works of social criticism—Alvin Toffler's *Future Shock*, Philip Slater's *Earthwalk*—and made extensive use of research from disciplines that had a long tradition in life-course research, such as sociology, psychology, and economics, as well as medicine and sexology. She cited the psychologist Eleanor Maccoby, the sociologist Mirra Komarovsky, and the economist Kenneth Galbraith, as well as Riesman, Frenkel-Brunswick, and Masters and Johnson, among others.[76]

"Sheehy goes beyond the academicians," the dust jacket of *Passages* announced, thus preempting criticism of her comprehensive perspective but also expressing Sheehy's stance toward academic research, which was often skeptical. She rarely employed the expository, laudatory tone characteristic of science writing.[77] Rather than seeking to make academic work accessible, she drew on it to prove a point of her own. For example, in an analysis of women's life course, Sheehy referenced Mead and Levinson to support her conclusions, based in part on her own experience: "It is rarely possible for a woman to integrate marriage, career and motherhood in her twenties, and it's about time some of us who have tried said so. It is quite possible to do so at 30 and decidedly at 35, but before then, the *personal* integration necessary as a ballast simply hasn't had a chance to develop. In discussions with Margaret Mead and Daniel Levinson, I found both agreed."[78]

Such confident usage of scientific results and academic theory was taught at the prestigious Columbia School of Journalism, where Sheehy had been a fellow in 1969–70, in the school's Interracial Reporting Program. Geared toward journalists with several years of experience, this midcareer course sought to communicate methods for deploying scientific research, especially from the behavioral and social sciences. Research, in content and method, was presented as a resource for contextualizing and making sense of contemporary issues. Setting out "to expose [journalists] to the behavioral sciences," the school declared that "reporting . . . begins in anthropology and psychology and political science and history and in other disciplines. The journalist will better understand the social significance of what he is reporting if he is able to relate this to larger bodies of knowledge."[79] One of six fellows, Sheehy attended Charles V. Hamilton's Black Politics political science course, a class on urban politics, and two anthropology courses taught by Mead, later involved in the *Passages* project as a mentor. She also got to know Dennis Watlington, then seventeen years old, as part of a year-long "participant observation" research project on the first Harlem teenagers admitted to Hotchkiss.[80]

The Columbia approach reflected the historical connection between journalism and the social sciences and tied in well with Sheehy's background. Under the banner of New Journalism, *New York*, Sheehy's head-quarters, celebrated its stories as implementations, even augmentations, of Max Weber's theory of social stratification, as "sociological studies of urban life that academic sociology had never attempted: the culture of Wall Street, the culture of political graft in New York, cop culture, Mob culture, . . . capital-S society and its discontents." Or it presented journalism as psychoanalysis by other means. In the words of Tom Wolfe, the style's chief theorist, "The whole Freudian revolution is not about sex, it's about the effect of subjective reality on people's actions."[81] Not a fan of Freud, Sheehy cut claims to universal knowledge down to size by likening science to folklore such as the "seven-year itch" and earlier life-cycle theories: "The poets and mystics always get there first. Shakespeare tried to tell us that man lives through seven stages. . . . And many centuries before Shakespeare, the Hindu scriptures described four distinct life stages."[82]

By no means anti-scientific, this critical engagement with social science provided the vantage point from which Sheehy joined the accusations of scientific androcentrism, which feminist academics advanced against the human and social sciences, and psychology and psychoanalysis in particular. In a 1968 conference paper, the Chicago psychologist Naomi Weisstein declared the discipline "relatively useless in describing, explaining, or predicting humans and their behavior" because it rested on sexist criteria. "Psychology has nothing to say about what women are really like, what they need and what they want, essentially, because psychology does not know," Weisstein famously stated. She received standing ovations, and her paper, "Kinder, Küche, Kirche, as Scientific Law: Psychology Constructs the Female," was widely circulated in the women's movement and reprinted in multiple feminist anthologies.[83]

In psychology and beyond, feminist scholarship multiplied rapidly through the 1970s, from one integrated women's studies program in 1970 (at San Diego State, with other pioneering programs in the California state university system following suit) to 150 in 1975 and 300 in 1980.[84] By the mid-1970s, critique of sexism and androcentrism in academia was widespread. For *Passages*, Sheehy consulted published and unpublished studies by the psychologist Matina Horner (on women's "fear of success"), the economist Margaret Hennig (on women executives), and the sociologist Harriet Zuckerman (on the careers of Nobel laureates). She cited Juliet

Mitchell's critique of "penis envy," the sociologist Jessie Bernard's assessment of the use and abuse of marriage for men and women, and the psychiatrist Mary Jane Sherfey's feminist redefinition of embryogenesis.[85] Of the subject of adult development, however, Sheehy noted that "most of the research was being done by men who were studying other men. Men and women may be isolated for the purpose of a scholar's study, but that is hardly how we live. We live together. How can we possibly expect to understand the development of men until we hear also from the people who bring them into the world, from the women they love and hate and fear and perform for, depend on and are depended on by, destroy and are destroyed by?"[86]

4 *Stages of Man*

The central target of Sheehy's critique was Erik Erikson, the psychoanalyst who had formulated one of the most widely circulating concepts of the human life cycle. Presented in the landmark study *Childhood and Society* (1950), the "Eight Stages of Man" delineated a normative sequence of identity development over the life course.[87] Based on Freud's theory of psychosexual development—from oral to anal to phallic, latent, and genital phases—Erikson's model devoted most space to early childhood and to the development of psychological qualities such as trust, autonomy, and industry in the first few years of life, followed by an adolescent "identity crisis" and the development of adult "intimacy" in stages five and six, respectively.

In "adulthood," the seventh, longest, and least differentiated stage, Erikson emphasized the cultural as much as biological character of reproduction. He defined the mature quality of "generativity" as the "establishment (by way of genes and genitality) of the next generation," but also as "productivity," "creativity," and assuming toward society generally "a parental kind of responsibility."[88] At a time when the relation between identity and work was publicly scrutinized, and worry about white-collar alienation was commonplace, the psychoanalyst suggested, instead, that careers were a pathway to authenticity. His phase model provided the base for the seminal theory presented in *Career Development* (1963) by the educationists David Tiedeman and Robert O'Hara, who noted that "Erikson . . . seems

1	2	3	4	5	6	7	8	STAGE
							EGO INTEGRITY VS. DESPAIR	8 MATURITY
						GENERATIVITY VS. STAGNATION		7 ADULTHOOD
					INTIMACY VS. ISOLATION			6 YOUNG ADULTHOOD
				IDENTITY VS. ROLE CONFUSION				5 PUBERTY AND ADOLESCENCE
			INDUSTRY VS. INFERIORITY					4 LATENCY
		INITIATIVE VS. GUILT						3 LOCOMOTOR-GENITAL
	AUTONOMY VS. SHAME, DOUBT							2 MUSCULAR-ANAL
BASIC TRUST VS. MISTRUST								1 ORAL SENSORY

FIG. 3.2 In the "Eight Stages of Man," the psychoanalyst Erik Erikson displayed the life course as a continuous, ascending ladder. Focusing on male development, this ubiquitous stage model was nonetheless importantly directed at women, as a guideline for child-rearing. Based on line drawings from Erikson's writings.

to believe that the attainment of an occupational identity is crucial for the fulfilment of the definition of ego identity."[89] Similarly, in a Harvard study of corporate leadership, Erikson's former student Daniel Levinson and the psychologists Abraham Zaleznik and Richard Hodgson described organization men climbing the corporate ladder as attaining "the stage of development that Erikson has entitled 'mature age,' the sociopsychological condition of integrity."[90]

"Integrity," the eighth and last stage, meant the "acceptance of one's own and only life cycle." Erikson's linear model left little room for regret and change, least of all in adulthood, when "the time is short, too short for the attempt to start another life and to try out alternate routes to integrity."[91] Doubt or fear of death signified a lack of ego integration, which the psychoanalyst "observed in middle-aged cases again and again. They are concerned with the question: If at one time in the past I had made a different decision, would I now be somebody else? And being somebody else, would I be able to handle this situation better? It is this which leads to many divorces."[92]

Erikson's stage theory focused on boys and men; as his Harvard colleague Ives Hendrick noted, this was a model of male, not female, development, in the Freudian tradition.[93] Yet as a postwar concept of childhood, it was about bringing up as much as growing up and, thus, importantly directed at women, as mothers. Erikson's biographer Lawrence Friedman has pointed out that the "Eight Stages" concerned the bonds between parents and children, and for Erikson, this intergenerational connectedness distinguished his theory from an orthodox "reconstruction of the infant's beginnings."[94]

As a guideline for mothers, the "Eight Stages" described as the primary task of women the parenting of children, especially boys, in a way that promoted trust and autonomy and, ultimately, produced citizens of integrity. This message became particularly clear in Erikson's contributions to a series of interdisciplinary preparatory meetings for the Midcentury White House Conference on Children and Youth in 1950, which sought to develop guidance for parents, educators, and social planners. The psychoanalyst was the first of four invited speakers, next to the parenting expert Lawrence Frank, the social psychologist Marie Jahoda, and the anthropologist Ashley Montagu. Helen Witmer, the director of the conference's fact-finding committee, found Erikson's concept of the life cycle so helpful that she wanted his statement copied and pasted into the conference report.[95]

At the meeting, much of the discussion about Erikson's model of child development centered on educating women, not children. Although the discussants often spoke of "parents" or "fathers and mothers" in the same breath, men were peripheral. Where they were discussed, the main concern was with fatherhood as a pathology: that they would father too much, verge on homosexuality.[96] The problem with women, by contrast, was a lack of identification with motherhood, envisioned as a full-time occupation. Lois Murphy, founder of the Sarah Lawrence Nursery School (today the Early Childhood Center), which offered courses for women in early childhood education, found the "Eight Stages" effective for instilling in female students a "deep acceptance" of maternity, thus helping them achieve "the fulfillment of their universal [biological] capacities."[97]

To the same end, the noted pediatrician and child-guidance expert Benjamin Spock, author of *The Common Sense Book of Baby and Child Care* (1946), wanted girls' education to emphasize empathy and family relations so that "the idea of eventually . . . being a mother will sound like an exciting aim through childhood." In young adulthood, higher educa-

tion needed to be kept separate lest women's identification with domesticity be damaged: "Education for women is still largely an imitation of
traditional education for men; it teaches them, especially in college, to
admire and to yearn for accomplishments in the fields of the arts, sciences,
industry. It belittles, not explicitly but by implication, human relations and
child rearing."[98]

Deviation from the maternal role meant maldevelopment. At the end
of the meeting, following Marie Jahoda's presentation ("Toward a Social
Psychology of Mental Health"), Erikson concluded the discussion by
describing "the mother [*sic*] who would refuse to have children" as the
epitome of a failed identity: "There is a very prevalent problem; namely
the American girl who can be very self-possessed, healthy, and direct as
long as she does not have to identify herself with her mother in the mother
role, and who has built into her identity, let us say, the image of a slim
body, of active behavior, and so forth. She may find that to have babies
contradicts all of these conditions of a sense of identity." The psychoanalyst assured his audience that "if all of this is not too deeply embedded in
a neurosis, the obstetrician's reassurances and alteration of social values
can help her to change."[99] But many women did not want to "change."

5 *Hole in the Head*

Betty Friedan—who had studied under Erikson at the University of California, Berkeley—rejected the interpretation of a woman's "role crisis"
or difficulties to adapt to full-time motherhood. She claimed Erikson's
theory of male identity development for women, too, including a developmental "identity crisis." Women's key problem was that they were "not
expected to grow up to find out who they are, to choose their human
identity. Anatomy is woman's destiny, say the theorists of femininity;
the identity of woman is determined by her biology." Experts thus over-
looked that women experienced an identity crisis, too, asking themselves:
"Where am I . . . what am I doing here? . . . In a sense that goes beyond
any one woman's life, I think that this is the crisis of women growing
up—a turning point from an immaturity that has been called femininity
to *full humanity*."[100] Part of a process of maturation and growth, women's
emancipation—on both an individual and a societal level—did not, as

Erikson and others implied, violate biological destiny but instantiated the principles of human development.[101]

Erikson objected. At the conference "The Woman in America," organized by the American Academy of Arts and Sciences (AAAS) and held in October 1963 in light of Friedan's book, he delivered a speech called "Inner and Outer Space," a pun on Cold War "space race" imagery and defense of separate spheres. The psychologist contradicted several other speakers—the sociologist Alice Rossi, the social psychologist Lotte Bailyn, and the historian Carl Degler—who explicitly confirmed Friedan's analysis.[102] Rossi's "immodest" proposal for "Equality between the Sexes" was nothing less than a rallying call for rekindling the "feminist spark . . . among American women."[103] Quoting from *The Feminine Mystique*, Erikson opined that "the now fashionable discussion . . . as to whether woman could and how she might become '*fully human*' in the traditional sense is really a cosmic parody."[104] The psychoanalyst clarified that he had not spoken about women precisely because he did not consider his concept of "identity crisis" and development to apply to them. As he infamously explained, "A woman's identity formation differ[s] by dint of the fact that her somatic design harbors an 'inner space' destined to bear the offspring of chosen men and, with it, a biological, psychological, and ethical commitment to take care of human infancy."[105]

Taken out of context, historians have read "Inner and Outer Space" as a "decidedly pro-feminist" celebration of women's qualities. Thus, Erikson's biographer Friedman makes no mention of *The Feminine Mystique* but holds that feminist responses to the analyst, from the 1970s, were "confusing Erikson's observations on differences between the sexes with an endorsement of inequality."[106] For the historian of psychology Ellen Herman, Erikson "anticipated" feminist care ethics, regardless of their well-known criticism of his focus on masculinity and concomitant marginalization of women and femininity.[107]

Yet "semblance is the source of error": the appearance of similarity is misleading.[108] Feminist theorists and activists have indeed used conceptions and activities of care and nurturance to reclaim the significance of venues traditionally associated with women and femininity and revalue the agency of those whose lives are centered in these sites. In the 1970s and '80s, this line of feminist thought was importantly involved in reframing and updating psychoanalysis.[109] Yet attempts to refurbish Erikson's "inner space" were rare, uninfluential, or even failed. When the psychologist and analyst Donna Bassin used the phrase as a metaphor to represent "a woman's interiority, and not her inferiority," she soon took this back, explaining that "my choice of the term 'inner space' . . . and its association with Erikson's model has been problematic." (She proposed the terms "inner subjectivity" or "inter-subjectivity" instead.)[110]

In fact, the comparison with feminist efforts to rethink psychoanalysis, and even his work, makes clear that Erikson had no intention to extend the "inner space" "beyond maternal and reproductive functions" (Bassin), a project of which he repeatedly disapproved. As with any idea or theory, to understand the historical meaning of "inner space," to decide what Erikson "intended to communicate," it is necessary, first of all, to "delineate the whole range of communications."[111] If Erikson was part of a conversation, who were his interlocutors? And what kind of message was the "inner space"?

Ultimately, Erikson's emphasis on feminine interiority constituted a response: he aimed to stop Friedan and, by extension, the women's movement. At the 1963 AAAS meeting, the analyst proved his point by drawing on observations of children's play done in 1939 and '40 as part of Jean Macfarlane's Berkeley Guidance Study. Originally, Erikson's experiment aimed at testing clinical hypotheses about child development, but, he explained some two decades later, that was "not the point to be made here."[112] In "Inner and Outer Space," he reinterpreted his study to argue for gender differences. In arranging toys into tableaus, "the girls emphasized inner and the boys outer space." This was "a matter of course" to the psychoanalyst: "sexual differences in the organization of play scenes seem to parallel the morphology of genital differentiation." Bolstering his point in a quick ride through Freudian theories about penis envy and the Oedipus complex, Erikson ascertained what Friedan had challenged: "Anatomy *is* destiny."[113]

Fifteen years later, the literary scholar Cynthia Griffin Wolff still remembered and invoked the "horror . . . felt (and voiced) by women who read Erikson's essay."[114] Friedan did not respond, but others stepped in. Feminist critiques abounded in response to a slightly revised version of Erikson's paper, "Womanhood and the Inner Space," published in more accessible form as part of the essay collection *Identity: Youth and Crisis* (1968), one of Erikson's most popular titles.[115] Weisstein cited him as an example of poor psychology in the opening paragraphs of "Kinder, Küche, Kirche," alongside the psychoanalyst Bruno Bettelheim, known for the *Ladies' Home Journal* column "Dialogue with Mothers."[116] A leaflet handed out by the Radical Caucus of the American Psychiatric Association at the May 1970 annual convention stated: "It's not penis envy or inner space . . . that determines our lives. It's an uptight, repressive male supremists social structure and set of social attitudes that prevents us from seeing ourselves as full human beings."[117]

Critique continued outside of psychological circles. According to the Australian activist and writer Germaine Greer, author of *The Female Eunuch* (1970), "Erik Erikson invented the concept of an 'inner space' in a woman's 'somatic design,' a hole in the head, as it were, which harbors the commitment to take care of the children."[118] Kate Millett's *Sexual Politics* (also 1970) devoted an entire section to the "Inner Space," next to analyses of novels by D. H. Lawrence, Henry Miller, and Norman Mailer. Before it led historians to misinterpret Erikson's agenda, Millett problematized his "chivalrous" perspective. Identifying his text as an updated version of Freud's biological determinism, she noted that "Erikson vacillates between two versions of woman, Freud's chauvinism and a chivalry of his own. He wishes to insist both that female anatomy is destiny (and personality as well) yet at the same time pleads that the preordained historical subordination of women be abridged by a gallant concession to maternal interests."[119] The following year, the author and critic Elizabeth Janeway presented her landmark study *Man's World, Woman's Place* as a book-length critique of Erikson's paper.[120]

In the mid-1970s, when the criticism had become commonplace, Jean Strouse, another former student, invited the psychoanalyst to revisit "Inner Space" as part of the anthology *Women and Analysis* (1974). Erikson used the opportunity to defend himself. Strouse's volume was composed of eleven classic essays on female psychology, including "Inner Space" as well as texts by Freud, Helene Deutsch, Clara Thompson, and others, each followed by a commentary by a contemporary expert, among them Janeway, Mead, and Juliet Mitchell. The auto-commentary by Erikson, the only "living legend" in the group, was an exception to this format. Strouse provided him with questions she felt had been raised in the controversy about "Inner Space": How had "the women's movement affected [his] thinking about women?" What was his answer to the charge, voiced by Millett and others, that he mistook for biology what was in fact learned behavior?[121]

A good decade after Friedan's use of the "identity crisis," Erikson's view was unchanged. In "Once More the Inner Space: Letter to a Former Student" he dismissed his critics' "intellectual militancy" and unscientific "pamphleteering." Making an example of Millett and Janeway, he reaffirmed his points in a philological manner, admonishing criticizers for ignoring "theoretical halftones" and the use of little words—"also," "and," "can"—or even italicizations in his work: this was the extent of the room he gave to alterations of women's roles. When Strouse asked him to respond to the argument that "anatomy . . . is only destiny insofar as it determines cultural conditioning," Erikson referred to a passage from "Womanhood," where he had written that "the basic modalities of woman's commitment and involvement naturally also reflect the ground plan of her body . . . : anatomy, history and personality are our combined destiny." He summoned Strouse and his readers to "take another look [and] . . . mark the little words. . . . 'Also' means that the modalities of a woman's existence reflect the ground plan of her body *among other things*—as men's modalities reflect that of the male body. 'And' says that history *and* personality *and* anatomy are our joint destiny. And if we should go all out and italicize 'combined' too, then an all-round relativity is implied."[122]

Erikson told Strouse: "You did not ask me what I would change if I could. . . . But as one of your anthology's last living authors, let me say that I would have felt like changing very little."[123] This loud and open resistance was a reason why, unlike Freud's, Erikson's theories were never fully revisited and redefined from a feminist perspective. However, he would not respond again when Sheehy redefined his stage theory for men and women.

❻ *Sexual Diamond*

Passages may be considered something of a sequel to *The Feminine Mystique*, the midlife crisis a new label for the "problem with no name." Change in middle age, Sheehy's central issue, had already played an important role for Friedan. The restless women of *The Feminine Mystique* were between thirty-five and forty years old—just in the age range of "midlife crisis." Drawing on Erikson's "identity crisis," Friedan reasoned that roughly fifteen years into their marriages, women were experiencing a "rebirth" and second adolescence. She depicted scenes of dissatisfaction as they would come to epitomize the midlife crisis, writing of the suburban American wife: "As she made beds, shopped for groceries, matched slipcover material, ate peanut butter sandwiches with her children, chauffeured Cub Scouts and Brownies, lay beside her husband at night—she was afraid to ask even of herself the silent question—'Is this all?'"[124]

A good dozen years later, Sheehy depicted the end of motherhood as a phase of empowerment in which women reached their "sexual peak" (the height of sexual desire and orgasmic capacity) and—more central in her description—reentered the working world. Case histories included "Kate," a Radcliffe graduate, housewife, and high school teacher, who at forty switched to publishing and before long was promoted to editor; at the same age "Peggy" went into real estate and filed for divorce, while Katharine Graham, after her husband's death, assumed leadership of the *Washington Post*.[125]

Such accounts confirmed the established feminist credo of women's self-fulfillment through work. As Friedan had written: "The only way for a woman, as for a man, to find herself, to know herself as a person, is by creative work of her own. There is no other way."[126] She went on to explain that volunteer or part-time work would do as little as housework: middle age was about careers. Sheehy corroborated this argument by pointing to the economic need for work. She underscored that for the majority of women, reentry into the working world had nothing to do with "the thrill of getting paid for selling whale-tooth pendants in one's own boutique": it was of necessity. "Husbands, after all, go off to fight, become prisoners of war, lose jobs, take mistresses, have heart attacks and leave their . . . wives in midlife with dismal regularity."[127]

If Friedan had claimed Erikson's concept of identity formation for women, Sheehy's description of women's midlife crisis challenged and recast the "Eight Stages." Throughout *Passages*, she disputed Erikson's definition of development: his notion of a period of delinquency in adolescence was not valid for girls—who risked, for example, stigmatization as "promiscuous"—and even problematic for many boys; the empty "inner space" was not a woman's uterus but an expression of a lack of career opportunities; the developmental goal of "intimacy"—stage six—was outdated by ideas of the autonomous self: "At the time Erikson was writing, the value system underlying psychoanalysis vaguely described 'genuine intimacy' as a selfless devotion to the other. . . . Then, the self was a blurred concept. Now that the focus has shifted to autonomy, theorists are struggling for even a primitive definition of intimacy, something to encompass the balancing act of giving to the other while still maintaining oneself."[128]

Sheehy's critique extended to Erikson's students and followers who spelled out his theory of adult development. When she introduced the work of Levinson, who formulated a theory of the male life course based on the "Eight Stages," Sheehy promptly took a swipe at the psychologist's male-centered perspective: "Levinson's outline of men's stages of adult growth . . . brought on a virulent case of reservations. How many men recognize that their wives and girlfriends have a need for development, too?"[129]

With regard to a paper by George Vaillant, another psychiatrist working in the Eriksonian tradition, Sheehy suggested that a man's self-fulfillment may be a woman's elimination: "Dr. Vaillant confuses me when he explains how the men who received the highest scores in overall adult adjustment mastered intimacy." Well-adapted men, Vaillant had written, achieved a stable marriage before thirty and stayed married. The psychiatrist "would seem to define intimacy as staying married," Sheehy noted. "One wonders how many of these wives enjoyed full adult development."[130] After all, the sociologist Jessie Bernard's recent research had shown that more married women than married men or unmarried women felt they were about to have a nervous breakdown; more had experienced psychological and physical anxiety; more had feelings of inadequacy in their marriages and blamed themselves for lack of adjustment.[131]

Most of all, Erikson's concept of adult generativity did not apply to women—serving others was what most women had been doing all along: "What is the first half of the female life course about if not nurturing children, serving husbands, and caring for others in volunteer work? If a young wife has any extra-familial career at all, it is most likely to be in teaching or nursing." It was not through more caregiving that a woman would find new purpose in the second half of her life. "It is through cultivating talents left half finished, permitting ambitions . . . , becoming aggressive in the service of her own convictions." Sheehy proposed to supplement Erikson's model: "If the struggle for men in midlife comes down to having to defeat stagnation through generativity, I submit that the comparable task for women is to transcend dependency through self-declaration."[132] This redefined the meaning of generativity for men, too.

In contrast to Friedan, Sheehy spoke about men and the "masculine mystique" at length and in detail.[133] The comparison of the male and female life courses was crucial to the layout of *Passages*; alternating between men's and women's lives, chapters, sections, and paragraphs focused on similarities and differences. Men's midlife crisis was depicted as the opposite of women's. When a woman was "brimming with ambition to climb her own mountain," a man felt himself "to be standing on a precipice, his strength, power, dreams, and illusions slipping away beneath him."[134] While women were said to experience a sexual surge, men had to cope with incipient impotence, which Sheehy also spoke of as the "male climacteric" or "male menopause." Women reentered the working world; men dropped out or phased out.

Sheehy inverted the double standard of middle age: middle age was a challenge for women but more of a crisis for men, who struggled with remorse, doubt, and uncertainty. Throughout *Passages*, Sheehy applied the term "midlife crisis" somewhat more frequently to men than to women. In part, or so she explained, men's entry into middle age was harder because they did not know how to read the signals of impending crisis, so that their midlife crisis was delayed and aggravated.[135] Men went through midlife crisis later than women—at forty rather than thirty-five. While such age lag seems to reiterate a double standard under which women grow old earlier than men, it also inverted scientific androcentrism by presenting male development as a deviation from female standards: men were "late," not women "early."

Sheehy's portrayal of the male midlife crisis reminds one of Riesman's *Lonely Crowd*—the best-selling book by a sociologist in the twentieth century—and other critiques of conformity, from the social-psychological study *The Authoritarian Personality* by Theodor Adorno and the Berkeley Public Opinion Study Group (also 1950) and the sociologist C. Wright

Mills's analyses of white-collar life to William Whyte's sociological and business commentary *The Organization Man* (1956).[136] Like Erikson, these authors saw a tight relation between work and identity but critiqued the self-alienation on the "personality market" (Mills).[137]

Sheehy similarly challenged the equation of professional success and identity fulfillment, suggesting that the corporate structure made middle age difficult for men: "In our society, turning 40 for a man is a marker event in itself. By custom, as if he were merchandise on a rack, he will be looked over by his employers and silently marked up or down, recategorized by his insurers, labeled by his competitors. Pyramids being what they are in the professional world, most men will have to adjust their dream downward to some degree."[138]

"Adjusting downward" could mean a severe cut in salary, relegation to a lower position, even job loss. In times of recession and restructuring, one often followed the other. "Ken Babcock" saw his dream of becoming company president going bust at forty-three, when the recession hit his company; he wasted his savings in a doomed attempt to renovate a Wall Street brokerage firm and had to sell the house he shared with his wife.[139]

But Sheehy emphasized that even the men whose dreams had come true were unhappy. A Manhattan architect received award after award and had his work shown in international exhibitions, yet "Aaron" (the alias possibly a reference to D. H. Lawrence's *Aaron's Rod*, a novel about a man who abandons his wife and children, known as a target of Kate Millett's *Sexual Politics*) felt depressed and inane.[140] Career success did not make him happy. Acting on the same experience, another interviewee quit a prestigious position in Washington, DC, for a lousy job in real estate that allowed him to live with his family in Maine. He told Sheehy: "I'll stay home and take care of the kids. I really mean it. I adore children. And to tell you the truth, at this time in my life, I would just love to paint houses and build cabins."[141]

If Erikson and his followers had spoken of generativity as productivity, Sheehy claimed achievement for women as much as caring for men. She praised "the man who devotes the same nurturing and succoring [to his wife] that wives normally provide their aspiring husbands," citing historical examples alongside her case studies: the poet Edna St. Vincent Millay's husband had cared for his emotionally fragile wife, so that her talents could be realized. Janet Travell, who was John F. Kennedy's physician, had a stockbroker-husband who retired at fifty; he "devoted the rest of his life to driving her on long professional trips and reading to her at night when she was exhausted."[142]

Feminist messages about men were not unusual in the 1970s, when writers and activists increasingly emphasized the inclusiveness of feminism, in part to preempt criticism of "man-hating." In the *Washington Post*, Gloria Steinem announced "'Women's Liberation' Aims to Free Men, Too," a message that was widely shared.[143] The ABC documentary "Women's Liberation" (1970), by the news correspondent and early National Organization for Women (NOW) member Marlene Sanders, quoted an activist called Linda Fisher, who highlighted the benefits of the women's movement for men: "The very first thing is that men will no longer have to be solely responsible for the financial health of their family; they don't have to get ulcers and other things because they are the only wage earners. . . . The other things that he has to gain have to do with emotional needs. A lot of men have said 'I wish I could cry,' but they're long past learning how because they've spent so long believing that it's inappropriate." Later in the same documentary, Friedan reiterated this thought. Asked "Who is the enemy?" she responded: "I don't think man is the enemy. I think man is a fellow victim."[144] Elaborating on these thoughts, in *The Second Stage* (1981), she would draw on the feminist concept of midlife crisis.[145]

Sheehy merged women's liberation and men's alienation. Taken together, men's and women's midlife crises meant a switch in gender roles: she, from housewife to full-time professional and breadwinner, he, from breadwinner to homemaker. Sheehy spoke of this pattern as the "Sexual Diamond": "The whole configuration can be seen in the shape of a diamond. That is, males and females . . . start out quite alike. In the twenties, they begin moving apart in every way. . . . By the late thirties and early forties, the distance across the diamond is at its greatest. In the fifties, they both go into a sexual involution, which eventually brings them together in the unisex of old age."[146]

The diamond was a trope of vaginal iconography, which Judy Chicago, whose sculpture *The Dinner Party* (1979) is a major example, defined as "a central focus (or void), spheres, domes, circles, boxes, ovals, overlapping flower forms and webs" that invoke female biology.[147] This was the imagery used by the graphic designer Barbara Nessim in a *New York* magazine

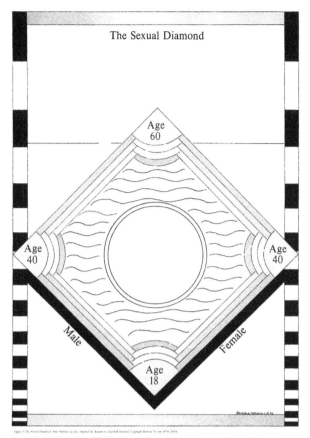

FIG. 3.3 The "Sexual Diamond." The graphic designer Barbara Nessim supplied Sheehy's *New York* article on the male and female life courses with illustrations of rhombi organized around pools and open space. She compared this midlife crisis diagram to a baseball field. © Barbara Nessim, 1976/2016.

excerpt from *Passages*. The figure of the diamond also alluded to social models of equality, used in the 1960s and '70s to criticize hierarchical social structures, such as in corporations.[148] Here, the diamond was presented as the opposite of the pyramid, in which "the majority of . . . individuals . . . rank very low." In contrast, the diamond represented societies organized around a higher number of middle-level jobs. Drawing on the imagery of feminism and social change, Sheehy presented the midlife crisis as a critique of the work and family values represented by the nuclear family and a step toward gender equality. Midlife crisis meant a reversal of gender roles that, ultimately, would lead to their dissolution.

By combining studies of men with research from women's studies, and comparing them, Sheehy challenged male as much as female gender norms. She participated in what the historian Joan Scott, writing some years later, described as the project of feminist research: critical supplementation. Drawing on a deconstructive understanding of supplementarity, Scott argued that new thinking about women as subjects of scholarly research filled gaps but also critically exceeded the ways in which scholarship had been conceived. "Supplementing," in Scott's understanding—and as Erikson and his followers knew—always also means "rewriting."[149]

7 *Reciprocity*

When asked what men could do to help advance women's public and professional participation, experts have repeatedly answered: "the laundry."[150] Sheehy agreed. Subverting Jaques's earlier definition, her concept of "midlife crisis" mutually vindicated women's careers and men's familial commitments. *Passages,* a book about women's liberation and the "masculine mystique," challenged middle-class work and family values and the scientific theories that sustained them. In the vein of contemporary feminist critiques of psychological and psychoanalytic androcentrism, Sheehy refuted Erikson's "Eight Stages of Man" and his understanding of work and family values. Friedan had previously applied Erikson's concept of "identity crisis" to women, to which the psychoanalyst objected, presenting instead a theory of female identity formation in marriage and motherhood. By supplementing Erikson's stage theory with a definition of female "generativity" as self-assertion, Sheehy recast the entire model, including a new understanding of male "generativity" as supporting women's careers.

Earlier accounts of the making of the midlife crisis, presented in academic studies, science writing, or self-help literature, tended to gloss over Sheehy's concept and ignore its original, critical implications. Yet Sheehy's place in the history of the midlife crisis is central, not only because *Passages* was more than popularized psychology but also because it had millions of readers. For many women and men, Sheehy's description of the midlife crisis provided perspective and orientation in times of social change.

4
Serious Sensation

Passages was a sensation. The *New York Times* called it "a revolution in psychological writing," the liberal *New Republic* spoke of a "damn *serious*" book, and *Ms.* magazine praised Sheehy's nuanced analysis of marriage and separation.[1] A best-seller within weeks of publication, it was the most-sold book in the United States throughout the summer of 1976. Perhaps two in ten American readers read Sheehy's book within the first two years of publication, and even more knew it from reviews, author interviews, and excerpts or from discussions with friends, relatives, and colleagues.[2] Widely read and publicly discussed, Sheehy's book seemed to express experiences felt by an entire community.[3] It was, in the words of the Chicago journalist Elaine Markoutsas, the book "thousands" of people identified with "as it stripped our fantasies, bared our souls, slapped us into reality, and confronted us with visions of who and what we are."[4]

Sheehy's success crucially depended on her feminist agenda and social-scientific approach. Existing scholarship on the Second Wave has focused on what changed or got lost in the coverage and communication of feminist ideas.[5] Complicating clear-cut dichotomies between the media and the movement, Sheehy's feminist best-seller suggests that slanted presentation and selective reception were not the only reasons for the popularity of feminism in the 1970s. The mass media—especially women's magazines—constituted a platform for visions of women's lives beyond domesticity even before the women's movement.[6] Moreover, in a period of economic crisis and changing social norms, feminism, with its critique of the family's dependence on the male breadwinner and its demands for careers for women and new roles for men, turned from an oppositional movement into a social and cultural tenet.

For millions of readers—many of them white, educated women—*Passages* replaced Erikson's, Spock's, and other experts' advice about child-rearing with guidance for living a feminist life. The great resonance of Sheehy's message among women past thirty challenges understandings of Second Wave feminism as a young women's movement and documents the involvement of married women and mothers in redefining gender roles for themselves and future generations.[7] If *Passages* encouraged midlife readers to reimagine their work and family lives, for younger, unmarried women the midlife crisis constituted a caveat of early marriage and motherhood, and an incentive to stay in their jobs and not drop out.

Sheehy's perspective and findings also appealed to academics and professionals—journals published more than a third of all *Passages* reviews—though they often dismissed Sheehy's book as inadequate by scientific standards. Historical scholarship and science and technology studies have focused on the ways in which such "boundary work" excluded or expelled "non-science" from the realm of "authentic" research.[8] Yet what seems significant is not that academics found methodological fault with journalistic work but that mass-media publishing was seen as social research. Reading *Passages* as insufficient science—but science nonetheless—psychologists, sociologists, and practitioners used Sheehy's bestseller as an inspiration and a starting point for research and counseling.

However, this success was not a matter of course, and Sheehy's right to speak as an autonomous thinker was disputed at first.

1 *Right to Write*

Sheehy's book created a scandal before it was even published. In an anonymous article put out two weeks before *Passages,* John Leo, editor of *Time* magazine's behavioral science section and an ardent anti-feminist, announced Sheehy's new book by reporting a plagiarism charge against her.[9] This had been leveled two years earlier by Roger Gould, an associate professor of psychiatry at the University of California, Los Angeles, also in private practice, who threatened to sue Sheehy, *New York* editor Clay Felker, and the New York Magazine Corporation for "plagiarism and copyright infringement, *inter alia.*"[10] The appendage was important; plagiarism was not an actionable civil offense, and American copyright protected verbatim expressions only, not ideas, so Gould (or his lawyer) reverted to contract law, a common procedure for plagiarism cases.[11]

The charges referred to an excerpt from Sheehy's book-in-progress in *New York* magazine, "Why Mid Life Is Crisis Time for Couples" (1974), a detailed case study, which prominently cited Gould.[12] Sheehy had interviewed the psychiatrist several months earlier, finding that his recently published paper "The Phases of Adult Life" (1972) resonated with her own interest in inner shifts of experience: "The words [he used] were almost identical to the ones I had been using . . . [;] the stages each of us had been outlining were in many ways consistent."[13]

Gould had done an observational study of adult personality development based on patients seen in age-homogenous groups for therapy at the UCLA Psychiatric Outpatient Clinic in 1968, and confirmed by a questionnaire administered to more than five hundred white middle-class nonpatients. As Sheehy noted approvingly, this survey probed the lives of men and, "yes, *women*."[14] The gender ratio, though nearly balanced for the total sample, was unevenly distributed, with "women being disproportionately represented over age 45," as the psychiatrist put it (he seemed less concerned about the overhang of young men).[15]

When Gould and Sheehy met in the summer of 1973, they discussed some of her biographical interviews as well as his research; the psychiatrist gave her a lecture manuscript, and Sheehy reported that they "decided to work together."[16] Collaborative work has systematically tended to exploit and eclipse women's efforts and contributions to their male partners' advantage—what the historian of science Margaret Rossiter has termed the "Matilda effect," named for the American suffragist and early sociologist of science Matilda Gage, who both experienced and articulated this phenomenon in the late nineteenth century.[17]

In Gould and Sheehy's case, restricting her right to authorship was also inextricable from silencing her critique of separate roles. While their topics of research and scales of analysis—his quantitative, hers qualitative—may have dovetailed, the psychiatrist, wedded to the Eriksonian model, was not at all interested in challenging gender dynamics. In the "Mid Life" piece, Sheehy critically asked: "Where, in all the reams of advice to wives of middle-aged men, is a word about how to build *her* ego?"[18] Adapting the "Phases" paper for *Psychology Today* three years after its initial publication (and one year after Sheehy's *New York* article), Gould pictured a woman's regrets in her forties as concerning authoritarian child-rearing practices, a worry that enforced motherly obligations: "I was young then. I did what the doctor told me. I didn't pick up the baby when he was crying even though I knew I should. If only I had followed my own judgment."[19] Gould's own book-length description of the midlife crisis, published in 1978 as a response of sorts to *Passages*, would demonstrate the persistent discrepancy in Gould's and Sheehy's fundamental outlooks.[20]

So whether Sheehy had lifted portions of her article from the professor's unpublished lecture or not, at stake was more than that. Seeking to protect an idea, not just his terminology, Gould's threat expressed worry about dissent as much as overlap. The struggle about who was authorized to speak and in which register was inseparable from the debate about gender roles.

When Sheehy put out the reportage about midlife couples, Gould accused her of paraphrasing and copying him, and—more legally relevant—of violating a "co-authorship agreement" by publishing the text under her "exclusive ostensible authorship." He demanded to be "fairly compensated," threatening that otherwise he might go to court.[21] Plagiarism cases against writers and journalists were not uncommon (although typically advanced by published authors) and were regularly settled to the claimant's advantage. The year *Passages* came out, two other top-bestsellers, Wayne Dyer's self-help book *Your Erroneous Zones* and Alex Haley's novel *Roots* (both 1976), were involved in similar cases, with Dyer charged for plagiarism by the psychologist Albert Ellis and Haley by the novelist Harold Courlander.[22] The "fair use" defense that allows the appropriation of copyrighted work in journalism and research became effective only four years later, and the use of unpublished sources remained difficult even then.[23]

After an unsuccessful attempt to quell Gould's complaints with an excuse and declaration of avoidance, then a smaller sum of money, Sheehy and *New York* kept him from bringing the action to law by offering to pay him $10,000 and 10 percent of the forthcoming book's royalties. This eventually included a $250,000 paperback sale, and within two years after the publication of *Passages*, Gould had already earned more than $75,000 in royalties and was ironically called "the first [academic] to make that much from someone else's book."[24]

As the literary scholar Marilyn Randall has argued, plagiarism arises from the judgment of readers more than from the intentions of authors. With reprise and repetition as necessary features of writing and thinking, "authorizing principles . . . are, unmistakably, a function of readership."[25] In publicizing Gould's accusation, Leo corroborated it, speaking of "plagiarism," not breach of contract, and turning a nonlitigation settlement into a "filed" lawsuit. He also updated and extended the charges from the magazine article to the forthcoming book, and from Sheehy's exchange with the psychiatrist to her "garbled" handling of scientific sources in general.

The science writer resented Sheehy's confident engagement with social science, dubiously noting that "Sheehy believes she has 'made a bridge between journalistic and academic methods.' As the author tells it, . . . *Passages* could easily have been published as a doctoral dissertation to establish her credentials in psychology." Instead, Leo objected, Sheehy merely reiterated existing studies: "Many of Sheehy's findings were . . . reported earlier by academics." By claiming originality, she "unfairly ripped off her professional mentors" and appropriated their research: "Where she does cite experts, they tend to be introduced as mere spear carriers in her own pageant." Clearly, the *Time* writer concluded, Sheehy was misled to think "she ought to be taken seriously as an independent researcher."[26]

Not everyone agreed. The Harvard economist Margaret Hennig, whose unpublished PhD thesis on the biographies of women executives Sheehy cited at length, refused the idea that she had been plagiarized, telling *Time* magazine that, on the contrary, Sheehy "gave me credit." Most of the scholars Sheehy had interviewed or whose unpublished manuscripts she cited—Margaret Mead, Bernice Neugarten, Matina Horner, George Vaillant, and others—said nothing at all. But Leo elicited an additional complaint about "unacknowledged borrowing" (a paraphrase for plagiarism) from the social and organizational psychologist Daniel Levinson, whose male-centered perspective Sheehy had challenged and who now accused her of being "incomplete . . . in acknowledging her use of my published and unpublished material."[27] Again, accusation of wrongful appropriation was a way of expressing disagreement with Sheehy's feminist agenda.

Sheehy rejected the charge of plagiarism as "wholly false." Not only was Gould's lecture "in the public domain and properly credited," as she reminded Leo. Moreover, she had made it clear at the beginning that the psychiatrist was to be a paid consultant on her book, not a collaborator. He had tried to force his way into the book against her will, as a coauthor, "play[ing] on my insecurities" as a nonacademic "without any letters after my name" and deprecating her writing skills, claiming he could write the book "in six weeks."[28]

In a letter to the *Time* editor, Sheehy called the science journalist Leo jealous and "unfair," pointing to the extensive footnotes and bibliography that detailed the sources of her writing. She explained that "the original theory came from Erik Erikson," not Gould or Levinson, and that she departed from it anyway: "Most of the current research . . . was being done by men who were studying other men. I focused on the life-stages of women, and . . . it became clear that the developmental rhythms of the sexes are strikingly unsynchronized." *Time* typically published letters to the editor within three weeks. Titled "No Pure Ideas," Sheehy's response appeared with an unusual delay of six weeks, after she and *New York* editor Clay Felker insisted it get into the magazine.[29]

Sheehy's case illustrates why it is difficult for women to be acknowledged as authors. The notion of authorship is intrinsically gendered, based on the equation of masculinity with originality and creativity, and femininity with copying, mechanical reproduction, imitation, and the absence of talent and work. Female authorship thus appears transgressive; women are understood to be not authors but a threat to authorship: the "author which is not one."[30] However, it was unusual for a female writer to be accused of plagiarism, a charge often cast in the language of rape and sexual assault against a feminized text and leveled mostly (by men) against men—as in the case of Sheehy's contemporaries Wayne Dyer and Harold Courlander.[31] The allegations against Sheehy thus indicate a perceived claim to authorship, borne out in her self-defense against Gould and Leo.

It was particularly complicated for women to protect scientific knowledge. When the world of science became professionalized in the nineteenth century, married women—not admitted to the category of "person" or citizen, and thus not allowed to hold property—were stripped of the right to own intellectual property, in the form of patents. This made it almost impossible for women to legally defend discoveries or inventions, even when produced and publicized under their name. Yet as the case of the physicist, chemist, and public intellectual Marie Skłodowska Curie illustrates, while the property road was closed for women, the celebrity road was not, and Curie resorted to this culture of publicness as an ownership strategy beyond science.[32] The media paved the way to public authority for Sheehy, too.

Scandals demonstrate social fault lines and mechanisms of exclusion but also attract attention and generate publicity. As the library scientist and sociologist Judy Anderson notes, authorship disputes can be a way to publicize a book, and some writers and publishers have deliberately used plagiarism as an effective and inexpensive marketing tool.[33] In Sheehy's case, one observer of the media noted, the size of the settlement with Gould turned out "paltry when compared with the cash value of attention that abetted the book's best-sellerdom."[34] Challenging credentialed authority, Sheehy was hailed as a counterexpert.

2 *Spock for Adults*

When *Passages* was published, the country's two largest book sections, the *New York Times Book Review* and *Washington Post Book World*, challenged Leo's account, painting a more complicated picture. The New York–based publishing insider Joyce Illig, renowned for the hard-news scoops recorded in her *Washington Post* "Book Business" column, suggested that Gould's work played a relatively minor role in *Passages*—his name appeared only "four or five times" in the book—and that Sheehy cited his work and even included him in the acknowledgments. Highlighting that the lawsuit was never filed, Illig also knew that there had been only an oral agreement, which Sheehy's agent had failed to nail down with a signed contract, and that Gould was now working on his own book, for Simon & Schuster.[35]

Meanwhile, the *New York Times* put the dispute into perspective, showing how it epitomized larger tensions between the specialist, "who knows something but can't write," and the skilled writer, who was able to engage a wide readership: "The specialist accuses the popularizer of glibness; the popularizer disdains the hermetic world of experts. Not to mention ego-conflicts and crass money matters revolving around how much the popularizer should profit from the specialist's research: or the specialist from the popularizer's writing flair."[36]

While commentators foregrounded balance and deliberation, reviewers of *Passages* delivered judgment and decided the dispute in Sheehy's favor. The *Washington Post* political columnist Roderick MacLeish (an expert on the midlife crisis by virtue of recently having turned fifty) introduced the new book as an updated version of pre-Homeric master myths, Shakespeare's *King Lear*, and Goethe's *Faust*. MacLeish avoided mentioning Gould, yet his discussion of Sheehy's use of scientific material read like a point-by-point rebuttal of Leo's accusations: "By her own assertion, Gail Sheehy is not the central theorist of her work. It has many sources. . . . What Sheehy has done is to gather together the material . . . , codify it into skillfully popularized form, invest it with the classy, vernacular prose style for which she is justifiably admired and arrive at a generalist's conclusions." With an eye on Sheehy's intended audience, MacLeish brushed aside the complaints of scientists (and science journalists): "I'm sure that specialists will quarrel with what she has done. That's what specialists are for. But the hope, wit and de-mythification of adulthood that permeates [sic] Sheehy's book make *Passages* a work of revelation for the layman."[37]

In the *New York Times*, Sara Sanborn, a freelance writer who regularly published in *Ms.* magazine, turned the tables on Gould. In an era that was critical of experts and technocrats, and when anti-psychiatry was rampant, he was easy prey. Sanborn stood up for *Passages* as a book by "a journalist, not a therapist," which respected its informants' experiential expertise as much as the interpretive independence of its readers. In contrast to a psychiatrist or counselor, Sheehy approached her subjects at eye level, "as an interviewer asking for help with her work and believing not only that their experience was valuable, but that they were competent to evaluate it. They in turn responded to her as to a co-seeker." As an author, the journalist did not lecture, order, or instruct: *Passages* was written "by an adult for other adults, instead of earnest but slightly backward adolescents." Where therapy "presume[d] to solve your life," Sheehy's observations instead provoked recognition and increased "awareness."[38]

The praise of Sheehy's friendly tone, reassuring message, and eye-level standpoint calls to mind earlier descriptions of Benjamin Spock's *Common Sense Book of Baby and Child Care* (1946), the influential child-rearing manual of the postwar era. A fourth, revised edition was published in 1976, raising sales numbers to 28 million copies by the following year—virtually one for every firstborn child in the country. The historian of paperbacks and publishing Kenneth Davis, who analyzes *Baby and Child Care* as a key postwar best-seller, sees Spock's tone as a main reason for its popularity and longevity.[39] The pediatrician's "gift [for conveying scientific] knowledge to people" was legendary and often invoked as an ideal for scientists and science writers.[40]

Advocating a new, permissive approach to parenting, the book also spoke with a voice of gentle encouragement rather than the condescendingly stern tones of medical authority. It was in *Baby and Child Care*'s famous opening line, the invitation to "trust yourself. You know more than you think you do."[41] As Spock commented, "The previous attitude was 'Look out, stupid, if you don't do as I say, you'll kill the baby.' I leaned over backwards not to be alarming and to be friendly with the parents."[42]

The pediatrician embodied the ideal of approachable expertise or "nonauthoritarian authority," shared by general readers and experts alike, who were impressed by his conversational style.[43] In the words of the US Children's Bureau educator Marion Faegre, in *Baby and Child Care*, "the print doesn't get between the author and his readers."[44] "I feel as if you were just talking to me," one mother told Spock. "You make me feel as if you thought I was a sensible person."[45] Similarly, Charles Anderson Aldrich, an earlier proponent of permissive child-rearing and coauthor, with his wife, Mary Aldrich, of *Babies Are Human Beings* (1938), was "immediately struck with [Spock's] friendliness," noting that "there is not a vestige of the carping criticism so often seen in such works."[46]

To commend Sheehy in terms of Spock was the ultimate accolade: here was a book both revolutionary and trustworthy, understanding and life-changing. It also implied her originality as a writer who presented her own ideas, skillfully, in casual language, rather than a conduit for someone else's conclusions. The acclaimed *New York Times* critic Anatole Broyard confirmed this. Selecting *Passages* as a "Book of the Times," he disagreed, once more, with the charges about unacknowledged borrowing, finding, on the contrary, "that Miss Sheehy's fundamental idea is more original— at least in the way she applies it—than she does." Challenging Leo's allegations of appropriation and presumptuousness, Broyard held that, if anything, Sheehy was too modest: "While she self-deprecatingly points out that Shakespeare spoke of the seven ages of man . . . , Sheehy does not give herself sufficient credit for adapting this notion with some ingenuity to contemporary life. Erik Erikson wrote of various stages of human life, too, but while she draws upon his ideas, she adds to them as well."[47] Sheehy was an expert on her own terms.

Yet *Passages* was no sequel to *Baby and Child Care*. Several reviewers compared Sheehy's book to Spock's and other popular parenting manuals. In the *New York Times*, Sanborn spoke of a book that did "for adult life what [the psychologist and pediatrician Arnold] Gesell and Spock had done for childhood"—drawing up a developmental sequence; *Ms.* magazine labelled *Passages* a "Dr. Spock for adults."[48] However, the Chicago child-rearing guru Joan Beck, author of the nationally syndicated advice column "You and Your Child" (1961–72) and long-seller *How to Raise a Brighter Child* (1967), was misled to suggest reading Sheehy's book as a guide for prolonged parenting into middle adulthood: "children are a concern for parents long after [adolescence]."[49]

At a time when Spock had come to be seen as emblematic of a system that urged women to stay home, "a symbol of male oppression— *just like Freud*," as Gloria Steinem famously put it at the 1971 National Women's Political Caucus Meeting, *Passages* was an anti-Spock of sorts.[50] Instead of repeating messages about maternity, Sheehy challenged the basic premise of parenting manuals—child-rearing as a woman's primary task—by providing an agenda for life beyond motherhood. "I barely made it past the introduction," reported Patricia O'Brien, a writer on marriage, divorce, and singleness, in *Ms.* magazine, "before I found myself underlining passages—not because I was learning startling new facts, but because finally somebody was putting universal human fears and uncertainties about change and growing old into a manageable perspective. . . . Gail Sheehy has . . . provide[d] all us adults with *our own* Dr. Spock."[51]

Rave reviews in some of the nationally most influential newspapers and periodicals set the tone for the media reception of Sheehy's book. *Passages* was critically acclaimed in the *Los Angeles Times Book Review* ("a deeply moving book"), the *Baltimore Sun* ("should be read by everyone"), and the *Atlanta Constitution* ("eye-opening"). Their attention documented as much as increased Sheehy's success.[52] Since the 1970s, media theorists have written off the book as more stable, self-contained, and even isolating than other periodical or electronic media.[53] Yet a main quality of the modern book was its ability to distribute a message in many forms and formats. By generating reviews, excerpts, and adaptations, comments, author interviews, and conversations, books reached audiences far beyond their immediate readership.[54] As the sociologist Gabriel Tarde observed at the advent of mass communication, "even those who do not read . . . , talking to those who do, are forced to follow the groove of their borrowed thoughts. One pen suffices to set off a million tongues."[55]

Passages seemed to be everywhere. In June 1976, within four weeks of publication, Sheehy's book was a national best-seller. It climbed the list in the following two months and was the number one seller in August. A new, sixth printing of 25,000 copies made 125,000 copies in print; by the end of the year, the hardcover was in its twelfth printing.[56] Bookstores sold it on its own little rack near the counter, the Literary Guild and other book clubs sent it to suburban households, and mass-market women's magazines like *McCall's* and *Family Circle* and then *Reader's Digest* brought excerpts to living rooms, kitchens, and bedside tables.[57] Sheehy discussed the midlife crisis in a *People* magazine at-home story, on television with Johnny Carson, and on Richard Heffner's PBS talk show *The Open Mind*, where she opened a series of dialogues on women, gender, and feminism, followed by interviews with Betty Friedan and Margaret Mead.[58]

"This book is getting a lot of attention," Robert Hassenger noted in the liberal and more highbrow *New Republic* in September, when *Passages* had been a best-seller for three months. "Paperback rights have already been sold for a quarter million. Can Truffaut and the Maysles be far behind?"[59] The New York sociologist, who appreciated Sheehy's "fine" work for *New York* magazine, would have been aware that *Grey Gardens* (1975), one of the most popular documentaries by Albert and David Maysles, was based on Sheehy's 1972 *New York* reportage "The Secret of Grey Gardens."[60] Indeed, the television network ABC planned a video adaptation of *Passages*, as a dramatized miniseries.[61] However, Hassenger continued, "I'd have to go with Woody Allen. For, while important, this book is too damn *serious*. It will scare the pants off a lot of people." Imagining "sending a marked-up copy to an ex-mate or former lover," the sociologist highlighted chapter 21, on the "Switch-40s," as "particularly intriguing."[62]

3 *Popular Feminism*

The popularity of *Passages* attested to the public standing of feminist issues in the 1970s. "This is the year of Women's Liberation," proclaimed Gloria Steinem in 1970. Or at least, it was the year the press had "discovered a movement that has been strong for several years now."[63] Through the decade, the women's movement evolved into an attractive media topic. Coverage in the *New York Times*, the setter of the nation's news agenda, increased markedly from the early to mid-1970s, with one or two stories on feminism per week in 1975 compared to none at all in 1969—an effect, not least, of the National Organization for Women's (NOW) media strategies.[64] The three dominant television networks produced more than twenty reports on the women's movement in 1970 alone, including an ABC documentary and multipart series on CBS and NBC.[65]

Coverage also grew more sympathetic. Earlier news accounts of feminism had often been dismissive, but during the 1970s, reporting became more supportive. Women's magazines routinely covered issues pushed by the women's movement such as abortion, rape, or sexism and included feminist columns and special sections—for example, the monthly *McCall's* feature "Right NOW," an eight-page insert of news clips about feminist activities. In 1972, the magazine named Steinem "Woman of the Year."[66]

The heightened presence of feminism in the mass media was mirrored on the book market, an effect that has been traced for fiction—the emergence of "consciousness-raising" best-sellers such as Erica Jong's *Fear of Flying* (1973) and Marilyn French's *The Women's Room* (1977)—and affected nonfiction in similar ways.[67] The success of Kate Millett's *Sexual Politics* (based on her PhD dissertation), Shulamith Firestone's *The Dialectic of Sex*, and Germaine Greer's *The Female Eunuch*—all published 1970, and all non-fiction—prompted mainstream publishers to take interest in feminist authors.[68] A section of Millett's book, in which she famously savaged Henry Miller and Norman Mailer, revived New American Library's (NAL) shaky literature and ideas magazine *New American Review*.[69] In 1973 and 1974, the first commercial edition of the Boston Women's Health Book Collective's *Our Bodies, Ourselves*, published with Simon & Schuster, was one of the five best-selling books on college campuses. Two years later, a revised and updated edition ranked on the *New York Times* best-seller list.[70] Random House published the collection *Sisterhood Is Powerful* (1970), edited by Robin Morgan, which made gray literature broadly available and turned texts such as Naomi Weisstein's "Kinder, Küche, Kirche" from pamphlets into classics.[71] The Basic Books anthology *Woman in Sexist Society* (1971), edited by the journalists Vivian Gornick (*Village Voice*) and Barbara Moran (*Woman's Day*), communicated feminist scholarship to a wide audience, reprinting Weisstein's piece along with papers by the sociologists Pauline Bart and Jessie Bernard, the psychologists Phyllis Chesler and Elizabeth Douvan, the literary scholars Elaine Showalter and Catharine Stimpson, and the art historian Linda Nochlin.[72]

In the early 1960s, when Friedan's *The Feminine Mystique* was published, "women's studies" had not been a category in the publishing industry.[73] A decade later, William Jovanovich, the chairman of Harcourt Brace Jovanovich, a large San Diego publishing firm, opined about the recent surge in feminist literature: "There's no question that publishers are aware that the whole society is thinking about women in a new way, and a good book about or by a woman is looked at with keener interest than it would have been 10 years ago."[74] Famed for having the right instinct, Dutton editor Hal Scharlatt had already commissioned a book from the *Life* magazine journalist Jane Howard on "how the feminist movement was affecting ordinary, regular American women—all American women." Howard spent two years crisscrossing the United States talking to many different women about their lovers and husbands, their jobs and how they spent their money, and what they would do differently if they had it all to do again. Her "liberated, apple-pie" travelogue *A Different Woman* was put out in 1973, making visible women's commitment to the principles of women's liberation all over the country.[75] The same year, Scharlatt offered Sheehy an advance for *Passages*.[76]

Feminism's popularity was selective and highly controversial. White, educated middle-class women and liberal perspectives dominated the public image of the Second Wave, while black and Chicana, working-class, and lesbian positions benefited less from the resonance of feminist messages.[77] The same was true of radical voices: in the women's movement, the early 1970s marked the disintegration of the so-called radical wing, and the year 1975 its collapse.[78] Radical feminists pointed out how the mass media modulated and commercialized political messages.

Gloria Steinem's feminist women's magazine *Ms.* was a prime target. In the anthology *Feminist Revolution* (1975), edited by the feminist action group Redstockings, the journalist and activist Ellen Willis denounced "*Ms.*-ism" as an "economistic" feminism that was hostile against the "sexual and emotional issues that radical feminists were raising."[79] Redstockings members do not seem to have commented on *Passages*, though they would later attack Sheehy in response to her *New York Times* portrait of Steinem, who apologized for having been the cause of "mail directed at you . . . by these putative Redstockings."[80]

Historical analyses tend to confirm the radical position, demonstrating how selection and adjustment shaped "popular feminism."[81] Perhaps most importantly, they show that media success did not always go hand in hand with social and political impact. Still, distortion and moderation were not the only reasons why feminist agendas such as Sheehy's spread. Not only did feminist writers and activists actively use the media as a resource.[82] Authors like Jane Howard, in *A Different Woman*, also emphasized the importance of "softening attitudes" as a means to remove barriers: "Nothing is less persuasive than a tirade from a rigidly orthodox heretic. . . . I have heard the message, *sorores*. I agree. But I'd rather be in the woodwind section than the percussion, and I don't think you can afford to alienate the piccolos. . . . Is not your cause more important than that?"[83] Moreover, feminist perspectives on work and the family also provided an explanation for the social and economic change that characterized the 1970s.

Passages was published in a period when economic crisis and changing social norms destabilized the model of the nuclear family with a male breadwinner and at-home wife and mother. The "male-breadwinner model" was prevalent in the white middle class, though more widely relevant as an ideal and the central paradigm for social policies. Its disintegration, in the late 1960s and the '70s, has been described as a classic example of an overdetermined phenomenon: the family wage ideal eroded, divorce rates rocketed, women's access to higher education was improved—midlife returns to school included. As real wages for men stagnated, their education was prolonged, while corporations ended the lockstep-career model, uncoupling the link between seniority and income and job security, an effect that early-retirement policies increased. The middle-aged parents of the baby boom, facing the rising cost of rearing children in late adolescence, struggled with what demographers called the "life-cycle squeeze": the gap between suburban lifestyle aspirations and family income.[84]

Critiques of the nuclear family and work ethic had circulated since the 1950s, yet in the 1970s, the dual-income model replaced the male-breadwinner family as an ideal. The shift toward a two-earner model meant the end of a life-course pattern of early marriages and separate spheres, challenging the plans and expectations of the baby boom generation as much as the life styles of "anyone over thirty." Gender was no longer an accurate predictor of a person's life course. Under these conditions of social change, feminist messages about work and family turned from an oppositional force into a powerful guideline and explanation.

Older models of the life course were ill equipped to account for what sociologists call the "de-standardization of the life course."[85] Erikson's linear concept of the "Eight Stages of Man," now more than twenty years old, was becoming dated. Benefiting from the paperback revolution, *Childhood and Society*—revised for the 1963 college edition paperback—had been widely successful during the 1960s, when "Eriksonian" was almost a household term on campuses and the psychoanalyst a public intellectual and hero to many campus student activists (although often against his will).[86] The biography *Erik H. Erikson: The Growth of His Work* (1970), by his student-turned-colleague Robert Coles, expressed as much as documented the psychoanalyst's sway.[87]

Yet in the early 1970s there was a turn away from Erikson, who was increasingly criticized as a social conservative, status quo theorist, not only by feminist thinkers. In *The Crisis of Psychoanalysis* (1970), the psychoanalyst and social philosopher Erich Fromm attacked Erikson for failure to pursue the theme that social organizations and values could cripple the individual self and leave a person with a fake sense of identity. For the Tufts political scientist Tony Smith, Erikson typified an oppressive, conservative social psychology that provided "ideological cover for the status-quo" to obscure the alienating power of social roles over the individual.[88] Erikson's sympathizers showed little interest in defending him. In psychoanalysis, his concept of "identity" was superseded by the idea of "narcissism," a debate he did not join.[89] Historians like John Demos, who had previously drawn on the "Eight Stages" and Erikson's psychohistorical biographies, "drifted away" in light of a heightened emphasis on the social structure in new studies of childhood and the family.[90]

Book sales plummeted. Norton had registered nearly 139,000 total paperback sales for all of Erikson's books at the height of his popularity, during the 1970–71 academic year. Five years later, in 1975–76, this number declined by more than half, to 66,400.[91]

The psychologist remembered the essay collection *Life History and the Historical Moment* (1975)—which included the infamous "Once More the Inner Space"—as his "least successful book."[92] When the political theorist Marshall Berman slated the anthology in a page 1 review in the *New York Times Book Review*, he ridiculed the "Eight Ages of Man" as a meaningless "multiplication table," reporting that Erikson "inevitably loses two-thirds of the audience whenever he hauls it out."[93]

In his 1976 biography *Erik H. Erikson: The Power and Limits of a Vision*, the political scientist and historian of psychoanalysis Paul Roazen (another former student) explained the lack of interest by pointing to Erikson's fascination with the prospective features of the life cycle as opposed to the focus on retrospection in earlier psychoanalysis. If more traditional Freudians overemphasized disability and failure, Erikson was "unduly optimistic" about human growth, seeing this only in terms of achievement of integration, not alienation. With all change resulting in improvement, even conflict and crisis were bound to be healthy and "developmental" rather than imposed, traumatic, and neurotic.[94]

This buoyancy came at a cost, as Roazen noted: there was no healthy place for dissatisfaction, regret, or divergency in Erikson's accumulative theory of life's stages. Of the analyst's definition of mature "integrity," Roazen wanted to know: "Why should wisdom be defined by the acqui-escence in the inevitable? It can just as well be argued that wisdom should also lead to dissatisfaction, even rage, at past personal mistakes, unfortu-nate chance, or uncorrected social injustices." Verging on an appeal for "keeping oneself together and functioning for others," Erikson's ideal of ego strength and success concealed suffering and human tragedy as well as sustaining social inequality. "One does not have to be a romantic to think that some personal upheavals . . . may in the long run be better than unthinking conformism."[95]

Put out at the moment of Erikson's decline, Sheehy's critique of his model of the life course and her revaluation of midlife discontent resonated widely. In the words of the psychiatrist Anthony Clare, *Passages* was "Erik Erikson's eight stages of personality growth and development brought up to date." As Broyard specified, Sheehy presented more than a "translation" and "update" of psychoanalytic terminology: "She has a talent for the concrete, partly because she is a good journalist and partly because she has talked with 115 people."[96] *Passages* provided a new, contemporary theory.

Focused on young age as the phase when development is initiated, linear models of the life course equated the yearning for change midway through with pathological "despair" rather than healthy "integrity," in Erikson's words. In *Passages*, on the contrary, the crack was how the light got in. Midlife disquiet held the potential for a new start, to change course, for men and women.

4 Excited Fans

"Excited fans" of *Passages* were known to be "legion."[97] "I felt she was talking directly to me," Alice Hilseweck Ball, a woman her midthirties, wrote her former classmates from Randolph-Macon Woman's College in Lynchburg, Virginia, and recommended Sheehy's book. "Sheehy's right about one thing," responded a thirty-year-old New York reader, a connoisseur of modern French literature, when asked what she liked about *Passages*. "The world brings you up through senior year of college, and then you get dumped." "That's an excellent book," said a young woman at the Harvard Coop, the nation's largest college bookstore, and pointed to *Passages*, in agreement with millions of other college students, who, when they read for their own pleasure, reached for what the rest were reading.[98] Focused on the lives of white, educated women, many married and with children in the home, *Passages*—like Friedan's *The Feminine Mystique*—was primarily (though not exclusively) read by this group; the major leisure-time readers of books, this audience could create and sustain best-seller success.[99]

Readers familiar with feminist messages welcomed *Passages* but hardly thought it new. Barbara Cady, critic-in-charge of books about women and gender at the *Los Angeles Times*, spoke for many when she noted that Sheehy described a "socially induced syndrome that the women's movement has certainly dealt with."[100] Appearing the same year as the psychoanalyst Jean Baker Miller's *Toward a New Psychology of Women* and the psychologist Dorothy Dinnerstein's *The Mermaid and the Minotaur*—two heavyweights on the psychology of women—and followed by Nancy Friday's controversial *My Mother/My Self* the next year (which cited *Passages*), Sheehy's book made little impression in feminist circles.[101] Its relevance lay in communicating feminist agendas, not changing gender theory or devising plans for activism.

Many of Sheehy's readers did not even have to buy her book to read about the midlife crisis; they came across portions of *Passages* in lifestyle magazines. In total, more than half of the chapters of *Passages* were excerpted, some repeatedly. Most excerpts were published in women's magazines: *Glamour* and *McCall's* (a major platform for book excerpts, second only to *Reader's Digest*) put out prepublications in April and May; *Family Circle* and *Bride's* magazine followed with excerpts in July and December.[102] Excerpts appeared in a couple of magazines for professional men, too: the Delta in-flight magazine *Sky* and newly founded business magazine *Wharton* (competitor of the *Harvard Business Review*) adapted Sheehy's chapters on men in crisis. Yet these were small-circulation outlets; larger magazines like *Playboy* and *Esquire*, though important publishers of book adaptations, did not excerpt *Passages*.[103] As Elaine Showalter observed, even Sheehy's depictions of "men's passages" were primarily read by "wives who will explain it to their husbands over the breakfast table. . . . But I hope," the literary scholar continued, "men will take the daring step of reading the book for themselves."[104]

The women's magazines' selection also influenced the choice of digest magazines: the excerpts from *McCall's* and *Family Circle* were reprinted in *Reader's Digest* and *Book Digest*, respectively. The *McCall's* excerpt "The Crisis Couples Face at Forty" was based on the sociologist Robert Hassenger's favorite chapter, on the "Switch-40s." Reprinted in *Reader's Digest*, this analysis of changing marriages midway through became the most widely distributed portion of *Passages*, circulating among more than 35 million magazine readers.[105] Bruce McCabe, the *Boston Globe*'s media critic, said the *Reader's Digest* version "is excellent and will make you want to get the book."[106]

At a time when readers reportedly relied on extracts to make purchas-

FIG. 4.1 "No matter what choice a woman makes, it's going to be very hard to live with." When *Book Digest* magazine adapted a portion from Sheehy's *Passages*, they supplied the excerpt with a new cover of sorts. In an interview with the magazine's editor, Sheehy observed that women had a particularly difficult confrontation with the passage of time because they were torn between the competing priorities of career, marriage, and family. *Book Digest*, September 1976.

ing decisions, magazine adaptations contributed to creating Sheehy's readership, while also enlarging it far beyond the book.[107] *McCall's* and *Family Circle* were two of the most widely read women's magazines in the United States. They belonged to a group known in the industry as the "Seven Sisters" (in reference to the women's colleges), together with the influential *Ladies' Home Journal* and *Good Housekeeping*, supermarket and domestic decoration magazines *Woman's Day* and *Better Homes and Gardens*, and *Redbook*, a magazine for young wives and mothers, the smallest member of the group. These magazines each reached an audience of 15 million to 22.5 million. Magazines were usually read by more than one person, meaning that even if paid circulation (that is, magazines bought) was below circulation (magazines printed), readership exceeded circulation rates, and often vastly so. In the mid-1970s, when *Family Circle* had just nosed out *McCall's* sales figures, both magazines recorded a combined readership of about 40 million, mostly white and college educated, and roughly between twenty and forty years old, in a population of little more than 50 million women that age.[108] The beauty magazine *Glamour* and the wedding guide *Bride's* added another million or so readers in their twenties.[109]

It was not unusual for mass-market women's magazines to print feminist content. Often criticized for maintaining separate spheres, these magazines still had a long-standing interest in publishing feminist ideas. Mass-market women's magazines in the 1940s to early '60s celebrated the public achievements of women in science, education, culture, and politics and contributed to a discourse of discontent with women's domestic roles.[110] In the 1950s, *Cosmopolitan* (then a middle-class family magazine) published reportage on American women—some by Betty Friedan—that stood in sharp contrast to the image of the happy, suburban housewife.[111] In January 1958, the magazine celebrated the 110th anniversary of the Seneca Falls Convention, the first American women's rights convention, with a special issue discussing women's careers in congress, law, and engineering and critiquing Sigmund Freud's definitions of femininity and women's sexuality.[112]

Similarly, women's magazines did not simply glorify domesticity but instead created a complex and contradictory discourse of discontent in which discussions of marital problems served as the key site for articulating dissatisfaction with women's roles. Articles about marriage crises not only enforced domestic ideology but also promoted women's rights. By documenting women's difficulties in finding satisfaction in their homes and personal lives, the magazines focused public attention on the problems of domesticity and cast it as a social issue.[113] In the mid-1950s, *Good Housekeeping* ran the writer and media critic Laura Hobson's monthly "Back Talk" (under the pseudonym Felicia Quist), which challenged "Man Talk," the marriage advice column written from the husband's perspective by renowned *New York Post* editor Samuel Grafton. Hobson found the "Man Talk" posts "either so sentimental they made me sick, or so macho they made me mad."[114] Her "Back Talk" appeared on the facing page and undercut Grafton's suggestions.

The magazines created and maintained a discourse of discontent that became increasingly politicized in the following years. In the 1970s, women's magazines turned into an important mass-media forum for the women's movement, offering an important route of access to feminist ideas for many women. Starting in 1971, Betty Friedan wrote a regular feature for *McCall's*, "Betty Friedan's Notebook," where she discussed her political activities alongside everyday experiences.[115] The previous year, an excerpt of Sheehy's programmatic novel *Love Sounds* had given the magazine one of its best-selling issues, and in June and July 1972, *McCall's* adapted Elaine Morgan's evolutionary intervention *The Descent of Woman*, which imagined woman, the sea-dweller, rather than man, the hunter, as the origin of the human species.[116] In the *Ladies' Home Journal*, Letty Cottin Pogrebin—activist and cofounder of *Ms.* magazine—started the frankly feminist column "The Working Woman," which ran for ten years.[117] *Bride's* excerpted the Boston Women's Health Book Collective's *Our Bodies, Ourselves*, which became a standard reference in the magazine's "Sex and You" column and recommended reading in *Redbook*, whose women's health articles often challenged traditional medicine.[118] Ever practical, *Woman's Day* compiled a Women's Rights Address Book, a directory of sixty national groups and agencies "currently devoted to helping women achieve equal rights and better status."[119] Even *Family Circle*, the quintessential guide to homemaking, reported on women's rights and celebrated the radical transformation of traditional women's organizations, from the reawakening of the League of Women Voters to the Woman's Christian Temperance Union (sending a delegate to International Women's Year meetings), the YWCA (making "liberated" marriage contracts available to its members), and Camp Fire Girls (teaching sex education).[120] In the summer of 1976, more than thirty magazines banded together to feature the Equal Rights Amendment (ERA) in their July issues, all supportive.[121]

Backtalk within might not have turned women's magazines into feminist organs, and the balance between conservative and critical messages was often asymmetrical. Yet some plurality was integral to the magazines. Diverging representations of femininity not only reflected the fact that female identities were themselves mobile and heterogeneous, often necessitating the negotiation of conflicting demands.[122] Like other periodicals, women's magazines were "miscellanies," driven by varied contributions. Middle-class magazines such as *McCall's* and *Ladies' Home Journal* had a particularly strong debating role and were known for creating controversy and inviting criticism. From the pragmatic perspective of mass-market publishers, including feminist content also enlarged readership numbers by increasing the chance any one reader would find something she liked; readers expected feminism and female emancipation as much as beauty and fashion, cooking, and child-rearing.[123] By embracing plurality and contradiction, the magazines provided forums for public deliberation about women's roles.

Not every reader (or editor) welcomed feminist messages—and by encouraging debate, the magazines affirmed their role as disinterested and trustworthy press services. When *Ladies' Home Journal* printed a special section on women's liberation in 1970 (following the occupation of its offices by the Media Women collective), editor John Mack Carter introduced this with a brief address to the readers, "Why You Find the Next Eight Pages in the *Ladies' Home Journal*." In this reading manual of sorts, Carter encouraged readers to join the debate: "You may find this New Feminism section enlightening, or baffling, or infuriating—or all three. It is an unusual section." Though he admittedly did not agree with many of the Media Women's assumptions, the editor insisted that "the point is: this is 1970. All people and both sexes are free to re-examine their roles. They are free to grow where they have been stunted, to move forward where they have been held back, to find dignity and self-fulfilment on their own. As a magazine that for 87 years has served as an emotional and intellectual forum for American women, we can do no less." Carter concluded with an invitation to send letters, "pro and con": "We think you will find this section provocative reading. Let us know what you think."[124] The twenty-five readers who responded by canceling their subscriptions were outweighed by far by some 150 previous nonreaders who declared their awakened interest in the magazine. Thousands of letters poured in, some pro, some con, many with mixed feelings, documenting that "women's liberation is a new fact of life on the American scene—and that [women's magazine] readers *are* involved."[125]

Responses to *Passages* excerpts were largely positive, though not all readers agreed with Sheehy. Critics often presented their own, crisis-free lives as counterevidence. What was wrong, asked thirty-year-old Carolyn Hogan from Harrison, New Jersey, about being a happy wife and mother?[126] Elizabeth Komanec, a *McCall's* reader from Parma Heights, Ohio, felt "cheated," explaining that her midlife crisis was "14 years overdue. I guess my husband and I have been floating along in a dream world—really enjoying our life together. Now I find that we are not doing it properly." But many women experienced a sense of recognition in the book's pages. "All my feelings and innermost thoughts for almost five years were staring at me from Gail Sheehy's article," wrote a *McCall's* reader from Gardiner, Washington, relieved that she was not alone with her problems.[127] Another letter writer, from Hastings-on-Hudson, a New York City suburb, found herself "emotionally exhilarated . . . , like a race horse." She told Sheehy: "You state so clearly what I've been through. *Passages are* my feelings—words used *are* the same I've written for myself in darkness. There, in the studies now being done and publicized by you, is a light at the end of what I thought was a long, dark, lonely passage."[128] A thirty-eight-year-old reader urged her friends to read the excerpt: "I know it will hit home for them, too!" And a woman in her fifties recognized her own midlife experience in Sheehy's analysis: "'The Crisis Couples Face at Forty' is the best and most sensitive article I have ever read on the subject. . . . If I had had this article before I went through it, I would have been better prepared and more understanding than I was."[129]

For these readers, *Passages* rendered personal experiences understandable as part of larger patterns. As Elayne Eskenazi, a New York NOW member who led consciousness-raising sessions for many years, described: "By sharing our experiences and perceptions, we come to feel the 'click'—the dramatic realization of how we have been affected by a society based on gender inequalities."[130] The feminist writer and theorist Sara Ahmed notes that "feminism is sensational" not only because it provokes great excitement and interest but also because it brings to consciousness a gut-level awareness of inequality: "Becoming a feminist might begin with an experience that you have that gives you a sense of injustice, a feeling that something is wrong or a feeling of being wronged. As you search for an understanding . . . , you begin to identify patterns and regularities. That sense of injustice becomes more and more sensible, as you acquire knowledge and understanding."[131] Sheehy's description of the midlife crisis identified and made tangible a situation many American women were experiencing.

Like Sheehy herself, who was thirty-nine years old when *Passages* came out, many of her readers were in their thirties and forties, often married and with children in their teens. Indeed, Sheehy noted that, while many people in their twenties seemed to have a "crawl-under-the-covers" reaction to the book and did not "want to believe it's going to happen to them, . . . people who are over 30 are ready to hear they are not alone in their hang-ups."[132] The resonance of Sheehy's message among women past thirty challenges the received notion of Second Wave feminism as a movement of younger women, confirming the historian Jessica Weiss's findings about the parents of the baby boom generation and their involvement in the social rebellions and transformations of the 1960s and '70s. Many women drew and redrew gender constructions as their lives evolved, and for many, midlife and women's liberation converged as they left middle-aged marriages and reentered the workforce.[133]

The difference between women of different generations was which feminist issues they cared about, not whether they wanted change at all. Bantam Books playfully illustrated that when, in February 1977, it put out the *Passages* paperback in four different colors—blue, green, orange, and magenta. The New York City salesperson covering Upper Manhattan and the Bronx reported that "blue sells best to over-40 readers, green to 35-year-old intellectuals, orange is picked up by 30-year-olds and magenta by the 20- to 30-year old reader."[134] Sociological research from the 1970s shows that while younger women were attuned to topics such as abortion, contraception, and rape, women approaching forty found divorce and equal economic and professional opportunities more important—these were central issues in *Passages*. (For elderly women, poverty and inequities in Social Security and pension rights were key concerns.)[135]

By distinguishing between youth and old age and privileging young age as the time of change, cohort thinking ignores cross-generational ties, including the ways in which mothers contributed to social change by shaping their daughters' life plans.[136] Even women who thought their own lives could no longer be changed—that they could not have a midlife crisis—were involved in transforming gender norms, often encouraging future generations to make choices different from those they themselves had made. Vera Watkins, a fifty-year-old at-home wife and mother from Logan, Utah, was one of the women who bought *Ladies' Home Journal* specifically for its August 1970 section on women's liberation. In a letter to the editor, Watkins explained that she did not expect to benefit from the movement herself but hoped "that my two teenage daughters will have a better life because of it. . . . I do not want them to feel socially disgraced if they never marry or have children. I also hope that they will find more doors open to them."[137] Far from suggesting a lack of interest, Watkins's presentation as selfless alluded to an established maternal virtue to rein-force the impact of her words.

Sheehy spoke to younger women as well, many of them unmarried (but often in a relationship with a man), most without children. College best-seller lists show that *Passages* circulated as widely among readers in their late teens and early twenties as among the rest of the population.[138] In an interview with the *Boston Globe*, Sheehy imagined the ideal reader of *Passages* to be no older than thirty: "They'd read the book . . . and feed the tape of life through their mind and then put the book away for three years, then take it out again and say: 'Oh, that stuff that I thought was a real crock is beginning to happen.'"[139]

A call for change for readers beyond thirty, the midlife crisis was a cautionary tale for younger women (and some men). Sheehy observed that "young people are a little more upset by the book than comforted. If you're 25 and you think you've got it all set out, you've got the One True Course all mapped out, you don't want to be told it's going to be bumpy."[140] She dispelled widespread warnings of middle-age regret about not getting married or having children, pointing out that, on the contrary, many women in their thirties regretted premature marriage and mother-hood.[141] In the *Glamour* excerpt "Why Do Men Marry? For Love, for Safety, for Freedom or All of the Above?," Sheehy warned young readers of marriage (a social convention, it stifled women's rights).[142] In *Bride's* magazine, she told marriage-minded women to postpone motherhood or at least stick it out in their jobs. An added questionnaire urged fiancées to "stop and think about the kind of marriage you'll have." Did they want children? How many? And when? What if they got pregnant before? Did they think they could handle being an employee, homemaker, and mother at the same time? Did their husband expect them to? Would they be able to support the family if they had to? And even if the couple now agreed on plans for work and children, what if, in a few years, one of them changed their minds?[143] Though Sheehy called the midlife crisis "predictable" for her own generation, she did not expect younger readers to experience the same: they were to avoid it by steering clear from traditional gender arrangements.

5 *Pop Science*

Passages was also read as social science. Sheehy's earlier writing had been reviewed occasionally by academic journals. In the *Journal of Contemporary Ethnography*, the sociologist Clarice Stoll praised the *New York* reportage on prostitution as "incisive urban ethnography" and declared that her profession might be able to learn a thing or two from Sheehy's journalistic work.[144] The psychiatrist and criminologist Park Dietz, who later became known for expert testimony in various high-profile trials including those of John Hinckley Jr. (who attempted to assassinate Ronald Reagan in 1981) and "Unabomber" Ted Kaczynski, recommended *Hustling* to forensic psychiatrists as a useful primer.[145] Celebrated for her psychology competence, Sheehy and her study of adult development received even greater attention among experts. More than one in three *Passages* reviews were put out in academic and professional journals, including *Contemporary Psychology* and *Contemporary Sociology*—the organs of the American Psychological and Sociological Associations respectively—and various periodicals in the fields of marriage, divorce, career counseling, social work, and adult education.[146]

Passages participated in moving feminist ideas into the academy and onto the couch. Feminist scholars were familiar with Sheehy's academic sources and message. Newly founded women's studies journals such as *Frontiers*, *Signs*, and *Sex Roles* (all established in 1975) or the influential *Psychology of Women Quarterly* (1976) did not need to review *Passages*. Many of their readers would have found, as did the sociologist Jessie Bernard, that Sheehy "confirmed" their own observations.[147] In the leadership journal *Group & Organization Studies*, Jean Campbell, head of the University of Michigan Center for Continuing Education of Women and known for her work on women "dropping back in" to higher education, called *Passages* "accurate, strong and insightful." She particularly praised Sheehy's parallel analysis of male and female life patterns, as well as her nontechnical language, noting of her presentation of degendering that "Sheehy manages to [describe] this without using the word 'androgyny.'"[148]

In contrast, scholars less well versed in feminist research and theory found *Passages* new and unusual. The *Personnel and Guidance Journal,* a monthly for all types of professional counselors as well as counseling professors and students, appreciated not only Sheehy's "top-notch" writing style but also her parallel analysis of male and female life patterns, finding that it filled "an embarrassing void by flipping up the female side of the adult development coin."[149] Experts were impressed by Sheehy's research: her interview data and case studies, integration of "disparate" facts and scholarly literatures, and the novelty of her theoretical model. The Association of Family and Conciliation Courts not only recommended *Passages* as "bibliotherapy" reading for clients but also found that it provided "insights for the further development of counseling theories and practices," generated "hypotheses for further research," and contained a "pool of subjective experience to illustrate future statistical findings."[150]

"Popular science," Ludwik Fleck famously wrote, "furnishes the major portion of every person's knowledge. Even the most specialized expert owes to it many concepts, many comparisons, and even his general viewpoint. . . . [Scientists] build up their specialized sciences around these concepts."[151] Sheehy's impact built on the established influence of journalistic reportage on American social science and on a tradition of operationalizing "everyday psychology."[152] Reviewers and commentators often called *Passages*—like some of Sheehy's earlier reportage—"pop sociology" or "pop psychology." This was not just an abbreviation for "popularization." Since the 1960s, "pop" had been closely tied to "Pop Art," which challenged the boundaries between high and low, art and everyday life, supermarket and museum.[153] "Pop science"—as a practice and a category of analysis—similarly redrew the hierarchy between journalistic and academic knowledge. In contrast to "popularization" (or "popular science"), it acknowledged the impact of best-sellers, magazines, and even cocktail-party chatter on scientific research, as the sociologist Sylvia Fava's contemporary definition illustrates: "Pop sociology must be distinguished from the attempts to 'translate' technical sociological concepts, language and findings into layman's terms. . . . Pop sociology may provide useful insights. One of the uses of pop sociology lies in providing hypotheses for new research."[154]

If Andy Warhol's paintings of something as trivial as Campbell's soup cans raised the question of what was art, Sheehy's journalistic description of emotional states provoked the question of what was social science. The sociologist and criminologist Renée Goldsmith Kasinsky, who reviewed *Passages* for the *Western Sociological Review*, spoke for many when she noted that journalists seemed to "have taken the lead in describing and analyzing major social problems of our time." Did social scientists just "follow suit" after the problem was named?[155] Academics and practitioners used reviews of *Passages* to dispel the notion that the book preempted or outperformed their expertise.

Critics commended Sheehy's "classy, vernacular prose," her insider's perspective, and her "shrewd understanding of the intellectual and social milieu to which the book is addressed."[156] Yet for many academic reviewers, these were signs of poor science, not journalistic excellence. In *Contemporary Sociology*, Michael Kimmel (then a sociology postdoc at Berkeley, later an eminent gender and masculinities scholar) pointed out Sheehy's class and racial biases—she discussed the lives of "upper middle class whites" only—and called *Passages* a "palliative to the upper middle class."[157] Adeline Levine, an associate professor of sociology at the State University of New York, Buffalo, who reviewed the book for *Contemporary Psychology*, spoke of a "painful" read. Expecting an explanatory style, the sociologist found Sheehy's literary journalism difficult to deal with, complaining that "bodies, faces, and inner feeling states are described with metaphors relating to food, fish, flowers, the sea, furniture, cloth, wallpaper, vinyl, gardening, luggage, and, most frequently of all, architecture." This was, Levine concluded, "obviously not the writer who will show social scientists the way out of the Thickets of Jargon to the Land of Lucid Prose."[158]

Even sympathetic reviews were often reserved against Sheehy's journalistic approach. In the *Adult Education Quarterly*, Stephen Chapman from the University of Tennessee, a practitioner in adult education, praised

Sheehy's collection of "mountains of interview data," "impressive" notes, and comprehensive bibliography, but made sure to add that, written for a general audience, the book was of "limited value" for professionals: "To be sure, it is interesting and informative. Sheehy has constructed a more extensive developmental model than existed before. But it *is* a layman's handbook; it is not the definitive research milestone of developmental psychology for adults."[159] *Family Court Review*, the official journal of the Association of Family and Conciliation Courts, after extolling the value of Sheehy's insights, findings, and data material, concluded that, for the professional, "the general weakness of [Sheehy's] research stems from the fact that she was writing a popular book . . . and did not follow the guidelines for strict research. As she did not state a clear hypothesis, give operational definitions, state her presuppositions or systematically present her findings, her work is not replicable and cannot be empirically generalized."[160]

Historians and sociologists have documented how such scientific "boundary work," which shores up the differences between science and other forms of knowledge, was used to delegitimize certain views or methods, individuals, and groups and expel them from the realm of science.[161] Yet what appears noteworthy is not that scientists pointed out a journalist's "failure" as a scientist or professional expert, but the very fact that reportage was read as social science and measured by academic standards, if only to be found wanting. Scientific demarcation indicated Sheehy's influence on academic thinking. As "pop science," the midlife crisis moved from the best-seller list into the academy. Several of the key experts on the topic published their own influential books on the topic in the wake of Sheehy's success.[162]

6 *A Narcissistic Disorder?*

Esteemed by critics, very widely read, and noted by social scientists, *Passages* created a serious sensation with a broad and lasting impact. Sheehy's feminist expertise provided life advice to millions of readers and also inspired academic research and therapeutic practice. The success was double-edged for Sheehy's publisher Dutton, whom it allegedly led to ramp up operations beyond its means.[163] But as a result, *Passages* also circulated internationally. Translated into twenty-eight languages, it reached readers throughout North America and Western Europe, as well as audiences in Asian, African, and Latin American countries and the South Pacific. Commentators spoke of a "global best-seller."[164]

How, then, did the feminist midlife crisis almost disappear? For all the success, Sheehy's book was not to everybody's liking. Christopher Lasch, the historian and social critic known for opposing the women's movement, rejected the midlife crisis as a "narcissistic disorder" besetting selfish women and idle men. In his ubiquitous *The Culture of Narcissism* (1979), he scolded Sheehy for "encouraging . . . self-scrutiny": "This is a recipe not for growth but for planned obsolescence."[165] (Lasch was not amused to see the paperback edition of his book promoted as ranking next to *Passages* as one of "the greatest books on society's changing values.")[166]

Sheehy repaid the professor in kind. Reviewing Lasch's later *The Minimal Self* (1984), an updated diatribe against narcissism, which also ridiculed feminist agendas as self-absorbed and misguided, she scoffed: "Has Mr. Lasch been out of the bunker lately? He ought to take [the Wall Street banker] Mary Cunningham to lunch. . . . Has he heard of [the physicist and astronaut] Sally Ride? [The physician and anti-nuclear activist] Helen Caldicott? [Democratic US representative] Geraldine Ferraro? These are not exactly dewy romantics standing over a pool and admiring their own reflections."[167] As Carolyn Heilbrun, a literary scholar at Columbia University, noted, the "real tension between Sheehy and Lasch" was that between "the fleeing woman and those who struggle to preserve the family."[168]

Critique of psychological self-help and therapeutic culture was a critical canard in the late 1970s—famously labeled the "Me Decade," after Tom Wolfe's 1976 *New York* essay—and regularly used to reject feminist agendas as egoistic and immoral.[169] In the following years and decades, *Passages* turned into a favorite example for critics of psychological culture, singled out as the typical expression of a self-centered "zeitgeist" that seemed to haunt women. These critiques indicated Sheehy's success and impact. When Charles Taylor, in *Sources of the Self* (1989), attacked therapy and social science for devaluing "community affiliations, the solidarities of birth, of marriage, of the family," he indicted Sheehy's *Passages* as Exhibit A.[170]

Yet the most influential criticism of Sheehy's model of the midlife crisis came from psychologists, psychiatrists, and psychoanalysts. Rather than rejecting the idea of middle life reinvention, they appropriated and reversed it. If Sheehy's feminist framework and engagement with social science made her concept of midlife crisis popular, they also constituted a critical target. In the wake of her success, Erikson's student Daniel Levinson and other psychological and psychiatric experts used boundary work to claim authority over the midlife crisis and change its meaning.

5

Psychology and the Crisis of Masculinity

Sheehy called 1978 the "Year of the Man," and she should know, the scholar and writer Jordan Pecile mused, "because she makes her living by keeping her finger on the pulse of social movements." All at once, Sheehy had noted in a *New York Times* piece, "men have become the salty peanuts of the social sciences." She was skeptical about the trend; after all, this was "hardly a new and not evidently an endangered species." With a view to the newly released *The Seasons of a Man's Life*, a study of the male midlife decade by the social psychologist Daniel Levinson, Pecile explicated: "What I think she means is that after the many molehills of books which have risen out of the burrowing activities of the feminists and which examined women's roles, life cycles, attitudes, desires and frustrations, there comes now the male *backlash*."[1]

The recoil against Sheehy took the form of three psychology books: Levinson's *Seasons* plus *Adaptation to Life* (1977), a survey of Harvard men by the psychiatrist George Vaillant, and the therapist Roger Gould's marriage advice book *Transformations: Growth and Change in Adult Life* (1978). Existing histories of the midlife crisis begin with these books, ignoring the fact that Levinson, Vaillant, and Gould responded to *Passages*.[2] Sheehy had criticized their psychoanalytic, Eriksonian premises, and while the identity theorist refrained from a response, his followers reacted. They put forward male-centered definitions of midlife rejuvenation that echoed *Playboy* fantasies and barred women from changing their lives.

The notion of popularization did important work in making this the dominant meaning of midlife crisis. Levinson, Vaillant, and Gould drew on the demarcation between "professional" and "popular" science to dismiss Sheehy and assert their own respectability.[3] This was successful:

the three experts received attention primarily because their books were read as more scientific, even more original versions of *Passages*. Seeing Levinson's *Seasons* as backlash, Pecile was one of the few to pick up on the struggle over gender. Anti-feminism was allowed to parade as better science.

1 *Psychoanalysts and Playboys*

"Since the publication of *Passages*," a critic complained, "it seems that anyone between the ages of 35 and 45 marginally capable of constructing a simple sentence can publish an autobiographical exegesis of the mid-life crisis."[4] Among the "procession" of books about the route to adulthood published in the wake of Sheehy's success, the central three were by the psychoanalytic experts Vaillant, Levinson, and Gould. In *Passages*, Sheehy had cited and criticized their work and its Eriksonian tenets; now came their retort.

Published first, George Vaillant's *Adaptation to Life*, put out as a trade edition with the respected Boston publisher Little, Brown, wore its politics on its sleeve, in the form of a cover image of the Vitruvian Man, an incarnation of scientific androcentrism. The book was based on a longitudinal study of Harvard graduates, a sample from the Grant Study in Social Adjustments, established in the late 1930s as an investigation into physiological masculinity (and named after its initial donor, the dimestore magnate William T. Grant).

A survey of Harvard student health, the Grant Study was typical of the college health work conducted at many elite men's and women's institutions in the United States from the late nineteenth century up to the 1970s.[5] Led by the physician Arlie Bock, it was dedicated to the collection of anthropomorphic data, including "posture pictures" taken of students in the nude in order to assess, by way of bearing, their health status, indicated, in case of the all-male Grant Study, by the degree of "masculinity" a student was seen to represent: the more virile, the healthier.[6] Among the original 268 participants, selected for their physical fitness, were John F. Kennedy and the later "Unabomber" Ted Kaczynski; Norman Mailer and Leonard Bernstein applied but were turned down.[7]

Though the study was originally envisioned as a five-year project, the

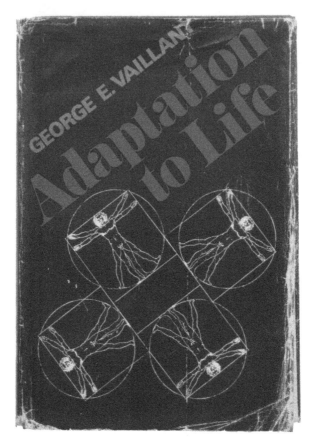

FIG. 5.1 The cover of the psychiatrist George Vaillant's *Adaptation to Life*, a study of male Harvard graduates, showed the image of the Vitruvian Man, an incarnation of scientific androcentrism. © Little, Brown, 1978.

researchers kept milking money from various donors throughout the following years and decades, and data from the men, through waves of questionnaires and, occasionally, personal interviews that continued up to 1972, when Vaillant became the principal investigator, and beyond.[8]

The Grant Study had not started out as a longitudinal study, and certainly not as an inquiry into the midlife crisis. It survived until the 1970s by shifting its outlook and adapting questionnaires and interpretations to new national politics or sponsors. During World War II, the study sought to determine selection criteria for officers.[9] After the researchers received a tobacco grant in 1955, the surveys included detailed sections on the men's smoking habits: How many cigarettes, pipes, or cigars did they smoke per day? Which kinds and what brands? And how? "Only a few puffs, about half way, two thirds, [or] nearly to butt"?[10] In the late 1960s, during the "brief Golden Age" of data management in the social sciences, the psychologist Charles McArthur, then head of the study, introduced IBM punch cards to code what he estimated to be more than five thousand items per participant.[11] Reckoned a way of making the study data accessible and thus manageable, punching and coding in fact multiplied the data—for example, when McArthur created correlations between what he himself called "apparently unrelated items," such as political orientation and fondness for sweet things: "Republicans eat little or no candy."[12]

Donors seemed not quite convinced by this approach, and McArthur faced accusations of unproductiveness, supported by an evaluation in which a group of noted peers—the developmental psychologist Jerome Kagan and the life-course sociologists Orville Brim and John Clausen—attested poor methodology and ignorance of comparable research.[13] Offended, McArthur resigned and was succeeded by Vaillant. The Grant Foundation had reservations about Vaillant's psychoanalytic framework, but funding continued on condition that a book, preferably with a trade publisher, drew together the research and hopefully lifted the study (and, therewith, its sponsors) out of oblivion.[14]

Based on open-ended interviews with ninety-four randomly selected Grant Study participants, then in their midforties, *Adaptation* was largely an elaboration of the theory of "defense mechanisms"—sublimation, projection, repression, and others—that Anna Freud had developed in the 1930s, and an essay on this topic had won Vaillant the Boston Psychoanalytic Society's annual award.[15] Ancillary to the overall issue of ego defenses was a chapter on middle age, "The Adult Life Cycle," which drew on Erikson's "Eight Stages of Man" and C. G. Jung, as well as on a paper by Levinson, to argue that the Harvardians' "midlife crisis" was a vital developmental step, not a sign of maladaptation.[16]

Daniel Levinson secured a book deal with a leading publisher, Alfred A. Knopf, in 1974, soon after Sheehy had reported about his research project on the career plateau, "A Psychosocial Study of the Male Mid-life Decade," concluded the previous year. "The *New York* piece [is] largely based on [Levinson's] work," noted Knopf editor Charles Elliott. He got in touch with the psychologist.[17]

The "Male Mid-life" project, begun in late 1968, had developed from

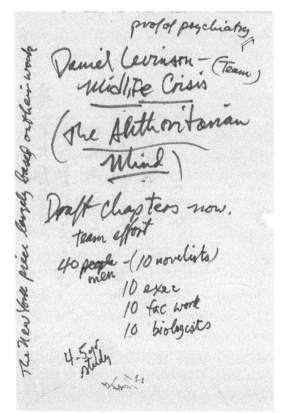

FIG. 5.2 "The *New York* piece based on [Levinson's] work." Knopf editor Charles Elliott got in touch with "prof of psychiatry" Daniel Levinson after reading Sheehy's *New York* magazine article about the midlife crisis. Knopf Records, box 795, folder 7, Harry Ransom Center, University of Texas at Austin.

Levinson's earlier work. Trained as a psychologist, he had studied with Erik Erikson (Betty Friedan was a fellow graduate student in the same year, 1942–43), and done his doctoral thesis as part of the Berkeley Public Opinion Study Group (1944–47), best known for *The Authoritarian Personality* (1950), to which Levinson contributed psychological scale-analyses, the Projective Question analysis, and statistical design and procedure.[18] In line with the legacy of authoritarianism research in American social science more broadly, criticism of conformity remained an important starting point for Levinson, whose focus soon shifted to organizational psychology—first at Harvard and, from 1966 onward, at Yale.[19]

Drawing on Erikson and borrowing from Jung, Levinson shared with

Vaillant a psychodynamic point of view that was not unusual in organizational psychology.[20] Typical of this field, Levinson's main interest was in managers, specifically questions of career development, and this resulted in publications such as *The Executive Role Constellation* (1965) or "Becoming the Director: Promotion as a Phase in Personal-Professional Development."[21]

In the "Male Mid-life" study, Levinson and his research team—the psychologists Maria Hertz Levinson (then his wife) and Edward Klein, the psychiatrist Braxton McKee, and the sociologist Charlotte Darrow were key members—studied the lives of forty men between thirty-five and forty-five years old when the project started, all American born and based somewhere between Boston and New York.[22] They came from different occupations: ten were executives from the Olin and GSI Corporations—Connecticut-based arms and electronics manufacturers, respectively—and ten each were workers (from the same companies), biologists (mostly from Yale), and novelists.[23] There were five black participants in the predominantly white sample: three workers and two novelists.

The men were interviewed several times during fall 1968 and spring 1969, with follow-up interviews in the early 1970s. As part of preparing the book with Knopf, the journalist Jack Shepherd reinterviewed the study participants again in 1976.[24] In addition, the sample was supplemented with descriptions of men's lives from biography and fiction, among them Dante and Shakespeare, the patriarch Abraham and Mahatma Gandhi, Paul Gauguin, King Lear, and Willy Loman (the protagonist of Arthur Miller's *Death of a Salesman*, 1949).[25]

Levinson and his team described the "mid-life decade" as a period of change, during which men reinvented themselves. The key case study in *The Seasons of a Man's Life*, "Jim Tracy," was a vice president and general manager of the Olin Firearms Division. After a series of sexual escapades, he divorced his wife and married a younger woman, then left the corporation to open his own business.[26] Levinson held that such a "mid-life crisis" or "mid-life transition" was a universal feature of the male life cycle: "[It] exists in all societies, throughout the human species, . . . grounded in the nature of man." However, the psychologist made one exclusion to the concept: he did not study women, interviewing the forty men's wives only "to obtain an additional perspective on the husband."[27]

Published last, by Simon & Schuster, Roger Gould's *Transformations: Growth and Change in Adult Life* (1978) redeemed the psychiatrist's claim to the midlife crisis, four years after charging Sheehy with plagiarism.[28] Without citing either Vaillant or Levinson, Gould built on the same psychodynamic tenets. A self-help book that introduced the "Seven-Step Inner Dialogue" to master marital problems, *Transformations* was based on the therapist's experience in private practice in Santa Monica, California. While *Seasons* and *Adaptation* spoke about men primarily, Gould included case studies of women, too, in discussions of relationships, motherhood, professional careers, and women's liberation. Yet like the two earlier titles, *Transformations* reserved midlife crisis for men.

Responding to *Passages* and sharing an analytical background, the three experts defined the midlife crisis in similar ways: it applied to men only and meant breaking out of conformity to the breadwinner role. Levinson, Vaillant, and Gould interlaced the received notion of male middle age as the "prime of life" with the criticism of soul-crushed breadwinners in "'gray flannel' straitjackets" that underlay much of postwar social science in the United States.[29] Criticism of other-directedness and the male-breadwinner family could go two ways and imply either renewed appreciation of fatherhood or escape into a playboy lifestyle. Tom Rath, the protagonist of Sloan Wilson's novel *The Man in the Gray Flannel Suit* (1955), recovered his integrity by confessing to his wife a previous case of infidelity and identifying with his role as a father.[30] Sheehy's definition of the male midlife crisis worked along similar lines, with disillusioned professionals moving into baking, gardening, and child care and supporting their wives' careers.

In contrast, Levinson's, Vaillant's, and Gould's depictions of a breakaway from monogamy reiterated stories made famous by Hugh Hefner's *Playboy* magazine, whose success was premised on adapting the notion of youthful masculinity to postwar consumerism.[31] One Grant Study man was "finally able" to let his inner "Brazilian jungle emerge into his conscious life" in the form of an "exciting" love affair; another built a "shamelessly exhibitionistic house"—a classic playboy emblem. A third Harvard graduate went scuba diving off the Barrier Reef "and mastered Australia's most challenging surfing beaches," then, in the company of a close friend, "plunged into the Amazon jungle to hunt for orchids—the most sensual of flowers" to discover an entirely new species.[32] Combining similar explorer myths with a sense for finance, a *Seasons* executive bought an island in the Caribbean, "partly as this fantasy of a home on an island, but also partly as an [offshore] investment."[33] Meanwhile, Gould explained that for a man, midlife was high time for questioning the assumption that "there is no life beyond this family." The demand for change was "so powerful that most of us forget our fifteen-to-twenty-five years investment in the [marital] relationship."[34]

Hefner's magazine may have become stale in the 1970s, but his ideas were carried on elsewhere.[35] Playboy imagery was not necessarily about reality; it was as much the gray-feeling breadwinner's dream: "of owning a fast sports car instead of a station wagon, of living in an urban skyscraper penthouse instead of a suburban ranch-style family home, of wearing elegant silk instead of gray flannel, and of loving pretty young bunnies instead of their wives."[36] In line with this male "double role," Levinson's, Vaillant's, and Gould's definition of midlife crisis advocated the combination of the breadwinner and playboy roles: sequentially throughout the life course and, possibly, concurrently through nonmonogamous marital arrangements.

2 *Second Adolescence*

"Adolescence" was the main metaphor the psychoanalysts used for the midlife crisis. They spoke of a "second" or "belated" youth in middle age, a "final surge of lasciviousness" (Levinson) in which men once again had to learn "how to handle their new sexuality, their bodily changes" (Gould).[37] In *Adaptation*, Vaillant challenged Elliott Jaques's earlier assumption that midlife troubles resulted from a fear of death: instead, middle age was about beginning a new life. Of his Harvard subjects, the psychiatrist wrote: "From age twenty-five to thirty-five they tended to work hard, to consolidate their careers, and to devote themselves to the nuclear family. . . . Rather than question whether they had married the right woman, rather than dream of other careers, they changed their babies' diapers and became lost in conformity."[38] Drawing on the Freudian idea that puberty is preceded by a latency stage, Vaillant depicted the forties as a phase in which men are "less inhibited" than in the "serious, practical, asexual" thirties: "Men in their forties ... are confronted by instinctual reawakening ... and their groping toward love seems *adolescent*."[39]

Reiterating the psychologist G. Stanley Hall's definition of adolescence as "recapitulation" of a "savage," audacious, and aggressive masculinity, the trope of a "second adolescence" and the notion of development more generally normalized the escapades of husbands and fathers as steps toward greater integrity.[40] Analogous to a teenager's breakaway from home, the midlife crisis designated a rupture in the realm of marriage. Vaillant described a shift in the perspective of one middle-aged Harvard physician, "Dr. Adam Carson," on his relationship. The "charming clinician" was the main midlife crisis case in *Adaptation*. At twenty-six, Carson had told the Grant Study researchers, "I treasure my marriage above everything else in the world; I get tremendous happiness from it." Yet when Vaillant prodded him to look back on that same marriage at forty-seven ("This is the hardest question that I shall ask: Can you describe your wife? ... What causes you concern about her?"), the physician—now divorced and remarried—recalled: "I felt that she was a rattlesnake, who would do something mean and awful." As Vaillant explained, Carson's wife had been "suitable for him as an immature twenty-six-year-old caterpillar," helpful for the young man's career advancement, but was now too "ascetic" and "conventional" for the man at midlife.[41]

Partially based on an earlier paper by Levinson, Vaillant's depiction of midlife crisis followed and confirmed the psychologist's observations.[42] Levinson explained men's distancing themselves from their wives as the result of midlife enlightenment. "Many men are able to consider seriously in their late thirties and early forties marital problems that they previously ignored," Levinson wrote. "A man may come to recognize that the marriage was flawed from the start." He might have married for reasons such as family pressure, convention, rebellion, social mobility, or even guilt. "Now a great fog of illusions has been lifted." And it dawns on the man that "there is no excitement" between him and his wife, that "he cannot share his main interests and concerns with her," or that she is "disappointed" and "resentful."[43]

The process of self-realization depicted by Vaillant and Levinson followed the gender dynamics of Erik Erikson's "Eight Stages of Man," which focused on men's growth and development, assigning women the role of

FIG. 5.3 A dream, a mentor, a career, and also a family: for the psychologist Daniel Levinson, a man's course in midlife depended on how he mastered these elements in his twenties and thirties. Illustration for an extract from *The Seasons of a Man's Life* in *Psychology Today*, January 1978. © Richard Grote.

helpmates. Levinson emphasized the importance of marriage to a man's professional advancement in his twenties and early thirties. As an organizational psychologist, he had worked on career development before, yet the attention to intimate relationships distinguished *Seasons* from his previous research.[44]

Levinson used the term "special woman" to describe the devoted at-home wife and mother who tried to further her husband's advancement or, in Levinson's terms, fulfill his "Dream." Her "special" quality, he explained, "lies in her connection to the young man's Dream." Her identity "is largely fashioned on and appended to the husband's. . . . His Dream thus serves as a vehicle for defining and pursuing her interests." She believes in the man as a "hero," helps him to shape and live out his goals, and creates a "boundary space" within which his aspirations can be imagined and his hopes nourished. At a psychological level, the "special woman" enables a man "to project onto her his own internal feminine figure"—what Jung called "the anima."[45]

The "special woman" was "primarily involved in her roles as wife and mother." If she had a job, it was as an unmarried woman "seeking a husband" or in an occupation such as teaching or nursing "where she is appropriately maternal, subordinate and non-competitive with men." Levinson stressed the importance of separate spheres—breadwinning father, homemaking mother—to a man's professional success and personal development by contrasting the "special" woman with the "liberated" woman whose involvement in a career produced "bitter discontent and conflict" in a marriage and was indeed against nature: "It is hard enough to form a life structure around one person's Dream. Building a structure that can contain the Dreams of both partners is a heroic task indeed, and one for which evolution and history have ill prepared us."[46]

The psychologist highlighted the motherly implications of a perfect wife's virtues. "Generally maternal and caring," she "makes things easier for him."[47] Drawing on the British psychoanalyst Donald Winnicott's definition of the "good enough mother," Levinson compared the "good enough" wife's relationship with her husband to that of a mother and child.[48] Like a boy's mother, too, the special woman was a "transitional figure": "During early adulthood, a man is struggling to outgrow the little boy in himself and to become a more autonomous adult. The special woman can foster his adult aspirations. . . . Later, in the Mid-life Transition, he will have to become a more individual person. With further development, he will be more complete in himself and will have less need of the . . . special woman."[49]

A man's midlife crisis, then, was a justification for abandoning his wife. The trope of adolescence was used to sanitize the breakout from marriage as an act of "free[ing] oneself more completely from the boy-mother relationship," as Levinson put it in his initial report.[50] As relevant as his wife had been in their twenties and early thirties, for the middle-aged man, she was "neither necessary nor desirable." The professional success the at-home wife had helped to build was no longer the established forty-year-old's priority; indeed, at middle age, her "special" qualities were considered "overly controlling," "smothering," "depriving and humiliating."[51] And just as for Winnicott, the child did not owe its mother anything—she was "devoted" by nature—so for Levinson, the husband had no obligations toward his wife.[52] With no strings attached and having made it, he was finally free to live the life he had always wanted.

Levinson emphasized the advantages of relationships with a younger woman; Hefner's "girl next door."[53] (Levinson put the ideal age difference between a man and his lover at ten years; Gould suggested a generational gap.)[54] Some of her features were defined in comparison to the middle-aged wife—the younger woman was "more understanding, sharing and sensually evocative"—and others with regard to the man, whom she made feel "more of a person."[55] Jungian theory, with its notion of femininity and masculinity as "archetypal structures," was central to anti-feminist thought, often used to strengthen traditional notions of masculinity by emphasizing gender polarities.[56] Drawing, again, on Jung's concept of psychic polarities, Levinson highlighted the psychodynamic relevance of intergenerational affairs: "We have to look at the extramarital relationship from a developmental perspective. It reflects a man's struggle with the Young/Old polarity: he is asserting his youthful vitality at a time when he fears that the Young in him is being crushed. . . . On the other hand, the exploration of new relationships with women of various ages may enable him to get more in touch with the feminine in himself and others and to resolve the Masculine/Feminine polarity."[57]

The midlife breakaway was not only from the man's current relationship but from the institution of marriage more generally. Informality and intimacy without commitment were main characteristics of extramarital affairs with younger women. An insignia of a man's success, the lover was a collective singular; "just another of his many conquests," she vanished in the "seemingly limitless supply of girls" and "anonymous women," or she was outsourced as in the case of a Grant Study man who "left home for several weeks to go to a foreign country and lose himself in the excitement of a love affair."[58] *Seasons* executive Tracy jumped from one woman's body to a multitude of affairs, from singular to plural, without catching his breath in between: "The first affair that was really other than totally casual was an infatuation. I can't say I loved her; I don't think it was that strong, but I felt a great desire for her. . . . The women were a mixture of some totally spur-of-the-moment casual types and others that weren't. It wasn't a pattern other than that they were pebbles on the beach."[59]

Speaking of an "exploration of alternatives," Levinson was reserved when it came to divorce and remarriage. Instead, he vaguely advised keeping the "other" woman (or women) next to the wife.[60] Vaillant, who referred to marital stability as an index of mental health, uncoupled this conventional Freudian wisdom from sexual satisfaction; he held that "enjoyable affairs" stabilized a marriage, which would benefit from the extramarital release of sexual tension.[61] This was a common belief in psychology. As the therapist O. Spurgeon English explained in his classic 1967 piece "The Affair," extramarital sex fulfilled deep personal needs.[62] The "open marriage" concept, which was prominently propagated in the 1970s by the anthropologists Elizabeth "Nena" and George O'Neill, advocated nonmonogamous arrangements, too.[63] Yet in contrast to the O'Neills, who placed the greatest importance on "open," free, and clear communication about both partners' needs and expectations, the theorists of the male midlife crisis did not think it necessary to negotiate the form of the relationship with any of the women involved. As one reader demanded to know of Levinson's remarks about younger women: "Where's the section on harassment?"[64] For Vaillant, only a man's—but not a woman's—sexual escapades correlated with marital stability: in a healthy marriage, the husband enjoyed many affairs, tolerated by the wife with "stoical acquiescence"; in an unhealthy marriage, a husband with lower sex drive tolerated his wife's affairs.[65]

Sheehy had countered Vaillant's, Levinson's, and Gould's ideas in *Passages*. With regard to Levinson's depiction of the at-home wife as the "special woman," she drew attention to her developmental needs. In earlier discussions of his research, Levinson had added a passing acknowledgment to the effect that, "of course," a relationship would be durable and further a man's development only if it also furthered a woman's. Sheehy answered: "Surely that is one of the biggest 'of courses' in the evolution of mankind." If women had wives to keep house for them, stay home with children, get the car fixed, fight with the painters, run to the supermarket, reconcile the bank statements, listen to everyone's problems, cater the dinner parties, and "nourish the spirit each night," "just imagine the possibilities for expansion"—the number of books that would be written, companies started, professorships filled, political offices that would be held, by women.[66]

According to Sheehy, what the three psychoanalysts depicted as healthy behavior was a panic reaction to physical aging, played out starkly in the biography of the sports-car magnate and notorious playboy John DeLorean. One of the interviewees who allowed Sheehy to quote his full name, DeLorean made national news repeatedly in the late 1960s to mid-1970s, when he left General Motors, got divorced and remarried twice, underwent facial surgery, and founded his own sports-car company: DeLorean Motor Company, DMC for short. In the words of one of several biographers, DeLorean "fulfilled a [male] fantasy"; his life was the stuff that men's magazines were made of, and in 1974 Playboy Press negotiated a contract to publish a biography.[67] Yet for Sheehy, the engineer was unable to admit his midlife crisis, which would "bring down the whole masculine mystique." Instead, he banished all reminders of his advancing age: "the fat, the same-aged wife, his own sagging face and graying hair. Like a sorcerer with a magic wand he has recreated for himself the face, the body, the wife . . . that belong to the dream of the 25-year-old man."[68]

Following the psychoanalyst Judd Marmor, Sheehy classified "sexual escapades" with younger women as "denial by overcompensation," the lowest, pathological level in Vaillant's hierarchy of defense mechanisms, a prominent feature of psychosis. (Vaillant's Grant Study sample contained many philanderers yet, as the psychiatrist emphasized, no cases of psychotic denial, except for a businessman unable to admit his addiction to sedatives.)[69] She introduced the term "Testimonial Woman," putting into perspective the younger partner's beneficial functions to a middle-aged man: "The root of the word *testimonial* is *testis* (plural *testes*). I read somewhere that when one aboriginal man bumped into another, he cupped the sexual parts of a tribesman in greeting. It was a 'testimonial to manhood' and the original basis for the handshake. Whether or not it's true, the Testimonial Woman offers the same service: She fortifies his masculinity."[70]

As Levinson, Vaillant, and Gould responded to Sheehy, they also reacted to the women's movement more generally. If their fantasy of the young girl—whether as first wife or lover—typified the ideal woman, the middle-aged wife stood for feminist opposition. She was a key addressee of male midlife crisis stories.

3 Backlash

Levinson wanted to "talk to men about our personal lives," yet in many ways, the male midlife crisis was a problem more for women.[71] If a woman had lived with a man for some fifteen or twenty years in a state of some satisfaction and equilibrium and suddenly he began changing, how was she to view it? When the science writer Maggie Scarf, writing for the women's magazine *McCall's*, asked Maria Levinson, Daniel's wife and a collaborator on the *Seasons* project, for advice for the wives of crisis-ridden husbands, the researcher appeared dumbstruck. Her first reply was evasive, yet the journalist insisted. "Suppose," Scarf asked, "a man moves into a time of great distress, and won't talk about it to his wife? Or suppose his dissatisfaction with himself has something to do with a dissatisfaction with her—and he finds some 'other' woman to talk about his problems to?" Maria Levinson, or so the journalist conveys it, "hesitates, looks at me, her gray eyes widening. 'Well, if that were the case, I'd say'—she blinks rapidly several times—'I'd say . . . That's too bad.'"[72] The Levinsons divorced a few years later, and he married a younger woman.[73]

In *Seasons*, Daniel Levinson indirectly answered the question about the implications of midlife crisis for women when he bemoaned that many wives did not fully "appreciate" their husbands' "need for a greater measure of autonomy and intimate sharing," and that some even acted as a "destructive witch or selfish bitch using both her strength and her weakness to keep him in line and prevent him from becoming what he truly wants to be." A wife should recognize that her husband was in a normal developmental period and "working on normal mid-life tasks," the psychologist urged. Midlife turmoil was a stage in the developmental process, not some kind of a virus to be cured or prevented: "The pathology is not in the desire to improve one's life but in the obstacles to pursuing this aim."[74]

Most explicitly directed at women, Gould's *Transformations* explicated at length the "very powerful push into extramarital sexuality" experienced by men in their forties: "We do what we can to avoid staring at our daughters' curves or their friends . . . ; we do what we can to keep our wives from knowing. Our sons' girls are awfully appealing, and sometimes we daydream about [them]." Women's (but never men's) attraction to other, younger men was touched on only briefly, as a fad. The dominant theme with respect to women was the distress that resulted from their husbands' extramarital activities, an issue Gould addressed by devaluing fidelity: he declared monogamy but a continuation of the Oedipal desire for parental love; women's "childish drive to possess" a man severely curtailed their husbands' "inner freedom." The therapist argued that the cheated woman's struggles were a perfidious weapon, acting on the husband as "a form of bondage much like our parents' worrying was during adolescence." An extramarital affair was a husband's "personal issue," and turning it into a marital one or asking for an apology meant restraining his ability to reach his "full measure of humanity."[75]

Yet women were not just instructed to accept and comply with their husbands' midlife crisis. Vaillant, Levinson, and Gould used gendered double standards to bar women from reimagining their own lives. By defining development in terms of men, they followed a tradition that dated back to Erikson and beyond. Carol Gilligan and other feminist psychologists would later read *Adaptation*, *Seasons*, and *Transformations* as androcentric in the sense of assuming the same developmental scheme for women as for men.[76] But the three studies did not simply imply that Man was the measure of all people; they also exempted women from transformation at middle age. Like Erikson before them, his followers made an argument for gender differences.

Levinson and Vaillant studied men only—they interviewed the wives to learn more about the husbands—and appeared undecided about how their developmental model applied to women. Levinson proposed that *Seasons* would serve as a "basis for the study of women." At the same time, he excluded women from his project, believing that they needed to be studied separately because the differences were too great, and dismissed comparisons between menopause and midlife crisis as useless, even ridiculous.[77] Where women figured in his book—especially as wives—he portrayed them as functions in men's lives, "obstacles to the quest [for autonomy] or as one of the rewards for his success."[78] Levinson's belated follow-up *The Seasons of a Woman's Life* (1996), posthumously published by his second wife and collaborator, Judy Levinson, would argue that at midlife, women—whether at-home wives or professionals—discovered that it was impossible for them to find fulfillment in work.[79]

Vaillant similarly avoided any comparative perspective. With some apologetic hand waving, he pointed to the "unforgivable omission" of women in the original Grant Study, yet he did not link his research to the plethora of similar studies conducted at women's colleges, excluding even a series of comparative studies on female students from Bryn Mawr and Swarthmore, which Grant Study researchers had conducted after World War II. In *Adaptation* he made clear that for him, Erikson's concept of generativity did not apply to mothers "raising young children."[80] Last but not least, even Gould, who considered men and women, reserved the midlife crisis for men; women were told how to cope.[81]

By excluding women from their concept of midlife crisis, the psychoanalysts barred them from redefining their lives and seeking self-fulfillment outside the home. Not all critics of the nuclear family endorsed women's liberation, and some opposed it. The career woman was *Playboy*'s ultimate enemy. In "How to Handle Women in Business," the columnist Shepherd Mead, author of the notorious *How to Succeed in Business without Really Trying* (1952), instructed men to create the impression that a woman executive was "always breaking into the middle of a dirty story" and, by implication, invading male space.[82]

In 1962, the magazine's editorial director, A. C. Spectorsky, informed the popular writer Philip Wylie, known for his infamous critique against middle-aged "Moms," that "Everybody here is completely flipped by your idea of doing the ultimate take-out on career women, compared to whom Mom is an absolute delight. We would really like a no-hold-barred tearing apart of this humanoid who calls herself a woman. . . . You are the man to do it," Spectorsky assured Wylie about the proposed article. "And we are the magazine to print it."[83] Wylie's misogynist assault on "Momism" has been interpreted as an endorsement of careers for women, yet the resulting piece, "The Career Woman," published the month before Friedan's *The Feminine Mystique*, lambasted women for intruding into the male realms of the professions and management and for using positions within the fashion, advertising, and television industries to exert influence on American culture. The professional woman, he wrote, has an "obscene compulsion:

She must compete with, and if necessary, cripple manhood and masculinity."[84] The problem with the career woman was that she challenged her place in a "man's world," as his helpmate.

Levinson agreed: women's liberation hindered men from releasing their full potential. The working woman had already been dangerous to the young man whose career advancement was limited by her "unnatural" professional ambition. In midlife, she also threatened a man's self-fulfillment. Drawing on the contemporary debate about a "new male impotence" induced by fear of self-confident women, not hormonal change, the psychologist held that a woman's "growing assertiveness and freedom" in middle age resulted in her partner's "severe decline." He problematized the moment when a wife "becomes the voice of development and change," "takes the initiative in reappraising the marriage," and "seeks to expand her own horizons and start new enterprises outside the home"—Sheehy's definition of the female midlife crisis. Levinson cautioned that "the husband may then become the voice of the status quo. Moreover, a man who feels that his own youthfulness is in jeopardy may be more threatened than pleased. . . . He has less authority . . . and feels increasingly obsolescent. . . . Where this occurs, it is a serious problem."[85]

If Levinson affirmed men's prerogative to initiate change, Gould prescribed "feminist-taming therapy." Concluding *Transformations* with a section called "Women's Liberation," he admitted that "it is true that men must change . . . their concept of women. However, this is not the whole truth." The primary problem was women's own psyches: "There are still two fronts for women to challenge—the external political structure and the limiting internal self-definition. And the most ferocious opponent is within." On some level, every woman knew this; women "talk about losing nerve and holding themselves back, as men rarely do." Yet presently, the psychiatrist observed, they had lost this insight, due to the women's movement: "[Women] fail to distinguish between the needs of a political movement to which they are committed and their own needs as individuals to grow. . . . Because the movement furnishes such powerful emotional support for individual growth . . . the two interests often seem to be indistinguishable."[86]

Feminist activism harmed, not furthered, a woman's self-fulfillment. Rather than critiquing "men's social-system bias against women"—let alone individual men—a woman should focus on "working out her own internal prohibitions. . . . So much unnecessary misery occurs when all a woman's aggression is directed at the men in her life, for everybody suffers and nobody benefits." Women in midlife were particularly susceptible to feminist agendas; many of them were now "seeking redress for twenty lost years," and *Transformations* concluded with a reminder to them that a woman's main problem was herself, always: many a husband had started a family and pursued a career at his wife's expense and continued to believe that women "can't add, subtract, or handle money," were "too 'soft'" for politics or business, and were "not capable of sustained serious thought." However, even if the husband was a "raving male chauvinist . . . , every woman's *first* project must be her own mind, her attitudes about herself, her own emotional constraints. . . . [Women] must always remember to look first for the enemy within."[87]

Framing middle life as "men's liberation," Levinson, Vaillant, and Gould leveled the double standard of aging against feminist agendas. Yet the anti-feminist overtones of the male midlife crisis were rarely publicly discussed.

4 *The Original* Passages

Vaillant, Levinson, and Gould presented their studies as better, even more original *Passages*. Mocking an earlier article by Vaillant, Sheehy had challenged his equation between mental health and marital stability: this did not apply to women. In *Adaptation*, the psychiatrist sidestepped and silenced her critique, reverting to the trope of media sensationalism to dismiss Sheehy. He suggested that, in the name of good copy, the journalist "made all too much of the midlife crisis. . . . The high drama in Gail Sheehy's bestselling *Passages* was rarely observed in the lives of the Grant Study men."[88] The allegation was easily turned against Vaillant himself, as the sociologist Alice Rossi noted: "While Vaillant rejects the high drama of the more popularized writings on the mid-life crisis, his case examples and summary statements project exactly this view."[89] Yet several months later, when Levinson's book was published, Vaillant's hierarchical distinction of science and the media was overlaid with a chronological one: "original" versus "popularization."

THE GROUNDBREAKING 10-YEAR STUDY
THAT WAS THE BASIS FOR
PASSAGES!
"THE MOST AMBITIOUS ACCOUNT
OF THE ADULT LIFE CYCLE."
–NEWSWEEK

THE
SEASONS
OF A
MAN'S
LIFE

THE
NATIONAL
BESTSELLER

DANIEL J.
LEVINSON
WITH
CHARLOTTE N. DARROW ● EDWARD B. KLEIN
MARIA H. LEVINSON ● BRAXTON McKEE

FIG. 5.4 Daniel Levinson's *The Seasons of a Man's Life* was marketed as "the basis for *Passages*" although, published two years after Sheehy's best-seller, it presented a contradictory definition of the midlife transition. © Ballantine, Penguin Random House.

Seasons was introduced as the original *Passages*. In the *New York* article, Sheehy had foregrounded the importance of Levinson's research for her book project, and in *Passages*, she included a "primary professional debt" to him in the acknowledgments.[90] Such affiliation elevated Sheehy's credibility, yet when Levinson's book was published, her references underpinned the psychologist's authority on the midlife crisis and bolstered a priority claim, put forward on the dust jacket, where *Seasons* was introduced as the "study that was the basis for *Passages*." Although Levinson was familiar with Sheehy's work and—despite declaring he preferred the term "midlife transition"—spoke of "midlife crisis" frequently, he dodged mention of *Passages* in his book. This supported the priority claim. (Why would he have bothered to refer to a popularization of his own work?)

With the same effect, the psychologist predated his idea of midlife crisis to the mid-1960s, when he changed universities, and explained that the "Male Mid-life" project was already "well under way" before 1970. He made sure to add that he had started planning *Seasons* in spring 1973, before Sheehy's *New York* article, and also before Knopf approached him.

Chuck Elliott had as much of a hand as Levinson in making this priority claim against Sheehy. Elliott's colleagues at the publishing house were initially skeptical of the quality and unique selling point of Levinson's work, knowing of previous titles such as Barbara Fried's *The Middle Age Crisis* (1967) and Eda LeShan's *The Wonderful Crisis of Middle Age* (1973) as well as about Sheehy's work, then still in progress.[91] The editor pitched *Seasons* by drawing on the demarcation between pop psychology and serious science. In a letter to editor in chief Robert Gottlieb, he explained: "He [Levinson] understands—having been told—that the number of schlock psychology books makes it imperative that his book be detailed, specific and authoritative."[92]

When *Seasons* was put out, its relation to *Passages* became a central selling point. The editorial fact sheet for Levinson's book, written by Elliott and sent to booksellers and the press, emphasized that Sheehy's *Passages* was based on Levinson's ideas and praised *Seasons* as "much more thorough, reliable and scientifically-grounded." It said: "Gail Sheehy's debased version of [the ideas set forth in this book] (she interviewed Levinson at length before the study had been completed, and then wrote *Passages*) has received wide attention, to say the least, but doesn't do justice to the depth of thinking and scientific rigor involved in Levinson's work." Elliott concluded with a list of selling points: "*The Seasons of a Man's Life* is much less journalistic than *Passages*, much more thorough, reliable, and scientifically grounded. *Passages* was an entertaining fly-by; but this is the real thing, and you can believe it."[93]

Gould proceeded similarly. In the introduction of *Transformations*, he evoked the plagiarism charges and extended them from his unpublished papers to the newly published book. By his own account, Sheehy had asked him "to join her in writing a book," but he turned her down because he did not want to write anything "superficial." Pointing out that Sheehy had started *Passages* in 1973, he predated the beginnings of his book: to a personal crisis "ten years ago," and more specifically to a 1972 paper, "The Phases of Adult Life," which tested the age classification of patients for group therapy at the UCLA psychiatric outpatient department.[94]

Drawing a line between "original" science and "popularization" allowed Vaillant, Levinson, and Gould to appropriate the concept of midlife crisis. Emphasizing the differences between academic and "popular" ways of knowing was a common means for credentialed psychologists to cash in on their discipline's increased public prestige at a time when 28 percent of all Americans were, at one time or another, in treatment. Even more sought advice from books or from radio and television programs. Starting in the early 1970s, psychologists increasingly turned from academe and private practice to writing books, articles, and scripts or consulting on broadcast shows.[95]

From the perspective of the American Psychological Association (APA), being able to use the media was a "survival skill."[96] The APA's Task Force on Self-Help Therapies devised a guideline for reaping the "tremendous potential" of popular psychology and making sure that academics would carry more weight than writers and journalists, whose work they dismissed as "exaggerated" and "sensationalized."[97] Part of professionalization processes through which scientists expand their expertise into new domains, monopolize public authority, or protect their autonomy and power, such boundary work has often classified women's work as undemanding and dismissed their contributions as derivative, irrelevant, or wrong, thus indicating women's particularly low status as makers and bearers of knowledge. At different points in history, discriminating between expertise and amateurism, midwifery and medicine, or clerical work and computer programming has been used to exclude women, claim their work and ideas, and mute critique or alternative views.[98]

Read for what they had to say about "the *Passages* subject matter," or the midlife crisis, the three experts received attention out of all proportion to their degree of popularity until then; this spoke to the continued interest in the midlife crisis.[99] They found acclaim not only among psychological, psychiatric, and sociological experts but also among an educated middle-class audience. Their books were reviewed in academic journals—among them the organs of the American Psychological and

Sociological Associations—as well as newspapers and weeklies such as the *New York Times*, the *Wall Street Journal*, and the *Nation*, excerpted in *Esquire* and *Psychology Today*, and distributed as a selection of *Playboy* and other book clubs.[100] Levinson and Vaillant were reviewed more often than Gould, receiving at least twenty-nine and twenty reviews, respectively, compared with eight for *Transformations*; taken together, this exceeded *Passages*, which had been reviewed at least forty-nine times.[101]

The psychoanalysts' claim to authority did not go unchallenged. Reviewing *Seasons*, the life-course sociologist Leonard Cain pointed out that Knopf would simply "like a best seller, duplicating the success of Gail Sheehy's *Passages*."[102] In the words of the *Nation* critic Richard Lingeman, Levinson practiced "literary cloning," "the technique of reproducing a credible likeness of a successful book," "suitably disguised," and "turned out in time to catch the market for the original."[103] Many noted the expert's stylistic shortcomings, and some even considered *Seasons* lesser psychology than *Passages*. In *Psychiatry*, Henry Maas—of the Maas-Kuypers longitudinal study on personality in men and women—pointed out that Levinson's text was about men only, gave an "inadequate account of its methodology," and provided "no bibliography, as such, at all." By contrast, Sheehy had included "women and couples as well as men in her book, and her footnote sources and bibliography are very good, in the best scholarly tradition."[104]

However, such critiques were outnumbered by discussions of *Seasons*, *Adaptation*, and *Transformations* as better takes on the midlife crisis. Reviewers justified Levinson's and Vaillant's androcentric approach as more "cautious" or exact.[105] The *Baltimore Sun* picked up on Vaillant's dismissal of *Passages* by comparing his and Sheehy's books as opera and pop music: "[*Adaptation*] is to *Passages* what [the operatic soprano] Beverly Sills is to [the popular singer] Linda Ronstadt."[106] In the influential *New York Review of Books*, Alex Comfort, physician and author of the sex manual *The Joy of Sex* (1972), included Levinson's *Seasons* in a multiple book review of men's self-help literature as a book that dealt "properly with the strand of value that underlies the popularity of Gail Sheehy's *Passages*."[107] The science writer Robert Kanigel went as far as advising against reading Sheehy: "If you never climbed aboard the bandwagon for *Passages*, . . . don't now. Because now comes *The Seasons of a Man's Life*, by

Daniel Levinson[,] and . . . it is by far the better book. Better, because it is solid and sure and wise. And most of all, credible."[108] If Kanigel "came away weak with wonder at the drama in every human life," for Richard Rhodes, the widely published writer and historian, Levinson's work was not just "authoritative" but indeed "as important and fully as extraordinary as Kinsey's [report on male sexual behavior]: it will be unfortunate if *Passages'* popularity distracts potential readers from [*Seasons*]."[109]

Levinson, Vaillant, and Gould had three advantages over Sheehy: their credentialed status as experts vis-à-vis a journalist undergirded their authority, and they reiterated the same double standard of middle age, so that their accounts of midlife crisis mutually confirmed each other. Moreover, there was little overlap with reviewers of *Passages*. Sheehy's book had mostly been reviewed by literary critics and journalists with a gender, marriage, and lifestyle beat, while reviews of *Seasons, Transformations*, and *Adaptation* were primarily by psychiatrists, psychologists, and sociologists, or science writers. Less familiar with Sheehy's message, they reiterated Vaillant's, Levinson's, and Gould's assertion that they had written better, even more original books on midlife crisis.

Reviewers often depicted the psychological publications as forerunners, not successors, of Sheehy's earlier best-seller, drawing—implicitly or explicitly—on the gendered juxtaposition between expert and amateur: "Prof. Levinson is the man we can thank for inventing the mid-life crisis— the crisis that Gail Sheehy popularized in *Passages*."[110] Or, again in the *Baltimore Sun*: "Daniel Levinson . . . first came up with many of the findings on which the Sheehy book was based."[111] Almost all reviews of Levinson's *Seasons* included sentences like these, often in similar wording, following from editor Elliott's pitch for *Seasons* as "the real thing." Most reviewers recognized the complications of casting *Passages* as a popularization of *Seasons* (or, sometimes, *Adaptation* and *Transformations*), but many were quick to rectify them by invoking standards of scientific popularization against Sheehy.[112] They called *Passages* untimely and blamed it, often in one long tirade, for "pre-empting" *Seasons*: "Levinson's study of adult development was initiated in 1967. . . . Funding continued through early 1973, but it was another five years before the book was published. In the meantime, Sheehy's *Passages* which contained some of Levinson's work became very popular."[113] And, in the *Wall Street Journal*: "There's some talk that Mr. Levinson should be distressed with Miss Sheehy, since she rushed out with a best seller based in part on his research."[114]

Reviewers also borrowed from the language of plagiarism to rectify the seemingly twisted order of publication. These allegations were brought up particularly frequently when Gould's *Transformations*, the "Father of *Passages*," was published, but they also applied to *Seasons*.[115] "If I were Daniel Levinson, I might have sued Gail Sheehy," the *Newsday* book critic Dan Cryer explained: "She is the writer who appropriated some of his best ideas." Admittedly, "Sheehy didn't literally steal from Levinson." But her book "attracted so much attention . . . that the element of surprise this book might otherwise have given us is lost." In addition, Cryer was annoyed by Sheehy's immodest "tendency to present herself as a discoverer rather than a popularizer."[116] Her criticism was thus turned into a popularizer's unjust claim to authorship.

Even reviewers who shared Sheehy's perspective saw the later books as the original *Passages*. Pecile, though aware of the anti-feminist implications of *Seasons*, described it as the study "that provided the basic research" for *Passages*.[117] For feminist scientists, keeping a distance from popular feminist works was also an attempt to preserve their own professional authority. In the *Journal of Marriage and the Family*, the sociologist Laurel Walum Richardson, an expert on gender and interested in publicly communicating feminist research, wanted Levinson credited as "first-comer," regretting Sheehy's earlier success: "Unfortunately, since much of Gail Sheehy's much publicized book, *Passages*, was 'borrowed' from the unpublished work of Levinson, many readers will view Levinson's work as yesterday's sport page."[118]

Drawing the line between science and journalism made the psychoanalytic trio expert authorities on the midlife crisis, and their anti-feminist account of midlife was carried forward in the following years, when attacks on the women's movement became pervasive.

5 *Crisis Time*

In the 1980s, anti-feminist backlash generated a mass-media phenomenon. More often than in men's liberation or masculinist activist groups, it was voiced in mass-market publishing, where articles alternately sneered at "superwomen" or pitied their burnout, identity crisis, and marriage panic, powerfully undergirded by psychologists and therapists who urged women to interpret the pressures of backlash as simply "their" personal problem and called for a "return to femininity."[119] The declaration of a "crisis of masculinity" was a key anti-feminist trope. Overreacting to women's modest progress, commentators depicted masculinity as a "fragile flower" threatened by the smallest advances in women's rights: "Nothing seems to crush the masculine petals more than a bit of feminist rain—a few drops are perceived as a downpour."[120] Depicting masculinity as threatened implied the desirability of the stability disrupted by change. At Columbia, Carolyn Heilbrun "heard men say, with perfect sincerity, that a few women seeking equal pay are trying to overturn the university."[121]

The male midlife crisis thrived in this climate. Psychological and psychiatric experts who published on the topic, often with reference to Vaillant, Levinson, or Gould, were now joined by physicians. In *The Middle Years* (1981), published with backing from the American College of Physicians (an honorary society of internists), Dr. Donald Donohugh, a former government medical officer in Pago Pago, advised men to "revamp" at midlife.[122] Others gave presentations at men's groups, advising their audience to do yoga and exercise more, keep diets, and switch jobs: "It not only will test your mettle but will rekindle your fire."[123]

Particularly prominent among the writing doctors was the surgeon William Nolen, who had successfully published before—about his doctoral internship and residency, his practice in Litchfield, Minnesota, and his own heart operation (as well as in several women's magazines).[124] In the wake of Levinson's *Seasons*, he received considerable attention for an autobiographical account of his 1978–79 midlife crisis, first published as a *McCall's* article ("Why Men Go Crazy in their Forties," 1980), then reprinted in *Reader's Digest*.[125] The two articles unleashed a flood of mail, explained Nolen: "The women said, 'Oh my God, that's what my husband's got and what can I do about it?' All I'd do was refer them to Gail Sheehy's *Passages* or to Daniel Levinson, who wrote *The Seasons of a Man's Life*, so I decided to look into it myself."[126]

Published in 1984, *Crisis Time! Love, Marriage, and the Male at Midlife* offered a "blend of medicalese and locker-room observations," in the words of an unusually critical reviewer, and covered familiar territory.[127]

Midlife crisis concerned all men but hit successful men (such as Nolen himself) particularly hard: "You've got serious obligations, a position in the community. But you have a need to change your life. You're sick of your job. You're having trouble with sexual potency. You think you need a new woman in your life. You turn in your station wagon for a sports car. You get a mod coiffure."[128] The surgeon made small amendments to the psychological model of midlife, for example, by expanding it to men around fifty years old. Nolen also believed that the midlife crisis was more than a psychological developmental stage, that there was "a chemical or organic change that goes on in the bodies and the minds of the men. . . . I wouldn't be at all surprised if we discovered sometime that if you draw blood from the man in the midst of a midlife crisis and test it you would find that his endorphin level was all screwed up."[129]

Most of all, the surgeon perceived the midlife crisis as an exclusively male phenomenon, to which their wives were bystanders, or from which they had escaped, at best. While reiterating a pattern that had been described by Levinson and Vaillant, Nolen was more explicit about this difference than his predecessors had been. If *Seasons* and *Adaptation* were sometimes read as androcentric books, this was hardly possible with Nolen's *Crisis Time*. Asked by *Chicago Tribune* reporter Connie Lauerman why the midlife crisis hit men, not women, the surgeon replied: "Now I hate to sound sexist, but I think women generally handle changes better than men." Nolen was "amazed" at "the women whose husbands went off and had affairs during the midlife crisis, some of them flagrant, and the women were so willing to forgive them if they'd only come back. . . . I think it's because women's sense of perspective when it comes to sexual matters is better than that of the average man. Maybe it's a sexist thing to say," he added. "Women make a greater commitment." (Which Nolen understood to mean that, unlike for men, love and sex were inseparable for women.) Armed with this knowledge about women, which he considered an "invitation to have an affair," Nolen admitted that in his own midlife crisis, he "felt so sure" of his wife (with whom he had six children) that he "never even considered" the possibility of her leaving him, although he was sure that would have made him "very miserable."[130]

This strict division between men and women, painting the midlife crisis as a men's problem, and explicitly setting it off against women, was a consistent feature of depictions of the midlife crisis in the 1980s. The psychiatrist Noel Lustig, who offered help for men in midlife crisis at the Northridge Hospital in California, believed that "men have a more difficult time adjusting to middle age than women."[131]

At the same time, midlife women remained important addressees of the male midlife crisis; advice to them was widespread. Nolen suggested they wait—two years seemed an appropriate benchmark—and consider the situation: "Can she absolutely not tolerate his relationships with other women? Or can she write it off as 'men will be men'?"[132] If they could not solve the problems on their own, women should seek professional help. The California psychiatrist Jim Stanley regularly treated men who were experiencing a midlife crisis—and their wives. In an interview with a local magazine, he advised women to be patient and understanding. A wife should "help her husband": "She should try to understand, communicate and empathize with him about the pressure he feels. She should also have patience to work through problems and not act precipitously, too, and give up on the relationship at the first sign of trouble." The therapist charged women with holding "unrealistic" expectations of men and advised them to be "more accepting" of their husbands' midlife behavior. Moreover, a woman might "discover that she expects too much of [her husband." This, Stanley held, often occurred after children left home, their departure resulting in a "tremendous vacuum" in the woman's life. "At that time, the wife may turn to the husband for the attention and the emotional support that her children gave her, and that isn't always appropriate."[133]

In short, the male midlife gospel continued throughout the 1980s, slightly updated. In 1989, Levinson himself capitalized on the continued success of his theory and turned *Seasons* into a documentary. Coproduced by David Keller and David Sutherland and broadcast on PBS, *Halftime: Five Yale Men at Midlife* chronicled the midlife crises of five white male Yale graduates, Class of 1963, selected by Levinson (out of a group of two hundred volunteers), who also interviewed them at length in front of the camera (individually and in a group session). In the opening shot, Steve Sohmer, a Hollywood executive complete with fat cigar, Rolls-Royce, and Rolex, recently fired as head of a major studio, talked about his experience of going through multiple marriages, love affairs, and jobs; later, the attorney Mike Redman aired anger over his wife's request for a divorce.

6 Rethinking Popularization

The male midlife crisis almost eclipsed Sheehy's earlier definition. In the following years and decades, journalistic and disciplinary histories of the midlife crisis continued to follow the lines laid out by Levinson, Gould, and Vaillant, who had drawn on the demarcation between academic and "popular" knowledge to silence Sheehy's feminist critique and assert their own scientific respectability. Often presented as introductions to articles and books about midlife crisis, these histories from within seldom failed to include a reference to at least two of the psychoanalytic books. According to the moral philosopher Kieran Setiya, the midlife crisis was "born" with Elliott Jaques's coinage, grew up with Daniel Levinson's and Roger Gould's studies, and came of age when Sheehy popularized the psychoanalysts, with "a knack for the memorable phrase . . . and a willingness to generalize."[134] Even those who shared Sheehy's feminist values spoke of Levinson's work as "the starting point for Gail Sheehy's more popular book *Passages*" or cited Vaillant, Levinson, and Gould as her "predecessors."[135]

These accounts are not simply wrong; they feed on and continue to nourish a narrative that has played important political roles. Turning upside down the publishing chronology obstructs the psychoanalysts' backlash agenda as much as Sheehy's original, feminist concept and her impact on the history of the midlife crisis. As a response and follow-up, Levinson, Vaillant, and Gould depended on Sheehy more than she on them: *Seasons, Transformation*, and *Adaptation* were advertised as the better *Passages* and read for what they had to say about the midlife crisis, and the experts' authority over the issue was created by way of comparison with the journalist.

The received tale of midlife crisis illustrates that after Vaillant, Levinson, and Gould, Sheehy's feminist midlife crisis was no longer authoritative. *Passages* continued to be read—by 1984, it was in its thirty-first printing—yet the term "midlife crisis" was now primarily connected to men and corroborated, rather than abolished, traditional gender hierarchies.[136] Still, the psychoanalysts did not have the last word. Feminist concepts of the life course continued to exist, and the male midlife crisis was contested soon and broadly by Carol Gilligan, Rosalind Barnett, and other psychologists and sociologists, who often used arguments similar to Sheehy's to turn the male midlife crisis into a chauvinist cliché.

6

Feminist Riposte

Backlash did not effect a setback. In the 1980s, feminist studies on middle life contributed to efforts to extend attention to women's lives beyond reproduction. The psychiatrist Myrna Weissman successfully campaigned for the removal of the diagnosis of "involutional melancholia"—depression in the menopausal years—from the third edition of the American Psychiatric Association's *Diagnostic and Statistical Manual*, or *DSM-III*.[1] Anthropologists, spearheaded by Judith Brown—known for her earlier work on menarche—confirmed from a cross-cultural perspective that in many societies middle age was the time when women enjoyed their greatest power and autonomy and came closer to the authority of men than in earlier years.[2] In her classic *The Female World* (1981), the sociologist Jessie Bernard drew on Sheehy's *Passages* to highlight the "female subworld" of midlife, challenging the understanding that a woman's "prime time" was between eighteen and the midtwenties. True prime began in the midthirties: "prime from the point of view of the woman herself."[3] For the American Academy of Political and Social Science, this body of research fundamentally "reconstructed middle age."[4]

It was "as though Gail Sheehy's *Passages* had been transported to ivied halls," noted the *New York Times* upon the book's tenth anniversary.[5] Yet as much as academic emphasis on women's midlife well-being resembled *Passages*, researchers did not reclaim the midlife crisis for feminist purposes. "One hears less today about women's 'mid-life crisis' and more about 'post-menopausal zest,'" observed the *Women's Review of Books*.[6] Most feminist social scientists rejected the idea of a midpoint change of life, associating this primarily with the male-centered concept put forward by Levinson, Vaillant, and Gould. Unaware of Sheehy's contribution, they also looked at midlife from new and different angles.

Psychologists were particularly invested in refuting the midlife crisis. The moral and developmental psychologist Carol Gilligan was its most famous antagonist, although she is not best known for criticizing it. Starting from a defense of women's right to choose abortion (a misremembered legacy), Gilligan's *In a Different Voice* (1982) famously challenged psychological theories of morality, arguing for an ethics of responsibility rather than rights and justice.[7] Based on an understanding of maturity as the acknowledgment of responsibility, Gilligan declared the male midlife crisis a sign of selfishness, negligence, and regression.

Gilligan was controversial in feminist circles, yet even those who disagreed with her emphasis on gender differences rejected the male midlife crisis, if on other grounds. In *Lifeprints* (1983), based on a study of three hundred women, the journalist Caryl Rivers and the Wellesley psychologists Grace Baruch and Rosalind Barnett, experts on education, motivation, and careers, found no indication of crisis in the lives of professional women now approaching midlife in larger numbers. Critiquing stage theories, they adopted a psychosocial perspective to attribute emotional turmoil in middle age, for men and women, to the limits of traditional roles, thus associating the midlife crisis with adherence to separate spheres.

Feminist critiques of the male midlife crisis resonated widely, notwithstanding the fact that Levinson, Vaillant, and Gould insisted on the validity of their diagnosis. When Levinson responded at book length, arguing that women had a midlife crisis, too, and that paid work interfered with their identity development, this was primarily a rearguard defense.[8] Feminist concepts of women's midlife well-being continued to circulate throughout the 1980s and '90s, in part with Gail Sheehy's best-selling menopause essay *The Silent Passage* (1992).[9] In 2000, the large-scale MIDUS survey on midlife in the United States confirmed the critique of the midlife crisis's universality from a quantitative perspective and showed that many Americans dismissed it as a "stupid excuse" for selfish behavior.[10]

1 *Voice and Choice*

As legend has it, Carol Gilligan had been "completely blind" to gender when she began research for *In a Different Voice: Psychological Theory and Women's Development* in the early 1970s: "I hadn't yet realized the degree to which women had been left out of my textbooks and models."[11] When her keystone book appeared in 1982, Gilligan was an associate professor of psychology at Harvard's Graduate School of Education. Born Carol Friedman in New York in 1936, she was one year Sheehy's senior, also having gained a BA in English literature (from Swarthmore, Pennsylvania), before going on to take a master's degree in clinical psychology at Radcliffe and marry the doctor-in-training James Gilligan (both in 1961), then complete a PhD in social psychology at Harvard.[12] A student of Walter Mischel, she collaborated with him on a study of temptation and delayed gratification, a forerunner of the famous "marshmallow test" experiments.[13] After two years at the University of Chicago, where Gilligan taught an introduction to modern social science, she returned to Harvard in 1967 as teaching assistant for Erik Erikson's Human Life Cycle course and as research and teaching assistant for the psychologist and moral theorist Lawrence Kohlberg, with whom she collaborated on several papers.[14] In 1971, she became an assistant professor at the Harvard Graduate School of Education, and for the following ten years she listened "to people talking about morality and about themselves" in a series of studies that became *In a Different Voice*.[15]

Gilligan was active in the anti-war and civil rights movements (doing voter registration), and, in countercultural spirit, her studies challenged psychological categories by exploring dissonances between scientific theory and lived experience. *In a Different Voice* started during protests against the Vietnam War with a college-student study, "Actual Experiences of Conflict and Choice" (1972–78). Gilligan interviewed twenty-five students—twenty men, five women—who had taken a course on ethical and political choice about their self-concepts and the making of life choices, with follow-up interviews planned the next year to probe the male senior students as they faced the draft.[16]

Yet Gilligan was not at all gender blind. Of twenty students who had dropped the ethics course, sixteen were women. By interviewing them in addition to the course participants, Gilligan contributed to an effort to understand above-average dropout rates among female students, and thus the gender gap in higher education at a time when elite universities were beginning to admit women undergraduates.[17] In late January 1973, soon after the beginning of the study, the Supreme Court legalized abortion, in the landmark case *Roe v. Wade*; then Nixon ended the draft. Gilligan turned her research from a moral problem that faced only men into a project on women and reproductive rights.[18]

Begun the year after the Supreme Court decision, when a sense of optimism and liberation accompanied the opening of legal abortion services, the "abortion-decision study" ("A Naturalistic Study of Abortion Decisions," 1974–78) became the book's core study. Together with Mary Belenky, her graduate student at the time, Gilligan interviewed twenty-nine women during their first trimester to understand how they constructed and resolved the choice of whether or not to continue pregnancy. Referred by storefront clinics, Planned Parenthood, and Harvard's University Health Service, the women were between fifteen and thirty-three years old, some single, some married, and a few the mother of a preschool child; some had had abortions before. A few came from working-class backgrounds, and one sixteen-year-old had a history of disorderly conduct and reform school, but most were highly educated, and some already in professional careers.[19]

The women were interviewed twice, first at the time they were making the decision, then at the end of the following year. In the initial part of the interview, they discussed the decision they faced: how they were dealing with it, the alternatives they were considering, their reasons for and against each option, the people involved, and the conflicts entailed. Of the twenty-nine women, twenty-one chose abortion, four decided to have the baby, two miscarried, and two could not be contacted again. The follow-up interview, conducted with the women who had chosen to have an abortion, discussed the decision retrospectively, also asking the women to resolve three hypothetical moral quandaries such as the so-called Heinz dilemma: Should a poor man steal an overpriced drug to save his wife's life? As was typical in moral theory, Gilligan and Belenky's analysis of the dilemmas focused not on the decision made but on the form in which it was justified: the ways in which the women used moral language—words such as "should," "ought," "better," "right," "good" and "bad"—the changes and shifts that appeared in their thinking, and the ways in which they reflected on and judged their own thought.[20]

Gilligan's starting point in the controversy about abortion meant that her perspective on the value of life choices and the costs tied to revaluation differed from the stance held by Sheehy or Friedan. In the abortion debate, the imperative to regret having behaved otherwise than socially expected was a way of maintaining conservative values. In the post-*Roe* period, and particularly after the election of President Ronald Reagan in 1980, when the anti-abortion movement ascended to a national stage, regret became a powerful threat lodged against women considering abortion.

Previously, deterministic arguments had simply insisted that women's reproductive potential obligated them to become mothers, leaving no other choice, and that motherhood was the only way of moving forward along the life course for an adult woman. Now that women did have a legal right to choose, anti-abortion activists told them that if they terminated a pregnancy, they would lament the decision and experience painful regret, or what came to be known as "post-abortion syndrome," a term coined by therapist and "pro-life" advocate Vincent Rue in testimony before Congress in 1981.[21] The anti-abortion pamphlet "How to Survive Your Abortion: A Guide to Rebuilding Your Life" warned women of "trivializing," "denying," or "rationalizing" shock, distress, and depression: "Society tells aborted women that they have no right to grieve, after all you were the one who made the decision, a 'choice' that is perfectly legal. Yet your grief is normal. . . . To *fail* to experience a sense of loss, of emptiness, of grief, is *abnormal.*"[22]

Pitting maternal happiness versus abortion grief, the notion of tragedy was used to shame, stigmatize, and silence women. This punitive notion of loss and remorse contrasted sharply with the understanding at the heart of the midlife crisis: that to question a path chosen meant challenging imposed or internalized social norms. In the 1980s, affirming women's freedom to terminate pregnancy implied ambivalence about doubt, sorrow, and the wish to undo the irreversible. Far from offering a route to self-fulfillment or marking the beginning of a new life, regret was "hegemony's watchdog, a normalizing mechanism aimed to restore each of us to the good graces of society."[23] In this light, consistency was a mark of integrity. In contrast to earlier feminist approaches, Gilligan devised a conception of identity and development based on the notion of self-continuity, not rupture.

By approaching abortion as a moral dilemma, Gilligan rejected the "pro-life" position that the termination of pregnancy was a selfish denunciation of human rights and duties. Part of a larger and continuing movement to decriminalize abortion, to which *Roe v. Wade* had contributed by changing the laws, Gilligan put forward a moral justification of women's choice, thus making ethics more relevant and useful for women's lives.[24]

The decision to have a child, she argued, could be immoral, too. Sociological accounts of single motherhood, notably Prudence Rains's and then Frank Furstenberg's well-known ethnographic studies of the "moral career" of unwed motherhood, from 1971 and 1976, respectively, argued for or defended abortion by depicting single "unplanned parenthood" as the outcome of a series of "choices" or actions, not a "natural," inevitable path: the decision to have premarital sex, the decision not to use contraceptives, and the decision not to have an abortion. Abortion was part of a larger process of planning and decision-making, not an exceptional choice.[25]

Gilligan followed a similar line of reasoning. Of the fifteen abortion-decision interviews cited in the book, more than half were with adolescents, some underage, and most of the remaining women were single. For Ruth, a twenty-nine-year-old married woman and mother of a preschool child, the timing of a second pregnancy conflicted with her completion of an advanced degree; Sandra, a Catholic nurse, who at the same age lived with her parents, considered her option to be either abortion or adoption. Having previously given up one child for adoption, she found that "psychologically there was no way I could hack another adoption. It took me about four and a half years to get my head on straight. There was just no way I was going through it again."[26] These cases, where pregnancy and motherhood threatened a woman's well-being, complicated the simple distinction between destiny and free choice. They illustrated Gilligan's argument that abortion could be a responsible, moral decision: "If there is no prospect for a future, that is, a happy future, then it is immoral to have a child."[27]

Historians as well as theorists have tended to neglect the relevance of Gilligan's starting point in changing debates about pregnancy termination, seeing *In a Different Voice* instead as a book about maternity.[28] Yet Gilligan relied on conceptions of motherhood to justify the termination of pregnancy, suggesting that the decisions for or against motherhood were equally valid and governed by the same moral principles, different points on a continuum rather than polar opposites.[29] By drawing on images of motherhood, nineteenth-century maternalist feminists had argued for women's innate benevolence and moral superiority to claim the vote and public positions, not least in jurisprudence.[30] Feminist scholars, writers, and activists who made similar arguments in the 1970s and '80s often relied on psychoanalysis, using its view of gender difference for their own purposes.

Gilligan felt a "profound affinity" with the psychoanalyst Jean Baker Miller, whose essay *Toward a New Psychology of Women* (1976) called for a new language to describe a female sense of self, "organized around being able to make and then to maintain affiliation and relationships," which previous psychoanalytic accounts had pathologized.[31] Miller saw in the self-in-relation "the possibilities for an entirely different (and more advanced) approach to living and functioning . . . [in which] affiliation is valued as highly as, or more highly than self-enhancement."[32] She advocated a view of mental health and maturity grounded in female rather than male psychology: hitherto devalued "feminine" traits of empathy and compassion were the true measure of psychological well-being.

Others put forward similar notions of superior femininity. In *The Reproduction of Mothering* (1978), the sociologist Nancy Chodorow—another important inspiration for Gilligan—critiqued the masculine sense of autonomy as the personality prototype of industrial capitalism and celebrated women's capacity for relationship as a source of redemption.[33] The philosopher Sara Ruddick suggested that the practices of mothering equipped women for resisting militarism and war and made them powerful negotiators for peace.[34] In history and philosophy of science, Evelyn Fox Keller, Donna Haraway, and Sandra Harding challenged the principles of objectivity as the basis of scientific inquiry and argued that "female" modes of knowing, based on imagination, integration, and empathy, constituted an alternative, valid, even superior epistemology.[35] Gilligan drove the underlying connection between women and virtuousness home by proposing a better, "feminine" understanding of morality. This became the main point of *In a Different Voice*: that something as basic as visions of the good and the right was strictly gendered.

2 *A Different View*

She was sitting at the kitchen table, Gilligan remembers, and looking through the abortion-decision interviews when it clicked. Her friend and colleague Dora Ullian, a psychologist at Harvard, came in, "and I said: 'Dora, these women—they are constructing self and they're constructing what's a moral problem differently'—and that's why they weren't fitting into the whole discussion of self in Freud and Erikson and objects relations and so forth that I'd been teaching, and that's why women were falling through the sieves of Kohlberg's categories." As she began writing up her findings, "I realized something that was just *stunning* to me, because I had never noticed that Erikson's work on identity was done with an all-male sample (returning war veterans); that Freud's work had a male voice, a male point of view, all through it; that the whole discussion of object relations theory was talking about a woman as an object; that Piaget had all boys in his *Moral Judgement of the Child* and Kohlberg's 20-year longitudinal research, heavily funded, was done with an all-male sample."[36]

Tales of oblivion and surprise, signaling a researcher's neutrality and objectivity, are a recurrent trope used to legitimize controversial research. By arguing that she came to her insight almost without any preexisting feminist consciousness, Gilligan and her supporters excluded the risk of bias. They combined the scientific discovery story with a tale of consciousness-raising—important in feminist autobiographies—thus aiding identification with Gilligan's not-yet-feminist journey.[37]

In the words of the journalist and intellectual historian Nicholas Bromell, Gilligan "made two discoveries virtually at the same moment: That women had been left out of most models of psychological development and that, indeed, women's experiences directly challenged the validity of these models."[38] Moral and psychological theory was built on observations of men's lives. When women failed to develop in the way men did, researchers concluded that something was wrong with women—all the more so, some senior professors argued when Gilligan wrote up her findings, because she worked with pregnant women, whom they saw as hysterical and unreasonable. (Someone suggested she "should study men having abortions.")[39] Gilligan concluded, instead, that the theory was wrong.

In her initial paper, "In a Different Voice: Women's Conceptions of Self and Morality" (1977), she joined recent critiques of gender bias in Kohlberg's stage theory for the measurement of moral maturity, put forward by the psychologists Norma Haan, Constance Holstein, and Elizabeth Simpson.[40] In Kohlberg's six-stage sequence—derived from a study of eighty-four boys—women appeared to be stuck at stage three, where moral decisions were made to help others and sustain interpersonal relations. They rarely rose to stage four, where relationships were subordinated to rules and the law, or stages five and six, where morality stemmed from ultimate principles of justice that transcend self-interest and social norms.[41] This, Kohlberg suggested, was "functional" for domestic and nurturing tasks, but insufficient in professional, business, and public roles.[42]

Gilligan argued that the differences represented by Kohlberg as steps in a developmental progression were instead a "contrapuntal theme."[43] He emphasized abstract principles of justice at the expense of virtues of responsibility and benevolence, muting women's voices and distorting the complex dialogue between fairness and care. Real-life morality asked not whose rights took precedence but how to act responsibly, carefully rather than carelessly. Gilligan's appeal for the acknowledgment of neglected, because "female," characteristics of ethical behavior became the best-known result of her research.

She supplemented Kohlberg's stage theory of moral development with a sequence in the development of the ethic of care, based on his notion of an expansion in moral understanding from an individual to a societal to a universal perspective or what Kohlberg termed the "preconventional," "conventional," and "postconventional" views of morality. In this scheme, conventional morality, or the equation of the right or good with the maintenance of existing social norms and values, was the point of departure. Preconventional moral judgment denoted an inability to construct a shared or societal viewpoint; postconventional judgment transcended that vision: "Preconventional judgment is egocentric and derives moral constructs from individual needs; conventional judgment is based on shared norms and values that sustain relationships, groups, communities, and societies; and postconventional judgment adopts a reflective perspective on societal values and constructs moral principles that are universal in application."[44]

In Gilligan's stage sequence of the development of an ethic of care, a preconventional, "selfish" focus on caring for the self in order to ensure survival was followed by the "conventional" acknowledgment of responsibility for the dependent and unequal that prioritized care to the point of self-abandonment. The third perspective dissipated the tension between selfishness and self-sacrifice through a new understanding of interconnection between other and self. Care became the self-chosen principle of a judgment that became universal—or "postconventional"—in its condemnation of exploitation and hurt.[45] Gilligan's ethics of care provided the basis for her critique of the midlife crisis.

In a Different Voice was no folie à deux between Gilligan and Kohlberg; it staked broader claims.[46] The inclusion of women challenged and changed the basic models and assumptions of psychological theory. Evoking Thomas Kuhn's notion of paradigm shift, Gilligan recounts: "It began to dawn on me that this was classic scientific paradigm extension."[47] Twenty years after publication, Kuhn's *The Structure of Scientific Revolutions* (1962) had evolved into a primary point of reference for critical voices of many kinds. Frequently drawn upon to show the constructedness and historicity of science, it was also used to stabilize scientific endeavors and often invoked by researchers to legitimize a discipline or field, a reading which might have been closer to Kuhn's own intentions.[48] Psychological theories of development—particularly by Jean Piaget—had been an early inspiration for Kuhn, and his sequential theory of scientific change resonated in the field. In the 1970s and '80s, psychologists habitually drew on *Structure*, thus giving a new twist to older debates about methodology, social relevance, and theoretical orientation.[49] A manual for scientific discovery as much as a tool for historical analysis, the Kuhnian model of scientific progress allowed scholars to argue for a new theory's superiority without falsifying alternative and conflicting interpretations.[50] Emphasizing gender difference allowed Gilligan to take the classic approach: look at the group that has been excluded from research, find disparate data, and redefine the models and theories that cannot explain this data.[51]

Morality was the first of several examples of Gilligan's larger target: "psychological theory and women's development." *In a Different Voice* was about developmental theory writ large, including in adulthood, or in Gilligan's own words: "I wrote the book . . . seeking to discover whether something had been missed by the practice of leaving out girls and women at the theory-building stage of research in developmental theory—that is, whether Piaget's and Kohlberg's descriptions of moral development, Erikson's description of identity development, [Daniel] Offer's description of adolescent development, Levinson's and Vaillant's descriptions of adult development, as well as more general accounts of human personality and motivation, contained a consistent conceptual and observational bias."[52] A final, "life cycle" study ("Development of Self and Morality," 1977–80)—the largest of the three surveys—explored and refined her conception of development in interviews with 144 white, educated middle-class girls and boys and men and women from six to sixty years old. They were asked about their conceptions of self and morality, experiences of moral conflict and choice, and judgments of hypothetical dilemmas.[53]

3 Regressive Masculinity

Throughout the life course, psychological theories described development as a process of separation, equating maturity with "individuation" or the distinction between self and others: "The arc of developmental theory leads from infantile dependence to adult autonomy, tracing a path characterized by an increasing differentiation of self from other."[54] In early childhood, progress was charted by measuring the distance between mother and child. Next, Peter Blos, a leading authority on adolescence, spoke of the "second individuation process" in which a teenager had to separate from the father.[55] And in the "second adolescence" chronicled by Levinson, Vaillant, and Gould, a man cut off ties to his wife, trading intimacy for achievement. From cradle to career, ending relationships gave way to identity; failing to do so restricted self-development.

Gilligan argued that the separation-individuation trajectory was skewed. Identity and intimacy were fused, not mutually exclusive; development entailed attachment as much as autonomy. To illustrate the existence and importance of continuing relationships, Gilligan drew on her interviews with women, who, when asked to describe themselves, often described a relationship, depicting their identity in the connection of future mother, present wife, adopted child, or past lover. Claire, a medical student and participant in the college-student study (after college, she worked as a counselor in an abortion clinic), found that "by yourself, there is little sense to things. It is like the sound of one hand clapping." Separateness was fictitious, "a human absurdity, the illusion of a person standing alone in a reality of interconnection."[56] No woman is an island.

The concern for others' needs and opinions represented a mature and complex morality, not a pathology. In the transition from childhood to adulthood, the activity of care was freed from the wish for approval by others; helping was distinguished from pleasing, and the ethic of responsibility became a "self-chosen anchor of personal integrity and strength."[57] The rejection of individualism implicated a moral and political position, as Gilligan explicated, in Claire's words: "It is the collective that is important to me."[58] Concern with relationships turned from a weakness into a human strength, social relations from an obstacle into a salient resource for identity.

This was more than an ancillary or alternative account; psychological theory was "wrong not just for women, it's wrong as a *human* story."[59] In Kuhn's terms, Gilligan's theory was "incommensurable" with previous constructions of development: "The proponents of competing paradigms practice their trades in different worlds. . . . [They] see different things when they look for the same point in the same direction." As in the famous rabbit-duck illusion, you could either see the rabbit or the duck but not both at the same time.[60] An ethics of care and cooperation exposed separateness as an impossible ideal, an "illusory and dangerous quest"; it made individuation look like a "process of dissociation," verging on isolation and indicating "indifference and unconcern" or a "problem in making connections."[61]

From this point of view, the midlife crisis indicated a problem. For Gilligan, Levinson and Vaillant depicted men who lived at a problematic personal distance from others and whose relationships were limited in their affective range. They lacked friends and had trouble even describing their wives, whose importance in their lives they nonetheless acknowledged. (As Gilligan reported, correctly, Vaillant told the men in his study that "the hardest question" he would ask was "Can you describe your wife?")[62] The men were compromised in their capacity for intimacy, having difficulty interacting with others and forming and sustaining meaningful connections. Their crisis pointed to "the limits of their adaptation"—that is, their ability to take in new ideas—or perhaps "to its psychological expense."[63] It was a sign of emotional and cognitive deficiencies, indicating psychological immaturity and a learning disability of sorts. Levinson's and Vaillant's construction of midlife crisis described a process not of development but of stagnation, even degeneration. More than that, it was cruel, malicious, and egoistical.

In speaking to Levinson's and Vaillant's celebration of midlife separation, Gilligan joined contemporary feminist criticism of marriage and divorce. Transferring into the marital realm arguments against abortion as egoistic and immoral, she suggested that terminating a long-term relationship was irresponsible. From the perspective of the one left behind, heroic accounts of self-actualization turned into narratives of loss, disappointment, and "extreme psychological violence."[64] By changing their lives, the men destroyed those of others. Their self-fulfillment at the expense of others was an "isolationist detachment from the claims of others," a selfish "flight from commitment," as the author Barbara Ehrenreich famously put it.[65]

For Gilligan, the male midlife crisis was a primary example for the lowest, preconventional stage of moral judgment. Unable to construct a shared or societal viewpoint, Levinson's and Vaillant's men egocentrically derived moral constructs from individual needs. They did not differentiate between "should" and "would," and other people influenced their decision only through their power to affect its consequences. Survival was the paramount concern, to the point of hurting and exploiting others. The midlife crisis was a sign of immaturity or moral regression.

To Gilligan, the observation that women's embeddedness in lives of relationship, their orientation toward interdependence, their subordination of achievement to care, and their conflicts over competitive success left them personally at risk, especially in midlife, indicated a "rather narrow vision" of identity and self-fulfillment, and was "more a commentary on the society than a problem in women's development."[66] She did not mention Sheehy's *Passages,* but when she considered women and middle age, as part of a study group at the Social Science Research Council, Gilligan rejected the idea of a change in adulthood.[67] There was no room for a "second adolescence" in her model of development.[68]

What happened for women in midlife was not a break with their pre-vious focus on intimacy. Women did not abandon their families, as the men Levinson described did. Nor did they switch from a preoccupation with care to an emphasis on achievement. Gilligan disliked the notions of androgyny and gender role reversal that were at the basis of Sheehy's "Sexual Diamond," suggesting it was impossible "to be male *and* female at the same time."[69]

Instead of rupture, women's lives illustrated a deepening of previously important traits, an uninterrupted development, focused on the recur-rent theme of empathy and activities of care. Women's experience delin-eated the path to a maturity realized through continuing connection, what Erikson had touched on in his concept of "generativity" but never fully spelled out, Gilligan suggested, because his theory was based on men's, not women's, life histories.[70] Distinguishing this from Erikson's develop-mental ladder and using classic movement vocabulary, she spoke of an ever-widening social circle and moral compass: like "the expanding rip-ples produced when a stone is dropped into a pond."[71]

By the time the little crimson book came out, Gilligan was no unknown within academic circles. *In a Different Voice* was her book debut, but her earlier article by the same title was already a citation classic, and a follow-up piece, "Woman's Place in Man's Life Cycle" (1979), had won the Asso-ciation for Women in Psychology's Distinguished Publication Award.[72] The *Boston Globe Magazine* reported at length on Gilligan's work as early as fall 1980, when she had barely finished the manuscript for Harvard Uni-versity Press.[73] *In a Different Voice* was broadly reviewed by prestigious journals including *Contemporary Psychology* and *Contemporary Sociology*, *Signs*, and the *Psychology of Women Quarterly* as well as in philosophy, law, political theory, social work, and education journals. Cross-disciplinary, Gilligan's audience extended beyond the academy, too. *In a Different Voice* was excerpted in *Psychology Today* ("Why Should a Woman be More like a Man?"), discussed in the *New York Times Book Review* ("consistently provocative and imaginative"), and praised by *Vogue* ("Thinking like a Woman").[74] The renowned critic Ellen Goodman recommended Gilli-gan's book as number one for summer reading.[75] It was no wonder, then, that on a transatlantic flight, the psychologist Helen Haste overheard a group of travel agents discussing *In a Different Voice* "with enthusiasm."[76]

FIG. 6.1 For the journalist and writer Amy Gross, Carol Gilligan's *In a Different Voice* "reframes qualities regarded as women's weaknesses and shows them to be human strengths." This portrait appeared in *Vogue*, May 1982. © Duane Michals, Courtesy DC Moore Gallery, New York.

Rarely read as a book about reproductive rights, *In a Different Voice* was widely used to understand women's public choices. The advertising trade magazine *Madison Avenue* asked Gilligan "What Does Woman Want from the Marketer?"[77] Before the 1984 elections, it was one of the top ten most-sold books in Washington, DC, drawn on to explain women's statistically lower support for Reagan: they voted for a "politics of caretaking," for a strong government and against individualism and free markets.[78]

Until Judith Butler's *Gender Trouble* (1990), Gilligan's was the most cited title of feminist theory.[79] Although not a national best-seller, 360,000 copies sold by the end of the 1980s and close to a million at its thirtieth

anniversary made *In a Different Voice* Harvard's most commercially successful book ever.[80] A classic, it was read on its own rather than as a reply to
other theory, generating further seminal works on "caring" and "women's
ways of knowing."[81] The foundation of the Center for the Study of Gender,
Education, and Human Development in 1983 allowed Gilligan to carry
on with her work in the large-scale Project on Women's Psychology and
Girls' Development, often credited with influencing the passage of the
1993 Gender Equity in Education Act.[82] She received tenure in 1986, the
same year the American Psychoanalytic Association, amid the backlash of
the Reagan-Bush years, reaffirmed its own pro-choice resolution, adopted
in the early 1970s.[83]

Importantly, you did not have to agree with Gilligan's feminist politics
to value her understanding of ethics. Gilligan's emphasis on cooperation,
not individualism, has been read as the central normative claim of her
work and called her "most radical" challenge to traditional developmental psychology.[84] Lawrence Kohlberg, while brushing aside the idea that
his hierarchy of development did not apply to women, considered Gilligan's redefinition of morality her "most important" contribution to moral
theory and redefined his conception of moral development to include a
"responsibility orientation."[85]

In developmental psychology, Gilligan contributed to a redefinition of
identity formation as a thoroughly social process, with cooperation and
altruism as key values. Infants and children were seen to learn because they
engaged with other people, while new concepts of adolescence showed
that this was not a period of separation.[86] Psychologists also used a lack of
social empathy and the failure to develop relations as the primary diagnostic criteria for autism, which went public as a developmental disorder, an
area of scientific research, and a health policy issue in the 1980s.[87]

More generally, in the long history of American anxiety about alienation and social fragmentation, Gilligan's relational understanding of identity resonated with contemporary attempts to reconcile self and society.
In the "age of fracture," worries about conformity, as adopted by Levinson, Vaillant, and Gould in the portrayal of "rebellious," "inner-directed"
middle-aged men, gave way to anxieties about absence of community and
lack of commitment, voiced prominently in *Habits of the Heart* (1985),
one of the central late twentieth-century interpretations of American cul-

ture, by the sociologist Robert Bellah and his colleagues.[88] Coauthor Ann Swidler, in her study of intimate relationships, described love as "a continuing process rather than a once-and-for-all culmination of life." Few people settled down after the choice of work and marital partner had been made, she observed; rather, the quest for identity and love became continuing preoccupations, and love became a "crucible for identity."[89]

The contemporary therapeutic and self-help literature, too, showed an increased concern for the quality of interpersonal relationships. Compromise and accommodation were seen as essential; self-sufficiency came under attack. Often, this was presented as an attack on the "psychoculture" of the 1970s. In his critique of the search of self-fulfillment, the pollster-turned-social-critic Daniel Yankelovich condemned the "root fallacy . . . that the human self can be wholly autonomous, solitary, contained, and 'self-created.'"[90] Intimacy was central to the development of identity. The self was, in the psychologist Kenneth Gergen's much-cited phrase, "created and re-created in relationships."[91] From this perspective, the midlife crisis did not seem like a sign of mental health.

However, there was criticism, too, and not just by Christopher Lasch, who, in response to subsequent research, frowned upon Gilligan's "[preoccupation] with questions of selfishness" and attacked her for claiming as "feminine" care and compassion and denigrating objective standards, industriousness, and the pursuit of perfection as "male."[92] *In a Different Voice* was particularly controversial in feminist circles. Many scholars disagreed with the notion of gender difference that was central to Gilligan's dialogue with psychoanalysis. Her conception of care could be understood as a call for the reconstruction of corporations, not women.[93] Yet set off against Matina Horner's "fear of success" and others who sought to help women overcome self-doubts, and thus read as a message to women, Gilligan's emphasis on care and critique of achievement seemed to suggest that femininity was at odds with a professional career.[94]

When *Signs* organized an interdisciplinary symposium in 1986, the eminent psychologist Eleanor Maccoby expressed the thoughts of many feminist scholars and writers, critiquing Gilligan for reinforcing traditional gender roles. Women had been "trapped for generations," Maccoby warned, "by people's willingness to accept their own intuitions about the truth of gender stereotypes." Representative of a trend toward quantitative research in psychology, she argued for statistical approaches to show that "there is no sphere of human thought, action, or feeling in which the two sexes are entirely distinct."[95]

Maccoby's interlocutors agreed. The legal historian Linda Kerber felt "haunted" by the sense of having heard Gilligan's argument before, as the doctrine of separate spheres. The inherent risk in Gilligan's work, Kerber contended, was "romantic oversimplification" and revisionism, a return to the world of the feminine mystique and the "angel in the house," this self-sacrificing figure that, as Virginia Woolf observed, a woman had to kill to be able to write.[96] The anthropologist Carol Stack, whose critique of racist constructions of the "normal" family Gilligan cited as a model, saw *In a Different Voice* evoking a monolithic image of woman as a universal category that transcended social and cultural differences.[97] Essentialism became the major argument against *In a Different Voice*, dominant in feminist assessments of Gilligan's work since the mid-1980s.[98]

Controversy was a currency of continued relevance, especially in universities, but the critiques not only attested to the fact that Gilligan's book had turned into a classic.[99] They also reflected the heated debates about difference and essentialism, which defined feminism in the 1980s.[100] The argument about the celebration of female difference and a separate "women's culture" came to a height around 1985, when this was misused as testimony in a landmark sex discrimination case filed six years earlier by the Equal Employment Opportunity Commission (EEOC) against Sears, Roebuck and Company, the world's biggest retailer and the nation's largest employer of women.

Started in 1973, the EEOC's investigation revealed major patterns of discrimination against women at Sears, who constituted a little over half of the company's employees. Significantly underrepresented in the company's most important managerial and administrative positions, women also held 77 percent of the lower-paying, noncommission sales jobs in retail stores and only 23 percent of the desirable commission sales positions. They worked part-time in disproportionately high numbers and, when promoted, were denied equal pay for equal work. Sears defended its hiring and promotion standards and contended that it was accommodating rather than restricting women by offering them so many part-time jobs.[101]

When the case went to court in 1984 and 1985, the historians Rosalind Rosenberg of Barnard College and Alice Kessler-Harris of Hofstra University testified as opposing witnesses, with Rosenberg defending Sears's hiring and promotion practices by arguing that women chose noncompetitive, low-wage jobs out of domestic interests. Kessler-Harris countered that discrimination was institutionally and socially ingrained. The judge, acquitting Sears in 1986, drew on Rosenberg's opinion that "women tend to be more interested than men in the social and cooperative aspects of the workplace. Women tend to see themselves as less competitive. They often view noncommission sales as more attractive than commission sales, because they can enter and leave the job more easily, and because there is ... less stress in noncommission selling."[102]

Yet blaming Rosenberg would be to overstate the effect of a lone historian. Initiated under the Carter administration but coming to trial during the Reagan administration, the Sears case was strongly influenced by the repositioning of federal policy. In light of such policy changes, the significance of Rosenberg's testimony lay in the debate it provoked in academic circles about the usage of research. In December 1985, the American Historical Association, its Conference Group on Women's History, and the Coordinating Council of Women in the Historical Profession passed resolutions in response to the case. The journal *Feminist Studies* published a critical commentary in the summer of 1986; *Signs* archived the court depositions of Rosenberg and Kessler-Harris.[103]

A widely known work, *In a Different Voice* became a catalyst of the debate over feminist epistemology. Voiced against the backdrop of Gilligan's wide reception, the criticism of her focus on women's difference reflected an increased worry about the cooptation of feminist ideas, such as when anti-feminist critics called upon Gilligan to argue that autonomy was unnatural and unhealthy for women, who had to pay a "psychic price" for professional success.[104]

Gilligan responded by contending that *In a Different Voice* was a book about theory. At the *Signs* symposium, she explained that she had set out to challenge ideas of self and morality, not reaffirm sex differences: "The book [about women's difference my critics] are discussing is different from the book I have written." Gilligan said. "My critics say that this story seems 'intuitively' right to many women but is at odds with the findings of psychological research. This is precisely the point I was making and exactly the difference I was exploring: the dissonance between psychological theory and women's experience."[105] The "different voice" hypothesis showed that by leaving women out from research samples, social science missed a different way of constituting the idea of the self and of what is moral. It was a shift introduced to the meanings of key terms of research. "If I had wanted to write a book about women's voices," Gilligan argued elsewhere, "I would have called it 'In a Woman's Voice.'"[106]

Presenting Gilligan's work as an antithesis to women's equality and exempting her and other difference feminists from the history of feminism as a "misadventure" and "blind alley," which—in the words of Londa Schiebinger—was "harmful to both women and science," contributed importantly to the notion of the end of feminism in the 1980s.[107] Yet even feminist psychologists who disagreed with Gilligan's conception of gender rejected the male midlife crisis.

4 *Superwoman Lives*

"If the study of midlife had begun with women, the midlife crisis would never have become part of our vocabulary!" Thus declared the psychologists Grace Baruch and Rosalind Barnett and the journalist and science writer Caryl Rivers in *Lifeprints: New Patterns of Love and Work for Today's Women* (1983), a book based on a study of employed women's well-being.[108] It showed that few women were dissatisfied or wished to change their lives in the middle years, experiencing instead a period of increased stability, achievement, and gratification.

The most direct book-length rebuttal of Levinson's *Seasons*, with cover art closely modeled on that book, *Lifeprints* also responded to a key backlash myth against women's economic advancement: that women could not "have it all," that it was impossible to fulfill the demands of both work and family life. Attempts to perform the multiple and "conflicting roles" of professional, wife, and mother resulted in "Superwoman syndrome," or symptoms of stress and exhaustion and feelings of guilt and failure as the predictable result of hyperbolic and unrealistic demands. Women had to choose between work aspirations and the desire to bear and raise children. Like Gilligan, the *Lifeprints* authors challenged the construction of a "hard choice" or dilemma specific to women's biographies. "Love" and "work" were not mutually exclusive for women, and combining them improved, not impaired, a woman's well-being.[109]

In the 1980s, stress, heart attacks, and other work-related ailments, primarily associated with men in high-paying prestige jobs, were revealed in women, too. Researchers and journalists reported a growing incidence of burnout among professional women. They appeared to be even more distressed than men, according to a typical message from a 1981 Stanford University study.[110] The "classy, capable, [and] confident" woman who had it all had "headaches, ulcers, chest pains, nausea and a nagging sense of doom. She sleeps fitfully, restlessly, plotting the events of the day in her head. . . . She smokes or drinks or pops pills to stay up or come down." Would professional women become "the next generation of dropouts"?[111]

In part, the new findings were an effect of including female study subjects in research on occupational risks. Organizational scholarship had persistently focused on "the organization *man*," as Rosabeth Moss Kanter, the leading authority on the "men *and* women of the corporation," pointed out, and biomedical research excluded women from major studies on cardiovascular disease.[112] Throughout the 1960s and '70s, stress had been related to overwork in men but to underwork—or the reproductive cycle—in women, following established gendered conceptions of work and its pathologies.[113] The emergence of studies on women and stress thus signaled a new and important awareness of women's afflictions beyond reproduction, supported by advocates for women's health, such as the Society for Women's Health Research (SWHR) founder Florence Haseltine, who pushed for a turn from reproductive to more general health issues for women.[114]

Yet the stress story could also be used to depict women as unfit for work, pathologize commitment outside the domestic sphere, and blame a lack of professional advancement on women, not organizations. Research on patterns of sickness and absenteeism characterized women as particularly prone to stress because of "role conflict" and "divided loyalties" between work and family responsibilities, as well as supposedly "constitutional" emotional instability.[115] Feminist scholars and writers who read the new findings against this backdrop cautioned against an attack on working women. Caryl Rivers warned in a commentary published first in the *Los Angeles Times*, then repeatedly reprinted: "There is a new kind of 'backlash,' emerging in response to women's drive for full equality, and these days it's voiced not with a snarl but with a sigh. The new message is, 'Oh, you poor dears! You're having such *problems*. And we only want to help.'" Rivers argued that the new "scare stories" aimed to keep women at home or in low-level jobs. Commiserations with professional women were "crocodile tears," shed to sugarcoat the old message: "Stay out of the boardroom, ladies, it's bad for your health."[116] In contrast, the Lifeprints survey showed that work improved women's well-being.

Based at the Wellesley Center for Research on Women, Baruch and Barnett were experts on college women's vocational planning and attitudes toward career achievement; Baruch was a developmental psychologist, Barnett a clinical psychologist in private practice.[117] They had previously collaborated on a monograph on women's career plans and the pathways and barriers to their success. *The Competent Woman* (1978) gave an overview of research on the topic and delineated areas of discrimination as well as of positive social changes and strategies that could be used by parents, educators, or women themselves.[118] The subsequent trade book *Beyond Sugar and Spice* (1979), coauthored with Rivers, synthesized research on female sex-role socialization into a girls' parenting manual.[119] (Parents were advised to encourage participation in team sports as well as the use of construction and science toys.) The collaboration was representative of a conscious effort, also by other feminist social scientists and writers, to combine scientific authority and journalistic skills so as to reach a wide audience and increase impact. Feminist research, in an often-quoted contemporary dictum, was "not research about women but research for women," to be used in transforming gender roles.[120]

Lifeprints continued along the life course. By turning the lens on women around forty years old, it aimed at helping educated women in their twenties and early thirties to make informed choices by providing them with a series of "blueprints" for life planning. Baruch, Barnett, and Rivers sought to dissipate women's anxieties about deviations from the life pattern of at-home wife and mother: if they did not marry, they would not be lonely, pitied "spinsters." If they married but did not have children, they would not be haunted by regrets when they were past the childbearing years. A high-powered career did not lead to "burnout," nor the career-woman/

wife/mother combination to an early coronary. But it was difficult for a woman to pick up the lost threads of a career when she was past thirty-five.[121]

The book was based on Baruch and Barnett's "Women in the Middle Years," a major National Science Foundation–funded study that interviewed approximately three hundred women between thirty-five and fifty-five (with an average age of forty-four years). Echoing earlier celebrations of women's prime of life, the psychologists looked at middle age as the time of professional achievement, and thus more significant for understanding work and success patterns than earlier, formative phases: "These are the years in which, for most women, the major aspects of life have settled into a stable pattern. Since we intended to study adult life patterns, we needed to look at the period of a woman's life that is most typical of a life as a whole. We wanted to go beyond the crises of young adulthood, during which women are often preoccupied with career choices and with such decisions as whom to marry or whether to have children."[122]

The Lifeprints study was an investigation into professional women's work lives and well-being, as distinct from relationships and problems. Limited to white women living in Brookline (part of Greater Boston), Baruch and Barnett's sample included married women with and without children, divorced mothers, and never-married women (understood to be without children). All were employed, except for a control group among the married women and mothers; although participants came from a range of economic levels, women in high-prestige jobs comprised a significant part of the sample. The average educational level was fourteen years (two years beyond high school), and many had taken a higher degree.[123] Although Baruch and Barnett emphasized the diversity of their sample, college-educated, professional women were at the center of the study, with other subsets used to compare and contrast.

Baruch and Barnett's survey comprised queries about employment and homemaking; marriage, divorce, and being single; and children and childlessness. It was upbeat in tone, balancing questions about rewards and pleasures with others about difficulties and complications: "How happy were they in their work?" "What were the problem areas in their marriages?" "What did they like about having children?" "What were the good things about being single?"[124] In the 1970s and '80s, feminist psy-

chologists employed inquiries about happiness and health to dispel negative stereotypes about women outside the nuclear family and as a basis
for devising empowerment strategies. As the psychologist and counselor
Judith Worell explained, by starting from the assumption of women's
mental health, they attempted to redirect the focus "from a woman's inner
pathology to the pathology of the system that keeps women imprisoned
by fear and lack of resources."[125] With regard to single motherhood, for
example, Worell moved the focus from the effects of "broken homes"
on children (boys in particular) to areas of competence and strength in
the families and sought to identify variables that affected single women's
lives and parenting opportunities, including poverty, isolation, and lack of
social support. Research on spouse abuse was reframed from the question
of "Why doesn't she just leave?" to others, such as "Why do some men
beat their wives?" or "What are the barriers that keep her from leaving?"[126]

Critiquing a focus in mental health research on women's intimate relationships, Baruch and Barnett focused instead on the advantages of public
and professional roles and sought to dispel "myths" about the benefits of
marriage and children.[127] Ultimately, they asked: What contributed to a
woman's well-being? What made a woman feel good about herself as a valued member of society? What gave her self-esteem and control of her life?

It was, Baruch and Barnett suggested, the very combination of multiple
roles that improved a woman's health, satisfaction, and self-esteem. They
refuted the idea that roles drained energy, so that the more roles a woman
occupied, the less energy she had, the more conflict she experienced, and
the more negatively her well-being was affected. Developed in the 1960s
to account for men's behavior in the workplace, this "scarcity hypothesis"
had been adapted to women's lives on the assumption that family roles
were "greedy," so that women had limited resources to meet the demands
of the workplace.[128]

By contrast, Baruch and Barnett argued for the benefits of multiple
roles, confirming and refining "spillover" theories, according to which
multiple roles increased the chances of being physically healthier, more
satisfied with life, and less depressed. Incumbents of multiple roles also
accrued privileges, and the increase in self-esteem, recognition, prestige, and financial remuneration more than offset the costs of adding on
roles.[129] In the 1970s, role expansion had been shown to improve well-

being for men, and Baruch and Barnett contributed to an effort to support the positive association between the number of roles occupied and psychological well-being for women, too, showing that multiple role involvement increased their psychological as well as physiological health.[130]

Regarding involvement in multiple roles as a prerequisite for well-being, the two psychologists also emphasized the importance of qualitative aspects of role involvement—autonomy, complexity, and impact, particularly in the world of work—for a woman's psychological health and happiness. Indeed, one of the findings from the study was that motherhood was a main source of distress, while working was a key to well-being. "The greatest sense of well-being," Baruch explained in a *New York Times* interview, "is among women who have high-level jobs, are mothers and are married. Juggling these multiple roles does not stress women. Work seems to be a buffer against the stresses of motherhood because it offers a sense of mastery that raising children does not."[131]

"Superwoman lives—and flies," proclaimed the *Vogue* science writer Suzanne Fields when Baruch and Barnett announced the results of their study.[132] While the *Lifeprints* authors were critical of the controversial figure of Superwoman, they also appropriated and humanized her. By advising women to "not get uptight about housekeeping," shed domestic tasks, and have their husbands help, they challenged the idea of "Supermom."[133] If women had to choose, Baruch and Barnett advised "a high-prestige job—rather than a husband."[134]

The most important finding of the Lifeprints study was that career women were happy; they did not have a midlife crisis. Baruch and Barnett did find women who were depressed, had little self-regard, and thought their lives had not turned out well, especially among the at-home wives and women working in lower positions. But professional women were satisfied. Their well-being was not compromised by age; they rarely experienced the upheavals, depression, and anxiety that defined the male midlife crisis, and they seldom spoke of feelings of stagnation and the wish to change their lives, nor of measuring their accomplishments against their expectations. In fact, many women found that the years of middle adulthood were turning out to be "much better than their youthful years."[135]

Looking back, working mothers did not regret their decision to combine work and family lives. Baruch, Barnett, and Rivers hoped that their findings about midlife bliss would encourage younger women who were struggling with the pressures of small children and a job and might be tempted to abandon or curtail their career goals to stick it out. The woman who managed to hang on to her career might experience more stress in her younger years when the pulls and tugs of family and career were, admittedly, more intense. Yet if she persisted, her chances for "much smoother sailing in her mature years" seemed very good.[136] If Superwoman lived— and flew—she was middle-aged.

5 *Inability to Change*

In light of research about stress, Baruch, Barnett, and Rivers reframed the meaning of midlife crisis. Unlike Gilligan, they did not propose a redefinition of developmental theory. Rather than reclaiming or redefining the midlife crisis, Baruch, Barnett, and Rivers refuted life-course theories altogether. Levinson was their main target, though their criticism applied to Sheehy's *Passages*, too, which they mistook for a "popularization" of *Seasons*: "Gail Sheehy's work drew on Levinson's *Seasons*. . . . One of the most popular notions emerging from these authors was that a 'midlife crisis' would inevitably occur around the age of forty. . . . Those who did not experience a crisis might wonder if they were normal. [We], in part because of personal experience and in part because of methodological concerns, doubted these models for women's lives."[137]

Not just concerned with interpreting the data, Baruch, Barnett, and Rivers had fundamental qualms about "[hauling] nature's authority into human affairs."[138] Committed to an anti-essentialist view of gender, they worried that the connection between biological age and social change suggested that women's problems would simply resolve themselves and go away and saw developmental theory as harmful to feminist causes. Barnett and Rivers later became some of Gilligan's fiercest opponents, arguing in their *Same Difference* (2004) that it was impossible to distinguish feminist from conservative arguments for gender differences.[139]

In *Lifeprints*, Baruch, Barnett, and Rivers attributed the absence of midlife crisis to the women's movement. Comparing mental health data from the 1950s and 1970s, they suggested that social change made it possible for women to cope better with growing older: "The women's movement, we would argue, not only is giving women permission to think about themselves in less limited ways than in the past, it has also led to real changes in opportunities."[140] Ideas about women's roles had been transformed, and women's freedom had increased; they entered and stayed in the workforce. Yet if women's well-being was linked to the social climate, then confidence, optimism, and satisfaction all could be dissipated if women stopped fighting and the gains of the movement slipped away.

Baruch, Barnett, and Rivers observed that few women in the Lifeprints survey saw what was happening in their lives in social and political terms. Most said things like "The women's movement hasn't had much impact on me *personally*" or "I don't see what the fuss is all about." The women's most frequent explanation for why they were happier now than when they were younger had to do with chronological age: "It's turning thirty-five." "When you're forty you know who you are." "Being fifty makes the difference." Even those in occupations only recently open to women failed to make the connection between their success and feminism, insisting on seeing achievement purely in personal terms. Failing to connect social change with their newfound pride and satisfaction, they assumed it must be their age.[141]

The *Lifeprints* authors argued that age did not influence well-being in a predictable way, as stage theories would suggest. Instead, they emphasized changing social and political contexts: "A woman of forty reentering the work-force after twenty years at home will be wrestling with very different life issues than a single woman the same age who is fighting for tenure at the university where she teaches." Similarly, a "man of fifty who has just lost a job because his company went out of business may be more similar in the psychological issues he is facing to a thirty-five-year-old in the same boat than to another fifty-year-old who has just been named vice-president of a company. If you studied thirty-five-year-old unemployed men in the midst of the Great Depression, they would probably look psychologically quite different from unemployed men of thirty-five in the mid-sixties."[142]

Many people faced the kinds of challenges Levinson (as well as Sheehy) described, but independent of age. Women in the Lifeprints study felt more uncertain and anxious in their early twenties than at midlife, thus confirming a classic sociological study about high stress levels among young adults, who coped with young children, wrestled with issues of becoming independent, and were particularly vulnerable to economic problems, in a life phase characterized by the disparity between escalating material needs and earnings. An unpublished study from the Harvard School of Business Administration showed men in their early thirties struggling with what were supposed to be midlife issues, asking themselves, "Was it worth it?" and "What shall I do with the rest of my life?"[143]

Moreover, the predictable "turning points" of a woman's life—marriage, childbirth, menopause, and children leaving the home—had little effect on the lives of the Lifeprints women. Predicated on reproductive events, the traditional evaluation of these transitions suggested that women were high in well-being as wives and mothers, happiest when the children were home and depressed when they left, and that menopause threatened women's identity. Yet only 20 percent of the married women mentioned marriage as a turning point (half of them, as a negative one). Expecting these marker events and having some idea about when they were likely to occur and what they looked like, women seemed to be equipped to cope with them without feeling forever marked or changed.

But how could the "midlife crisis" be explained, if it was not linked to aging? Baruch, Barnett, and Rivers, like Gilligan, recast the midlife crisis against the backdrop of values of stability, continuousness, and sustenance. In the 1980s, stress, construed as a prime cause as well as a symptom for ill health and unhappiness, emerged as a new "social theory" of sorts, a "means of generating and organizing a whole complex of beliefs and ideas about the nature of social order."[144] Vehicles for articulating and validating concerns about the attainability of happiness, well-being, and economic security, narratives of stress also highlighted notions of personal balance, security, and resilience in a changing world. It was in linking stress to social change, and culture to health, that Baruch, Barnett, and Rivers turned the midlife crisis into an individual and social pathology.

What the Lifeprints women most frequently mentioned as turning points were unexpected events such as divorce, a sudden job transfer, a car crash, or a parent's premature death. These "life events" were rarely predictable in the sense that women rehearsed for them and had in mind an appropriate time for them to happen. Foiling plans and crushing expectations, they were much more likely to precipitate crisis and shaped the life course more decisively.[145]

Rooted in social work and community research, the concept of life events emphasized the effect of social circumstances on mental health. In contrast to stress research that highlighted the role of personality and individual perception, studies of life events linked psychological health to social adversity, paying attention to events and circumstances rather than a person's appraisal of and reaction to them as being stressful. Life-event research was typically geared to devising plans for political or occupational reform rather than strategies for coping and personal adjustment. In the 1960s, the Seattle-based psychiatrists Thomas Holmes and Richard Rahe found the onset of disease to be associated with changes in personal and economic circumstances. The influential Holmes and Rahe Stress Scale (1967) related "psychosocial life crises" to personal health, occupational change, and financial hardship.[146] In the 1970s, Barbara and Bruce Dohrenwend, a New York social psychologist and psychiatrist, respectively, studied urban communities to show that greater prevalence of social disorders was the product of situational rather than constitutional or personality factors: stress was a socioeconomic phenomenon.[147] In the 1980s, research on life events came to include everyday events or "daily hassles," with a particular focus on the demands of work and marriage, such as status incongruity between spouses, sex-role conflicts, the demands of children and aged parents, and work overload and underload.[148]

By adopting a psychosocial perspective, Baruch, Barnett, and Rivers reframed the meaning of the midlife crisis for women and men. As a reaction to life events, it indicated a socioeconomic problem: the persistence of traditional gender roles. "The old sex roles too often operate as a straitjacket, preventing men and women from acting in the most 'adaptive' way—that is, the most effective way to deal with the situation at hand."[149]

Baruch, Barnett, and Rivers concluded their book by warning about the danger and insecurity tied to the at-home pattern. The high point of employed women's lives, midlife was a period of great anxiety for at-home women. The homemaker role easily became a trap: divorce, the death of a spouse, economic need, or changing personal and social conditions could leave a woman in this "lifeprint" in an untenable situation.

As Baruch and Barnett had noted in their earlier analysis *The Competent Woman*, women who had lived traditional lives as wives and mothers often found themselves ill equipped to deal with an array of personal and social changes at midlife. Some were able to face such predictable events as the increasing independence of their children and to find alternative foci and skills, "but others are overtaken by unpredictable events: an unemployed spouse, divorce, widowhood." These events often caused women to reassess their established patterns, creating in them a desire or need for financial and economic independence. Yet many women were beset by a lack of confidence and paralyzed by the absence of means to achieve their goals, questioning "not only their ability to undertake new projects successfully but the very legitimacy of any plans that might be seen as 'selfish.'" And because the skills they had exercised in the domestic sphere did not usually constitute a source of capital readily transferable to the world of work, women often perceived themselves as less competent than they really were.[150] Five years later, in *Lifeprints*, the assessment was more drastic. Options for reentry were rapidly disappearing in a changing economy, and reentry jobs were typically low-level jobs, which made life more difficult than careers: "A physician can earn a good income on a part-time basis, can arrange her professional life so she can get out to her child's school concert during the day, but a nurse can't. Professors don't ask a boss for permission to bring a child to work, if that's necessary; secretaries do."[151]

Betty Friedan was thrilled. She cited the Lifeprints study enthusiastically and repeatedly; it seemed to confirm the diagnosis she had made twenty years before about the relevance of work to women's well-being. As Friedan wrote in the preface to the anniversary edition of *The Feminine Mystique*, Baruch and Barnett's research showed that professional and business women with children were not succumbing to type A stress, heart attacks, and ulcers: "Women don't seem to be falling into the 'superwoman' trap so easily."[152]

Yet concerns had shifted. A revolutionary demand in 1963, women's paid work had become a necessity twenty years later. Not just reiterating earlier constructions, Baruch and Barnett's research documented a new normality at a time when 43 percent of all US households were dual-earner couples, 37 percent were traditional married couples, 14 percent families headed by a woman, and 4 percent families headed by a man. In 1985, three-fifths of all women in the United States with children were in the labor force, and half of the mothers with infants under one year of age worked outside the home. Many couples, having abandoned traditional, male-breadwinner family models without giving up on marriage, were struggling to reconcile the demands of two jobs with a happy family life.

Wives' incomes counted, and counted substantially. Their contribution to the family income was not supplemental but essential. Even in middle-class families, the incomes of wives often made a difference between economic marginality and a comfortable standard of living. In 1985, the median income of couples where the wife did not work was $24,556; that of couples with the wife in the paid labor force was $36,431. Joint incomes were necessary to raise a family, buy a home, and maintain a middle-class lifestyle. In the affluent 1950s and '60s, parents could do this on a single income, but in the 1980s and '90s, couples found it harder to maintain a similar lifestyle without both working. A family wage no longer supported a family. But many men (and women) did not realize this.[153]

For Baruch and Barnett, the male midlife crisis indicated a problematic adherence to traditional gender roles, an idea spelled out in a related research project, "Correlates of Fathers' Participation in Family Work," begun in 1980, which studied men's multiple role involvement in white, middle-class, two-parent families with young children. The two psychologists looked at the working father's role in the family to examine how the male role was reassessed in the light of the women's movement and the increased labor-force participation of married women with children. Baruch and Barnett showed that men's higher levels of participation in home activities was associated with feeling more involved and competent as the parent.[154]

Earlier research on the benefits of multiple roles suggested that simultaneous commitment to work and family roles enhanced men's well-being and life satisfaction.[155] Baruch and Barnett attributed male symptoms of midlife crisis to a narrow, "sorely impoverished" view of male identity,

a lack of engagement in domestic and familial roles, and resulting failure to cope with the decline of the breadwinner role.[156] The male midlife
crisis indicated "tradition-directedness," in the words of David Riesman,
who noted the "inability" of characters in traditional societies "to change
roles."[157] It was a sign of rigidity, a chauvinist depression.

Reflecting an assessment of the women's movement, Baruch and Barnett's pathological concept of midlife crisis described the problem that
barely half of Sheehy's program had been fulfilled. Her vision about simultaneous and equal change in men *and* women had not come true.

Women had changed, but little else had. Most workplaces remained
inflexible in the face of the family demands of their workers, and at home,
most men had yet to really adapt to the changes in women. The wife was
still the primary parent and remained ultimately responsible for keeping
house. Women's paid work was still seen as a "job," in contrast to a man's
career. In a 1986 study, 54 percent of women in their early twenties and
13 percent of the men expected to be the one who would miss an important meeting at work for a sick child; another survey of undergraduates
at six different campuses across the country found that half the women
planned to put the husband's job first, but two-thirds of the men said they
planned to put their own job first.[158]

The stagnancy problem was noted by others, too. When the political
scientist Anne Machung asked undergraduate men at Berkeley in 1985 if
they expected to marry a woman who held a job outside the home, most
answered: "She can work if she wants." When asked if they would be willing to marry a woman who wanted them to do half the housework and
child care, one man replied, "Yes, I could always hire someone." Another
said, "It would depend on how much I liked her and how she asked." A
number of them were willing to "help out" but expressed fear that their
wives might draw up "lists," assign chores, tell them what to do, and tally,
measure, and compare their contributions.[159]

"The old way of being a woman in a patriarchal but stable family system
is fading," the Berkeley sociologist Arlie Hochschild observed. "But an
equal new relationship with men at work and at home is not yet in reach."
Building on Baruch and Barnett's study of men's domestic involvement,
Hochschild's landmark study *The Second Shift* (1989) challenged the perception that the conflict between work and family was a woman's issue

and asked "how to do without a change in men, how to be a woman who is different from her mother, married to a man not much different from her father." One of the best-known analyses of the "stalled revolution," Hochschild's study illustrates a wider concern with men's roles in debates about gender, work, and the family in the 1980s.

Was it possible, the sociologist wondered, that "one reason that half the lawyers, doctors, business people are not women is because *men do not share the raising of their children and the caring of their homes*"?[160] Interviews and ethnographical research conducted in collaboration with Machung between 1980 and 1988 showed that men who did share the load at home seemed just as pressed for time as wives, and as torn between the demands of career and small children. But the majority of men did not get involved at home, refusing either outright or more passively, often offering a loving shoulder to lean on and an understanding ear as their working wives faced the conflict they both saw as hers. Even when husbands happily shared the hours of work, their wives felt more responsible for home and children, keeping track of doctors' appointments, play dates, and birthday presents and checking in by phone with the babysitter. Moreover, men and women did different work at home: while women did two-thirds of the daily jobs that fixed them to a rigid schedule, such as cooking, child care, and cleaning, men had more control over when they made their contributions, such as repairs of household appliances.[161] For Hochschild, how involved men were at home related to deeper issues of male power: not assuming responsibility at home was a way of maintaining gender hierarchies. The "second shift" at home kept women from fully engaging in paid work, testified to the devaluation of domestic work, and created marital tensions.[162]

Dealing with different issues and looking from a different perspective, Baruch, Barnett, and Rivers arrived at a conclusion remarkably similar to Gilligan's. Both *Lifeprints* and *In a Different Voice* critiqued traditional notions of masculinity and men's social roles by redefining the midlife crisis as a pathology. The broad opposition against the idea of midlife crisis, extending across the divisions that characterized feminism in the 1980s, illustrates that critique of traditional masculinity was what many feminists identified with. These critiques decisively changed the understanding of midlife crisis. The pathological view of the male midlife crisis as immoral and chauvinist became mainstream within psychology as well as in public discourse. When Levinson, Vaillant, and Gould attempted to defend their idea, this failed.

6 *Chauvinist Cliché*

Vaillant, Levinson, and Gould did not debunk Gilligan or the Lifeprints research as lesser science but disagreed with the new interpretations of the life course. Vaillant insisted on the developmental relevance of separation and maintained that the Harvard graduates in his study were well adapted.[163] Gould continued using the psychoanalytic concept of adult development in therapeutic practice and introduced it into computer-assisted and web-based therapy. His "Therapeutic Learning Program" was a ten-session computer-based treatment designed to help "unblock natural psychological development processes."[164] Levinson expanded the midlife crisis to women. Beginning in 1980, he conducted biographical interviews with forty-five women between thirty-five and forty-five years old (thirty businesswomen and scholars, fifteen at-home women) to argue that careers for women and dual-earner families were "completely unworkable."[165] Initially sponsored by the Financial Women's Association of New York and the Teachers Insurance and Annuity Association, funding for the project ended in 1982. In the wake of Gilligan's success and the Lifeprints study, it proved difficult to secure support for a project that applied the male-centered concept of midlife crisis to women's lives. Levinson continued to promote the study throughout the 1980s, yet it was his wife, Judy, who—having been involved in the research from the beginning—analyzed the interviews and wrote large portions of the book. When she published *The Seasons of a Woman's Life* (1996), two years after her husband had passed away, it was under his name, listing herself only as a collaborator.[166]

Levinson's book opened with the assertion that no studies of women's lives had been done, that the question of how women's lives evolved had "rarely been asked in psychology or the other human sciences."[167] This was a sweep against critics. Neither Sheehy nor Baruch, Barnett, and Rivers were cited, and *The Seasons of a Woman's Life* did not engage with Gilligan. It refuted the idea of women's different developmental course and their midlife stability. "Unfortunately," Levinson continued—thus suggesting some knowledge of more recent literature—the midlife crisis had come to be seen as an "inappropriate or maladaptive response to a stressful event" that was "entirely negative and to be avoided."[168] However, it was a developmental crisis that applied to women, too: they went through the same stages as men, at the same ages.

The at-home women in *Seasons of a Woman's Life*—most from working-class backgrounds—experienced a period of emotional turmoil in middle age. They were often forced to confront the end of their marriages or to understand, as Levinson put it, that "traditional marriage . . . simply doesn't work."[169] Many took a new job, and some went to school. However, work and education did not make them any happier. Insisting that this reflected a general pattern in women's lives, Levinson applied it to career women, too, echoing much older critiques of the detrimental effect of women's education: this did "not necessarily help a lot."[170] Career women experienced profound conflicts, too. For a professional woman at midlife "it became evident that she was not, despite the media hype and her own private wish, a Superwoman."[171] Combining marriage and a family with a full-time career did not bring satisfaction.

To the psychologist Joan Bean and the anthropologist Margery Fox, Levinson's depiction indicated at-home women's problems with professional reentry and glass ceilings imposed on women's career achievement, yet Levinson suggested that work was the problem, not the solution.[172] Women had to accept their experience of a developmental crisis at midlife. The women who fared best were those who developed new kinds of motherly relations with their adult children. Levinson rejected the idea of the "empty nest," finding that "parents and offspring continue a relation." If women experienced an empty nest syndrome, "something is wrong": depression or anger in midlife indicated a woman's failure as a mother or wife.[173]

The Seasons of a Woman's Life was a rearguard defense, and not only because of its belated publication. It received little attention and did not succeed in turning the midlife crisis into an experience associated with women's lives. Much more widespread was the view of midlife as a period of women's liberation, as illustrated by the success of Sheehy's 1992 essay *The Silent Passage: Menopause*—probably the most widely discussed title on middle age in the 1990s.[174] Now based at *Vanity Fair*, Sheehy returned to the subject after portraits of Corazón Aquino, Margaret Thatcher, and Mikhail Gorbachev and a decade of political writing.[175] She did not reclaim the midlife crisis, yet confirmed her observations for women.

The Silent Passage was a slim volume; based on interviews with more than one hundred women and seventy-five medical experts, it reiterated many of the ideas presented some fifteen years earlier and extended them into the sixth decade of life. By bringing the "menopausal passage" forward to include "perimenopause" (when egg cells are still released but the production of estrogen begins to decrease), Sheehy extended menopause to women in their thirties and forties, thus aligning it with midlife crisis.[176] She discussed the "Sexual Diamond," comparing relatively high levels of testosterone in some postmenopausal women to the gradual decline in men's testosterone level with age, and drew on Margaret Mead's life as an example of "post-menopausal zest"—the anthropologist went back to fieldwork to study child-rearing in New Guinea at the age of fifty-one.[177] The biggest difference from *Passages* was probably that *The Silent Passage* had little to say about men, other than as sympathetic bystanders.[178]

Drawing on older critiques of gender and aging, the motif of "silence" was about social "taboos," misinformation, and ignorance as much as shame, fear, and the stigma of aging. Breaking the "conspiracy of silence" was a radical move: "No one wants us to find out how much power we have."[179] Noting a "scandalous" lack of research into menopausal therapies, Sheehy critiqued experts and policy-makers who ignored women's suffering and devalued their experience. The medical profession was stuck in the "dark ages" of medical androcentrism, a lack of attention to women's medical issues beyond reproduction, and an indifference to their suffering.[180] For Sheehy, "activism was the only answer. I had to talk to the few women in Congress about pushing for a government-controlled study of menopause and the impact of treatments on women's health. And I had to upend the stereotype."[181]

The "Change"—a term introduced by Germaine Greer—was not a curse that turned older women into victims; it was a freedom that allowed them to stop trying so hard to please.[182] Sheehy spoke of a period of "coalescence," the moment when women discarded "the shell of the reproductive self," which encased them in adolescence, and were no longer confined by the culture's definition of woman as a primarily sexual object and "breeder": "A full unity of her feminine and masculine sides is possible . . . [as] she moves beyond gender definition."[183] Marked by the "courage to go against," midlife allowed a woman, at last, to "integrate the rebellious boy in herself, left back when she was ten or eleven. . . . Given the added status and confidence of the postmenopausal state, women are in an optimal position to voice their convictions and make a powerful public impact." Echoing much older conceptions of the "table mount" of middle age, Sheehy spent a few days alone in the mountains to mark her own rite of passage through menopause.[184]

Widely successful, *The Silent Passage* turned 1992 into the "Year of the Menopause."[185] As Sheehy's literary agent explained to a publisher: "The demographics alone—forty-three million American women—do the figures yourself."[186] For Sheehy, it wasn't just postmenopausal zest. "It was the accumulated force of the women's movement that coalesced around that time." Making menopause public was an important part of the "long, slow, never-give-up, nonviolent war" to represent women.[187] With the menopause essay, she returned to writing about the life course, updating her earlier conception of the life course in *New Passages* (1996), followed by a series of "passages" titles.[188] Throughout the 1990s, positive accounts of women's midlife permeated feminist treatises, scholarly publications, and "midlife memoirs," often drawing on Sheehy, Gilligan, and the Lifeprints study.[189]

The feminist riposte was followed by new research on middle age. In 1990, the MacArthur Foundation's Research Network on Successful Midlife Development, or "Midmac," was established to explore what its director, Orville Brim, a social psychologist, claimed as the "last uncharted territory in human development."[190] Building on emerging "life-span" theories within the scholarship of aging, which promoted a positive image of old age, psychologists worked with sociologists, demographers, and medical scholars. By casting aging as part of a lifelong developmental process, they discarded the notion of a break in midlife as marking the shift from growing up to growing old.[191]

Midmac's main project was the large-scale longitudinal MIDUS study of midlife in the United States, a national survey of health and well-being administered to three thousand people between twenty-four and seventy-four years old beginning in 1995. Subsequently sponsored by the National

Institute on Aging, the MIDUS dataset on aging remains one of the most frequently used and cited in the United States.[192] This quantitative analysis—as distinct from case studies of middle-age experience—confirmed the status of the midlife crisis as an idiosyncrasy.

As Brim noted when the first MIDUS findings were released in 1999, for most people, midlife was a time of general satisfaction with life: "We find that midlifers report feeling better about their lives now than they did ten years ago and, except for health, they expect to feel better about their lives ten years in the future." "Normal" people recognized that life brings change, regardless of age, that a "healthy response to change is to make the necessary adjustments," and that changes which occur during midlife did not differ from changes and adjustments made during any other time of life.[193]

Those who suffered a midlife crisis were "people who typically cannot adjust to the changes that midlife brings. They do not, for example, confront the realization that their lives are moving swiftly by, and adjust their goals, aspirations, timetables and expectations accordingly."[194] In short, midlife crisis was a pathology, a measure of neuroticism rather than healthy development, simply one more incident in a lifelong history of maladjustment, which now expressed itself in job dissatisfaction and marital troubles.

The MIDUS survey was well-known within academia and beyond. The *New York Times*, the *Chicago Tribune*, *USA Today*, and National Public Radio reported on it at length ("New Study Finds Middle Age Is Prime of Life"), followed by further stories in *Newsweek* and *Jet*, the *Washington Post*, the *LA Times*, the *San Francisco Examiner*, and multiple small-town newspapers.[195] In the 2000s, Midmac's refutation was the most commonly cited research on midlife crisis.[196] Even those who defended the concept of midlife crisis had to acknowledge this "most significant challenge" to it. Yet descriptions of the network as having "radically changed scientific orthodoxy" are as misleading as Brim's claim to virgin lands.[197] Thanks to Gilligan, Baruch, Barnett, and others, "midlife crisis" was no accepted diagnostic category.

Indeed, Midmac's own research documented that many people thought of the midlife crisis as a social pathology before the study's publication. In a 1997–98 study done as part of the project, the Cornell psychologist Elaine Wethington showed that the vast majority of the population did not report having experienced age-linked turmoil during midlife. Wethington's 2000 paper "Expecting Stress: Americans and the 'Midlife Crisis'" showed that only 8 percent of the participants related a midlife crisis such as defined by Levinson, Vaillant, and Gould, although women were as likely as men to report having experienced this. The psychologist ruled out another 18 percent of respondents who reported a crisis in earlier or later periods of life or as the result of specific life events, such as children leaving home, divorce, job loss, job insecurity, or serious financial problems. Indeed, when asked for their conception of midlife crisis, most participants described this as a reaction to stressful life events, tending to involve for men, either job or marriage, and for women, health, family deaths, and marriage.[198]

Indicating that people framed the midlife crisis in terms of stress and life events, Wethington's study also suggested that one of the reasons why relatively few respondents even reported having had a midlife crisis might have been that they did not accept the label. When the psychologists asked for their ideas about (rather than experience of) midlife crisis, most respondents were critical of its existence. Ninety percent of the participants could provide a definition of the midlife crisis, which tended to fall in line with the concept of the male midlife crisis defined by Vaillant, Levinson, and Gould. Yet only a few respondents (less than 1 percent of the men and 1.6 percent of the women) shared the three psychologists' positive view of this as a "learning experience" and liberation. Most beliefs about the midlife crisis were negative.[199]

Respondents drew on notions of immaturity and irresponsibility to criticize the idea of midlife crisis or those who claimed that they were having one; 16.8 percent of men and 21.9 percent of women believed that the midlife crisis did not exist. Some refused to define the term, saying, "That term doesn't mean anything," "It's just an excuse," or "It's stupid and immoral." "Some people are always in crisis, that's what I think it is," one respondent explained. A few respondents defined the midlife crisis as a mental health problem. Many condemned people who had a midlife crisis, criticizing those who made big life changes without "taking the feelings of others into account." Others criticized the concept as a justification for making bad choices, not dealing with reality, living in a fantasy world, "abandoning moral values," acting childishly, or justifying selfish actions that hurt their families: "The midlife crisis is about not growing up," "not taking responsibility," or "copping out when your family needs you the most."[200]

Midmac's refutation of the midlife crisis as deviance and pathology was not new. It expressed, confirmed, and extended an existing consensus, shared by social scientists and in the public sphere, that the midlife crisis was a myth to bolster chauvinism. Other research from the network qualified these findings. In addition to the MIDUS survey, Midmac carried out a cluster of eleven related studies, which involved another five thousand subjects in the United States, not counting comparative studies done in England, Germany, and Japan. This research highlighted the variety of adult experiences, compounded by gender as well as differences in backgrounds, education, income, and social place.[201]

In looking at gender, Midmac researchers confirmed and updated earlier findings on women and middle age in a series of collaborative projects with the Henry A. Murray Research Center of Radcliffe College. This repository for social and behavioral science data on women had been established in 1976 under the name Radcliffe Data Resource and Research Center (it was renamed in 1980) to sponsor scholarly research on the impact of social change on women's lives. Focusing on studies from psychology, sociology, and education, with additional data sets from economics and political science, the center preserved coded, machine-readable data along with original records such as transcripts of in-depth interviews, behavioral observations, and responses to projective tests for secondary analyses, which interrogated the material from new perspectives and with different scoring procedures. The center acquired new studies each year; Baruch and Barnett donated the Lifeprints materials—interview records and coded data—in 1983, and Gilligan submitted the interview transcripts and information on demographic background for the participants of the abortion-decision study in 2002.[202] In 1991, at the time of the Midmac collaboration, the center developed a major collection of long-term studies: 73 of 216 datasets were longitudinal, providing an alternative to retrospective studies, which relied on people's memory.[203]

Midmac researchers used the archival material to challenge the notion of age linkage in shifts in family values of and work ethic. Finding that respondents of different ages changed their value systems in the 1970s, they related this to the influence of the women's movement and economic recession.[204] Newly scoring data on the life courses of women from Lewis M. Terman's study of gifted children, begun at Stanford in the early 1920s (the Radcliffe center had a duplicate), confirmed the diversity of women's biographies to challenge linear models of the life course whose "clearly delineated steps of development deny the multiplicity of paths that women might pursue."[205]

Finally, a reanalysis of Baruch and Barnett's Lifeprints data shed new light on the relatively weak impact of marriage and relationships on women's health, asking if this perhaps indicated the costs that women incurred within their intimate relationships, which mitigated against a wholly beneficial effect of social embeddedness on health and well-being. While relationships with husbands and children did provide rewards to women, they also engendered highly distressing concerns. Could some of these be avoided or reduced? Did women fail to insist on reciprocity in their relationships because they "*valu[ed] others over self*"? The report recommended "examining values (e.g. self-sacrifice) derived from long-entrenched patriarchy."[206]

In contrast to earlier research on middle age, Midmac looked beyond the white middle class, and indeed the United States. Anthropologists, failing to find the construct of midlife outside many North American and European cultures, spoke of this as a "cultural fiction."[207] In Japan, as shown by the Canadian medical anthropologist Margaret Lock, whose subsequent *Encounters with Aging* (1993) was a key contribution to the continued research on gender and midlife, a woman's aging was framed as a process of increasing responsibility and advancement through the social hierarchy rather than in terms of biology and decline. The Kisii people of Western Kenya, whose men and women in their forties were "deeply concerned with continued childbearing," did not care about midlife or midlife crisis either.[208]

Nor was middle age the average experience within the United States. Poor black women and men living in New York City's Harlem rarely talked about middle age as a separate phase of life. They linked major discontinuities in their lives to history, place, and race rather than chronological age, speaking of the migration from the rural South between the two world wars as well as the civil rights movement. Similarly, for middle-aged Latinos living in the city, "middle age" had no meaning. There was no Spanish equivalent in Puerto Rican, Mexican, or Dominican communities, and open-ended questions about life stages "never yielded a single example" of "middle age" as a subcategory of adulthood, much less a distinctive phase of life.[209]

One of the striking differences in midlife was the social gradient in well-being: differences were "not just associated with poverty[;] ... health becomes progressively better with increasing status, throughout the socioeconomic distribution."[210] This meant that the poor aged faster than their middle-class contemporaries. In midlife, impoverished people were battered by the cumulative effects of mediocre or curtailed education, joblessness, single motherhood, ill health, and poor care.[211]

Education was a particularly stable predictor of ill health, followed by household income and the area where people lived. The level of education influenced respondents' own conception of well-being and agency. While 60 percent of college-educated respondents mentioned leisurely enjoyment as a central category of well-being, this was central to only 38 percent of high school graduates, who instead focused on family relationships, financial security, and job stability.[212]

Challenging the universality of midlife itself, not just the crisis, Midmac researchers demonstrated that the dialectic between regret and sense of control characteristic for middle-age retrospection was based on the values and capacities of the educated middle class. In discussing their position of agency, college graduates emphasized being "able to make choices," having a purpose, and accomplishing their goals. They talked about self-confidence and endurance, doing the right thing, and not giving up. Asked why her life had gone well, a college-educated woman responded: "All the good things in my life? Yeah, I think I made them myself. I mean, I think I created the situations, and I think everybody has that ability." By contrast, a high-school graduate explained: "I'm not looking to be rewarded for what I do. I just think . . . that there are certain things in life everybody has to fulfill, and one thing is . . . to be able to take care of themselves and take care of others and be helpful and kind and generous." Another high-school-educated woman offered: "I didn't have to deal with a lot of bad things during our kids' teenage years. Sometimes

I think I just had it really well. When I listen to other people, things that have happen with them and their kids."[213]

Few high school graduates saw the course of their lives in terms of their own skills and ability. Tending to describe themselves as incorporating expectations and obligations, adapting rather than influencing, they were also more focused on the present than the future, implying that the future might not be able to be controlled or predicted. The immediate contingencies "preclude[d] the opportunity to focus on one's own interests and enjoyment. Instead, the needs and requirements of others are what seem to structure everyday life."[214]

Midmac gave the midlife crisis the coup de grâce. Consolidating and extending earlier findings on gender and the life course, the researchers also put these into perspective. By rejecting a focus on white middle-class American men as the average human being and pointing to the impact of race, class, and culture as well as gender, Midmac contributed to particularizing the midlife crisis as a diagnosis about chauvinism.

7 *Feminist Legacy*

Feminist research invented the midlife crisis, and feminism abolished it, too. Feminist scholarship did not revive Sheehy's concept. Though Gilligan and Baruch, Barnett, and Rivers shared Sheehy's critique of Eriksonian conceptions of identity, they did not engage with her work. They not only understood midlife crisis as a concept primarily defined by Levinson, Vaillant, and Gould—thus perceiving *Passages* as a popularization of androcentric concepts of development—but also differed from Sheehy in their understanding of the life course. Most importantly, while Sheehy had advocated the normalcy of change, the later studies foregrounded concepts of adult mental health as stability and continuity. There was more than one feminist concept of middle age.

The concepts of women's midlife in the 1980s and '90s illustrate the long legacy of feminist concepts of the life course, which permeated public and academic debates even at a time of backlash. Feminist researchers turned upside down the concept of human development put forward by Levinson and other masculinist experts by using images of midlife stability gleaned from women's lives to dismiss negative images of women outside domestic roles. From Carol Gilligan's point of view, the male midlife crisis was irresponsible behavior; the Lifeprints study suggested that it indicated an insistence on traditional gender roles despite their limits. This research turned the midlife crisis into a widely used tool of feminist critique.

As a result, those who depicted midlife-crisis-typical behavior became defensive and often rejected the label. "The midlife crisis has become a joke," complained the therapist and marriage counselor Andrew Marshall, which was "usually at the expense of a man" and used by his partner to blame and accuse him. "Nobody has ever arrived at my office saying 'Help, I'm having a midlife crisis' but I've had lots of people accusing their partner of having one." Dismissing the "midlife crisis" diagnosis, Marshall still drew on Jaques as well as Jung to assure those whose lives had descended into chaos "with affairs, heartbroken children, or clinical depression" that he admired their courage in engaging with the truly great issues of identity and the meaning of life in middle age.[215]

Yet feminism did not entirely eliminate the midlife crisis. As "midlife crisis" turned into a cliché, many people avoided using the term. But ideas about turmoil in middle age continued to exist, for women and men.

7
Oldness

Does the midlife crisis exist? By making visible the feminist origins and legacy of the midlife crisis as well as backlash against it, this book has proposed that we reframe the question, that we ask instead how to define "midlife crisis." It has revealed the significance of gender in conceptions of the life course and recovered the rich and influential feminist traditions in thinking about and contributing to public debates about the meaning and making of life, human existence, and social relations. Lastly, it has challenged analyses based on the distinction between academia and the public sphere: this did not reflect the shape of debates but provided an effective tool for scientists to dismiss critical voices and obstruct their ideas even to those who shared at least part of the message.

Today, the controversy about the midlife crisis continues. In the 2010s, the midlife crisis was rediscovered by economists of happiness who, to broad public attention, spoke of the "U-shape" of satisfaction over the life course: well-being is supposed to decline in the forties, then rise again. Neurologists confirmed this: stress levels rise from age twenty-two but then fall off after fifty. Sadness and worry peak at midlife; after the middle years, positive emotions increase. Starting with findings gleaned from the lives of American men, researchers collected evidence of similar patterns in subsamples of women and from more than seventy other countries to declare the U-curve a universal phenomenon. Not even apes were spared. "It [is] a statistical regularity," said Carol Graham, an economist at the Brookings Institution in Washington, DC. "Something about the human condition."[1]

This book has proposed a different perspective. Instead of looking at biographical change in middle adulthood as a timeless and universal occurrence, I have shown how the term and idea of "midlife crisis" became popular in the United States in the 1970s. The notion of an age-linked imperative to reappraise one's way of living lent sense to the decline of the male-breadwinner family as an ideal and a lifestyle and the emergence of two-job models in the white, educated middle class. Sheehy's *Passages* defined "midlife crisis" as the end of separate gender roles for men and women. Her plea for the reexamined life was endorsed in the public sphere as well as in academia.

When the psychoanalytic experts Daniel Levinson, George Vaillant, and Roger Gould refuted Sheehy in the late 1970s, they turned the midlife crisis into a male-only concept that described the end of a man's family obligations as a rite of passage to manhood. This "crisis of masculinity" confirmed and defended gender hierarchies. By excluding women from their conceptions of self-development, Levinson, Vaillant, and Gould prevented them from reimagining their lives. In subsequent studies, Carol Gilligan, Grace Baruch, Rosalind Barnett, and other feminist scholars rejected and denounced the male midlife crisis as a sign of selfishness, immaturity, and chauvinism, thus turning it into a social pathology.

Historical analysis has not debunked the midlife crisis. By showing that this was neither an inevitable nor a universal part of the human life cycle, it has documented why this "essentially contested" conception of midlife reconsideration emerged.[2] Proponents and adversaries invoked, dismissed, or reclaimed the midlife crisis to negotiate gender roles for women and men in the context of social and political transformation. The longer we look at the midlife crisis, the more it becomes clear that this is a social, political, and ethical as much as a psychological concept. Questions about the temporal dimensions of human nature, about options and constraints, success and failure, choice, regret, and responsibility, probe the intersection of self and social order. Questions of what human life is about and how it should—or can—be lived cannot be answered once and for all. The debate has resumed today, and so it should.

*

Feminist conceptions of "midlife crisis" continue to exist, though the term is rarely used. The idea of changing your life midway through is central in Sara Ahmed's conception of "living a feminist life." As she relates about herself: "In the middle of my life . . . I left a certain kind of life and embraced a new one." For Ahmed, the act of rejecting one life and choosing another typifies the feminist critique of traditional lifestyles as the only right choices. In this sense, she argues, "it is good to think of life as always potentially in crisis, to keep asking the question: how to live?"[3]

Middle age and the life course also remain prominent in the ongoing debate about gender, paid work, and family life, where the problems have not been fixed. Mental load, emotional labor, and glass ceilings weigh heavily on the lives and time of many women. The Facebook executive Sheryl Sandberg famously advises women with children to "lean in" and stay in the workforce as long as possible for the sake of their careers. She cites Rosalind Barnett and Caryl Rivers's follow-up research to the Life-prints study to argue that women's careers benefit family relationships and guarantee a purpose in life independent from motherhood. While Sandberg demands workplace structures that make it easier for employees with family responsibilities to remain on a leadership track, the political scientist and former US State Department official Anne-Marie Slaughter seeks to ensure that those who temporarily step out of the workforce or reduce their work hours are not permanently derailed by the decision. Drawing on Gilligan and echoing Myrdal and Klein, Slaughter uses the concept of sequencing to push back against linear "up or out" career tracks and advocate for women's—and men's—freedom to work part-time or even take some time out and come back in the "third phase" of life. Both Sandberg and Slaughter emphasize the importance of egalitarian familial involvement and feminist parenting.[4]

The midlife crisis has not disappeared. It has simply changed. According to the CNN journalists Lia Macko and Kerry Rubin, we are dealing with a new kind of midlife crisis, which plagues not at-home mothers but young career women, who are successful and "on track" at work but alone, unhappy, and anxious in their personal lives.[5] As this suggests, new norms of femininity, while tied to professional achievement, also continue to sustain the ideal of procreation. "Being a woman you can't just say you don't want a child," remarks Sheila Heti in her inquiry into childlessness and the choice of motherhood. "You have to have some big plan or idea of what you're going to do instead. And it better be something great." When the meaning of a woman's life is tied to marriage and maternity, when it is implied "that a woman is not an end in herself [but] a means to a man," time and aging bring relief and independence at last: "Now that I am older . . . , my life is not a speculative life, or a blueprint for a future life. It's just my life. This oldness is a good feeling—a feeling of nothing more to be decided. What happens now will be something other than the strain of making a decision, or the stress of fighting with nature. . . . You start life all over again, this time with yourself."[6]

The female and feminist discourse about the meaning of life has dropped almost completely out of scholarly records and public memory. Even historians have forgotten or misremembered women's contributions and critiques. Potted histories that present *Passages* as a popularization of psychological accounts of midlife crisis perpetuate Vaillant's, Levinson's, and Gould's backlash against Sheehy. These three experts weaponized the notion of popularization to sideline Sheehy's book and silence her critique. "Popularization" did not just discredit Sheehy's authority, as other instruments of boundary work would have done; it also created expert competence over a concept of popular culture. Casting Sheehy's book as a watered-down version of their own research allowed the experts successfully to coopt the midlife crisis. Scientific demarcation hid Sheehy's feminist agenda even from Gilligan, Baruch, Barnett, and other scholars who shared much of her perspective. Until today, many people remain unaware of the anti-feminist stance that motivated the idea of men's midlife crisis.

✳

We are now in a position to reassess the two central themes of gender and social science in this history of the midlife crisis: the double standard of aging and the notion of science popularization. Historians and sociologists of science have long acknowledged that the communication of ideas and theories is more diverse than received understandings of "popularization" suggest. This book has adopted and developed this perspective by showing that the concept of midlife crisis was popular before psychologists turned it into an academic idea. It has demonstrated how a writer created her own scientific precursor. Sheehy used and repurposed the psychoanalyst Jaques's term "midlife crisis" to support her own points. Above all, it has countered the assumption that journalistic accounts seek to translate, explain, and publicize scientific findings. Rather than following and affirming psychoanalytic conceptions of gender and identity, Sheehy often contested them. Her definition of men's and women's reciprocal midlife crises challenged gender bias in the social and human sciences.

Uncovering the feminist origins of the midlife crisis sheds new light on constructions of aging, and thus the relationships between gender and the social and human sciences. Centering on medical and pathological definitions of middle age, early feminist scholarship delineated the ways in which the notion of the end of reproductive activity and capacity thwarted women's rights. A second, revisionist round of investigations complicated the dichotomy between controlling doctors and powerless women. This demonstrated the limits of medical power as well as of female patients' requests for professional help, yet did little to change our understanding of age and gender.

By looking at therapy as well as psychology, sociology, and economics, at social policy, the law, and activism, and, importantly, at journalism, best-selling books, and their readers, I have expanded our understanding of who discussed midlife and how. I have demonstrated that the oppressive double standard of aging, though powerful, was not the only concept of female identity beyond reproduction. Experts, writers, and activists frequently used notions of middle age to reject and redefine traditional gender roles and hierarchies. Critical and empowering concepts of gender and the life course challenged the understanding of middle age as the end of a woman's life, instead displaying it as the beginning of public and professional lives. Not only a bait to tie young women to the home, celebrations of maturity comprehensively detached women's lives from domesticity. In the 1970s, for example, younger women perceived "midlife crisis" as a warning and an incentive to postpone marriage and motherhood in favor of careers. For many women, the idea of midlife typified liberation from traditional gender roles.

This little-studied tradition of writing about middle age formed an important part of the debate about identity and the life course. In the last third of the twentieth century, Sheehy participated in an older tradition of conceptualizing midlife and gender from a feminist vantage point, which stretched back to the First Wave of feminist activity and persisted into the postwar period, as Myrdal and Klein's influential demand for midlife reentry illustrates. The backlash from Vaillant, Levinson, and Gould highlights that the double standard was often promoted in reaction against women's celebration of aging. In the 1980s, studies by Gilligan and by Baruch and Barnett documented the continuity of feminist traditions in speaking about midlife as well as their changing perspectives. The different professional backgrounds and diversity of their work, its broad reception, and the backlash it elicited illustrate the stability and impact of the critique of the gendered double standard as well as alternative, empowering concepts of middle age.

The history of the midlife crisis, gender, and social science points to the significance of feminist perspectives in debates about identity, the life course, and the social order. Discriminatory double standards were influential but not universally accepted. They competed with feminist critiques and variant concepts. These constitute an important part of the history of gender and the social and human sciences. This book has supplemented accounts of gender inequalities by illuminating critical attitudes and alternative conceptions of the meaning of life, and made visible another history.

*

Reconsidering the feminist origins of the midlife crisis today does not necessarily mean adopting Sheehy's concept of midlife crisis. Too much has changed anyway, although the end of traditional gender roles has only partially been realized. But to point out that the midlife crisis emerged at a particular time and place and delineate its functions and effects in controversies about the social world turns a set idea—that all men have a midlife crisis—into a matter for reasoned argument. It enlarges our understanding of what it may mean to start anew in middle life and opens a debate about the impact of time on women's and men's options and experiences and about the chronologies of inequality.

The look back demonstrates that the debate about gender, paid work, and personal responsibilities has a long continuity. Some of the concepts put forward today sound like those proposed forty, sixty, or more than a hundred years ago. Recent demands for a "succession principle" to allow women with children to leave the workforce and then start anew revive

Myrdal and Klein's proposition for women's reentry.[7] The rerun can be read as a sign of stagnation, an indication that inequalities persist, that barely anything has changed and too little been achieved. To some, society has failed; yet others blame the shortcomings of earlier critics and activists for the impasse. There is another way of thinking about, and with, feminism's oldness.

The historical perspective illuminates the legacy of feminist thought and practice. Women's expressions of autonomy do not just come in waves or as a fashion. Even when gender roles ossified after World War II and then during the backlash of the 1980s, critical voices spoke out. Much more than an anomaly or defensive reaction, feminism forms an integral part of the public sphere as much as specialist debates. Being aware of this feminist presence makes it important to better comprehend who suppressed it and how. Practices of demarcation and cooptation have allowed anti-feminist experts to claim authority, even impartiality, on the back of women's own claims. Appreciation of feminist continuances also broadens our understanding of the breadth and diversity of feminist participants and agendas and makes visible the variety of forums, concerns, and strategies. Feminism was never a monolithic ideology, an analytical insight that tends to get lost in normative acts of defining and tidying the space of women's causes, whether as stereotype or ideal. Finally, then, nurturing connections encourages a fuller engagement with feminist pasts, crucial both within feminist circles and beyond. Earlier feminist voices were not marginal at their time; nor are their perspectives obsolete today. Not just failed attempts or limited, less sophisticated perspectives that need to be overcome and left behind, they provide a basis and resource for contemporary feminist visions and approaches. Moreover, feminist expertise and action constitute an important and influential part of our society's past, present, and future.

Acknowledgments

I am indebted to the many people who made this book possible.

First, Nick Hopwood's advice, encouragement, and devotion of time and energy, Peter Mandler's faith in this project, and Anke te Heesen's guidance and mentoring have been invaluable. The late John Forrester brought to the project intellectual breadth and curiosity, wit, and warmth. From early on, Karen Merikangas Darling, together with Susannah Engstrom and Tristan Bates, made this book real.

The Cambridge Department of History and Philosophy of Science supported me in many ways, and I am especially grateful for the close interest and criticism of Helen Curry, Jim Secord, and Nick Jardine as well as Mary Augusta Brazelton, Hasok Chang, and Patricia Fara. In addition, I am thankful for the help of Tamara Hug. Special thanks go to Lucy Delap in the Faculty of History for her time and feedback.

Substantial parts of the book have been researched and written at Harvard's Department of the History of Science; further portions, at the Max Planck Institute for the History of Science in Berlin. At Harvard, Rebecca Lemov was an insightful and charitable sponsor, and Allan Brandt took generous interest in the project. For their warm welcome and feedback, I am also indebted to Anne Harrington, Alex Csiszar, and especially Liz Lunbeck. At the Max Planck Institute, my thanks go to Christine von Oertzen, Jamie Cohen-Cole, Erika Milam, Dan Bouk, Julia Voss, and Ohad Parnes as well as Hansjakob Ziemer and the Journalistic Practices working group. At Free University Berlin, Sebastian Conrad and the Center for Global History provided an ideal home for finishing the manuscript. I would also like to thank Birgit Aschmann for very early support.

I greatly appreciate the generosity and feedback of audiences at Harvard and Princeton; the Max Planck Institute for the History of Science, the Charité, Humboldt University, and the Free University in Berlin; ETH Zurich; the German Historical Institute in Washington, DC; the Universities of Exeter, Lübeck, and Regensburg; the Forschungszentrum Gotha; the University of Cambridge, many a time; and the annual conferences of the History of Science Society, the Gesellschaft für Geschichte der Wissenschaften, Medizin und Technik, the Society for the History of Recent Social Science, the Science in Public research network, and the Independent Social Research Foundation.

I had a lot of help from archivists and librarians, first and foremost from Ellen Shea, Amanda Strauss, Zoe Hill, and others at the Schlesinger Library at Harvard, whose collections have been invaluable, as well as Monica Blank at the Rockefeller Archive Center, Bruce Kirby and Ryan Reft at the Library of Congress, Elizabeth Dunn at Duke University's Rubenstein Rare Book and Manuscript Library, Chido Muchemwa and Elizabeth Garver at the Harry Ransom Center at the University of Texas at Austin, Alex Asal at the Smith College collection of women's history, Anne Cox from the State Historical Society of Missouri, Heidi Stover at the Penn State Special Collections Library, and Bernd Hoffmann in the Archives of the Max Planck Society in Berlin. Gerald Rosen graciously shared materials from the American Psychological Association's Task Force on Self-Help Therapies. Countless books have been borrowed from and hours spent in Cambridge's Whipple, Social and Political Sciences, and University Libraries, Harvard's Widener, Countway, and Baker Libraries, the libraries of the Max Planck Institutes for the History of Science and for Human Development, the Patricia D. Klingenstein Library of the New-York Historical Society, and the Staatsbibliothek zu Berlin.

The book would not have been possible without support from the German National Academic Foundation, the Arts and Humanities Research Council, and the Cambridge History and Philosophy of Science Trust Fund, as well as the Rockefeller Archive Center, the Kurt Hahn Trust, the University of Cambridge and the Lundgren Fund, and Clare College, Cambridge.

I am thankful for comments from and conversations with Claire Sabel, Kira Jürjens, Moritz Neuffer, Linda Conze, Julia Pelta Feldman, Jenny Bangham, Boris Jardine, and Johannes Schreyer. Thanks are also due to Hannes Bajohr, Ettina Blaison, Lucy Bollington, Robert Brennan, Stijn

Conix, Till Großmann, Nils Güttler, Nina Toudal Jessen, Lisa Malich, Edda Mann, Andrew McKenzie-McHarg, James Morris, Philipp Müller, Philipp Nielsen, Jesse Olszynko-Gryn, Olga Osadtschy, Tom Pye, Charlotte Reichow, Hardy Schilgen, Britt Schlünz, Alrun Schmidtke, Sandra Schnädelbach, Kathryn Schoefert, Caspar Schwietering, Antje Stahl, and Alice-Marie Uwimana.

My deepest thanks, to Felix Lüttge, go far beyond this project. The love and support of our families have been invaluable.

Notes

Chapter 1

1   Sheehy 1976f, 3–4.
2   Sheehy 1972a.
3   Sheehy 1976f, 12.
4   Sheehy 1976f, 3–12. On the NWPC, see, for example, Greer 1972; Steinem 2015, 150–154.
5   Quoted in Sheehy 2014, 217.
6   Hanisch 1970; see also Morgan 1970b. On war and masculinity: Mosse 1996; Dudnik, Hagemann, and Tosh 2004.
7   Sheehy 1976f, 307–308; Jaques 1965.
8   Sheehy 1976f, 390–400. Sheehy's later portrayal of Glaser, her colleague at *New York* magazine, closely resembles the description in *Passages*; see Sheehy 2014, 81–82.
9   Friedan 1963a; Riesman, Glazer, and Denney 1950.
10 Sabine and Sabine 1983, 38; Fein 1991.
11 Combaz 1978, 74.
12 Whitbourne 2012; similarly, Whitbourne 2010, 160–169.
13 See, for example, Cohen 2012, 12, 115–116; Mintz 2015, 300; Hagerty 2016, 17–19; Setiya 2017, 6, 10–12. Rauch (2018) does not mention Sheehy at all.
14 Levinson 1978c; Vaillant 1977a; Gould 1978.
15 On science communication, see Shinn and Whitley 1985; Cooter and Pumfrey 1994; Secord 2004; Topham 2009; Hopwood et al. 2015; "popularization" and boundary work: Gieryn 1983; Hilgartner 1990.
16 Friedan 1963a, 68–72; Erikson 1950a; Erikson 1958.
17 Erikson 1964.
18 Gilligan 1982c; Baruch, Barnett, and Rivers 1983.
19 Rodgers 2011, 163.
20 Wethington 2000; Lachman 2001; Brim 2004. See also the Midlife in the United States website, MIDUS.wisc.edu (accessed November 19, 2018).
21 Friedman 2008.
22 Blanchflower and Oswald 2008; Weiss et al. 2012; Steptoe, Deaton, and Stone 2014; Graham and Pozuelo 2017.
23 Setiya 2017, esp. 25–27, 54–76, 127–154; 15, 143 quoted.
24 Gergen 1997, 475.
25 Williams and Nagel 1976; Williams 1981, esp. 26–27, 37; see also the critiques by Friedman 1993, 163–170; Card 1996.

26 Setiya 2017, 2, 55–57, 136–138, 142–143; see also Cusk 2014, 90–131.

27 Coontz 1992; Coontz 2005, esp. 247–262; Creighton 1999; Lewis 2001; Self 2012.

28 Ariès 1962. Ariès became the target for many historians' own interpretative claims; see esp. Orme 2001; Ozment 2001; and, for an overview of the debate, Hutton 2004, 92–112.

29 Joerißen and Will 1983; Cole 1992; Ehmer 1996; Hartog 2012; Willer, Weigel, and Jussen 2013. For an overview on old age: Thane 2005; see also the history of gerontology: Achenbaum 1995; Katz 1996; Park 2016. On modern developmental series more generally: Hopwood, Schaffer, and Secord 2010.

30 Bouk 2018; see also Parnes, Vedder, and Willer 2008; Onion 2015. On adolescence: Gillis 1974; Kett 1978; DeLuzio 2007; Marland 2013; "youth" as metaphor: Frank 1997.

31 Gilligan 1982c, 18.

32 Sontag 1972, 29.

33 Balzac 1901.

34 Smith-Rosenberg 1985; Bell 1987; Lock 1990; see also Banner 1992; Berger 1999; and, more recently, Wiel 2014b; as well as the edited volumes Formanek 1990; and Komesaroff, Rothfield, and Daly 1997; and the more popular Foxcraft 2009. For a comprehensive, journalistic history of middle age: Cohen 2012; see also Gullette 1997; Mintz 2015; on Britain: Benson 1997; Heath 2009.

35 Key texts include Ehrenreich and English 1978; Showalter 1985; Poovey 1988; Jordanova 1989; Russett 1989.

36 Houck 2006; Watkins 2007a; for a critique of Houck's book, see Bell and Reverby 2006.

37 Rose 1990; Rose 1998; Herman 1996; Frank 1997; Mirowski 2002; Illouz 2008; Moskowitz 2008.

38 On the "open mind," see Cohen-Cole 2014; consumers as political subjects: Cohen 2003; Trentmann 2008; Mead: Mandler 2013; countercultural science: Moore 2008; Kaiser and McCray 2016. See also Jewett 2014; Lunbeck 2014; Plant 2015; Herzog 2017; for an overview: Aubry and Travis 2015; on Britain: Savage 2010; Evans 2017; and the British empire: Tilley 2011; Linstrum 2016.

39 Foucault 2007; Foucault 2001. See also Sarasin 2007; and, on the reception and politics of French theory in the United States, Cusset 2008.

40 For a survey history of feminist science, technology, and medicine, see Schiebinger 1999; also Creager, Lunbeck, and Schiebinger 2001; on feminism and social science: Rosenberg 1982; Tarrant 2009; psychology, psychiatry, and psychoanalysis: Lunbeck 1994; Morawski 1994; Pandora 1997; Buhle 1998, and also the biographical encyclopedia Psychology's Feminist Voices, directed by Alexandra Rutherford, FeministVoices .com; on women's health activism in the 1960s and '70s: Davis 2007; Kline 2010; Murphy 2012; and before: Morantz-Sanchez 1985; Bittel 2009; Leng 2013. On women's research and inquiry beyond the academy, see Gates 1998; Lightman 2007, esp. 95–165; Oertzen, Rentetzi, and Watkins 2013. On the significance of self-hood and individuality for feminist thought and practice, see Fraisse 1988; Scott 1996; Delap 2007.

41 On feminism beyond movement chronologies and the complex and ambivalent politics of self-identification: Meyerowitz 1994; Misciagno 1997; Hewitt 2010; Hewitt 2012; Laughlin et al. 2010; Laughlin and Castledine 2012; Bereni 2012; on the term "feminism": Offen 1987; Cott 1989, 3–6.

42 For an overview on Second Wave feminism and the media: Barker-Plummer 2010; see also Farrell 1998; Bradley 2003; Dow 2014. On backlash in the 1980s: Faludi 1991.

43   Myrdal and Klein 1956.
44   Mosher, c. 1916, quoted in Houck 2006, 36; Spencer 1913, esp. 232.
45   Rosin 2012, 227.
46   Sandberg 2013; Slaughter 2015; Macko and Rubin 2004; on egg-freezing: Wiel 2014a; Wiel 2015.

Chapter 2

1   Sontag 1972, 31.
2   The literature is extensive; classic studies include Smith-Rosenberg 1985; Bell 1987; Lock 1990; see also the more recent Houck 2006; Watkins 2007a. On Sontag's studies of illness: Brandt, esp. 203–204; Clow 2001.
3   Zola 1972; Conrad and Schneider 1980. The language of the clinical pathologized men, too: Tiefer 1986; Benninghaus 2012.
4   Here and for the following: Stolberg 2007a; Stolberg 2007b; see also Palm 2011; Verheyen 2014. For the Hippocratic definition of "crisis": Langholf 1990, 73–117.
5   Bras 2000, 257–343.
6   Stolberg 2007a, 107–108. Women's omission is discussed in Schäfer 2015, 162–172.
7   Halford 1813, 323. The paper was a typical starting point for writings on the climacteric; see, for example, Good 1835 2:23–26; in psychiatry: Skae 1865. On Halford, see Munk 1895; on the reception and continued influence of his paper: Stolberg 2007b, 113.
8   Dewees 1826, 149. Similar complaints were made by German physicians; for example, Adelmann 1840. See also Lock 1990, 307–317.
9   Menopause became a subject apart from menstruation in 1927, when the *Index Medicus* was merged with the American Medical Association's *Quarterly Cumulative Index to Current Literature*, which had listed menopause separately since its establishment in 1916. In 1928, the *Index-Catalogue of the Library of the Surgeon-General's Office* listed fewer than twenty articles about menopause published in American medical journals compared to more than fifty articles about "painful menstruation"; Houck 2006, 246n7.
10   Freidenfels 2009, 74–119; DeLuzio 2007, 50–89; Delaney, Lupton, and Toth 1988, 55–66. For a transnational comparison: Rowold 2010, on menstruation esp. 32, 41–43, 59–60, and 123.
11   West 1858, 34–78, esp. 49–51.
12   Martin 1989, 51; see also Banner 1992, 277.
13   Erikson 1964, 596.
14   Millett 1970, 218.
15   For positive readings of the lack of attention to menopause, see Lock 1990, esp. 307–317. On female physicians' complaints: Houck 2006, 16–17.
16   Wilbush 1980. On the French discourse, see Stearns 1980.
17   Tilt 1851b; Tilt 1857; see also Tilt 1851d; Tilt 1851c; Tilt 1851a.
18   Gardanne 1816. He changed the name to *ménopause* in the second edition (1821); see also Théré 2015.
19   Tilt 1857, 66, 3, 11, 15, 35, 237–246.
20   Wilbush 1980, 263.
21   Wilbush 1981, 7n9.

22 Currier 1897. The Chicago physician Alice Stockham added a chapter on "menopause" in the revised edition of her widely circulating women's guidebook *Tokology* (1883); see Stockham 1887, 276–285.

23 Bell 1987; Hirshbein 2009.

24 Currier 1897, vii–viii.

25 Currier 1897, 153.

26 Similarly, Currier used the example of prostitutes to illustrate the problems of "excessive" sexual activity; see Currier 1897, 153. On class and hormonal cycles: Fuchs 2005, 51; Houck 2006, 4.

27 Currier 1897, 151, and see also 35–39, 270–272; Smith-Rosenberg 1985, esp. 192–193; Lock 1990, 319, 321; Banner 1992, 284–287.

28 Taylor 1871, 92–93. Rest cures were an important target of feminist critique; see Lee 1997, 182–186; Berman 1992; Allen 2009, 20–25; Bittel 2009, 126–135, 142–144.

29 Reed 1901, 742.

30 Bell 1987; see also Oudshoorn 1994; Sengoopta 2000; Sengoopta 2006.

31 Weisman 1951, 55.

32 Watkins 2007a; Houck 2006.

33 Wilson and Wilson 1963; Wilson 1966.

34 On this last aspect, see Houck 2006, 102–103.

35 Lock 1990, 329, also 330–341; Banner 1992, 297–305; Houck 2006, 40–57.

36 Freud 1965, 167.

37 Deutsch 1945, 459–460, 474–475. On masochism as the elemental power of feminine mental life, see Deutsch 1930. On the influence of psychoanalysis on postwar American culture: Burnham 2012.

38 Wylie 1942, 186–187. On Wylie's antimaternalism, see Plant 2010, 19–54; also Buhle 1998, 125–164; May 1988, 73–74.

39 Reuben 1969, 365–366.

40 Martin 1989, esp. 42–46, 51–52.

41 Palmatier 1995; "Empty Nest" 2013. For uses in the 1950s and '60s, see Komarovsky 1953, 244; Lawrence 1956; Deykin et al. 1966; Kinney 1968. There is, to my knowledge, no analysis of this human-animal metaphor, which historians regularly use as an analytical category; see, for example, Houck 2006, 99–101. But note Lisa Malich's analysis of pregnancy and the "nesting instinct," which displayed women's domestic roles as the "natural" expression of motherly feelings and was linked to improved standards of living and separate children's rooms: Malich 2017, 329–342.

42 Stolberg 2007a, 117–119. On twentieth-century debates about the male climacteric, see Sengoopta 2006, 177–186; Hofer 2007; Watkins 2007b; Watkins 2008.

43 Scott 1898, 70–71.

44 Reed 1904, 741–742.

45 Wilson and Wilson 1963, 347.

46 Pitkin 1932, 26; Pitkin 1930; Pitkin 1937.

47 Perkin 1996; see also Bledstein 1976; Chandler 1977; Zunz 1990.

48 Pitkin 1932, 19.

49 Pitkin 1932, 73–74, 75.

50 Neugarten 1968a, 96. See also, on the rise and fall of professional men's wages over the life course, Ghez and Becker 1975.

51 Sontag 1972, 31; Neugarten 1968a, 96. For a helpful, class-focused analysis of aspiration and contentment, see Komarovsky 1967, 202–204, 330–347; "status panic": Mills 1951; the longer history of failure in American business: Sandage 2005.

52　Hall 1922, 11. For an overview of the history of adolescence: Kett 2003. On adolescence and masculinity, see the classic Kett 1978; Gillis 1974; Macleod 1983. But note also, with regard to girls and young women: Smith-Rosenberg 1985; Hunter 2002; DeLuzio 2007; Marland 2013.

53　Bergler 1954; also Bergler 1946; Bergler 1948; Bergler 1949. On Bergler's punitive approach: Herzog 2017, 63; on his anti-feminist stance: Gerhard 2001, esp. 41.

54　Bergler 1954, 3, 9.

55　Bergler 1954, 311–312.

56　Sontag 1972, 38.

57　Sommers 1974, 5. On race and infantilization, see Nandy 1987; McClintock 1995; Stoler 1995, 150–164.

58　Newman 1998, 282–283.

59　Engels 1892, 159–160, 242, 160; this applied on both sides of the Atlantic, see Shergold 1982, esp. 73–74.

60　Chase 1929, 340; Chase 1932.

61　Williams 1920, 39.

62　Edwards 1979, 169–170; Ransom and Sutch 1986, 27–29.

63　On race and the Lynds, see Igo 2007, 54–60; race and medicine: Epstein 2007, 203–231. For a comparable European survey, see the Marienthal Study of unemployment: Jahoda, Lazarsfeld, and Zeisel 1933.

64　Lynd and Lynd 1929, 30, 35; on "compulsory education" laws and schooling patterns, see 181–187.

65　Lynd and Lynd 1929, 33, 34.

66　Burnett 1994, 217–218.

67　Segrave 2001, 99–102; on age discrimination from 1860 to 1920: Hushbeck 1989.

68　Connell 1987, 183; see also Connell and Messerschmidt 2005.

69　Sontag 1972, 32.

70　Lynd and Lynd 1929, 27n4.

71　Lynd and Lynd 1929, 28. Most of the Lynds' interviews took place during the day, and thus included few women who were continuously employed away from home; see ibid., 29.

72　Newman 1998.

73　Spencer 1913, 230–231, 233, 234. Spencer's early use of the metaphor "new deal" suggests that it was rooted in the context of social reform, even before Chase's 1932 *New Deal*. On gender and legal subjectivity: Scott 1996.

74　Spencer 1913, 232.

75　On positive definitions of middle age as confirming the double standard, see Banner 1992, 7. Judith Houck argues that celebrations of midlife release reinforced women's domestic roles: Houck 2006, esp. 30, 89–91, 94, 102–103, 105, 111–112.

76　Degler 1974; Smith-Rosenberg 1985, 194–195.

77　Drake 1902, 43–44. Reissued repeatedly, well into the 1930s, Drake's book was also translated into German and French: Drake 1910; Drake 1942. For later uses of the "panorama" metaphor, see Edsall 1949, 121; Davis 1951, 149.

78　See, for example, Drake 1902, 44–45; Lowry 1919, 144–145.

79　Steeholm and Fisher published under the pseudonym Sara Trent; see Trent 1934, 173.

80　Mosher 1916; also Mosher 1901; and, for similar arguments, Jacobi 1877; Hollingworth 1914. On Mosher: Degler 1974; Tunc 2010.

81　Mosher 1916, 32–34.

82   Mosher 1916, 33, 34–35.

83   On menopause and "community housekeeping," see Houck 2006, 30–32. On maternalist politics in medicine: Morantz-Sanchez 1985; more generally: Offen 1988;
Gordon 1990; Koven and Michel 1990; Koven and Michel 1993; Bock and Thane 1991;
Ladd-Taylor 1994, esp. 104–132; Delap 2007, 139–179; Klein et al. 2012. See also, on the
gendered structure of the American political sphere, Baker 1984; Fraser 1992.

84   "Is Forty the Limit?" 1922; see also, in the following decades: Albert 1930; Miller 1939;
"I Like Being Forty!" 1941; Sherwood 1949.

85   Coyle 1928, esp. 92–101.

86   Lowry 1919, 156–165.

87   Spencer 1913, 236, 238.

88   Palmer and Greenberg 1936, 103, also 102–104, 107–108. See also Hansl 1927; Knopf
1932, 238–241.

89   Lock 1990, 330–360; Banner 1992, 297–310.

90   May 1988; Coontz 1992; Meyerowitz 1994; Weiss 2000; Laughlin 2000; on "interwave" psychology: Rutherford 2017; Johnson and Johnston 2010; Johnston and Johnson 2017; advice for mothers: Plant 2010, esp. 88, 115–116. On working women past
thirty-five: United States Department of Labor 1956, 19–21; United States Department
of Labor 1960, 27–31; United States Census Bureau 1957.

91   On Levine, see "Lena Levine Dies" 1965; Chesler 1992, 289, 307n, 415–416; Gordon
1976, 265–275. On Doherty: Doherty 1949; Kamen 1985, esp. 257, 273, 325n20; Nissley
2017.

92   Levine 1938. The brochure was renamed *The Doctor Talks to the Bride and Groom* in
1950; reprints appeared as late as 1964. See also Stone and Levine 1956.

93   "Women Needn't Worry" 1953, 170; see similarly Shepherd 1952.

94   Levine and Doherty 1952, 25.

95   Levine and Doherty 1952, 57, 116–117. On housework and technology: Cowan 1983;
Bernard 1981, 393–412; on industrial metaphors in medical writing: Martin 1989.

96   "Student and Teacher of Human Ways" 1959, 147 (my italics); see also Mead 1946,
xxiv–xxv, 339–341.

97   Lutkehaus 2008, 73.

98   On the genesis of the project: Myrdal and Klein 1956, ix; on the primacy of the
middle class: 2, 8–10; for Klein's earlier work: Klein 1946. Myrdal and Klein's book was
part of a shift of attention to professional women and employment; see Lewis 1990;
Laughlin 2000; Allen 2005, 223–225; Lyon 2007; Oertzen 2007; Tarrant 2009, esp.
154–161; Johnson and Johnston 2010; McCarthy 2016. On pressures on professional
women: Solomon 1985, esp. 186–206; Rossiter 1995.

99   Myrdal and Klein 1956, 32–39, 159–161, 163–164.

100   Quoted in McCarthy 2016, 299; see also University Grants Committee 1964, esp. 109–
110, 136–140. On Sweden as well as Norway: Sejersted 2011, 248–249; see also, on West
Germany: Oertzen 2007, esp. 49–52.

101   Commission on the Education of Women of the American Council on Education
1955; Commission on the Education of Women of the American Council on Education 1960. See Eisenmann 2006, esp. 17–27, 87–111; Rutherford 2017.

102   Jahoda and Grant 1955; see also Jahoda 1958.

103   Maccoby 1958; see also National Manpower Council 1957; National Manpower Council 1958.

104   President's Commission on the Status of Women 1963, 76 (quoting Executive Order
10980); Eisenmann 2006, 141–178; Cobble 2010.

105 Friedan 1963a, 8; see also 390n3, 401n34, 406n15.

106 Sontag 1972, 38.

107 Hacking 2002, 37; see also Ong 1982, 12.

108 Note especially the slightly earlier essay by sociologist Bell 1970; also Beauvoir 1972.

109 Sontag 1972, 38.

Chapter 3

1 Koselleck 2006, 358–359. Diagnostic concepts can be normative, too; as Canguilhem observes, "Health is at once a state and an order": Canguilhem 2008, 476; see also Canguilhem 1978.

2 Mintz 2015, 300. See also, in psychology: Elkind 1994, 192–193; Wethington 2000, 91–92; Whitbourne 2010, 160–169; journalism: Cohen 2012, 12, 115–116; Hagerty 2016, 17–19.

3 Shinn and Whitley 1985; Secord 1994; Cooter and Pumfrey 1994; Lewenstein 1995; Secord 2004; Topham 2009. The notion of "popularization" bolsters scientific authority; see Hilgartner 1990; Nelkin 1987; Lewenstein 1992.

4 On "popular science" as validation: Fleck 1979, 112–117; see also Nelkin 1987.

5 On Erikson as "pro-feminist," see Friedman 1999, esp. 423–426, and Herman 1996, esp. 293, 391n78.

6 Sheehy's biography and career are reconstructed on the basis of Gail Sheehy, "Cultural History," February 17, 1970, and "Alicia Patterson Fellowship Application," October 23, 1972, Margaret Mead Papers, Library of Congress, Washington, DC, box D51, folder 2; Gail Sheehy, "Biography," 1975, Penney-Missouri Journalism Awards Records, State Historical Society of Missouri, Columbia, MO, folder 603; Sheehy 2014, esp. 5–49.

7 Sheehy 2014, 6. See also Gail Sheehy to Helen Gurley Brown, March 29, 1968, Helen Gurley Brown Papers, Smith College Archives, Northampton, MA, box 9, folder 9. On Sheppard and the *Herald Tribune*'s fashion pages, see Bender 1967, 76–85; Kluger 1986, 622–625, 672, 691–692.

8 Mills 1988; Bradley 2005; Voss and Speere 2007; Whitt 2008; see also the detailed literature overview by Barker-Plummer 2010.

9 "Gail Sheehy" [1976], Clay Felker Papers, Rubenstein Library, Duke University, Durham, NC, box 2; Sheehy 2014, 7–10. On New York City's infant mortality in the 1960s and '70s, see Wallace and Wallace 1990.

10 On the end of the New York *Herald Tribune* and the beginnings of *New York* magazine, see Kluger 1986, 703–741; *New York*'s first decade: Weingarten 2005; the magazine's politics: Greenberg 2008, 71–96.

11 Wolfe 1970.

12 Thom 1997, 200.

13 See her comment on the takeover: Sheehy 1977b.

14 Weingarten 2005, 207.

15 Sheehy 1976f, 77. For "sex" and "gender" in 1970s academic feminist debates, see Oakley 1972; Rubin 1975. On the physical and social qualities of "sex," see Tarrant 2009.

16 See the classic Hull, Bell-Scott, and Smith 1982; also Hewitt 2010; Laughlin et al. 2010. On 1970s feminism in the media: Farrell 1998; Bradley 2003; Dow 2014.

17 Sheehy 1968c; Sheehy 1968b. Arbus's photographic perspective overlapped with New Journalism's interest in nonelites and "freaky humanity," see Johnson 1979, 35–36.

18   Sheehy 1971a; Sheehy 1971c; Sheehy 1968a; Sheehy 1969a; Sheehy 1969b.

19   Sheehy 1971e.

20   Sheehy 1970a; Sheehy 1972b; Sheehy 1970b; Sheehy 1970d; Sheehy 1971d, esp. 36–41.

21   Cleveland 1970, 16.

22   Sheehy 1971d.

23   Sheehy 1972b. On Sheehy's impact on city politics: Waggoner 1973; Smith 1973; her use of composite characters: Lehmann-Haupt 1973; Pinkerton 1971; and the New Journalism controversy more generally: Weber 1974; Schudson 1978, 160–194.

24   Kilday 1975; Sheehy 1973a.

25   Sheehy 1974a, 33; Sheehy 2014, 210. Alicia Patterson Foundation, press release, December 18, 1972, and Alicia Patterson Foundation to Margaret Mead, December 1973, Mead Papers, box C106, folder 2. Alicia Patterson Foundation to Clay Felker, November 1974, Felker Papers, box 2. On Dutton, see: Tebbel 1981, 156–157.

26   Côté 2000, 2.

27   On midlife vs. middle age: Sheehy 1976f, 304–305.

28   Sternbergh 2006; Rosen 1989.

29   Wolfe 1970; Wolfe 1976; Blum 1987.

30   Quoted in Ken Emerson, "Gail Sheehy's *Passages*: Growing Up Takes a Life Time," *Boston after Dark*, 1976, Felker Papers, box 2; Sherman 1995. For the various neologisms, see Sheehy 1976f, 99–105, 163–177, 345–346 and 358–376.

31   Sheehy 1976f, 435.

32   Canguilhem 2005, 199–200. In the nineteenth and early twentieth centuries, female "popularizers" avoided open controversy to maintain their authority, see Gates 1998, 36–38; Lightman 2007, 155–163. See also, on disciplinary histories: Brannigan 1979; Graham, Lepenies, and Weingart 1983; Skopek 2011.

33   In an interview, Jaques stated that he presented the paper as part of the process of becoming a member and had started conceptualizing it in 1952; see Kirsner 2004, 200–201.

34   G. S. 2005; Pugh and Hickson 2016. On the "time-span of discretion," see esp. Jaques 1956. On the significance of wartime developments for psychological expertise, see Herman 1996, 82–123.

35   Beard 1881, 243.

36   Beard 1881, 198–199, 235–243. On Beard, see Rosenberg 1962; Lutz 1991; Rabinbach 1992, 153–162. Quantitative biographical work was not uncommon in psychology; see, for example, Bühler 1933; Frenkel-Brunswik 1936; Maslow 1943.

37   Jaques 1965. On Dante and midlife literature: Hirdt 1992.

38   Jaques 1965, 502, 505.

39   Jaques 1965, 512, 506.

40   On menopause, see Jaques 1965, 502.

41   Lavietes 2003; see also the *Oxford English Dictionary*'s entry "Mid-life."

42   According to GoogleScholar and the Psychoanalytic Electronic Publishing (PEP-Web) Archive.

43   Kirsner 2004, 201.

44   For an exception, see Wilhelm Fliess and Sigmund Freud's correspondence on the "male menopause," Freud to Fliess, March 1, 1896, Freud 1954, 159.

45   King and Steiner 1990.

46   Kirsner 2004, 198, 197; see also Jaques 1998; Twemlow 2005.

47   See, for example, Wind 1968; Rapoport 1970, 136, 219.

48   Gould 1972; Lowenthal and Chiriboga 1972.

49   *Work in America* 1973, 41.

50   Jaques 1970; Brook 1971, 314.

51   Soddy 1967.

52   Neugarten 1968b. Similarly, the psychoanalyst Judd Marmor, whose *Psychiatry in Transition* (1974) included a chapter titled "The Crisis of Middle Age," made no mention of Jaques, see Marmor 1974.

53   Daniel Levinson, "A Psychosocial Study of the Male Midlife Decade" (1972), Jessie Bernard Papers, Penn State Special Collections Library, University Park, PA, box 10, folder 21; Wolfe 1972.

54   Jaques was mentioned in correspondence, as an insider's tip; see Elliot G. Mishler to Orville Brim, February 28, 1974, Social Science Research Council Records, Rockefeller Archives, Sleepy Hollow, NY, Record Group 2/2, Series 1/106, box 648, folder 7928.

55   Skopek 2011, 211.

56   See GoogleScholar and PEP-Web. There was also an additional review of Jaques's essay collection: de Grazia 1976.

57   Levinson 1978c, 26. Bernice Neugarten and Nancy Datan did not refer to Jaques in their 1974 "The Middle Years" but cited him when this was reprinted several years later; compare Neugarten and Datan 1974 and Neugarten and Datan 1996. Similarly, the Harvard psychiatrist George Vaillant made no mention of Jaques in a 1972 paper but discussed him five years later, see Vaillant and McArthur 1972; Vaillant 1977a, 221–223.

58   Sheehy 2014, 211; Sheehy 1974a, 44.

59   Sheehy 1976f, 19–21. Sheehy emphasized the variety of her subjects' geographical distribution, but in the various cases presented, New York is by far the most frequently mentioned place.

60   Tavris 1995.

61   Sheehy 1976f, 268–276; Sheehy 1973b; see also Mead 1972, 271. On Mead's involvement in the war effort and her more positive initial reaction to the news of the dropping of the atomic bomb: Mandler 2013, esp. 45–176, 189–190.

62   Sheehy 1976f, 178. See also Plate 2007, 126–128.

63   Sheehy 1974a.

64   Sheehy 1976f, 143.

65   Sheehy 1976f, 108.

66   Sheehy 1976f, 241–242, 209–311. See similarly, on Friedan, Coontz 2011, 130–132.

67   Sheehy 1976f, 54, 63, see also 52–65, and for Arthur Mitchell, 235. See also Watlington's recollections of Sheehy's interviews, in Watlington 2006, 150–151, 170–171, 175–176.

68   Sheehy 1976f, 20.

69   Lemov 2015, 193.

70   Hapgood 1903; Hapgood 1909; see also Lindner 1996, 145, 150; Lemov 2015, 188–189. On life histories and the social scientific interview, see also Bulmer 1986, 89–108; Forrester 1999; Forrester 2016; Heesen 2014.

71   The two most influential statements on consciousness-raising were Sarachild 1970 and Allen 1970. See also Long 1999, 75–80, 98–100; and the critiques by Echols 1989, e.g., 83–98, 140–153; Herman 1996, 297–302.

72   The slogan plays on the early twentieth-century labor songwriter Joe Hill's "Don't Mourn—Organize!"; see Huckle 1991, 185, 195; Rosen 2000, 276.

73 For women's life histories: Ruddick and Daniels 1977; Sidel 1978. Beginning in 1977, the women's studies journal *Frontiers* published a series of special issues on women's oral history; see the compilation: Armitage, Hart, and Weathermon 2002. For an introduction and overview of women's life histories and feminist biographies: Long 1999, esp. 73–116.

74 Keller 1981; Keller 1983; see also Comfort 2001, 5.

75 Sheehy 2014, 133; see also Morgan 1970b.

76 Toffler 1970; Slater 1974.

77 On science writing as promotion: Nelkin 1987; Lewenstein 1992; Mellor 2003, 511–512.

78 Sheehy 1976f, 277.

79 Richard Baker, "Proposal for a Program [in Race Relations and the Mass Media]," November 27, 1967, Rockefeller Foundation Records, Rockefeller Archives, Sleepy Hollow, NY, A76/200, box 54, folder 400. On Columbia's science-writing program: Boylan 2007, 139–142.

80 "Report of the 1969–1970 Interracial Reporting Program of the Columbia University Graduate School of Journalism" [ca. 1970], Rockefeller Foundation Records, A76/200, box 54, folder 401. See also Gail Sheehy to Margaret Mead, April 26, 1971, Mead Papers, box C94, folder 1.

81 Wolfe 2008, 84; quoted in Robinson 1974, 71. On journalism and social science, see also Lindner 1996; Heesen 2014.

82 Sheehy 1976f, 16, 17. A similar statement has been attributed to Freud: "The poets and philosophers before me discovered the unconscious. What I discovered was the scientific method by which the unconscious can be studied." However, as Jeffrey Berman points out, this statement is nowhere to be found in Freud's writings; it started circulating in the 1940s and '50s; see Berman 1987, 304n40.

83 Weisstein 1970, 206. The paper was first read at a feminist conference, then at the 1968 American Studies Association (ASA) meeting, see Kitzinger 1993, 189. On the ovations at the ASA meeting: Weisstein 1989, 9. The paper was first published in pamphlet form: Weisstein 1968. See also 1993b; Herman 1996, 280–284; Rutherford, Vaughn-Blount, and Ball 2010; Cohen-Cole 2014, 228–230. On the history of the "3 K" slogan: Paletschek 2001.

84 Boxer 2002; Boxer 1998. The Princeton case is illustrative; see Malkiel 2016, 296–299.

85 Horner 1968; Horner 1970; Horner 1972; Hennig 1970; Hennig and Jardim 1977; Mitchell 1974; Bernard 1972; Sherfey 1972.

86 Sheehy 1976f, 18.

87 Erikson 1950a, 219–234; and the early presentation in Erikson 1950b. In the 1963 edition, Erikson spoke of "Eight Ages" instead of "Stages." For a comparison of his life-cycle model in 1950 and 1963: Friedman 1999, 336–337.

88 Erikson 1950b, 142; Erikson 1950a, 231.

89 Tiedeman and O'Hara 1963, 54.

90 Hodgson, Levinson, and Zaleznik 1965, 229, see also 31–37; Osipow 1973, 105–122.

91 Erikson 1950b, 143, 144.

92 Senn 1950, 38.

93 Senn 1950, 46–47. Erikson's subsequent psychohistorical biographies were of men only—Martin Luther, Mahatma Gandhi, Albert Einstein; see Erikson 1958; Erikson 1969; Erikson 1982.

94 Erikson 1961, 151; Friedman 1999, 222, 225.

95 Senn 1950, 38–39.

96 See, for example, Senn 1950, 62, 69–70.

97   Senn 1950, 72–73. On neo-Freudian perspectives on motherhood and child care in the 1950s, see Michel 1999; Stoltzfus 2003; Plant 2010; and especially Vicedo 2013.

98   Senn 1950, 74, 78. Historians have shown how Spock's permissive child-rearing ideology intensified maternal obligations by requiring mothers to provide care "on demand"; see Weiss 1977; Grant 1998, esp. 201–244; Apple 2006, 107–134; see also, on role differentiation, Graebner 1980b, 620–622.

99   Senn 1950, 293–294.

100   Friedan 1963a, 71–72 (my italics). Friedan also used Erikson to claim careers for women; see 322. On Friedan as Erikson's student: Horowitz 1998, 95–96.

101   Friedan 1963a, 322.

102   See the references to Friedan's *Feminine Mystique*: Rossi 1964, 613n; Degler 1964, 668–669; Bailyn 1964, 709n2.

103   Rossi 1964, 608.

104   Erikson 1964, 583 (my italics). Erikson's quote is from the last sentence of Friedan's chapter on women's identity crisis: "I think women had to suffer this crisis of identity . . . to become fully human" (Friedan 1963a, 72). See also Erikson's recollections: Erikson 1974a, 322.

105   Erikson 1964, 586.

106   Friedman 1999, 423; see also 423–426.

107   Herman 1996, 391n78; see also 293. For prominent criticism, see Gilligan 1977 and 1982c, 11–15, 98, 103–105, 107, 155.

108   Kant 1923, 54; see also 55–57.

109   See esp. Dinnerstein 1976; Miller 1976; Chodorow 1978; Benjamin 1988.

110   Bassin 1982, 200; Bassin 1988, 347–348; see also Buhle 1988, esp. 278–279.

111   Skinner 1969, 49; see also Latour 2005, esp. 21–156.

112   Erikson 1964, 588, 589. For a discussion of the experiment, see Erikson 1950a, 97–108; on his brief stint as a research associate at the Berkeley Guidance Study: Friedman 1999, 150–155.

113   Erikson 1964, 590, 591, 600.

114   Wolff 1979, 356.

115   Erikson 1968.

116   Weisstein 1968, 206; see also Bettelheim 1962.

117   Cited in Herman 1996, 289.

118   Greer 1970, 88. See also Hole and Levine 1971, 177–178; Chesler 1972, 76–77; Chodorow 1971, 167; as well as the later Caplan 1979; Wolff 1979; Hopkins 1980.

119   Millett 1970, 212; see also 210–220. This ambivalence was the starting point for criticism in Wolff 1979, esp. 355–358.

120   Janeway 1971, esp. 8, 28, 34–36, 93–96.

121   Erikson 1974a, 320. The text was republished in Erikson 1975, 225–247. "Womanhood and the Inner Space" was also reprinted in Strouse's volume; see Erikson 1974b.

122   Erikson 1968, 285; Erikson 1974a, 323.

123   Erikson 1974a, 327.

124   Friedan 1963a, 11.

125   Sheehy 1976f, 287, 306–319, 253–254, 348–350, 412–413.

126   Friedan 1963a, 332.

127   Sheehy 1976f, 309, 243.

128   Sheehy 1974a, 30, 33; Sheehy 1976f, 71–72, 83–84.

129   Sheehy 1974a, 35. See also Sheehy 1976f, 17.

130   Sheehy 1976f, 217; Vaillant and McArthur 1972, 421.

131   Sheehy 1976f, 234; Bernard 1972, esp. 15–53.

132   Sheehy 1976f, 345.

133   Sheehy 1976f, 327.

134   Sheehy 1976f, 19.

135   Sheehy 1976f, 36–37, 320–321.

136   Riesman, Glazer, and Denney 1950; Adorno et al. 1950; Mills 1951; Mills 1956; Whyte 1956. See also Wilson 1955. On Riesman's success: Gans 1998.

137   Mills 1951, 186–187.

138   Sheehy 1976f, 321.

139   Sheehy 1976f, 414–416.

140   Sheehy 1976f, 390–400; Millett 1970, 269–280.

141   Sheehy 1976f, 334.

142   Sheehy 1976f, 236.

143   Steinem 1970; see also the later *Ms.* "Special Issue on Men" 1975; as well as Dow 2014, 133–139; and Hogeland 1994.

144   Dow 2014, 134–135.

145   Friedan 1981, 159–160.

146   Sheehy 1976f, 361.

147   Cited in Gerhard 2013, 81, see also 81–83, 137–142, 217–219.

148   Barber 1968. For an older critique of the pyramid of power, see Mills 1956.

149   This argument runs through Scott's writing, for early formulations, see Scott 1983, esp. 145; Scott 1989, esp. 8–9; Scott 1996.

150   The original response is attributed to the Harvard Business School professor Rosabeth Moss Kanter: Steward 2011; see also Sandberg 2013, 104–121.

Chapter 4

1   Broyard 1976; Hassenger 1976, 30; O'Brien 1976.

2   In the 1970s, about 35 million Americans regularly read books, typically obtained from friends, relatives, or public libraries, so that many of the 3.9 million *Passages* copies in print by May 1978 were read by more than one or two people. On *Passages* sales: "PW Paperback Bestsellers" 1978; *Bowker Annual of Library & Book Trade Information* 1978, 434; reading statistics and habits: Gallup Organization 1978, 12; Yankelovich 1978, 17–18; Damon-Moore and Kaestle 1991.

3   This is how James Secord defines literary sensations in Secord 2000, 11–37, 39.

4   Markoutsas 1978, 1.

5   Echols 1989; Douglas 1994; Farrell 1998; Hogeland 1998; Bradley 2003; Dow 2014. For a contemporary critique of "mainstream feminism," see Zeisler 2016. Bernadette Barker-Plummer proposes a more dialogic approach to feminism and the media; see esp. Barker-Plummer 2010.

6   See esp. Meyerowitz 1993.

7   See also Weiss 2000. For rethinking the Second Wave, see esp. Laughlin et al. 2010; Hewitt 2010.

8   See, for example, recent historical studies on pseudo-science: Gordin 2012; Rupnow et al. 2008; Wessely 2014. On "boundary-work": Gieryn 1983.

9   Leo 1976. On Leo's authorship, see the letter by *Time* editor in chief Henry Grunwald to Gail Sheehy, May 18, 1976, Henry Grunwald Papers, Library of Congress, Washington, DC, box 6. Leo would soon lash out against Shere Hite's *Report on Male Sexuality* (1981) and is known for attacking *Thelma & Louise* (1991); see Leo 1981; Leo 1991; also Leo 1994, 235–264; Leo 2001, 101–121.

10   Robert E. Hinerfeld to Clay S. Felker, November 15, 1974, Felker Papers, box 2.

11   For a historical discussion of the idea-expression divide, see Biagioli 2011. On copyright and contract law: Kirsch 1995, 7–12; Vaidhyanathan 2003, 23, 33–34.

12   Sheehy 1974b, esp. 32.

13   Sheehy 1974a, 38; Gould 1972.

14   Sheehy 1974a, 38.

15   Gould 1972, 41.

16   Sheehy 1974a, 38.

17   Rossiter 1993; see also Gage 1870. On collaboration between scientific couples, see also Pycior, Slack and Abir-Am 1996; Lykknes, Opitz, Van Tiggelen 2012.

18   Sheehy 1974a, 33.

19   Gould 1975, 74. On how postwar permissive child-rearing ideology heightened maternal responsibilities, see the classic Weiss 1977.

20   Gould 1978.

21   Hinerfeld to Felker, 1974.

22   Ellis 2010, 485–490; Courlander 1979.

23   Leaffer 2009.

24   "*Passages* II" 1978.

25   Randall 2001, 29, also esp. 99–125.

26   Leo 1976, 66, 69.

27   Both quoted in Leo 1976, 69.

28   Quote in Leo 1976, 69, and "Book Ends" 1976.

29   Sheehy 1976e; Henry Grunwald to Gail Sheehy, May 18, 1976, Grunwald Papers, box 6; see also Sheehy 2014, 222.

30   Howard 2000, 475; Irigaray 1985.

31   Howard 2000. On plagiarism as male, see also Randall 2001, 272n4.

32   On Marie Skłodowska Curie, see Hemmungs Wirtén 2015, esp. 16–19, 32–37. On the women as "persons" and citizens, see Scott 1996; as well as Naffine 2004; Davies 2007; Hamilton 2009. On gender and patenting, Merritt 1991; Khan 1996; and also, on literary property, Homestead 2005. On gender, celebrity culture, and the public sphere: Berlanstein 2004, 2007; Brock 2006; Berenson and Gioli 2010.

33   Anderson 1998, 13; for scandal in cultural and intellectual history, see Surkis 2014.

34   Rosen 1980, 13.

35   Illig 1976. Illig also researched and reported on the publishing industries for *Publishers Weekly*, the Literary Guild Newsletter, the Book-of-the-Month Club News and others; see "Joyce Illig Bohn, Columnist" 1976; "Joyce Illig" 1976. For a comparison of book sections, see Pool 2009, esp. 16.

36   "Book Ends" 1976.

37   MacLeish 1976.

38   Sanborn 1976.

39   Davis 1984, 7; see also Weiss 1977, 540–541; Levey 2000, esp. 283–284. For Spock's sales: Weiss 1977, 520n3; Swinth 2018, 65.

40   Here, by Helen Witmer, director of the Fact Finding Committee of the Midcentury White House Conference on Children and Youth: Witmer 1950, 13.

41   Spock 1946.

42   Quoted in Davis 1984, 7.

43   Hulbert 1996.

44   Faegre 1946.

45   Quoted in Maier 1998, 155.

46   Aldrich 1946; Aldrich and Aldrich 1938. See also the reviews by Mackenzie 1946; Wegman 1946. On prewar permissive child-rearing advice, see Jensen 2014, 31.

47   Broyard 1976.

48   O'Brien 1976, 112; Sanborn 1976. For similar comparisons, see Colander 1976; Abraham 1978. For Gesell's stage theory, see his parenting guides: Gesell 1943; Gesell 1946.

49   Beck 1976; Beck 1967. On Beck: Breslin 1998.

50   Quoted in Maier 1998, 353; for an overview of feminist criticism, see 352–362.

51   O'Brien 1976, 112 (my italics).

52   Cady 1976, 1; Henkel 1976; Ryback 1976. On the dynamics of book reviewing, see Pool 2009, esp. 15–32.

53   For Hans Magnus Enzensberger, the printed book even encouraged the repression of opposition, see Enzensberger 1982, esp. 70–72.

54   Priscilla Coit Murphy's analysis of Rachel Carson's *Silent Spring* (1962) documents the relation between a book and other formats, see Murphy 2005, esp. 48–52, 155–156; see also Radway 1984, esp. 19–45; and Gérard Genette on the "public epitext": Genette 1997, esp. 344–346.

55   Tarde 1969, 304.

56   "PW Hardcover Bestsellers" 1976a; "Best Seller List" 1976; "PW Hardcover Bestsellers" 1976b.

57   Lague 1977; on marketing best-sellers in the 1960s and '70s: Miller 2000. *Passages* was a main selection of the Literary Guild, Macmillan, Psychology Today, and Contempo book clubs.

58   Lee Wohlfert, "Catch-30 and Switch-40s Are Just Two Stages of Growing Up Adult, Says Gail Sheehy," *People*, Felker Papers, box 2; Sheehy 2014, 226; C. Smith 1976.

59   Hassenger 1976, 30.

60   Sheehy 1972c; Maysles and Maysles 1975.

61   Maksian 1977.

62   Hassenger 1976, 30.

63   Steinem 1970.

64   Barker-Plummer 1995; Barker-Plummer 2002; Huddy 1997; for an overview: Bradley 2003.

65   Dow 2014, 2, 52–94, 120–143.

66   "Gloria Steinem" 1972.

67   On the consciousness-raising novel, see esp. Hogeland 1998; also Payant 1993; Whelehan 2005; Onosaka 2006.

68   Millett 1970; Firestone 1970; Greer 1970.

69   Davis 1984, 323. On the reception of Millett's *Sexual Politics*, see also Poirot 2004.

70   Boston Women's Health Book Collective 1976a; Davis 2007, 24.

71   Morgan 1970a.

72   Gornick and Moran 1971.

73   Davis 1984, 304–305.

74   Quoted in Pace 1972.

75   Howard 1973; "Review of *A Different Woman*" 1973. On Scharlatt: Howard 1974; Stern 1974.

76   Sheehy 2014, 210.

77   For critical appraisals of the "wave" chronology of feminism, see Laughlin et al. 2010; Hewitt 2010.

78   Echols 1989.

79   Willis 1975, 108; also 1975; on radical feminist opposition to *Ms.*: Echols 1989, 265–269; Farrell 1998, 81–83; Bradley 2003, 184–187.

80   Gloria Steinem to Gail Sheehy [n.d., c. 1980], Gloria Steinem Papers, Smith College Archives, Northampton, MA, box 90, folder 1; Sheehy 1980.

81   Farrell 1998; Hogeland 1998; Dow 2014; also McCracken 1993.

82   For an example of feminist media activism, see Barker-Plummer (1995, 2000) on NOW's media strategies.

83   Howard 1973, 409–410.

84   Creighton 1999; Lewis 2001; Waite and Nielsen 2001; Coontz 1992; Coontz 2005, 247–262; Self 2012. On women's education: Eisenmann 2006; Malkiel 2016; the "life-cycle squeeze": Oppenheimer 1974; Oppenheimer 1976; Oppenheimer 1977; retirement: Costa 1998, 6–31, 160–187; Graebner 1980a, 242–262; Atchley 1982.

85   Kohli 1986; Brückner and Mayer 2005.

86   Erikson 1950a; Friedman 1999, 240–241, 303, 351; Herman 1996, 293. On the "paperback revolution," see the classic Mercer 2011.

87   Coles 1970.

88   Fromm 1970, 21; T. Smith 1976, 5. For an account of Erikson's decline, see Friedman 1999, 420–423. A similar effect has been observed for other postwar social thinkers; see, on David Riesman and Abraham Maslow, respectively, Geary 2013; Weidman 2016. See also, for criticism of Benjamin Spock's psychoanalytic approach, Maier 1998, 352–361, 408–412.

89   Lunbeck 2014, esp. 224–251.

90   Demos 1993, 439; see also Manuel 1971; Weinstein and Platt 1975.

91   Friedman 1999, 434.

92   Quoted in Friedman 1999, 420, see also 426–436; Erikson 1975.

93   Berman 1975, 1. On Berman's review and its effects, see Friedman 1999, 426–436.

94   Roazen 1976, 109–110.

95   Roazen 1976, 115–116, 192.

96   Clare 1977, 557; Broyard 1976.

97   Lague 1977, 8; see also Marty 1978, K2.

98   "Class of 1961," 1976, 40; McCain 1977, 1; Lague 1977, 8.

99   On Friedan's reception, see Coontz 2011. On the omission of race in 1970s literature on professional women: King 2003; and on labor feminist agendas: Cobble 2004. On white middle-class women as a large and influential group of readers: Rubin 1992; Radway 1997; Bradley 2003, 5–7; also Gallup Organization 1978, 14; Yankelovich 1978, 26–28, 50–52; Damon-Moore and Kaestle 1991.

100   Cady 1976, 10; see also Hassenger 1976.

101   Miller 1976; Dinnerstein 1976; Friday 1977, 424. Shere Hite's controversial *Report on Female Sexuality* and Friedan's movement memoir *It Changed My Life* were also published that year; see Friedan 1976; Hite 1976.

102   Sheehy 1976g; Sheehy 1976b; Sheehy 1976c; Sheehy 1976d. On book extracts in *McCall's*: Faulstich and Strobel 1986, 56–57.

103   Sheehy 1976h; Sheehy 1976a. On book excerpts in *Playboy*: Faulstich and Strobel 1986, 40, 57–58.

104   Showalter 1998.

105   Sheehy 1976b; Sheehy 1977a. On *Reader's Digest,* see Shaw 1990.

106   McCabe 1977.

107   On book selection: Yankelovich 1978, 176–177; on the importance of magazine excerpts: Faulstich and Strobel 1986, 56; Murphy 2005; Polsgrove 2009; on book distribution: Radway 1984; Genette 1997.

108   Miller 1979, 56–60; Aronson 2010, esp. 40–44.

109   On *Glamour,* see White 1970, 248; McCracken 1993, 151–153; Endres 1995b; on *Bride's*: Endres 1995a; Howard 2006, 87–89, 97.

110   Meyerowitz 1993. On earlier women's magazines, see Aronson 2002; Scanlon 1995; Zuckerman 1998. See similarly on the Canadian *Chatelaine,* Korinek 2000; and on the German *Brigitte,* Müller 2010.

111   Friedan 1956. On *Cosmopolitan,* see Scanlon 2009; Landers 2010.

112   James 1958.

113   Moskowitz 1996.

114   Hobson 1983, 152–153. Hobson also wrote *Good Housekeeping's* literary column "Thumbing Through" and "Trade Winds" in the *Saturday Review of Literature.* On "Man Talk/Back Talk," see also Walker 2000, 165–166; Blix 1992, 63, 67–68.

115   Reprinted in Friedan 1976, 233–322. The *Ladies' Home Journal, McCall's,* and *Mademoiselle* had excerpted *The Feminine Mystique;* see Friedan 1962; Friedan 1963c; Friedan 1963b.

116   Sheehy 1970c; Faulstich and Strobel 1986, 57; Morgan 1972b; Morgan 1972a; see also Milam 2013.

117   Some of Pogrebin's columns are reprinted in Pogrebin 1975.

118   Boston Women's Health Book Collective 1976b; on *Redbook*: Kline 2010, 166n27.

119   Moran 1972, 25.

120   Anderson 1976; on *Family Circle's* conservatism, see Sammon 1969.

121   Butler and Paisley 1978; Farley 1978.

122   Macdonald 1995. See also Kathrin Friederike Müller's perceptive analysis in Müller 2010, 330, 336, 356–357.

123   Aronson 2010; on *McCall's* and the *Ladies' Home Journal* in particular, see White 1970, 250–51. On women's voices in the public sphere more generally: Fraser 1992.

124   Carter 1970. On the *Ladies' Home Journal* sit-in, see Jay 1970; Brownmiller 1999, 83–92; also Dow 2014, 95–119. On readers' letters as forums for debate, see Hynds 1991; Wahl-Jorgensen 2001; Wahl-Jorgensen 2007, esp. 66–67; and on reading instructions: Bourdieu and Chartier 1985, 221–223.

125   "Women's Lib and Me" 1970, 69.

126   Gail Sheehy, "'Vox Pop' on a Theory in Labor (IV)," November 6, 1974, Felker Papers, box 2; see also "Letters" 1974; "Letters from Readers" 1976, 16.

127   "Letters to the Editor" 1976b, 1976a.

128   Gail Sheehy, "'Vox Pop' on a Theory in Labor (III)," October 30, 1974, Felker Papers, box 2.

129   "Letters to the Editor" 1976b.

130   Quoted in Reger 2012, 55; see also O'Reilly 1971; on CR and emotions: Sarachild 1970; Allen 1970.

131   Ahmed 2013; see also Ahmed 2017, 21–31.

132   King 1976.

133   Weiss 2000, esp. 62–81, 188–222; see also Rupp 2001.

134   Sheehy 1976f; Mitgang 1977.

135 Bernard 1974, 127–129.

136 See the demographer Norman Ryder's influential work on "the cohort as a concept in the study of social change," first presented in 1959: Ryder 1965. For historical critiques of generational thinking: Parnes, Vedder, and Willer 2008, esp. 275–276; also Bouk 2018. On the impact of mothers in the 1970s: Weiss 2000, 206–207.

137 "Women's Lib and Me" 1970, 69.

138 McCain 1977.

139 Levey 1976, 52.

140 Quoted in Levey 1976, 52; see also King 1976, Gail Sheehy, "'Vox Pop' on a Theory in Labor (III)," October 30, 1974, Felker Papers, box 2.

141 For a forceful contemporary version of this argument, see Donath 2017.

142 Sheehy 1976g.

143 Sheehy 1976d, 88.

144 Stoll 1973b; Stoll 1973a.

145 Dietz 1973. Sheehy's op-ed "Divorced Mothers as a Political Force" (1971) was included in an anthology on *The Future of the Family*, see Sheehy 1972b.

146 In addition, some of the reviews in newspapers and magazines were written by psychological and psychiatric experts, see Ryback 1976; Clare 1977.

147 Bernard 1981, 168; Bernard referred to her earlier study of remarriage, see Bernard 1956, esp. 277–278. For a historical perspective on feminist and women's studies journals, see McDermott 1994.

148 Campbell 1976; see also Campbell 1973; on Campbell's work: Eisenmann 2006, 210–227.

149 Wachowiak 1977, 376.

150 Guild and Neiman 1976.

151 Fleck 1979, 112. See also Shinn and Whitley 1985; Cooter and Pumfrey 1994. On "popularization" and communication between specialists: Bunders and Whitley 1985.

152 On journalism and social science, see Lindner 1996; on "everyday psychology": Ash and Sturm 2007, 9–11.

153 Danto 2009, 26–37.

154 Fava 1973, 122. Note the different use of the term in Basalla 1976.

155 Kasinsky 1977, 239.

156 MacLeish 1976.

157 Kimmel 1977, 492, 493.

158 Levine 1977, 285.

159 Chapman 1977, 75, 76.

160 Guild and Neiman 1976, 34–35.

161 See esp. studies of pseudo-science: Gordin 2012; Rupnow et al. 2008; Wessely 2014; also Gieryn 1983.

162 See esp. Vaillant 1977a; Levinson 1978c; Gould 1979.

163 Milliot 2014.

164 Combaz 1978.

165 Lasch 1978, 48, 214, see also 45–50, 209–214; as well as Lasch's previous *Passages* review, Lasch 1976; and his book-length critique of changing family lifestyles, Lasch 1977.

166 Narr 1980, 71.

167 Sheehy 1984. For more critique of Lasch's gender politics, see Breines, Cerullo, and Stacey 1978; Engel 1980; Hochschild 1983, 195–196; Gornick 1980; Barrett and McIntosh 1985.

168 Heilbrun 1979, 178.

169 Wolfe 1976. On narcissism in particular, see Lunbeck 2014, esp. 74–77. See also Buhle 1998, 280–317; Zaretsky 2007, 183–221; Aubry and Travis 2015, 1–23, esp. 8–14; Cooper 2017, 8–12. The claim that feminism was "kitchen psychology" also implied that serious science maintained the social order; see Schmidt 2018.

170 Taylor 1989, 507–508, 81n48. See also Marty 1978; Hochschild 1983, 56, 75.

Chapter 5

1 Sheehy 1978; Pecile 1978.

2 See, for example, Whitbourne 2010, 160–169; Cohen 2012, 12, 115–116; Mintz 2015, 300; Hagerty 2016, 19; Setiya 2017, 11–12.

3 On boundary work, see Gieryn 1983. On the demarcation between science and popularization in particular: Hilgartner 1990; Cooter and Pumfrey 1994; Secord 2004; Topham 2009.

4 Beal 1977.

5 Prescott 2007, 30–46; on the Grant Study, 19–27.

6 Heath 1945, esp. 59–60 and figures I–IV.

7 Vaillant 1977a, 366; Klemesrud 1977; Shenk 2009; Saur 2013, 38.

8 For a detailed history of the Grant Study, see Eva Milofsky, "The Grant Study: A Panoramic View after Half a Century" (1985), Harvard Grant Study, William T. Grant Foundation Records, Rockefeller Archives, Sleepy Hollow, NY, box 6a, folder 44. See also Vaillant 1977a, 30–52; Vaillant 2012, 54–107. In 2003, Robert Waldinger succeeded Vaillant as director of the Grant Study, which is now administered at Massachusetts General Hospital.

9 See Woods, Brouha, and Seltzer 1943. The key Grant Study publications before Vaillant's *Adaptation* were Heath 1945; Hooton 1945; Monks 1957.

10 Milofsky, "The Grant Study," 29; Grant Study Questionnaire, May 1964, Grant Study Records, box 6a, folder 51.

11 Lemov 2015, here 248.

12 Proposal by Charles McArthur, 1968, Grant Study Records, box 6a, folder 51.

13 The Grant Study was evaluated in November 1971 by Orville Brim, John Clausen, Ernest Haggard and Jerome Kagan. See Philip Sapir to Orville Brim, John A. Clausen, Ernest Haggard and Jerome Kagan, November 1, 1971, John Clausen to Philip Sapir, November 22, 1971, and Orville Brim to Philip Sapir, November 30, 1971; Grant Study Records, box 6a, folder 48.

14 Philip Sapir to George E. Vaillant, June 24, 1971, Grant Study Records, box 6a, folder 48.

15 Freud 1937. Vaillant's prizewinning essay was titled "A Theoretical Hierarchy of Adult Ego Mechanisms of Defense"; see "Progress Report," 1969, Grant Study Records, box 6a, folder 49. Vaillant continued to publish on ego-mechanisms of defense; see Vaillant 1986; Vaillant 1992.

16 Vaillant 1977a, 195–236.

17 Charles Elliott, "Daniel Levinson" [1974], Alfred A. Knopf, Inc. Records, Harry Ransom Center, University of Texas at Austin, box 795, folder 7. "A Psychosocial Study of the Male Mid-Life Decade" was funded by the National Institute of Mental Health from 1969 to 1973: National Institute of Mental Health 1969–72 (1969, 15; 1970,

14; 1971, 14; 1972, 16); Levinson 1978c, xi. Sheehy learned about Levinson's project in spring 1973, see Sheehy 1974a, 35.

18 Friedan 1993, 110; Adorno et al. 1950.

19 On the legacy of *The Authoritarian Personality*: Cohen-Cole 2014, esp. 35–62; on non-conformity and management theory: Frank 1997.

20 See Samuel Osipow's overview of organizational psychology in the 1970s: Osipow 1973.

21 Hodgson, Levinson, and Zaleznik 1965; Klerman and Levinson 1969. For similar work in the field, see Rapoport 1970.

22 Levinson 1978c, 12.

23 On the companies, see "Executives, Workers, Biologists, Novelists," n.d., Knopf Records, box 795, folder 7.

24 Jack Shepherd to Charles Elliott, May 2, 1976, Knopf Records, box 795, folder 7.

25 Levinson 1978c, 16.

26 Levinson 1978c, 65–66, 112–125, 166–170, 305–313.

27 Levinson 1978c, 322, 13.

28 Gould 1978.

29 Vaillant 1977a, 220. On criticism of conformity in postwar social science, see Cohen-Cole 2014.

30 Wilson 1955; see Martschukat 2011.

31 On *Playboy* and youthfulness: Osgerby, 139–141; on "youth" and consumerism more generally: Frank 1997, esp. 24–25, 120–121, 171–175.

32 Vaillant 1977a, 221, 223, 100. On *Playboy* and architecture, Preciado 2014; on masculinity and imperial fantasies of exploration: Pratt 1992; Kroll 2008, esp. 9–36. See also the contemporary advice on emerging offshore financial centers in the Caribbean: Grundy 1974; Langer 1975.

33 Levinson 1978c, 294.

34 Gould 1978, 267.

35 On the end of *Playboy* in the 1970s: Fraterrigo 2009, 167–204; its afterlife: Preciado 2014, 215–223.

36 Martschukat 2011, 22. On the typical *Playboy* reader: Pitzulo 2011, 72, 82; Fraterrigo 2009, 50. On style and aspiration: Wilson 1985, esp. 246; Craik 1993, 50–51.

37 Levinson et al. 1974, 255; Gould 1978, 221.

38 Vaillant 1977a, 220–221, 216–217.

39 Vaillant 1977a, 220, 222 (my emphasis).

40 Hall 1904. See also Kett 1978, esp. 173–198; DeLuzio 2007, 95–113.

41 Vaillant 1977a, 205, 387.

42 Levinson et al. 1974.

43 Levinson 1978c, 256.

44 For Levinson's description of a man's midlife breakaway from his professional mentor, see Levinson 1978c, 96–101, 147–149.

45 Levinson 1978c, 109, 110. On the "Dream," see Levinson 1978c, 91–97.

46 Levinson 1978c, 110, 232.

47 Levinson 1978c, 248.

48 Levinson 1978c, 92–93; see Winnicott 1988; Winnicott 1965; Winnicott 1971, esp. 10–11.

49 Levinson 1978c, 109.

50 Levinson et al. 1974, 255.

51 Levinson 1978c, 237, 256.

52   On the "ordinary devoted mother," see esp. Winnicott 1988; on the devaluation of motherhood as instinctual: Vicedo 2013.

53   On the "girl next door": Fraterrigo 2009, 105–133; Preciado 2014, 51–65. See also Ouellette 1999.

54   Levinson 1978c, 164; Gould 1978, 269.

55   Levinson 1978c, 256.

56   Connell 1994, esp. 22.

57   Levinson 1978c, 258.

58   Levinson 1978c, 124, 118; Vaillant 1977a, 66, 155.

59   Levinson 1978c, 118.

60   Levinson 1978c, 58, 256n21.

61   Vaillant 1977a, 320–326, 223.

62   English 1967. See similarly Bach and Wyden 1968, 263–274; Neubeck 1969.

63   O'Neill and O'Neill 1972; for an analysis of the problems entailed in criminalizing adultery, see also Rhode 2016.

64   Handwritten comments in a copy of Levinson's *Seasons* in Widener Library, Harvard University, call number WID LC BF 724.6 .S 42 1978.

65   Vaillant 1977a, 66–67.

66   Sheehy 1976f, 129.

67   Levin 1983, 52; Wright 1979, vii–ix.

68   Sheehy 1976f, 328.

69   Sheehy 1976f, 436n7. See also Marmor 1974, 75; Vaillant 1977a, 80–81, 83, 383.

70   Sheehy 1976f, 170.

71   Quoted in "Three Sticky Subjects" 1978.

72   Scarf 1976b, 281; reprint of Scarf 1972. The focus on men in studies on heart disease had a similar effect, conveying to women the message that coronary disease could make them widows; see Epstein 2007, 59–60.

73   Brown 1987.

74   Levinson 1978c, 157, 199.

75   Gould 1978, 269, 274, 275.

76   Gilligan 1982c, esp. 151–152.

77   Levinson 1978c, 8–9, 24; Scarf 1976a, 226. See similarly Vaillant 1977a, 220, 224.

78   Gergen 1997, 475.

79   Levinson and Levinson 1996. See also Brown 1987.

80   Vaillant 1977a, 13, 202; see also Muson 1977, 48–49; Prescott 2002, 25.

81   Gould 1978, esp. 229–262.

82   Mead 1957. The piece was excerpted from *How to Succeed with Women without Really Trying* (1957), then reprinted in the September 1963 issue, possibly in response to Friedan's *The Feminine Mystique*.

83   Quoted in Fraterrigo 2009, 125.

84   Wylie 1963; see Fraterrigo 2009, 124–127. On "Momism" and careers: Plant 2010.

85   Levinson 1978c, 257. On the "new impotence": Nobile 1972; McLaren 2007, 227–234.

86   Gould 1978, 332–333. On "feminist-taming therapy," see Faludi 1991, 348–352.

87   Gould 1978, 333–334.

88   Vaillant 1977a, 222–223. On "media sensationalism" as a means of scientific demarcation: Green 1985.

89   Rossi 1980, 10, and also 6.

90   Sheehy 1974a, 35; Sheehy 1976f, xi.

91   AMS to Charles Elliott, May 21, 1974, Knopf Records, box 795, folder 7. See Fried 1967; LeShan 1973.

92   Charles Elliott to Robert Gottlieb, October 27, 1975, Knopf Records, box 795, folder 7.

93   "Knopf Editorial Fact Sheet," September 1977, Knopf Records, box 795, folder 8.

94   Gould 1978, 14–15; Gould 1972.

95   Smith 1983.

96   Smith 1983, C6.

97   "Report of the Task Force on Self-Help Therapies," submitted to the American Psychological Association, October 1978, Gerald Rosen, personal collection, 1–2. See also Rosen 1978; Rosen 2004.

98   On boundary work and "popularization": Gieryn 1983; Hilgartner 1990; on gender and "popular science," Gates and Shteir 1997; Gates 1998; Maitzen 1998; Lightman 2007, esp. 95–165; science: Rossiter 1982; Kohlstedt 1995; Laslett et al. 1996; technology: Oldenziel 1999; Ensmenger 2010; and medicine: Morantz-Sanchez 1985; Reverby 1987.

99   Rosenblum 1979.

100 Levinson's *Seasons* was distributed by the *Playboy*, *Psychology Today*, and Macmillan book clubs, see Anne McCormick to Charles Elliott, November 7, 1977, and Debbie to Charles, November 15 and December 5, 1977, Knopf Records, box 795, folder 8. *Seasons* was also excerpted in *Esquire*; see Levinson 1978a. For the *Psychology Today* excerpts: Gould 1975; Vaillant 1977b; Levinson 1978b.

101 Though never listed as such, Levinson's *Seasons* was sometimes called a "national best-seller"; see, for example, Raymond 1980.

102 Cain 1979, 548.

103 Cain 1979, 548; Lingeman 1978, 544. Lingeman's article did not mention specific titles, but was printed right next to a review of Levinson's *Seasons*.

104 Maas 1979, 190; Maas and Kuypers 1974.

105 Bunke 1978, 6. See also Allen 1978, 545.

106 Jay 1977.

107 Comfort 1978. See also the response by Levinson's Yale colleague: Newton 1978.

108 Kanigel 1978.

109 Rhodes 1978; see Kinsey, Pomeroy, and Martin 1948.

110 Gartner 1978.

111 Kanigel 1978.

112 On the standards of science writing and popular science: Nelkin 1987, esp. 14–32; Hilgartner 1990; Lewenstein 1992; Kiernan 2006.

113 Rose 1980.

114 Gartner 1978.

115 Krier 1978.

116 Cryer 1978.

117 Pecile 1978; see also Scarf 1978.

118 Richardson 1979, 915. See also Richardson 1977; Richardson 1991; and, for another example of feminist scientists' critique of a popular work, Milam 2013, 229–230, 233.

119 Faludi 1991, esp. 89–124, 345–371.

120 Faludi 1991, 76, see 73–79; also: Connell 1995, 84; Traister 2000.

121 Quoted in Faludi 1991, 79.

122 Donohugh 1981. See also Osherson 1980; Barnett 1981; Pesmen 1984; Nichols 1986; Sharp 1988.

123　McLellan 1982.

124　Nolen 1968; Nolen 1972; Nolen 1976.

125　Nolen 1980; Nolen 1981.

126　Lauerman 1984.

127　Lewis 1984; Nolen 1984.

128　Christy 1984.

129　Lauerman 1984.

130　Lauerman 1984. On the children, see Christy 1984; Nolen 1968.

131　"Hospital Offers Treatment for Mid-life Crisis" 1987.

132　Sifford 1985. See also Nolen 1984.

133　Quoted in Bawden 1988, 202–203.

134　Setiya 2017, 11–12.

135　Elkind 1994, 193; Giele 1980, 153. On the uses and functions of disciplinary histories, see esp. Graham, Lepenies, and Weingart 1983.

136　Sheehy 1976f.

Chapter 6

1　Weissman 1979; American Psychiatric Association 1980; see also Bookspan and Kline 1999, 1238–1313; Hirshbein 2009. On backlash in the 1980s, see Faludi 1991.

2　Brown 1981; Brown et al. 1982; Agassi et al. 1982; Brown and Kerns 1985; see also Brown 1963.

3　Bernard 1981, 169, see also 141–147, 168–175.

4　O'Rand and Henretta 1982, 58.

5　Neustadtl 1986. On backlash in the 1980s, see Faludi 1991.

6　Hess 1985, 7.

7　Gilligan 1982c.

8　Levinson and Levinson 1996.

9　Sheehy 1992.

10　Wethington 2000; see also Wethington, Kessler, and Pixley 2004.

11　Gilligan 1994, 409; quoted in Bromell 1985, 14.

12　For Gilligan's biography, see Gilligan 2009a; Gilligan 2009b; Gilligan 2011.

13　Mischel and Gilligan 1964; Gilligan 1964; see also Mischel 2014, 73–75.

14　Gilligan et al. 1971; Kohlberg and Gilligan 1971; Kohlberg and Gilligan 1977. On teaching for Erikson: Friedman 1999, 426.

15　Gilligan 1982c, 1.

16　Gilligan 1982c, 2–3, 158.

17　Gilligan 1982c, 2–3; Gilligan 1982b, 21–23. For debates about women dropping out of higher education: Patterson and Sells 1973; Eisenmann 2006, 62, 99–100; Rossiter 2012, 99–100; on coeducation: Malkiel 2016.

18　Gilligan 2009b.

19　Gilligan 1982c, 3, 71–72, 109; Gilligan 1982b, 27; see also Belenky 1978; and on post-*Roe* optimism: Schoen 2015, 23–154.

20　Gilligan 1982c, 3, 72, 108, 74–75. For the Heinz dilemma: Kohlberg 1981.

21　*Constitutional Amendments Relating to Abortion: Hearings on S.J. Res. 18, S.J. Res. 19, and S.J. Res. 110 before the Subcomm. on the Constitution of the S. Comm. on the Judiciary*, 97th Cong. 329–378 (1981) (testimony of Vincent Rue, associate professor of family relations, UCLA). See also Siegel 2008, 1657–1658.

22 McKinney [1981?]. See also Haugeberg 2017, 40–45; Schoen 2015, esp. 146–150, 204–205. On abortion stigma and abortion silence, see Kumar, Hessini and Mitchell 2009 and Beynon Jones 2017, respectively; also Millar 2017.

23 Donath 2017, 57; see also 3, 15, 52–58.

24 For a comparison of the pro-choice and "pro-life" movements: Luker 1984, esp. 92–191.

25 Rains 1971; Furstenberg 1976; see also Luker 1975.

26 Gilligan 1982c, 85; see also 75–98, 109–124.

27 Gilligan 1982b, 22.

28 See, for example, Buhle 2000, 262–269; Dow 1996, 164–202. Similarly, histories of abortion do not mention or discuss Gilligan; see, for example, Luker 1984; Reagan 1997; Schoen 2015.

29 For a similar line of argument, see Donath 2017, esp. xxv, 1–28.

30 On maternalist feminism, see above, 44–45; on gender and morality in jurisprudence: Schnädelbach 2017, 197–208.

31 Gilligan 1982c, xii, see also 48–49, 168–170; Miller 1976, 83; see also Miller 1973; Buhle 1998, esp. 267–269.

32 Miller 1976, 83.

33 Chodorow 1978, 37, 180–190; see Gilligan 1982c, 7–11; also: Buhle 1998, 242–244, 249–265.

34 Ruddick 1980; Ruddick 1989.

35 Keller 1983; Keller 1985; Haraway 1988; Haraway 1989; Harding 1986.

36 Gilligan 1994, 409.

37 On consciousness-raising: Herman 1996, 297–303; feminist "confessions": Felski 1989, 86–121. See also "The Feminist Memoir Project": DuPlessis and Snitow 1998.

38 Bromell 1985, 15.

39 Quoted in Robb 1980, 70. On psychosomatic perspectives on pregnancy, see Malich 2017.

40 Gilligan 1977; Haan 1975; Haan 1977; Holstein 1976; Simpson 1974; on cultural bias: Edwards 1975.

41 For Kohlberg's stages of moral development, see Kohlberg 1969b; Kohlberg 1969a; Kohlberg 1976; Kohlberg 1981; also the classic scoring manual: Colby and Kohlberg 1987–88.

42 Kohlberg and Kramer 1969, 108.

43 Gilligan 1982c, 1.

44 Gilligan 1982c, 73; Kohlberg 1976.

45 Gilligan 1982c, 73–100.

46 Broughton 1983, 635.

47 Quoted in Bromell 1985, 15.

48 Kuhn 1962; Isaac 2012.

49 On Kuhn's psychology readings: Isaac 2012, 216–217; Kaiser 2016. On his use in psychology: Faye 2012; in psychoanalysis: Lunbeck 2014, 53.

50 On falsification: Popper 1963.

51 For feminist uses of Kuhn: Giele 1982a, 199; Harding 1986; Longino 2003; also Friedan 1997.

52 Kerber et al. 1986, 325. On adolescence: Offer 1969; Offer and Offer 1975.

53 Gilligan 1982c, 3.

54 Gilligan 1977, 481.

55 Blos 1967; Blos 1979.

56   Gilligan 1982c, 160.

57   Gilligan 1982c, 171.

58   Gilligan 1982c, 160.

59   Gilligan, cited in Bromell 1985, 44.

60   Kuhn 1962, 150, 126–127.

61   Gilligan 1982c, 48, xiii, 22, 43.

62   Gilligan 1982c, 154; Vaillant 1977a, 400.

63   Gilligan 1982c, 154. Gilligan's use of "adaptation" was informed by Piaget's theory of learning, e.g., Piaget 1980.

64   Gilligan 1982b, 23.

65   Ehrenreich 1983, 169. For contemporary views of marriage and commitment, see also Pearce 1978; Swidler 1980; Swidler 2001; Quinn 1982.

66   Gilligan 1982c, 16, 171.

67   Gilligan 1982a; see also Giele 1982b.

68   Gilligan 1982c, 170; also Notman 1982, 142.

69   Gilligan 1982b, 25. For a critique of achievement motivation: Gilligan 1982c, 14–15; see also Simmons 2016, 120–121.

70   Gilligan 1982c, 98, 153.

71   Cited in Vaillant 2012, 149.

72   On "In a Different Voice" as a Citation Classic: Gilligan 2009a. For "Woman's Place in Man's Life Cycle": Gilligan 1979, "Past Distinguished Publication Awards," Association for Women in Psychology, https://www.awpsych.org/distinguished _publication.php (accessed December 19, 2017).

73   Robb 1980.

74   Gilligan 1982d; Tavris 1982; Gross 1982.

75   Goodman 1982a.

76   Haste 1994, 339.

77   Milbauer 1983.

78   "Washington Best Sellers" 1984; Goodman 1982b; also, Mann 1983; Auerbach et al. 1985. For a historical perspective on Reagan's "gender gap": Chappell 2012.

79   Rodgers 2011, 163; Butler 1990.

80   Faludi 1991, 365; Rosen 2013.

81   Noddings 1984; Belenky et al. 1986; Ruddick 1989.

82   Key works from the Project on Women's Psychology and Girls' Development include Gilligan, Ward, and Taylor 1988; Gilligan, Lyons, and Hanmer 1989; Gilligan, Rogers, and Tolman 1991; Brown and Gilligan 1992; Taylor, Gilligan, and Sullivan 1996; Brown 1998; Lamb 2001; Brown 2003. On the Gender Equity in Education Act, see the influential report by the American Association of Women 1992, esp. 20–21, 114, 144.

83   On abortion and the American Psychoanalytic Association: Buhle 1998, 274.

84   England 1999, esp. 266–267; Prose 1990, 45.

85   Kohlberg 1982, 513. On gender: Walker 1984.

86   On child development: Astington, Harris, and Olson 1988; Tomasello 2009; adolescence: Offer and Sabshin 1984; Apter 1990.

87   Wing 1974; Wing and Gould 1979; Newson and Newson 1975; Tager-Flusberg, Baron-Cohen, and Cohen 1993; for a historical perspective: Evans 2017, 285–316; Silverman 2012; Göhlsdorf 2014.

88   Bellah et al. 1985. On self and society in the 1980s, see Thomson 2000, esp. 107–120, and Thomson 2005; Rodgers 2011.

89　Swidler 1980, 127, 130; see also Swidler 2001.

90　Yankelovic 1981, 237.

91　Gergen 1991, 146.

92　Lasch 1992, 36.

93　Sassen 1980; see Gilligan 1982c, 14–15.

94　Horner 1970; Horner 1972; see also Symonds 1974; Moulton 1977; Moulton 1986; as well as Buhle 1998, 271–274; Simmons 2016.

95　Kerber et al. 1986, 315–316. See also Maccoby 1968; Maccoby and Jacklin 1974.

96　Kerber et al. 1986, 306, 309.

97　Kerber et al. 1986, 321–324; see Gilligan 1982, 168–169; Stack 1974.

98　See also Auerbach et al. 1985.

99　On controversy, ambiguity, and success in social science: Davis 1971, 1986; for Gilligan: Davis 1992, 221–222.

100　Weed and Schoor 1994; Young 1998; Stone 2004.

101　For an overview of the case from 1973–79, see Milius 1979.

102　*EEOC v. Sears, Roebuck, & Co.*, 628 F. Supp. 1264 (N. D. Ill. 1986), 1308.

103　McDermott 1994, 142–157; see also Faludi 1991, 411–422.

104　Salholz 1986, 59; see also Faludi 1991, 342.

105　Kerber et al. 1986, 326, 325.

106　Gilligan 2009b.

107　Schiebinger 1999, 3, 5; see also Faludi 1991, 329–342; and, on the reception of Keller's *Feeling for the Organism*, Comfort 2001, 6–7.

108　Baruch, Barnett, and Rivers 1983, 241.

109　Shaevitz 1984. On Superwoman and backlash, see Faludi 1991, 57–60; on "hard choices": Gerson 1985.

110　Morris 1981a.

111　Mellin 1984; Morris 1981b.

112　Kanter 1977, 16–17. On heart disease: Schiebinger 1999, 113; Epstein 2007, 47–48, 60.

113　On the strains of domesticity, see Kury 2012, 136–142; "menstrual stress": Jackson 2013, 81, 203–204. For earlier constructions of gender and exhaustion: Myerson 1920; Wylie 1942; historical perspectives: Barke, Fribush, and Stearns 2000, 570–571; Plant 2010.

114　Haseltine 1997; Schiebinger 1999, 116–117.

115　Jackson 2013, 201–203.

116　Rivers 1983.

117　Barnett 1967; Barnett 1971; Baruch 1973a; Baruch 1973b.

118　Barnett and Baruch 1978a.

119　Rivers, Barnett, and Baruch 1979.

120　Cook and Fonow 1986, 13; see also Baruch and Kaufman 1987; Richardson 1991, 284.

121　Baruch, Barnett, and Rivers 1983, 3; see also Barnett and Baruch 1978b.

122　Baruch, Barnett, and Rivers 1983, 17–18.

123　Baruch, Barnett, and Rivers 1983, 4–9.

124　Baruch, Barnett, and Rivers 1983, 265.

125　Worell 2000, 189. For earlier feminist uses of mental health, see Jahoda and Grant 1955; Jahoda 1958.

126　Worell 2000, 189; Worell 1978; Worell 1988. On the politics of well-being, see Davies 2015; Alexandrova 2017.

127　Baruch, Barnett, and Rivers 1983, 4–5, 12–22, 58–59, 80–82.

128   Goode 1960; Slater 1963; Coser 1974.

129   Sieber 1974; Marks 1977.

130   Verbrugge 1982; Thoits 1983; Crosby 1984; Gove and Zeiss 1987.

131   Quoted in Goleman 1984, C2. See also Barnett and Baruch 1985; Baruch and Barnett 1986b; Baruch, Biener, and Barnett 1987.

132   Fields 1981.

133   Rivers quoted in Longcope 1984; see also Baruch, Barnett, and Rivers 1983, 59–64, 144–145; for a similar argument about housekeeping: Cowan 1983. For feminist appropriations of "superwoman" in the late twentieth century: Schiebinger 1999, 94–95; Lepore 2014, 283–296; and before: Delap 2007, 249–291.

134   Quoted in Fields 1981.

135   Baruch, Barnett, and Rivers 1983, 24.

136   Baruch, Barnett, and Rivers 1983, 146, 148–149.

137   Baruch and Kaufman 1987, 56.

138   Daston and Vidal 2004, 10.

139   Barnett and Rivers 2004; see also Barnett and Rivers 2011.

140   Baruch, Barnett, and Rivers 1983, 237.

141   Baruch, Barnett, and Rivers 1983, 237–238.

142   Baruch, Barnett, and Rivers 1983, 241.

143   Baruch, Barnett, and Rivers 1983, 239, 241; Pearlin and Johnson 1977; see also Whitbourne 1986, 7–12.

144   Pollock 1988, 383. On stress in the 1980s, see also Jackson 2013, esp. 4–10, 181–264.

145   Baruch, Barnett, and Rivers 1983, 234–235.

146   Rahe et al. 1964; Holmes and Rahe 1967. On the history of "life events": Cooper and Dewe 2004, 41–51; Jackson 2013, 188–198; Hayward 2014; in popular culture: Brown 2005.

147   Dohrenwend and Dohrenwend 1969; Dohrenwend and Dohrenwend 1974; Dohrenwend and Dohrenwend 1981; see also Srole et al. 1962; Duhl 1963; Rabkin and Struening 1976; Theorell 1976. On studies about the impact of urbanization on health: Ramsden 2014.

148   Kanner et al. 1981; Kanner et al. 1987.

149   Baruch, Barnett, and Rivers 1983, 245.

150   Baruch and Barnett 1978a, 16.

151   Baruch, Barnett, and Rivers 1983, 248; see also Baruch and Barnett 1986b and 1988; on reentry in the 1980s and '90s: Wheeler 1997, 116–117.

152   Friedan 1983, xxiii–xxiv; see also Tyrer et al. 1983, 190; Friedan 1993, 139–140; as well as Crosby 1991.

153   United States Census Bureau 1986, 6; Gerson 1985; Machung 1989, 43.

154   Baruch and Barnett 1983.

155   Gove and Tudor 1973.

156   Barnett and Baruch 1987, 125; see also Baruch and Barnett 1981; Baruch and Barnett 1986a; Barnett and Rivers 1998, esp. 55–85; Rosenfield 1980.

157   Riesman, Glazer, and Denney 1950, 246.

158   Catalyst 1987; Hochschild 1989, 278–279.

159   Machung 1989, esp. 46–47.

160   Hochschild 1989, 277, 30, xiii; on Baruch and Barnett, see 3, 286.

161   Hochschild 1989, xiii, 7–9.

162   Hochschild 1989, esp. 231–235.

163   Vaillant 1985; Vaillant 1992; Vaillant 1993; Vaillant 2002; Vaillant 2012.

164 Maheu et al. 2005, 179. See also Gould 1986; Colby, Gould, and Aronson 1989; Gould 1990a; Gould 1990b; Gould 1992.

165 Quoted in Newton 1994, 147.

166 Levinson and Levinson 1996, xi–xiii.

167 Levinson and Levinson 1996, 3.

168 Levinson and Levinson 1996, 3, 35.

169 Quoted in See 1996.

170 Quoted in Forman 1988.

171 Levinson and Levinson 1996, 372.

172 Bean and Fox 1988.

173 Quoted in Forman 1988.

174 Sheehy 1992; see also Sheehy 1991; Watkins 2007a, 235–238.

175 Sheehy 1986; Sheehy 1988; Sheehy 1989; Sheehy 1990.

176 Sheehy 1992, 8–14, 66–94.

177 Sheehy 1992, 145–147.

178 Sheehy 1992, 46–47.

179 Sheehy 1992, 7.

180 Sheehy 1992, 21–23, 35–37.

181 Sheehy 2014, 365.

182 Greer 1991.

183 Sheehy 1992, 135, and see 40–41, 135–150.

184 Sheehy 1992, 138, 151–153.

185 Watkins 2007a, 222.

186 Sheehy 2014, 370.

187 Sheehy 2014, 372.

188 Sheehy 1996; Sheehy 1998; Sheehy 2006; Sheehy 2010.

189 See, for example, Fodor and Franks 1990; Friedan 1993; Apter 1995. For memoirs: Brown 1993; Jong 1994.

190 Brim 1992, 171. Primary Midmac members were the psychologists Paul Baltes, Margie Lachman, Hazel Markus, Carol Ryff, the sociologists David Featherman and Alice Rossi, the medical scholars William Hazzard and Michael Marmot, the medical sociologists Paul Cleary and Ronald Kessler, the demographer Larry Bumpass, and the anthropologist Richard Shweder; see "Changing Family and Work Life During Middle Age" (1994), *Midmac Bulletin* 2, Paul Baltes Papers, Archives of the Max Planck Society, Berlin.

191 See esp. Baltes 1987. On gerontological visions of growth more generally: Park 2016; also Achenbaum 1995; Katz 1996.

192 MIDUS is the most downloaded dataset from the National Archive of Computerized Data on Aging (NACDA), located within the Inter-university Consortium for Social Science Research (ICPSR) data archive. For a full bibliography of publications using MIDUS data, see the study website, MIDUS.Wisc.edu, or the repository, ICPSR .UMich.edu (accessed December 19, 2017). See also Brim 2004; Radler 2014; and for key Midmac publications, Rossi 1994; Lachman and James 1997; Shweder 1998; Rossi 2001.

193 "Release of the Midmac MIDUS Findings," February 1999, Paul Baltes Papers.

194 "Release of the Midmac MIDUS Findings."

195 "Media Summary: MacArthur Research Network on Successful Midlife Development," February 16–March 31, 1999, Paul Baltes Papers.

196 See, for example, Lachman's comprehensive *Handbook of Midlife Development* (2001).

197 Setiya 2017, 14; see similarly Cohen 2012, 129–130.

198 Wethington 2000, esp. 90, 95, 97–98.

199 Wethington 2000, 91–92.

200 Wethington 2000, 92–93.

201 "MacArthur Foundation Research Network on Successful Midlife Development" [n.d., ca. 1999], Paul Baltes Papers.

202 Grace Baruch and Rosalind Barnett, "Women in the Middle Years, 1979–80" and "Correlates of Father Participation in Family Work, 1979–81"; Carol Gilligan, "Abortion Decision Study, 1975–76," Henry Murray Research Center, Institute for Quantitative Social Science. Harvard University, Cambridge, MA.

203 Colby 1997, xi; see also Colby 1985.

204 Parker and Aldwin 1997; see also James and Lewkowicz 1997; MacDermid, Heilbrun, and deHaan 1997.

205 Vandewater and Stewart 1997, 368.

206 Thomas 1997, 284.

207 Shweder 1998.

208 Lock 1998; Levine and Levine 1998.

209 Newman 1998, 292n15.

210 "Changing Family and Work Life During Middle Age," 1994, Paul Baltes Papers.

211 Marmot and Fuhrer 2004.

212 Markus et al. 2004; see also Rossi 2001.

213 Markus et al. 2004, 307–308, 314.

214 Markus et al. 2004, 313.

215 Marshall 2017, 10.

Chapter 7

1 Quoted in Rauch 2014; see Nikolova and Graham 2015; Graham and Pozuelo 2017; Weiss et al. 2012; Stone et al. 2010; Blanchflower and Oswald 2008; also Schwandt 2015; Cheng, Powdthavee, and Oswald 2017; and, for a defense of midlife crisis in evolutionary and philosophical terms, respectively: Bainbridge 2012; Setiya 2017.

2 Gallie 1956.

3 Ahmed 2017, 48, 196.

4 Sandberg 2013; Slaughter 2015; see also Barnett and Rivers 1998; Moravscik 2015; Rhode 2017.

5 Macko and Rubin 2004.

6 Heti 2017, 51, 158, 266–267.

7 Corino 2018.

Bibliography

Archives

Alfred A. Knopf, Inc. Records. Harry Ransom Center, University of Texas at Austin.

Baltes, Paul. Papers. Archives of the Max Planck Society, Berlin.

Bernard, Jessie. Papers. Penn State Special Collections Library, University Park, PA.

Brown, Helen Gurley. Papers. Smith College Archives, Northampton, MA.

Felker, Clay. Papers. Rubenstein Library, Duke University, Durham, NC.

Grunwald, Henry. Papers. Library of Congress, Washington, DC.

Harvard Grant Study. William T. Grant Foundation Records. Rockefeller Archives, Sleepy Hollow, NY.

Henry A. Murray Research Archive. Institute for Quantitative Social Science. Harvard University, Cambridge, MA.

Mead, Margaret. Papers. Library of Congress, Washington, DC.

Penney-Missouri Journalism Awards Records. State Historical Society of Missouri, Columbia, MO.

Rockefeller Foundation Records. Rockefeller Archives, Sleepy Hollow, NY.

Social Science Research Council Records. Rockefeller Archives, Sleepy Hollow, NY.

Steinem, Gloria. Papers. Smith College Archives, Northampton, MA.

"Report of the Task Force on Self-Help Therapies," submitted to the American Psychological Association, October 1978. Gerald Rosen, personal collection.

Literature

Abraham, Amrita. 1978. "A Manual for the Middle-Aged." *India Times*, August 13, 10.

Achenbaum, W. Andrew. 1995. *Crossing Frontiers: Gerontology Emerges as a Science*. Cambridge: Cambridge University Press.

Adelmann, Georg. 1840. "Etwas über das Wort 'Climacterisch.'" *Medicinisches Correspondenz-Blatt bayerischer Aerzte* 1:12–14, 20–21.

Adorno, Theodor W., Else Frenkel-Brunswik, Daniel J. Levinson, and R. Nevitt Sanford. 1950. *The Authoritarian Personality*. New York: Harper.

Agassi, Judith Buber, Haim Hazan, Judith Posner, and Judith K. Brown. 1982. "On Middle-Aged Women." *Current Anthropology* 23 (3):352–353.

Ahmed, Sara. 2013. "Feminism Is Sensational." October 3. https://feministkilljoys.com /2013/10/03/feminism-is-sensational/.

———. 2017. *Living a Feminist Life*. Durham, NC: Duke University Press.

Albert, Dora. 1930. "The Fatal Forties and Beyond." *Independent Woman*, May, 197–198, 221.

Aldrich, Charles Anderson. 1946. Review of *Common Sense Book of Baby and Child Care*, by Benjamin Spock. *Parents Magazine*, February, 140.

Aldrich, Charles Anderson, and Mary M. Aldrich. 1938. *Babies Are Human Beings: An Interpretation of Growth*. New York: Macmillan.

Alexandrova, Anna. 2017. *A Philosophy for the Science of Well-being*. Oxford: Oxford University Press.

Allen, Ann Taylor. 2005. *Feminism and Motherhood in Western Europe, 1890–1970: The Maternal Dilemma*. New York: Palgrave Macmillan.

Allen, James Sloan. 1978. "I Want to Be as Much of Me as I Can Be." Review of *The Seasons of a Man's Life*, by Daniel J. Levinson. *Nation*, May 6, 545–546.

Allen, Judith A. 2009. *The Feminism of Charlotte Perkins Gilman: Sexualities, Histories, Progressivism*. Chicago: University of Chicago Press.

Allen, Pamela. 1970. *Free Space: A Perspective on the Small Group in Women's Liberation*. New York: Times Change.

American Association of Academic Women. 1992. *How Schools Shortchange Girls—The AAUW Report: A Study of Major Findings on Girls and Education*. New York: Marlowe. Reprint, 1995.

American Psychiatric Association. 1980. *Diagnostic and Statistical Manual of Mental Disorders*. 3rd ed. Washington, DC: American Psychiatric Association.

Anderson, Judy. 1998. Introduction to *Plagiarism, Copyright Violation and Other Thefts of Intellectual Property: An Annotated Bibliography*, 1–36. Jefferson, NC: McFarland.

Anderson, Peggy. 1976. "Women's Organizations: It's a Whole New Scene." *Family Circle*, April, 19–22.

Apple, Rima D. 2006. *Perfect Motherhood: Science and Childrearing in America*. New Brunswick, NJ: Rutgers University Press.

Apter, Terri E. 1990. *Altered Loves: Mothers and Daughters during Adolescence*. New York: St. Martin's.

———. 1995. *Secret Paths: Women in the New Midlife*. New York: Norton.

Ariès, Philippe. 1962. *Centuries of Childhood: A Social History of Family Life*. London: Jonathan Cape.

Armitage, Susan H., Patricia Hart, and Karen Weathermon, eds. 2002. *Women's Oral History: The "Frontiers" Reader*. Lincoln: University of Nebraska Press.

Aronson, Amy Beth. 2002. *Taking Liberties: Early American Women's Magazines and Their Readers*. Westport, CT: Praeger.

———. 2010. "Still Reading Women's Magazines: Reconsidering the Tradition a Half Century after *The Feminine Mystique*." *American Journalism* 27 (2):31–61.

Ash, Mitchell G., and Thomas Sturm, eds. 2007. *Psychology's Territories: Historical and Contemporary Perspectives from Different Disciplines*. Mahwah, NJ: Erlbaum.

Astington, Janet W., Paul L. Harris, and David R. Olson, eds. 1988. *Developing Theories of Mind*. Cambridge: Cambridge University Press.

Atchley, Robert C. 1982. "Retirement as a Social Institution." *Annual Review of Sociology* 8:263–287.

Aubry, Timothy, and Trysh Travis, eds. 2015. *Rethinking Therapeutic Culture*. Chicago: University of Chicago Press.

Auerbach, Judy, Linda Blum, Vicki Smith, and Christine Williams Source. 1985. "On Gilligan's *In a Different Voice*." *Feminist Studies* 11 (1):149–161.

Bach, George R., and Peter Wyden. 1968. *The Intimate Enemy: How to Fight Fair in Love and Marriage*. New York: Morrow.

Bailyn, Lotte. 1964. "Notes on the Role of Choice in the Psychology of Professional Women." *Daedalus* 93 (2):700–710.

Bainbridge, David. 2012. *Middle Age: A Natural History*. London: Portobello.

Baker, Paula. 1984. "The Domestication of Politics: Women and American Political Society, 1780–1920." *American Historical Review* 89:620–649.

Baltes, Paul B. 1987. "Theoretical Propositions of Life-span Developmental Psychology: On The Dynamics between Growth and Decline." *Developmental Psychology* 23 (5):611–626.

Balzac, Honoré de. 1901. *A Woman of Thirty*. New York: Macmillan.

Banner, Lois W. 1992. *In Full Flower: Aging Women, Power, and Sexuality*. New York: Knopf.

Barber, Bernard. 1968. "Social Stratification Structure and Trends of Social Mobility in Western Society." In *American Sociology: Perspectives, Problems, Methods*, edited by Talcott Parsons, 184–195. New York: Basic Books.

Barke, Megan, Rebecca Fribush, and Peter N. Stearns. 2000. "Nervous Breakdown in 20th-Century American Culture." *Journal of Social History* 33 (3):565–584.

Barker-Plummer, Bernadette. 1995. "News as a Political Resource: Media Strategies and Political Identity in the U.S. Women's Movement, 1966–1975." *Critical Studies in Mass Communication* 12:306–324.

———. 2000. "News as a Feminist Resource? A Case Study of the Media Strategies and Media Representation of the National Organization of Women, 1966–1980." In *Gender, Politics, and Communications*, edited by Annabelle Sreberny and Liesbet van Zoonen, 121–159. Cresshill, NJ: Hampton Press.

———. 2002. "Producing Public Voice: Resource Mobilization and Media Access in the National Organization for Women." *Journalism and Mass Communication Quarterly* 79 (1):188–204.

———. 2010. "News and Feminism: A Historic Dialog." *Journalism and Mass Communication Monographs* 12:145–203.

Barnett, Joe R. 1981. *Mid-life Crisis*. Aylmer, ON: Pathway.

Barnett, Rosalind C. 1967. "Vocational Planning of College Women: A Psycho-social Study." *Proceedings of the Annual Convention of the American Psychological Association* 2:345–346.

———. 1971. "Personality Correlates of Vocational Planning." *Genetic Psychology Monographs* 83 (2):309–356.

Barnett, Rosalind C., and Grace K. Baruch. 1978a. *The Competent Woman: Perspectives on Development*. New York: Halsted.

———. 1978b. "Women in the Middle Years: A Critique of Research and Theory." *Psychology of Women Quarterly* 3 (2):187–197.

———. 1985. "Women's Involvement in Multiple Roles and Psychological Distress." *Journal of Personality and Social Psychology* 49:135–145.

———. 1987. "Social Roles, Gender, and Psychological Distress." In *Gender and Stress*, edited by Rosalind C. Barnett, Lois Biener, and Grace K. Baruch, 122–143. New York: Free Press.

Barnett, Rosalind C., and Janet Shibley Hyde. 2001. "Women, Men, Work, and Family: An Expansionist Theory." *American Psychologist* 56:781–796.

Barnett, Rosalind C., and Caryl Rivers. 1998. *She Works/He Works: How Two-Income Families Are Happier, Healthier, and Better Off*. Cambridge, MA: Harvard University Press.

———. 2004. *Same Difference: How Gender Myths Are Hurting Our Relationships, Our Children, and Our Jobs*. New York: Basic Books.

———. 2011. *The Truth about Girls and Boys: Challenging Toxic Stereotypes about Our Children*. New York: Columbia University Press.

Barrett, Michèle, and Mary McIntosh. 1985. "Narcissism and the Family: A Critique of Lasch." *New Left Review* 135:35–48.

Baruch, Grace K. 1973a. "Feminine Self-esteem, Self-ratings of Competence, and Maternal Career Commitment." *Journal of Counseling Psychology* 20 (5):487–488.

———. 1973b. "Maternal Influences upon College Women's Attitudes toward Women and Work." *Developmental Psychology* 6 (1):32–37.

Baruch, Grace K., and Rosalind C. Barnett. 1981. "Fathers' Participation in the Care of Their Preschool Children." *Sex Roles* 7 (10):1043–1055.

———. 1983. "Correlates of Fathers' Participation in Family Work: A Technical Report." Working paper no. 106. Wellesley, MA: Wellesley College, Center for Research on Women.

———. 1986a. "Consequences of Fathers' Participation in Family Work: Parents' Role-Strain and Well-being." *Journal of Personality and Social Psychology* 51 (3):983–992.

———. 1986b. "Role Quality, Multiple Role Involvement, and Psychological Well-being in Midlife Women." *Journal of Personality and Social Psychology* 5:578–585.

———. 1988. "Women: Dependence and Independence." In *Prevention, Powerlessness, and Politics: Readings on Social Change*, edited by George W. Albee, Justin M. Joffe, and Linda A. Dusenbury, 171–179. Newbury Park, CA: Sage.

Baruch, Grace K., Rosalind C. Barnett, and Caryl Rivers. 1983. *Lifeprints: New Patterns of Love and Work for Today's Women*. New York: McGraw-Hill.

Baruch, Grace K., Lois Biener, and Rosalind C. Barnett. 1987. "Women and Gender in Research on Work and Family Stress." *American Psychologist* 42 (2):130–136.

Baruch, Grace K., and Debra Renee Kaufman. 1987. "Interpreting the Data: Women, Developmental Research and the Media." *Journal of Thought* 22 (1):53–57.

Basalla, George. 1976. "Pop Science: The Depiction of Science in Popular Culture." In *Science and Its Public: The Changing Relationship*, edited by Gerald Holton and William A. Blanpied, 261–278. Dordrecht: Reidel.

Bassin, Donna. 1982. "Woman's Images of Inner Space: Data towards Expanded Interpretive Categories." *International Review of Psychoanalysis* 9(2): 191–203.

———. 1988. Interview with Donna Bassin. In *Women Analyze Women: In France, England, and the United States*, edited by Elaine Hoffman Baruch and Lucienne J. Serrano, 337–354. New York: New York University Press.

Bate, Barbara. 1983. Review of *In a Different Voice*, by Carol Gilligan. *Women's Studies in Communication* 6 (2): 105–106.

Bawden, Julie. 1988. "Coping with a Midlife Crisis: An Interview with Jim Stanley, M.D." *Orange Coast*, June, 200–203.

Beal, Suzanne. 1977. "The Heroine Is Too Close for Comfort." Review of *Endangered Species*, by Sandra Hochman. *Baltimore Sun*, October 30, D4.

Bean, Joan P., and Margery Fox. 1988. "Women's Goals: Plus Ça Change." *New York Times*, January 10, 24.

Beard, George Miller. 1881. *American Nervousness: Its Causes and Consequences*. New York: Putnam.

Beauvoir, Simone de. 1972. *The Coming of Age*. New York: Putnam.

Beck, Joan. 1967. *How to Raise a Brighter Child*. New York: Simon & Schuster.

———. 1976. "How to Rear the Child Who Is between 20 and 50." *Chicago Tribune*, May 24, A2.

Belenky, Mary. 1978. "Conflict and Development: A Longitudinal Study of the Impact of Abortion Decisions on Moral Judgments of Adolescent and Adult Women." PhD diss., Harvard University.

Belenky, Mary, Blythe McVicker Clinchy, Nancy Rule Goldberger, and Jill Mattuck Tarule. 1986. *Women's Ways of Knowing: The Development of Self, Voice, and Mind*. New York: Basic Books. Reprint, 1997.

Bell, Inge Powell. 1970. "The Double Standard." *Trans-action* 8 (1–2):75–80.

Bell, Susan E. 1987. "Changing Ideas: The Medicalization of Menopause." *Social Science and Medicine* 24:535–542.

Bell, Susan E., and Susan M. Reverby. 2006. "Sweating It Out." Review of *Hot and Bothered*, by Judith Houck. *Women's Review of Books* 23 (6):9–10.

Bellah, Robert N., Richard Madsen, William M. Sullivan, Ann Swidler, and Steven M. Tipton. 1985. *Habits of the Heart: Individualism and Commitment in American Life*. Berkeley: University of California Press.

Bender, Marilyn. 1967. *The Beautiful People*. New York: Coward-McCann.

Benhabib, Seyla. 1987. "The Generalized and the Concrete Other: The Kohlberg-Gilligan Controversy and Feminist Theory." In *Feminism as Critique: On the Politics of Gender*, edited by Seyla Benhabib and Drucilla Cornell, 77–95. Minneapolis, MN: University of Minnesota Press.

Benjamin, Jessica. 1983. Review of *In a Different Voice*, by Carol Gilligan. *Signs* 9 (2):297–298.

———. 1988. *The Bonds of Love: Psychoanalysis, Feminism, and the Problem of Domination*. New York: Pantheon.

Benninghaus, Christina. 2012. "Beyond Constructivism? Gender, Medicine and the Early History of Sperm Analysis, Germany, 1870–1900." *Gender & History* 24 (3):647–676.

Benson, John. 1997. *Prime Time: A History of the Middle Aged in Twentieth-Century Britain*. New York: Routledge.

Bereni, Laure. 2012. "Penser la transversalité des mobilisations féministes: l'espace de la cause des femmes." In *Les féministes de la deuxième vague*, edited by Christine Bard, 27–41. Rennes: Presses Universitaires de Rennes.

Berenson, Edward, and Eva Gioli, eds. 2010. *Constructing Charisma: Celebrity, Fame, and Power in Nineteenth-Century Europe*. New York: Berghahn.

Berger, Gabriella E. 1999. *Menopause and Culture*. London: Pluto.

Bergler, Edmund. 1946. *Unhappy Marriage and Divorce: A Study of Neurotic Choice of Marriage Partners*. New York: International Universities Press.

———. 1948. *Divorce Won't Help*. Madison, CT: International Universities Press.

———. 1949. *Conflict in Marriage: The Unhappy Divorced*. New York: Harper.

———. 1954. *The Revolt of the Middle-Aged Man*. Madison, CT: International Universities Press.

Berlanstein, Lenard. 2004. "Historicizing and Gendering Celebrity Culture: Famous Women in Nineteenth-Century France." *Journal of Women's History* 16 (4):65–91.

———. 2007. "Selling Modern Femininity: *Femina*, a Forgotten Feminist Publishing Success in Belle Époque France." *French Historical Studies* 30 (4): 623–649.

Berman, Jeffrey. 1987. *The Talking Cure: Literary Representations of Psychoanalysis*. New York: New York University Press.

———. 1992. "The Unrestful Cure: Charlotte Perkins Gilman and 'The Yellow Wallpaper.'" In *The Captive Imagination: A Casebook on "The Yellow Wallpaper,"* edited by Catherine Colden, 211–241. New York: Feminist Press.

Berman, Marshall. 1975. "Erik Erikson, the Man Who Invented Himself." Review of *Life History and the Historical Moment*, by Erik Erikson. *New York Times*, March 30, BR1–2, 22.

Bernard, Jessie. 1956. *Remarriage: A Study of Marriage*. New York: Russell & Russell. Reprint, 1971.

———. 1972. *The Future of Marriage*. New Haven, CT: Yale University Press.

———. 1974. "Age, Sex and Feminism." *Annals of the American Academy of Political and Social Science* 415:120–137.

———. 1981. *The Female World*. New York: Free Press.

"Best Seller List." 1976. *New York Times*, August 28, 224.

Bettelheim, Bruno. 1962. *Dialogues with Mothers*. New York: Free Press.

Beynon-Jones, Siân M. "Untroubling Abortion: A Discourse Analysis of Women's Accounts." *Feminism & Psychology* 27 (2):225–242.

Biagioli, Mario. 2011. "Genius against Copyright: Revisiting Fichte's Proof of the Illegality of Reprinting." *Notre Dame Law Review* 86 (5):1847–1868.

Bittel, Carla. 2009. *Mary Putnam Jacobi and The Politics of Medicine in Nineteenth-Century America*. Chapel Hill: University of North Carolina Press.

Blanchflower, David G., and Andrew J. Oswald. 2008. "Is Well-being U-Shaped over the Life Course?" *Social Science and Medicine* 66:1733–1749.

Bledstein, Burton J. 1976. *The Culture of Professionalism: The Middle Class and the Development of Higher Education in America*. New York: Norton.

Blix, Jacqueline. 1992. "A Place to Resist: Reevaluating Women's Magazines." *The Journal of Communication Inquiry* 16 (1):56–71.

Blos, Peter. 1967. "The Second Individuation Process of Adolescence." *Psychoanalytic Study of the Child* 22:162–186.

———. 1979. *The Adolescent Passage: Developmental Issues*. New York: International Universities Press.

Blum, David. 1987. "Couch Potatoes: The New Nightlife." *New York*, July 20, 24–30.

Bock, Gisela, and Pat Thane. 1991. *Maternity and Gender Politics: Women and the Rise of European Welfare States, 1880s–1950s*. London: Routledge.

"Book Ends." 1976. *New York Times*, May 30, 161.

Bookspan, Phyllis T., and Maxine Kline. 1999. "On Mirrors and Gavels: A Chronicle of How Menopause Was Used as a Legal Defense against Women." *Indiana Law Review* 32:1267–1318.

Boston Women's Health Book Collective. 1976a. *Our Bodies, Ourselves*. New York: Simon & Schuster.

———. 1976b. "Your Bodies, Yourselves: Feeling at Home with Your Sexuality." *Bride's*, June, 150–151, 212–213.

Bouk, Dan. 2018. "The Generation That Causes Crisis: How Population Research Defined the Baby Boomers." *Modern American History* 1 (3):321–342.

Bourdieu, Pierre, and Roger Chartier. 1985. "La lecture, une pratique culturelle." In *Pratiques de la lecture*, edited by Roger Chartier, 217–239. Paris and Marseille: Editions Rivages.

Bowker Annual of Library and Book Trade Information. 1978. New York: Bowker.

Boxer, Marilyn J. 1998. *When Women Ask the Questions: Creating Women's Studies in America*. Baltimore: Johns Hopkins University Press.

———. 2002. "Women's Studies as Women's History." *Women's Studies Quarterly* 30 (3/4):43–51.

Boylan, James. 2007. *Pulitzer's School: Columbia University's School of Journalism, 1903–2003*. New York: Columbia University Press.

Bradley, Patricia. 2003. *Mass Media and the Shaping of American Feminism, 1963–1975*. Jackson: University Press of Mississippi.

———. 2005. *Women and the Press: The Struggle for Equality*. Boston: Northwestern University Press.

Brandt, Allan. 1991. "Emerging Themes in the History of Medicine." *Milbank Quarterly* 69 (2):199–214.

Brannigan, Augustine. 1979. "The Reification of Mendel." *Social Studies of Science* 9 (4):423–454.

Bras, Hervé Le. 2000. *Naissance de la mortalité: l'origine politique de la statistique et de la démographie.* Paris: Gallimard/Le Seuil.

Breines, Wini, Margaret Cerullo, and Judith Stacey. 1978. "Social Biology, Family Studies, and Antifeminist Backlash." *Feminist Studies* 4:43–67.

Breslin, Meg McSherry. 1998. "Joan Beck, 75, Pioneering Journalist." *Chicago Tribune,* December 12, 14.

Brim, Orville G. 1992. *Ambition: How We Manage Success and Failure throughout Our Lives.* New York: Basic Books.

———, ed. 2004. *How Healthy Are We? A National Study of Well-being at Midlife.* Chicago: University of Chicago Press.

Brock, Claire. 2006. *The Feminization of Fame, 1750–1830.* London: Palgrave Macmillan.

Bromell, Nicholas. 1985. "Feminist Perspectives: Five Local Theorists Talk about Challenging Society's Fundamental Beliefs." *Boston Review,* January 13, 12–15, 44–45, 53–58.

Brook, A. 1971. Review of *Work, Creativity, and Social Justice,* by Elliott Jaques. *British Journal of Industrial Medicine* 28 (3):313–314.

Broughton, John M. 1983. "Women's Rationality and Men's Virtues: A Critique of Gender Dualism in Gilligan's Theory of Moral Development." *Social Research* 50 (3):597–642.

Brown, Helen Gurley. 1993. *The Late Show: A Semiwild but Practical Survival Plan for Women over 50.* New York: Morrow.

Brown, Judith K. 1963. "A Cross-Cultural Study of Female Initiation Rites." *American Anthropologist* 65:837–853.

———. 1981. "Cross-Cultural Perspectives on the Female Life-Cycle." In *Handbook of Cross-Cultural Human Development,* edited by Ruth H. Munroe, 581–610. New York: Garland STPM Press.

Brown, Judith K., Jeanine Anderson, Dorothy Ayers Counts, Nancy Datan, Molly C. Dougherty, Valerie Fennell, Ruth S. Freed, David L. Gutmann, Sue-Ellen Jacobs, Douglas Raybeck, and Sylvia Vatuk. 1982. "Cross-cultural Perspectives on Middle-Aged Women (and Comments and Replies)." *Current Anthropology* 23 (2):143–156.

Brown, Judith K., and Virginia Kerns, eds. 1985. *In Her Prime: New Views of Middle-Aged Women.* South Hadley, MA: Bergin & Garvey.

Brown, Lyn Mikel. 1998. *Raising Their Voices: The Politics of Girls' Anger.* Cambridge, MA: Harvard University Press.

———. 2003. *Girlfighting: Betrayal and Rejection among Girls.* New York: New York University Press.

Brown, Lyn Mikel, and Carol Gilligan. 1992. *Meeting at the Crossroads: Women's Psychology and Girls' Development.* Cambridge, MA: Harvard University Press.

Brown, Patricia Leigh. 1987. "Studying Seasons of a Woman's Life." *New York Times,* September 14, B17.

Brown, Steven D. 2005. "The Worst Things in the World: Life Events Checklists in Popular Stress Management Texts." In *Ordinary Lifestyles: Popular Media, Consumption and Taste,* edited by David Bell and Joanne Hollows, 231–242. Buckingham: Open University Press.

Brownmiller, Susan. 1999. *In Our Time: Memoir of a Revolution.* New York: Dial Press.

Broyard, Anatole. 1976. "Clearing Our Passages." Review of *Passages,* by Gail Sheehy. *New York Times,* August 16, 60.

Brückner, Hannah, and Karl Ulrich Mayer. 2005. "De-Standardization of the Life Course: What It Might Mean? And if It Means Anything, Whether It Actually Took Place?" In *The Structure of the Life Course: Standardized? Individualized? Differentiated?*, edited by Ross Macmillan, 27–54. Amsterdam: JAI Press.

Buhle, Mari Jo. 1998. *Feminism and Its Discontents: A Century of Struggle with Psychoanalysis.* Cambridge, MA: Harvard University Press.

Bühler, Charlotte M. 1933. *Der menschliche Lebenslauf als psychologisches Problem.* Leipzig: Hirzel.

Bulmer, Martin. 1986. *The Chicago School of Sociology: Institutionalization, Diversity, and the Rise of Sociological Research.* Chicago: University of Chicago Press.

Bunders, Joske, and Richard Whitley. 1985. "Popularisation within the Sciences: The Purposes and Consequences of Inter-Specialist Communication." In *Expository Science: Forms and Functions of Popularisation*, edited by Terry Shinn and Richard Whitley, 61–77. Dordrecht: Reidel.

Bunke, Harvey C. 1978. "The Editor's Chair." *Business Horizons*, August, 4–8.

Burnett, John. 1994. *Idle Hands: The Experience of Unemployment, 1790–1990.* New York: Routledge.

Burnham, John C., ed. 2012. *After Freud Left: A Century of Psychoanalysis in America.* Chicago: University of Chicago Press.

Butler, Judith. 1990. *Gender Trouble: Feminism and the Subversion of Identity.* New York: Routledge.

Butler, Matilda, and William Paisley. 1978. "Magazine Coverage of Women's Rights." *Journal of Communication* 28 (1):183–186.

Cady, Barbara. 1976. "Crises of Midlife: The Search for Personal Identity." *Los Angeles Times Book Review*, June 20, 1, 10.

Cain, Leonard D. 1979. "Adding Spice to Middle Age." Review of *The Seasons of a Man's Life*, by Daniel J. Levinson. *Contemporary Sociology* 8 (4):547–550.

Campbell, Jean W. 1973. "Women Drop Back In: Educational Innovation in the Sixties." In *Academic Women on the Move*, edited by Alice S. Rossi and Ann Calderwood. New York: Russell Sage Foundation.

———. 1976. Review of *Passages*, by Gail Sheehy. *Group & Organization Studies* 1 (4):514.

Canguilhem, Georges. 1978. *On the Normal and the Pathological.* Boston: Reidel. Original edition, 1966.

———. 2005. "The Object of the History of Sciences." In *Continental Philosophy of Science*, edited by Gary Gutting, 198–207. Malden, MA: Blackwell. Original edition, 1983.

———. 2008. "Health: Crude Concept and Philosophical Question." *Public Culture* 20 (3):467–477.

Caplan, Paula J. 1979. "Erikson's Concept of Inner Space: A Data-Based Reevaluation." *American Journal of Orthopsychiatry* 49 (1):100–108.

Card, Claudia. 1996. *The Unnatural Lottery: Character and Moral Luck.* Philadelphia: Temple University Press.

Carter, John Mack. 1970. "Why You Find the Next Eight Pages in the *Ladies' Home Journal*." *Ladies' Home Journal*, August 1970, 63.

Catalyst. 1987. *New Roles for Men and Women: A Report on an Educational Intervention with College Students.* New York: Catalyst.

Chandler, Alfred D., Jr. 1977. *The Visible Hand: The Managerial Revolution in American Business.* Cambridge, MA: Harvard University Press.

Chapman, Stephen. 1977. Review of *Passages*, by Gail Sheehy. *Adult Education Quarterly* 28 (1):74–76.

Chappell, Marisa. 2012. "Reagan's 'Gender Gap' Strategy and the Limitations of Free-Market Feminism." *Journal of Policy History* 24 (1):115–134.

Chase, Stuart. 1929. "Laid Off at Forty." *Harper's Monthly*, August, 340–347.

———. 1932. *A New Deal*. New York: Macmillan.

Cheng, Terence C., Nattavudh Powdthavee, and Andrew J. Oswald. 2017. "Longitudinal Evidence for a Midlife Nadir in Human Well-being: Results from Four Data Sets." *Economic Journal* 127 (599):126–147.

Chesler, Ellen. 1992. *Woman of Valor: Margaret Sanger and the Birth Control Movement in America*. New York: Simon & Schuster.

Chesler, Phyllis. 1972. *Women and Madness*. Garden City, NY: Doubleday.

Chodorow, Nancy. 1971. "Being and Doing." In *Woman in Sexist Society: Studies in Power and Powerlessness*, edited by Vivian Gornick and Barbara K. Moran, 259–291. New York: Basic Books.

———. 1978. *The Reproduction of Mothering: Psychoanalysis and the Sociology of Gender*. Berkeley, CA: University of California Press.

Christy, Marian. 1984. "Overcoming a Mid-life Crisis: How a Noted Surgeon-Author Kicked the Booze and Pills." *Boston Globe*, November 25, A9, A14.

Clare, Anthony. 1977. "Taking Off." Review of *Passages*, by Gail Sheehy. *New Society* 41 (780):557–558.

"Class of 1961." 1976. *Randolph-Macon Woman's College Alumnae Bulletin* 70, 40.

Cleveland, Amory. 1970. "Trade Winds." *Saturday Review*, November 21, 16–18.

Clow, Barbara. 2001. "Who's Afraid of Susan Sontag?" *Social History of Medicine* 14 (2):293–312.

Cobble, Dorothy Sue. 2004. *The Other Women's Movement: Workplace Justice and Social Rights in Modern America*. Princeton, NJ: Princeton University Press.

———. 2010. "Labor Feminists and President Kennedy's Commission on Women." In *No Permanent Waves: Recasting Histories of U.S. Feminism*, edited by Nancy A. Hewitt, 144–167. New Brunswick, NJ: Rutgers University Press.

Cohen, Lizabeth. 2003. *A Consumers' Republic: The Politics of Mass Consumption in Postwar America*. New York: Knopf.

Cohen, Patricia. 2012. *In Our Prime: The Invention of Middle Age*. New York: Scribner.

Cohen-Cole, Jamie. 2014. *The Open Mind: Cold War Politics and the Sciences of Human Nature*. Chicago: University of Chicago Press.

Colander, Pat. 1976. "Books to Beat the Doldrums." *Chicago Tribune*, August 8, D5.

Colby, Anne. 1985. *A Guide to the Data Resources of the Henry A. Murray Research Center of Radcliffe College*. Cambridge, MA: Henry A. Murray Research Center.

———. Foreword to *Multiple Paths of Midlife Development*, edited by Margie Lachman and Jacquelyn Boone James, ix–xii. Chicago: University of Chicago Press.

Colby, Anne, and Lawrence Kohlberg. 1987–88. *The Measurement of Moral Judgment*. 2 vols. Cambridge: Cambridge University Press.

Colby, Kenneth Mark, Roger L. Gould, and Gerald Aronson. 1989. "Some Pros and Cons of Computer-Assisted Psychotherapy." *Journal of Nervous & Mental Disease* 177 (2):105–108.

Cole, Thomas R. 1992. *The Journey of Life: A Cultural History of Aging in America*. Cambridge: University of Cambridge Press.

Coles, Robert. 1970. *Erik H. Erikson: The Growth of His Work*. Boston: Little, Brown.

Combaz, Christian. 1978. "Petites misères de la quarantaine." *Jeune Afrique*, April 19, 74–75.

Comfort, Alex. 1978. "The Male Animal." Review of *Beyond the Male Myth*, by Anthony Pietropinto and Jacqueline Simenauer; *Male Sexuality*, by Bernie Zilbergeld; *The Seasons of a Man's Life*, by Daniel J. Levinson. *New York Times*, March 12, BR4.

Comfort, Nathaniel C. 2001. *The Tangled Field: Barbara McClintock's Search for the Patterns of Genetic Control*. Cambridge, MA: Harvard University Press.

Commission on the Education of Women of the American Council on Education. 1955. *How Fare American Women?* Washington, DC: American Council on Education.

———. 1960. *The Span of a Woman's Life and Learning*. Washington, DC: American Council on Education.

Connell, R. W. 1987. *Gender and Power*. Sydney: Allen & Unwin.

———. 1994. "Psychoanalysis on Masculinity." In *Theorizing Masculinities*, edited by Harry Brod and Michael Kaufman, 11–38. Thousand Oaks, CA: Sage.

———. 1995. *Masculinities*. Berkeley: University of California Press.

Connell, R. W., and James W. Messerschmidt. 2005. "Hegemonic Masculinity: Rethinking the Concept." *Gender & Society* 19 (6):829–859.

Conrad, Peter, and Joseph W. Schneider. 1980. *Deviance and Medicalization: From Badness to Sickness*. St. Louis: Mosby.

Cook, Judith A., and Mary M. Fonow. 1986. "Knowledge and Women's Interests: Issues of Epistemology and Methodology in Feminist Sociological Research." *Sociological Inquiry* 56 (1):2–29.

Coontz, Stephanie. 1992. *The Way We Never Were: American Families and the Nostalgia Trap*. New York: Basic Books.

———. 2005. *Marriage, a History: How Love Conquered Marriage*. New York: Viking.

———. 2011. *A Strange Stirring:* The Feminine Mystique *and American Women at the Dawn of the 1960s*. Philadelphia: Basic Books.

Cooper, Cary L., and Philip Dewe. 2004. *Stress: A Brief History*. Malden, MA: Blackwell.

Cooper, Melinda. 2017. *Family Values: Between Neoliberalism and the New Social Conservatism*. New York: Zone.

Cooter, Roger, and Stephen Pumfrey. 1994. "Separate Spheres and Public Places: Reflections on the History of Science Popularization and Science in Popular Culture." *History of Science* 32 (3):237–267.

Corino, Eva. 2018. *Das Nacheinander-Prinzip: Vom gelasseneren Umgang mit Familie und Beruf*. Berlin: Suhrkamp.

Coser, Lewis A. 1974. *Greedy Institutions*. New York: Free Press.

Costa, Dora L. 1998. *The Evolution of Retirement: An American Economic History, 1880–1990*. Chicago: University of Chicago Press.

Côté, James E. 2000. *Arrested Adulthood: The Changing Nature of Maturity and Identity*. New York: New York University Press.

Cott, Nancy F. 1989. *The Grounding of Modern Feminism*. New Haven, CT: Yale University Press.

Courlander, Harold. 1979. "*Roots, The African,* and the Whiskey Jug Case." *Village Voice*, April 9, 33–35.

Cowan, Ruth Schwartz. 1983. *More Work for Mother: The Ironies of Household Technology from the Open Hearth to the Microwave*. New York: Basic Books.

Coyle, Grace L. 1928. *Jobs and Marriage? Outlines for the Discussion of the Married Woman in Business*. New York: Womans [*sic*] Press.

Craik, Jennifer. 1993. *The Face of Fashion: Cultural Studies in Fashion*. London: Routledge.

Creager, Angela N. H., Elizabeth Lunbeck, and Londa Schiebinger, eds. 2001. *Feminism in Twentieth-Century Science, Technology, and Medicine*. Chicago: University of Chicago Press.

Creighton, Colin. 1999. "The Rise and Decline of the 'Male Breadwinner Family' in Britain." *Cambridge Journal of Economics* 23:519–541.

Crosby, Faye J. 1984. "Job Satisfaction and Domestic Life." In *Management of Work and Personal Life*, edited by Mary Dean Lee and Rabindra N. Kanungo, 41–60. New York: Praeger.

———. 1991. *Juggling: The Unexpected Advantages of Balancing Career and Home for Women and Their Families*. New York: Free Press.

Cryer, Dan. 1978. "Pre-empted by *Passages*." Review of *The Seasons of a Man's Life*, by Daniel J. Levinson. *Newsday*, April 9, B21.

Currier, Andrew F. 1897. *The Menopause*. New York: Appleton.

Cusk, Rachel. 2014. *Outline*. London: Faber.

Cusset, François. 2008. *French Theory: How Foucault, Derrida, Deleuze, & Co. Transformed the Intellectual Life of the United States*. Minneapolis, MN: University of Minnesota Press.

Damon-Moore, Helen, and Carl F. Kaestle. 1991. "Gender, Advertising, and Mass-Circulation Magazines." In *Literacy in the United States: Readers and Reading since 1880*, edited by Carl F. Kaestle, Helen Damon-Moore, Lawrence C. Stedman, Katherine Tinsley, and William Vance Trollinger Jr., 245–271. New Haven, CT: Yale University Press.

Danto, Arthur C. 2009. *Andy Warhol*. New Haven, CT: Yale University Press.

Daston, Lorraine, and Fernando Vidal. 2004. "Doing What Comes Naturally." In *The Moral Authority of Nature*, edited by Lorraine Daston and Fernando Vidal, 1–20. Chicago: Chicago University Press.

Davies, William. 2015. *The Happiness Industry: How the Government and Big Business Sold Us Well-being*. London: Verso.

Davies, Margaret. 2007. *Property: Meanings, Histories, Theories*. Oxford: Routledge.

Davis, Kathy. 1992. "Toward a Feminist Rhetoric: The Gilligan Debate Revisited." *Women's Studies International Forum* 15 (2):219–231.

———. 2007. *The Making of "Our Bodies, Ourselves": How Feminism Travels across Borders*. Durham, NC: Duke University Press.

Davis, Kenneth C. 1984. *Two-Bit Culture: The Paperbacking of America*. Boston: Houghton Mifflin.

Davis, Maxine. 1951. *Facts about the Menopause*. New York: McGraw-Hill. Original edition, 1948.

Davis, Murray. 1971. "That's Interesting! Towards a Phenomenology of Sociology and a Sociology of Phenomenology." *Philosophy of the Social Sciences* 1:309–344.

———. 1986. "That's Classic! The Phenomenology and Rhetoric of Successful Social Theories." *Philosophy of the Social Sciences* 16:261–301.

Degler, Carl N. 1964. "Revolution without Ideology: The Changing Place of Women in America." *Daedalus* 93 (2):653–670.

———. 1974. "What Ought to Be and What Was: Women's Sexuality in the Nineteenth Century." *American Historical Review* 79 (5):1467–1490.

de Grazia, Sebastian. 1976. Review of *Work, Creativity, and Social Justice*, by Elliott Jaques; *The Harried Leisure Class*, by Staffan B. Linder; *Work in America: Report of a Special Task Force to the Secretary of Health, Education, and Welfare*; *Work, Society, and Culture*, by Yves Simon. *American Political Science Review* 70 (4):1273–1276.

Delaney, Janice, Mary Jane Lupton, and Emily Toth. 1988. *The Curse: A Cultural History of Menstruation*. Chicago: University of Illinois Press.

Delap, Lucy. 2007. *The Feminist Avant-Garde: Transatlantic Encounters of the Early Twentieth Century*. Cambridge: Cambridge University Press.

DeLuzio, Crista. 2007. *Female Adolescence in American Scientific Thought, 1830–1930*. Baltimore: Johns Hopkins University Press.

Demos, John. 1993. "Interview with John Demos, by Roger Adelson." *Historian* 55 (3):430–446.

Deutsch, Helene. 1930. "The Significance of Masochism in the Mental Life of Women." *International Journal of Psycho-analysis* 11:48–60.

———. 1945. *Psychology of Women: A Psychoanalytic Interpretation*, vol. 2, *Motherhood*. New York: Grune & Stratton.

Dewees, William. 1826. *A Treatise on the Diseases of Females*. Philadelphia: H. C. Carey and I. Lea.

Deykin, Eva Y., Shirley Jacobson, Maida Solomon, and Gerald Klerman. 1966. "The Empty Nest: Psychosocial Aspects of Conflict between Depressed Mothers and Their Grown Children." *American Journal of Psychiatry* 122 (12):1422–1425.

Dietz, Park Elliott. 1973. Review of *Hustling*, by Gail Sheehy. *Journal of the American Academy of Psychiatry and the Law* 1 (4):294–295.

Dinnerstein, Dorothy. 1976. *The Mermaid and the Minotaur: Sexual Arrangements and Human Malaise*. New York: Harper & Row.

Doherty, Beka. 1949. *Cancer*. New York: Random House.

Dohrenwend, Barbara Snell, and Bruce P. Dohrenwend, eds. 1974. *Stressful Life Events: Their Nature and Effects*. New York: Wiley.

———, eds. 1981. *Stressful Life Events and Their Contexts*. New Brunswick, NJ: Rutgers University Press.

Dohrenwend, Bruce P., and Barbara Snell Dohrenwend. 1969. *Social Status and Psychological Disorder: A Causal Inquiry*. New York: Wiley-Interscience.

Donath, Orna. 2017. *Regretting Motherhood: A Study*. Berkeley, CA: North Atlantic Books.

Donohugh, Donald. 1981. *The Middle Years: A Physician's Guide to Your Body, Emotions and Life Challenges*. New York: Saunders.

Douglas, Susan. 1994. *Where the Girls Are: Growing Up Female with the Mass Media*. New York: Random House.

Dow, Bonnie J. 1996. *Prime-Time Feminism: Television, Media Culture, and the Women's Movement since 1970*. Philadelphia: University of Pennsylvania Press.

———. 2014. *Watching Women's Liberation, 1970: Feminism's Pivotal Year on the Network News*. Urbana: University of Illinois Press.

Drake, Emma F. 1902. *What a Woman of Forty-Five Ought to Know*. Philadelphia: Vir.

———. 1910. *Was eine Frau von 45 wissen muß*. Konstanz: Hirsch.

———. 1942. *Ce que toute femme de 45 ans devrait savoir*. Paris: Fischbacher.

Dudink, Stefan, Karen Hagemann, and John Tosh, eds. 2004. *Masculinities in Politics and War: Gendering Modern History*. Manchester: Manchester University Press.

Duhl, Leonard. 1963. *The Urban Condition: People and Policy in the Metropolis*. New York: Basic Books.

DuPlessis, Rachel Blau, and Ann Snitow. 1998. *The Feminist Memoir Project: Voices from Women's Liberation*. New York: Three Rivers.

Echols, Alice. 1989. *Daring to Be Bad: Radical Feminism in America, 1967–1975*. 6th ed. Minneapolis: University of Minnesota Press. Reprint, 2003.

Edsall, Florence S. 1949. *Change of Life: A Modern Woman's Guide.* New York: Grosset & Dunlap.

Edwards, Carolyn P. 1975. "Societal Complexity and Moral Development: A Kenyan Study." *Ethos* 3:505–527.

Edwards, Richard. 1979. *Contested Terrain: The Transformation of the Workplace in the Twentieth Century.* New York: Basic Books.

Ehmer, Josef. 1996. "'The Life Stairs': Aging, Generational Relations, and Small Commodity Production in Central Europe." In *Aging and Generational Relations over the Life Course: A Historical and Cross-Cultural Perspective,* edited by Tamara K. Hareven, 53–74. Berlin and New York: W. de Gruyter.

Ehrenreich, Barbara. 1983. *The Hearts of Men: American Dreams and the Flight from Commitment.* Garden City, NY: Anchor Press/Doubleday.

Ehrenreich, Barbara, and Deirdre English. 1978. *For Her Own Good: 150 Years of the Experts' Advice to Women.* Garden City, NY: Anchor Press/Doubleday.

Eisenmann, Linda. 2006. *Higher Education for Women in Postwar America, 1945–1965.* Baltimore: Johns Hopkins University Press.

Elkind, David. 1994. *Ties That Stress: The New Family Imbalance.* Cambridge, MA: Harvard University Press.

Ellis, Albert. 2010. *All Out! An Autobiography.* Amherst, MA: Prometheus Books.

"Empty Nest." 2013. In *The American Heritage Dictionary of Idioms: American English Idiomatic Expressions and Phrases,* edited by Christine Ammer, 131. Boston: Houghton, Mifflin, Harcourt.

Endres, Kathleen L. 1995a. "*Bride's* & *Your New Home.*" In *Women's Periodicals in the United States: Consumer Magazines,* edited by Kathleen L. Endres and Therese L. Lueck, 38–43. Westport, CT: Greenwood.

———. 1995b. "Glamour." In *Women's Periodicals in the United States: Consumer Magazines,* edited by Kathleen L. Endres and Therese L. Lueck, 107–113. Westport, CT: Greenwood.

Engel, Stephanie. 1980. "Femininity as Tragedy: Re-examining the New Narcissism." *Socialist Review* 10 (5):77–103.

Engels, Friedrich. 1892. *The Condition of the Working-Class in England in 1844.* London: Allen & Unwin.

England, Paula. 1999. "The Impact of Feminist Thought on Sociology." *Contemporary Sociology* 28 (3):263–268.

English, O. Spurgeon. 1967. "Values in Psychotherapy: The Affair." *Voices* 3 (4):9–14.

Ensmenger, Nathan. 2010. *The Computer Boys Take Over: Computers, Programmers, and the Politics of Technological Expertise.* Cambridge, MA: MIT Press.

Enzensberger, Hans Magnus. 1982. "Constituents of a Theory of the Media [1970]." In *Hans Magnus Enzensberger: Critical Essays,* edited by Reinhold Grimm and Bruce Armstrong. New York: Continuum.

Epstein, Steven. 2007. *Inclusion: The Politics of Difference in Medical Research.* Chicago: University of Chicago Press.

Erikson, Erik H. 1950a. *Childhood and Society.* New York: Norton.

———. 1950b. "Growth and Crises of the 'Healthy Personality.'" In *Symposium on the Healthy Personality: Transactions of Special Meetings of Conference on Infancy and Childhood,* edited by Milton J. E. Senn, 91–146. New York: Josiah Macy Jr. Foundation.

———. 1958. *Young Man Luther: A Study in Psychoanalysis and History.* New York: Norton. Reprint, 1962.

———. 1961. "The Roots of Virtue." In *The Humanist Frame*, edited by Julian S. Huxley, 145–165. London: Allen & Unwin.

———. 1964. "Inner and Outer Space: Reflections on Womanhood." *Daedalus* 93 (2):582–606.

———. 1968. "Womanhood and the Inner Space." In *Identity: Youth and Crisis*, 261–294. New York: Norton.

———. 1969. *Gandhi's Truth: On the Origins of Militant Nonviolence*. New York: Norton.

———. 1974a. "Once More the Inner Space: Letter to a Former Student." In *Women and Analysis: Dialogues on Psychoanalytic Views of Femininity*, edited by Jean Strouse, 320–340. New York: Grossman.

———. 1974b. "Womanhood and the Inner Space [1968]." In *Women and Analysis: Dialogues on Psychoanalytic Views of Femininity*, edited by Jean Strouse, 291–319. New York: Grossman.

———. 1975. *Life History and the Historical Moment*. New York: Norton.

———. 1982. "Psychoanalytic Reflections on Einstein's Centenary." In *Albert Einstein: Historical and Cultural Perspectives*, edited by Gerald Holton and Yehuda Elkana, 151–173. Princeton, NJ: Princeton University Press.

Evans, Bonnie. 2017. *The Metamorphosis of Autism: A History of Child Development in Britain*. Manchester: Manchester University Press.

Faegre, Marion L. 1946. Review of *Common Sense Book of Baby and Child Care*, by Benjamin Spock. *Child*, November, 94–95.

Faludi, Susan. 1991. *Backlash: The Undeclared War against American Women*. London: Vintage. Reprint, 2006.

Farley, Jennie. 1978. "Women's Magazines and the Equal Rights Amendment: Friend or Foe?" *Journal of Communication* 28 (1):187–192.

Farrell, Amy Erdman. 1998. *Yours in Sisterhood: Ms. Magazine and the Promise of Popular Feminism*. Chapel Hill: University of North Carolina Press.

Faulstich, Werner, and Ricarda Strobel. 1986. *Bestseller als Marktphänomen: Ein quantitativer Befund zur internationalen Literatur 1970 in allen Medien*. Wiesbaden: Harrassowitz.

Fava, Sylvia. 1973. "The Pop Sociology of Suburbs and New Towns." *American Studies* 14 (1):121–133.

Faye, Cathy. 2012. "American Social Psychology: Examining the Contours of the 1970s Crisis." *Studies in History and Philosophy of Biological and Biomedical Sciences* 43 (2):514–521.

Fein, Esther B. 1991. "The Book That Made the Most Difference in People's Lives." *New York Times*, November 20, C26.

Felski, Rita. 1989. *Beyond Feminist Aesthetics: Feminist Literature and Social Change*. Cambridge, MA: Harvard University Press.

Fields, Suzanne. 1981. "The Importance of Being Important." *Vogue*, December, 155.

Firestone, Shulamith. 1970. *The Dialectic of Sex: The Case for Feminist Revolution*. New York: Morrow.

Fleck, Ludwik. 1979. *Genesis and Development of a Scientific Fact*. Chicago: University of Chicago Press.

Fodor, Iris G., and Violet Franks. 1990. "Special Issue: Women in Midlife and Beyond." *Psychology of Women Quarterly* 14 (4):445–623.

Forman, Gail. 1988. "Rethinking the Empty Nest Syndrome." *Washington Post*, September 6, E5.

Formanek, Ruth, ed. 1990. *The Meanings of Menopause: Historical, Medical, and Cultural Perspectives*. Hillsdale, NJ: Analytic Press.

Forrester, John. 1999. "If *p*, then What? Thinking in Cases." *History of the Human Sciences* 9 (3):1–25.

———. 2016. *Thinking in Cases.* Cambridge: Polity.

Foucault, Michel. 2001. *The Hermeneutics of the Subject: Lectures at the Collège de France, 1981–82.* New York: Palgrave Macmillan.

———. 2007. "What Is Critique? [1978]." In *The Politics of Truth*, edited by Sylvère Lotringer, 41–81. Cambridge, MA: Semiotext(e).

Foxcraft, Louise. 2009. *Hot Flushes, Cold Science: A History of the Modern Menopause.* London: Granta.

Fraisse, Geneviève. 1988. "La constitution du sujet dans la pensée féministe: paradoxe et anachronisme." In *Penser le sujet aujourd'hui*, edited by Elisabeth Guibert-Sledziewksi and Jean-Louis Vieillard-Baron, 257–264. Paris: Méridiens Klincksieck.

Frank, Thomas. 1997. *The Conquest of Cool: Business Culture, Counterculture, and the Rise of Hip Consumerism.* Chicago: University of Chicago Press.

Fraser, Nancy. 1992. "Rethinking the Public Sphere: A Contribution to the Critique of Actually Existing Democracy." In *Habermas and the Public Sphere*, edited by Craig Calhoun, 109–194. Cambridge, MA: MIT Press.

Fraterrigo, Elizabeth. 2009. *Playboy and the Making of the Good Life in Modern America.* Oxford: Oxford University Press.

Freidenfels, Lara. 2009. *The Modern Period: Menstruation in Twentieth-Century America.* Baltimore: Johns Hopkins University Press.

Frenkel-Brunswik, Else. 1936. "Studies in Biographical Psychology." *Journal of Personality* 5 (1):1–34.

Freud, Anna. 1937. *The Ego and the Mechanisms of Defence.* London: Hogarth.

Freud, Sigmund. 1954. *The Origins of Psycho-analysis: Letters to Wilhelm Fliess, Drafts and Notes, 1887–1902.* Edited by Marie Bonaparte, Anna Freud and Ernst Kris. New York: Basic Books.

———. 1965. "Femininity [1933]." In *New Introductory Lectures on Psycho-analysis*, edited by James Strachey, 139–168. London: Strachey.

Friday, Nancy. 1977. *My Mother/My Self: The Daughter's Search for Identity.* New York: Delacorte.

Fried, Barbara. 1967. "The Middle-Age Crisis." *McCall's*, March 1967, 88–89, 169–175.

Friedan, Betty. 1956. "Millionaire's Wife." *Cosmopolitan*, September, 78–87.

———. 1962. "The Feminine Fulfillment: 'Is This All?'" *Mademoiselle*, May, 146–147, 205–209.

———. 1963a. *The Feminine Mystique.* New York: Dell. Reprint, 1977.

———. 1963b. "The Fraud of Femininity." *McCall's*, March, 81, 130–132.

———. 1963c. "Have American Housewives Traded Brains for Brooms?" *Ladies' Home Journal*, January, 24–26.

———. 1976. *It Changed My Life: Writings on the Women's Movement.* Cambridge, MA: Harvard University Press. Reprint, 1998.

———. 1981. *The Second Stage.* New York: Summit Books.

———. 1983. "Twenty Years After." In *The Feminine Mystique*, ix–xxviii. New York: Norton.

———. 1993. *Fountain of Age.* New York: Simon & Schuster.

———. 1997. "Defining a Paradigm Shift." In *Beyond Gender: The New Politics of Work and Family*, edited by Brigid O'Farrell, 1–16. Baltimore: Johns Hopkins University Press.

Friedman, Lawrence J. 1999. *Identity's Architect: A Biography of Erik H. Erikson.* Cambridge, MA: Harvard University Press.

Friedman, Marilyn. 1993. *What Are Friends For? Feminist Perspectives on Personal Relationships and Moral Theory.* Ithaca, NY: Cornell University Press.

Friedman, Richard A. 2008. "Crisis? Maybe He's a Narcissistic Jerk." *New York Times,* January 15, F5.

Fromm, Erich. 1970. *The Crisis of Psychoanalysis: Essays on Freud, Marx, and Social Psychology.* New York: Holt, Rinehart & Winston.

Fuchs, Rachel G. 2005. *Gender and Poverty in Nineteenth-Century Europe.* Cambridge: Cambridge University Press.

Furstenberg, Frank F. 1976. *Unplanned Parenthood: The Social Consequences of Teenage Childbearing.* New York: Free Press.

G. S. 2005. "Jaques, Elliott." In *Encyclopedia of History of American Management,* edited by Morgen Witzel, 267–270. Bristol: Thoemmes Continuum.

Gage, Matilda. 1870. *Woman as Inventor.* Fayetteville, NY: Darling.

Gallie, Walter B. 1956. "Essentially Contested Concepts." *Proceedings of the Aristotelian Society* 56: 167–198.

Gallup Organization. 1978. *Book Reading and Library Usage: A Study of Habits and Perceptions.* Princeton, NJ: Gallup Organization.

Gans, Herbert J. 1998. "Best-sellers by American Sociologists: An Exploratory Study." In *Required Reading: Sociology's Most Influential Books,* edited by Dan Clawson, 19–27. Amherst, MA: University of Massachusetts Press.

Gardanne, Charles-Pierre-Louis de. 1816. *Avis aux femmes qui entrent dans l'âge critique.* Paris: Gabon.

Gartner, Michael. 1978. "The Wonderful World of Mid-life Crisis." Review of *The Seasons of a Man's Life,* by Daniel J. Levinson. *Wall Street Journal,* May 5, 12.

Gates, Barbara T. 1998. *Kindred Nature: Victorian and Edwardian Women Embrace the Living World.* Chicago: University of Chicago Press.

Gates, Barbara T., and Ann B. Shteir, eds. 1997. *Natural Eloquence: Women Reinscribe Science.* Madison, WI: University of Wisconsin Press.

Geary, Daniel. 2013. "Children of *The Lonely Crowd*: David Riesman, the Young Radicals, and the Splitting of Liberalism in the 1960s." *Modern Intellectual History* 10 (3):603–633.

Genette, Gérard. 1997. *Paratexts: Thresholds of Interpretation.* Cambridge: Cambridge University Press.

Gergen, Kenneth. 1991. *The Saturated Self: Dilemmas of Identity in Contemporary Life.* New York: Basic Books.

Gergen, Mary. 1997. "Finished at 40: Women's Development within the Patriarchy." *Psychology of Women Quarterly* 14 (4):471–493.

Gerhard, Jane F. 2001. *Desiring Revolution: Second-Wave Feminism and the Rewriting of American Sexual Thought, 1920–1982.* New York: Columbia University Press.

———. 2013. *The Dinner Party: Judy Chicago and the Power of Popular Feminism, 1970–2007.* Athens: University of Georgia Press.

Gerson, Kathleen. 1985. *Hard Choices: How Women Decide about Work, Career, and Motherhood.* Berkeley: University of California Press.

Gesell, Arnold. 1943. *Infant and Child in the Culture of Today: The Guidance of Development in Home and Nursery School.* Oxford: Harper.

———. 1946. *The Child from Five to Ten.* New York: Harper & Row.

Ghez, Gilbert, and Gary S. Becker. 1975. *The Allocation of Time and Goods over the Life Cycle.* New York: National Bureau of Economic Research.

Giele, Janet Z. 1980. "Adulthood as Transcendence of Age and Sex." In *Themes of Work and Love in Adulthood,* edited by Neil J. Smelser and Erik H. Erikson, 151–173. Cambridge, MA: Harvard University Press.

———. 1982a. "Women in Adulthood: Unanswered Questions." In *Women in the Middle Years: Current Knowledge and Directions for Research,* edited by Janet Z. Giele, 1–35. New York: Wiley.

———, ed. 1982b. *Women in the Middle Years: Current Knowledge and Directions for Research.* New York: Wiley.

Gieryn, Thomas F. 1983. "Boundary-Work and the Demarcation of Science from Non-Science: Strains and Interests in Professional Ideologies of Scientists." *American Sociological Review* 48 (6):781–795.

Gilligan, Carol. 1964. "Responses to Temptation: An Analysis of Motives." PhD diss., Harvard University.

———. 1977. "In a Different Voice: Women's Conceptions of Self and of Morality." *Harvard Educational Review* 47 (4):481–517.

———. 1979. "Woman's Place in Man's Life Cycle." *Harvard Educational Review* 49 (4):431–446.

———. 1982a. "Adult Development and Women's Development: Arrangements for a Marriage." In *Women in the Middle Years: Current Knowledge and Directions for Research,* edited by Janet Z. Giele, 89–114. New York: Wiley.

———. 1982b. "Gibt es eine weibliche Moral? Das *Psychologie Heute*-Gespräch mit Carol Gilligan." *Psychologie Heute,* 20–27, 34.

———. 1982c. *In a Different Voice: Psychological Theory and Women's Development.* Cambridge, MA: Harvard University Press. Reprint, 1993.

———. 1982d. "Why Should a Woman Be More Like a Man?" *Psychology Today,* June, 68–77.

———. 1994. "Listening to a Different Voice: Interview with Carol Gilligan, by Celia Kitzinger." *Feminism & Psychology* 4 (3):408–419.

———. 2009a. "Curriculum Vitae." https://its.law.nyu.edu/facultyprofiles/index.cfm?fuseaction=profile.full_cv&personid=19946 (accessed December 19, 2017).

———. 2009b. "Interview with Carol Gilligan, by Leeat Granek." http://www.feministvoices.com/assets/Feminist-Presence/Gilligan/Carol-Gilligan-Oral-History.pdf (accessed December 19, 2017).

———. 2011. *Joining the Resistance.* Malden, MA: Polity.

Gilligan, Carol, Lawrence Kohlberg, Joan Lerner, and Mary Belenky. 1971. "Moral Reasoning about Sexual Dilemmas: The Development of an Interview and Scoring System." In *Technical Report of the U.S. Commission on Obscenity and Pornography* 1:141–147. Washington, DC: FRIEDMAN 1999 Government Printing Office.

Gilligan, Carol, Nona P. Lyons, and Trudy J. Hanmer, eds. 1989. *Making Connections.* Cambridge, MA: Harvard University Press.

Gilligan, Carol, Annie G. Rogers, and Deborah L. Tolman, eds. 1991. *Women, Girls and Psychotherapy: Reframing Resistance.* New York: Harrington Park.

Gilligan, Carol, Janie Victoria Ward, and Jill McLean Taylor, eds. 1988. *Mapping the Moral Domain: A Contribution of Women's Thinking to Psychological Theory and Education.* Cambridge, MA: Harvard University Press.

Gillis, John R. 1974. *Youth and History: Tradition and Change in European Age Relations, 1770–Present.* New York: Academic Press.

"Gloria Steinem, Woman of the Year." 1972. *McCall's,* January, 67–69.

Göhlsdorf, Novina. 2014. "Störung der Gemeinschaft, Grenzen der Erzählung: Die Figur des autistischen Kindes." *Jahrbuch der Psychoanalyse* 68:17–34.

Goleman, Daniel. 1984. "Psychology Is Revising Its View of Women." *New York Times*, March 20, C1–C2.

Good, John Mason. 1835. *The Study of Medicine*. 5 vols. Vol. 2. New York: Harper.

Goode, William J. 1960. "A Theory of Strain." *American Sociological Review* 25:483–496.

Goodman, Ellen. 1982a. "A Little Reading List for the Beach." *Boston Globe*, August 3, 17.

———. 1982b. "Political Gender Gap." *Boston Globe*, October 19, 19.

Gordin, Michael D. 2012. *The Pseudoscience Wars: Immanuel Velikovsky and the Birth of the Modern Fringe*. Chicago: University of Chicago Press.

Gordon, Linda. 1976. *The Moral Property of Women: A History of Birth Control Politics in America*. Chicago: University of Illinois Press. Reprint, 2002.

———. 1990. *Women, the State and Welfare*. Madison: University of Wisconsin Press.

Gornick, Vivan. 1980. "One Man's Narcissism . . . May Be a Woman's Self-Emergence." Review of *The Culture of Narcissism*, by Christopher Lasch. *Savvy*, February, 76–78.

Gornick, Vivian, and Barbara K. Moran. 1971. *Woman in Sexist Society: Studies in Power and Powerlessness*. New York: Basic Books.

Gould, Roger L. 1972. "The Phases of Adult Life: A Study in Developmental Psychology." *American Journal of Psychiatry* 129 (5):521–531.

———. 1975. "Adult Life Stages: Growth toward Self-Tolerance." *Psychology Today* 8:74–78.

———. 1978. *Transformations: Growth and Change in Adult Life*. New York: Simon & Schuster.

———. 1979. "Transformations in Mid-life." *New York University Education Quarterly* 10 (2):2–9.

———. 1986. "The Therapeutic Learning Program (TLP): A Computer-Assisted Short-term Treatment Program." *Computers in Psychiatry/Psychology*, September.

———. 1990a. "Clinical Lessons from Adult Development." In *New Dimensions in Adult Development*, edited by Robert A. Nemiroff and Calvin A. Colarusso, 345–370. New York: Basic Books.

———. 1990b. "The Therapeutic Learning Program." In *Fostering Critical Reflection in Adulthood: A Guide to Transformative and Emancipatory Learning*, edited by Jack Mezirow, 134–156. San Francisco: Jossey-Bass.

———. 1992. "Adult Development and Brief Computer-Assisted Therapy in Mental Health and Managed Care." In *Managed Mental Health Care: Administrative and Clinical Issues*, edited by Judith L. Feldman and Richard J. Fitzpatrick, 347–358. New York: American Psychiatric Press.

Gould, Stephen Jay. 1980. *The Mismeasure of Man*. New York: Norton.

Gove, Walter R., and Jeanette Tudor. 1973. "Adult Sex Roles and Mental Illness." *American Journal of Sociology* 78:812–835.

Gove, Walter R., and Carol Zeiss. 1987. "Multiple Roles and Happiness." In *Spouse, Parent, Worker: On Gender and Multiple Roles*, edited by Faye J. Crosby, 125–137. New Haven, CT: Yale University Press.

Graebner, William. 1980a. *A History of Retirement: The Meaning and Function of an American Institution, 1885–1978*. New Haven, CT: Yale University Press.

———. 1980b. "The Unstable World of Benjamin Spock: Social Engineering in a Democratic Culture, 1917–1950." *Journal of American History* 67:612–629.

Graham, Carol, and Julia Ruiz Pozuelo. 2017. "Happiness, Stress, and Age: How the U-curve Varies across People and Places." *Journal of Population Economics* 30 (1):225–264.

Graham, Loren, Wolf Lepenies, and Peter Weingart. 1983. *Functions and Uses of Disciplinary Histories*. Dordrecht: Reidel.

Grant, Julia. 1998. *Raising Baby by the Book: The Education of American Mothers*. New Haven, CT: Yale University Press.

Green, Jeremy. 1985. "Media Sensationalisation and Science: The Case of the Criminal Chromosome." In *Expository Science: Forms and Functions of Popularisation*, edited by Terry Shinn and Richard Whitley, 139–161. Dordrecht: Reidel.

Greenberg, Miriam. 2008. *Branding New York: How a City in Crisis Was Sold to the World*. New York: Routledge.

Greer, Germaine. 1970. *The Female Eunuch*. London: MacGibbon & Kee.

———. 1972. "McGovern, the Big Tease." *Harper's*, October 1972, 56–72.

———. 1991. *The Change: Women, Aging and the Menopause*. New York: Knopf.

Gross, Amy. 1982. "Thinking like a Woman." *Vogue*, May, 268–269, 333–335.

Grundy, Milton. 1974. *Tax Havens: A World Survey*. London: Sweet & Maxwell.

Guild, Laura, and Wayne Neiman. 1976. "A Journey into the Forgotten Realm of Adult Personality Development." Review of *Passages*, by Gail Sheehy. *Family Court Review* 14 (2):34–35.

Guilder, George. 1984. "Women in the Work Force: Gender Disparity in the Workplace Might Have Less to Do with Discrimination than with Women Making the Choice to Stay at Home." *Atlantic*, September, 20–24.

Gullette, Margaret Morganroth. 1997. *Declining to Decline: Cultural Combat and the Politics of the Midlife*. Charlottesville, VA: University of Virginia Press.

Haan, Norma. 1975. "Hypothetical and Actual Moral Reasoning in a Situation of Civil Disobedience." *Journal of Personality and Social Psychology* 32:255–270.

———. 1977. *Coping and Defending: Processes of Self-Environment Organization*. New York: Academic Press.

Hacking, Ian. 2002. *Historical Ontology*. Cambridge, MA: Harvard University Press.

Hagerty, Barbara Bradley. 2016. *Life Reimagined: The Science, Art, and Opportunity of Midlife*. New York: Riverhead.

Halford, Henry. 1813. "On the Climacteric Disease." *Medical Transactions of the Royal College of Physicians of London* 4:316–328.

Hall, G. Stanley. 1904. *Adolescence: Its Psychology and Its Relations to Physiology, Anthropology, Sociology, Sex, Crime, Religion and Education*. New York: Appleton.

———. 1922. *Senescence, the Last Half of Life*. New York: Appleton.

Hamilton, Sheryl N. 2009. *Impersonations: Troubling the Person in Law and Culture*. Toronto: University of Toronto Press.

Hanisch, Carol. 1970. "The Personal Is Political." *Notes from the Second Year*, 76–78.

Hansl, Eva von Baur. 1927. "What about the Children? The Question of Mothers and Careers." *Harper's*, January, 220–227.

Hapgood, Hutchins. 1903. *The Autobiography of a Thief*. New York: Johnson Reprint. Reprint, 1970.

———. 1909. *An Anarchist Woman*. New York: Duffield.

Haraway, Donna. 1988. "Situated Knowledges: The Science Question in Feminism and the Privilege of Partial Perspective." *Feminist Studies* 14 (3):575–599.

———. 1989. *Primate Visions: Gender, Race, and Nature in the World of Modern Science*. New York: Routledge.

Harding, Sandra. 1986. *The Science Question in Feminism*. Ithaca, NY: Cornell University Press.

Hartog, Hendrik. 2012. *Someday All This Will Be Yours: A History of Inheritance and Old Age.* Cambridge, MA: Harvard University Press.

Haseltine, Florence. 1997. Foreword to *Women's Health Research: A Medical and Policy Primer,* edited by Florence Haseltine and Beverly Jacobson, xiii–xviii. Washington, DC: Health Press.

Hassenger, Robert. 1976. Review of *Passages,* by Gail Sheehy. *New Republic,* September 18, 30–31.

Haste, Helen. 1994. "'You've Come a Long Way, Babe': A Catalyst of Feminist Conflicts." *Feminism & Psychology* 4 (3):399–403.

Haugeberg, Karissa. 2017. *Women against Abortion: Inside the Largest Moral Reform Movement of the Twentieth Century.* Urbana: University of Illinois Press.

Hayward, Rhodri. 2014. "Sadness in Camberwell: Imagining Stress and Constructing History in Postwar Britain." In *Stress, Shock, and Adaptation in the Twentieth Century,* edited by David Cantor and Edmund Ramsden, 320–342. Rochester, NY: University of Rochester Press.

Heath, Clark W. 1945. *What People Are: A Study of Normal Young Men.* Cambridge, MA: Harvard University Press.

Heath, Kay. 2009. *Aging by the Book: The Emergence of Midlife in Victorian Britain.* Albany: State University of New York Press.

Heesen, Anke te. 2014. "'Ganz Aug', ganz Ohr': Hermann Bahr und das Interview um 1900." In *Echt inszeniert: Interviews in Literatur und Literaturbetrieb,* edited by Thorsten Hoffmann and Gerhard Kaiser, 129–150. Wilhelm Fink: Paderborn.

Heilbrun, Carolyn G. 1979. *Reinventing Womanhood.* New York: Norton.

Hemmungs Wirtén, Eva. 2015. *Making Marie Curie: Intellectual Property and Celebrity Culture in an Age of Information.* Chicago: University of Chicago Press.

Henkel, Wayne J. 1976. "Going through Some Changes." Review of *Passages,* by Gail Sheehy. *Baltimore Sun,* July 25, 1976, D5.

Hennig, Margaret. 1970. "Career Development for Women Executives." PhD diss., Harvard Business School.

Hennig, Margaret, and Anne Jardim. 1977. *The Managerial Woman.* Garden City, NY: Anchor Press/Doubleday.

Herman, Ellen. 1996. *The Romance of American Psychology: Political Culture in the Age of Experts.* Berkeley: University of California Press.

Herzog, Dagmar. 2017. *Cold War Freud: Psychoanalysis in an Age of Catastrophes.* Cambridge: Cambridge University Press.

Hess, Beth B. 1985. "Prime Time." Review of *Lifeprints,* by Grace Baruch, Rosalind Barnett, and Caryl Rivers; *Women in Midlife,* by Grace Baruch and Jeanne Brooks-Gunn; and *In Her Prime,* by Judith Brown and Virginia Kerns. *Women's Review of Books,* June, 6–7.

Heti, Sheila. 2017. *Motherhood.* New York: Holt.

Hewitt, Nancy A., ed. 2010. *No Permanent Waves: Recasting Histories of U.S. Feminism.* New Brunswick, NJ: Rutgers University Press.

———. 2012. "Feminist Frequencies: Regenerating the Wave Metaphor." *Feminist Studies* 38 (3):658–680.

Hilgartner, Stephen. 1990. "The Dominant View of Popularization: Conceptual Problems, Political Uses." *Social Studies of Science* 20 (3):519–539.

Hirdt, Willi. 1992. "Lebensmitte: Zu archetypischen Vorstellungen im Zusammenhang mit 'Inferno I,1.'" *Deutsches Dante-Jahrbuch* 67 (1):7–32.

Hirshbein, Laura D. 2009. "Gender, Age, and Diagnosis: The Rise and Fall of Involutional Melancholia in American Psychiatry, 1900–1980." *Bulletin of the History of Medicine* 83 (4):710–745.

Hite, Shere. 1976. *The Hite Report: A Nationwide Study of Female Sexuality.* New York: Dell. Reprint, 1981.

Hobson, Laura Z. 1983. *Laura Z: A Life.* New York: Arbor House.

Hochschild, Arlie Russell. 1983. *The Managed Heart: Commercialization of Human Feeling.* Berkeley: University of California Press.

Hochschild, Arlie Russell, with Anne Machung. 1989. *The Second Shift: Working Parents and the Revolution at Home.* New York: Viking.

Hodgson, Richard C., Daniel J. Levinson, and Abraham Zaleznik. 1965. *The Executive Role Constellation: An Analysis of Personality and Role Relations in Management.* Boston: Harvard University Press.

Hofer, Hans-Georg. 2007. "Medizin, Altern, Männlichkeit: Zur Kulturgeschichte des männlichen Klimakteriums." *Medizinhistorisches Journal* 42 (2):210–246.

Hogeland, Lisa Maria. 1994. "'Men Can't Be That Bad': Realism and Feminist Fiction in the 1970s." *American Literary History* 6 (2):287–305.

———. 1998. *Feminism and Its Fictions: The Consciousness-Raising Novel and the Women's Liberation Movement.* Philadelphia: University of Pennsylvania Press.

Hole, Judith, and Ellen Levine. 1971. *Rebirth of Feminism.* New York: Quadrangle.

Hollingworth, Leta Stetter. 1914. *Functional Periodicity: An Experimental Study of the Mental and Motor Abilities of Women during Menstruation.* New York: Teachers College, Columbia University.

Holmes, Thomas H., and Richard H. Rahe. 1967. "The Social Readjustment Rating Scale." *Journal of Psychosomatic Research* 11 (2):213–218.

Holstein, Constance B. 1976. "Irreversible, Stepwise Sequence in the Development of Moral Judgment: A Longitudinal Study of Males and Females." *Child Development* 47 (1):51–61.

Homestead, Melissa J. 2005. *American Woman Authors and Literary Property, 1822–1869.* Cambridge: Cambridge University Press.

Hooton, Ernest. 1945. *Young Man, You Are Normal.* New York: Putnam.

Hopkins, Linda B. 1980. "Inner Space and Outer Space Identity in Contemporary Females." *Psychiatry* 43 (1):1–12.

Hopwood, Nick, Peter Murray Jones, Lauren Kassell, and Jim Secord. 2015. "Special Issue: Communicating Reproduction." *Bulletin of the History of Medicine* 89 (3).

Hopwood, Nick, Simon Schaffer, and Jim Secord. 2010. "Seriality and Scientific Objects in the Nineteenth Century." *History of Science* 48 (161):251–285.

Horner, Matina S. 1968. "Sex Differences in Achievement Motivation and Performance in Competitive and Non-Competitive Situations." PhD diss., University of Minnesota.

———. 1970. "Femininity and Successful Achievement: A Basic Inconsistency." In *Feminine Personality and Conflict*, edited by Judith M. Bardwick, Elizabeth M. Douvan, Matina S. Horner, and David Gutmann, 97–122. Belmont, CA: Brooks-Cole.

———. 1972. "Toward an Understanding of Achievement-related Conflicts in Women." *Journal of Social Issues* 28 (2):157–175.

Horowitz, Daniel. 1998. *Betty Friedan and the Making of* The Feminine Mystique*: The American Left, the Cold War, and Modern Feminism.* Amherst: University of Massachusetts Press. Reprint, 2000.

"Hospital Offers Treatment for Mid-life Crisis." 1987. *Los Angeles Times*, July 27, V8.

Houck, Judith A. 2006. *Hot and Bothered: Women, Medicine, and Menopause in Modern America*. Cambridge, MA: Harvard University Press.

Howard, Jane. 1973. *A Different Woman*. New York: Dutton.

———. 1974. "Hal Scharlatt, 1935–1974." *Village Voice*, March 14, 26.

Howard, Vicki. 2006. *Brides, Inc.: American Weddings and the Business of Tradition*. Philadelphia: University of Pennsylvania Press.

Huckle, Patricia. 1991. *Tish Sommers, Activist, and the Founding of the Older Women's League*. Knoxville: University of Tennessee Press.

Huddy, Leonie. 1997. "Feminists and Feminism in the News." In *Women, Media, and Politics*, edited by Pippa Norris, 183–204. New York: Oxford University Press.

Hulbert, Ann. 1996. "Dr. Spock's Baby." *New Yorker*, May 20, 82.

Hull, Gloria T., Patricia Bell-Scott, and Barbara Smith. 1982. *All the Women Are White, All the Blacks Are Men, but Some of Us Are Brave*. New York: Feminist Press.

Hunter, Jane. 2002. *How Young Ladies Became Girls: The Victorian Origins of American Girlhood*. New Haven, CT: Yale University Press.

Hushbeck, Judith. 1989. *Old and Obsolete: Age Discrimination and the American Worker, 1860–1920*. New York: Garland.

Hutton, Patrick H. 2004. *Philippe Ariès and the Politics of French Cultural History*. Amherst: University of Massachusetts Press.

Hynds, Ernest C. 1991. "Editorial Page Editors Discuss Use of Letters." *Newspaper Research Journal* 13 (1):124–136.

"I Like Being Forty!" 1941. *Independent Woman*, February, 47.

Igo, Sarah E. 2007. *The Averaged American: Surveys, Citizens, and the Making of a Mass Public*. Cambridge, MA: Harvard University Press.

Illig, Joyce. 1976. "Book Business." *Washington Post*, May 23, L10.

Illouz, Eva. 2008. *Saving the Modern Soul: Therapy, Emotions and the Culture of Self-Help*. Berkeley, CA: University of California Press.

Irigaray, Luce. 1985. *This Sex Which Is Not One*. Ithaca, NY: Cornell University Press.

"Is Forty the Limit?" 1922. *Independent Woman*, November, 21.

Isaac, Joel. 2012. *Working Knowledge: Making the Human Sciences from Parsons to Kuhn*. Cambridge, MA: Harvard University Press.

Jackson, Mark. 2013. *The Age of Stress: Science and the Search for Stability*. Oxford: Oxford University Press.

Jacobi, Mary Putnam. 1877. *The Question of Rest for Women during Menstruation*. New York: Putnam.

Jahoda, Marie. 1958. *Current Concepts of Positive Mental Health*. New York: Basic Books.

Jahoda, Marie, and Joan (Havel) Grant. 1955. "Psychological Problems of Women in Different Social Roles: A Case History of Problem Formulation in Research." *Educational Record* 36 (4):325–333.

Jahoda, Marie, Paul F. Lazarsfeld, and Hans Zeisel. 1933. *Die Arbeitslosen von Marienthal: Ein soziographischer Versuch*. Frankfurt am Main: Suhrkamp. Reprint, 2015.

James, T. F. 1958. "The American Wife." *Cosmopolitan*, January, 20–37.

James, Jacquelyn Boone, and Corinne J. Lewkowicz. 1997. "Themes of Power and Affiliation across Time," in *Multiple Paths of Midlife Development*, edited by Margie E. Lachman and Jacquelyn Boone James, 109–144. Chicago: University of Chicago Press.

Janeway, Elizabeth. 1971. *Man's World, Woman's Place: A Study in Social Mythology*. New York: Dell.

Jaques, Elliott. 1956. *Measurement of Responsibility: A Study of Work, Payment and Individual Capacity*. London: Tavistock.

———. 1965. "Death and the Mid-life Crisis." *International Journal of Psychoanalysis* 46:502–514.

———. 1970. *Work, Creativity, and Social Justice.* New York: International Universities Press.

———. 1998. "On Leaving the Tavistock Institute." *Human Relations* 51 (3):251–257.

Jay, Karla. 1970. "The Man's Media—*Ladies' Home Journal.*" *Rat*, April 4, 4, 22.

Jay, Peter A. 1977. "Tales of Some Travelers." Review of *Adaptation to Life*, by George Vaillant. *Baltimore Sun*, December 28, A14.

Jensen, Uffa. 2014. "Mrs. Gaskell's Anxiety." In *Learning How to Feel: Children's Literature and Emotional Socialization, 1870–1970*, edited by Ute Frevert et al., 21–39. Oxford: Oxford University Press.

Jewett, Andrew. 2014. *Science, Democracy, and the American University: From the Civil War to the Cold War.* Cambridge: Cambridge University Press.

Joerißen, Peter, and Cornelia Will. 1983. *Die Lebenstreppe: Bilder der menschlichen Lebensalter.* Köln: Rheinland-Verlag.

Johnson, Ann, and Elizabeth Johnston. 2010. "Unfamiliar Feminisms: Revisiting the National Council of Women Psychologists." *Psychology of Women Quarterly* 34 (3):311–327.

Johnson, John W. 1979. "The 'New Journalism' and the 'New' American Studies: Some Relationships and Points of Comparison." *Indian Journal of American Studies* 9 (1):32–43.

Johnston, Elizabeth, and Ann Johnson. 2017. "Balancing Life and Work by Unbending Gender: Early American Women Psychologists' Struggles and Contributions." *Journal of the History of the Behavioral Sciences* 53 (3):246–264.

Jong, Erica. 1994. *Fear of Fifty: A Midlife Memoir.* New York: HarperCollins.

Jordanova, Ludmilla. 1989. *Sexual Visions: Images of Gender in Science and Medicine between the Eighteenth and Twentieth Centuries.* Madison: University of Wisconsin Press.

"Joyce Illig Bohn, Columnist, Wrote 'Book Business.'" 1976. *Washington Post*, August 24.

"Joyce Illig Dies; Weekly Columnist." 1976. *New York Times*, August 24, 32.

Kaiser, David. 2016. "Thomas Kuhn and the Psychology of Scientific Revolutions." In *Kuhn's "Structure of Scientific Revolutions" at Fifty: Reflections on a Science Classic*, edited by Robert J. Richards and Lorraine Daston, 71–95. Chicago: University of Chicago Press.

Kaiser, David, and W. Patrick McCray, eds. 2016. *Groovy Science: Knowledge, Innovation, and American Counterculture.* Chicago: University of Chicago Press.

Kamen, Martin David. 1985. *Radiant Science, Dark Politics: A Memoir of the Nuclear Age.* Berkeley: University of California Press.

Kanigel, Robert. 1978. "The Passing of the Seasons." Review of *The Seasons of a Man's Life*, by Daniel J. Levinson. *Baltimore Sun*, April 23, D5.

Kanner, Allen D., James C. Coyne, Catherine Schaefer, and Richard S. Lazarus. 1981. "Comparison of Two Modes of Stress Measurement: Daily Hassles and Uplifts versus Major Life Events." *Journal of Behavioral Medicine* 4 (1):1–39.

Kanner, Allen D., S. Shirley Feldman, Daniel A. Weinberger, and Martin E. Ford. 1987. "Uplifts, Hassles, and Adaptational Outcomes in Early Adolescents." *Journal of Early Adolescence* 7 (4):371–394.

Kant, Immanuel. 1923. *Gesammelte Schriften*, edited by Preussische Akademie der Wissenschaften. 24 vols. Vol. 9, *Logik*. Berlin: de Gruyter.

Kanter, Rosabeth Moss. 1977. *Men and Women of the Corporation.* New York: Basic Books.

Kasinsky, Renée Goldsmith. 1977. Review of *Passages*, by Gail Sheehy. *Western Sociological Review* 8 (2):239–241.

Katz, Stephen. 1996. *Disciplining Old Age: The Formation of Gerontological Knowledge.* Charlottesville, VA: University of Virginia Press.

Keller, Evelyn Fox. 1981. "McClintock's Maize." *Science '81,* October, 54–59.

———. 1983. *A Feeling for the Organism: The Life and Work of Barbara McClintock.* San Francisco: Freeman.

———. 1985. *Reflections on Gender and Science.* New Haven, CT: Yale University Press.

Kerber, Linda K., Catherine G. Greeno, Eleanor E. Maccoby, Zelia Luria, Carol B. Stack, and Carol Gilligan. 1986. "On *In a Different Voice:* An Interdisciplinary Forum." *Signs* 11 (2):304–333.

Kett, Joseph F. 1978. *Rites of Passage: Adolescence in America, 1790 to the Present.* New York: Basic Books.

———. 2003. "Reflections on the History of Adolescence in America." *History of the Family* 8 (3):355–373.

Khan, B. Zorina. 1996. "Married Women's Property Laws and Female Commercial Activity: Evidence from the United States Patent Records, 1790–1895." *Journal of Economic History* 56 (2):356–388.

Kiernan, Vincent. 2006. *Embargoed Science.* Urbana: University of Illinois Press.

Kilday, Gregg. 1975. "Rule in Plea for 'Good Taste.'" *Los Angeles Times,* April 3, J15.

Kimmel, Michael. 1977. Review of *Passages,* by Gail Sheehy. *Contemporary Sociology* 6 (4):490–493.

King, Pearl, and Riccardo Steiner. 1990. *The Freud-Klein Controversies, 1941–45.* London: Routledge.

King, Peter H. 1976. "Gail Sheehy's Book Probes Changing Passages of Life." *Atlanta Constitution,* September 4, 1976, 5B.

King, Toni C. 2003. "'Who's That Lady?' *Ebony* Magazine and Black Professional Women." In *Disco Divas: Women and Popular Culture in the 1970s,* edited by Sherrie A. Inness, 87–102. Philadelphia: University of Pennsylvania Press.

Kinney, Jean Brown. 1968. *Start with an Empty Nest.* New York: Harcourt, Brace & World.

Kinsey, Alfred Charles, Wardell Baxter Pomeroy, and Clyde Eugene Martin. 1948. *Sexual Behavior in the Human Male.* Bloomington: Indiana University Press.

Kirsch, Jonathan. 1995. *Kirsch's Handbook of Publishing Law for Authors, Editors, and Agents.* Los Angeles: Acrobat.

Kirsner, Douglas. 2004. "The Intellectual Odyssey of Elliott Jaques: From Alchemy to Science." *Free Associations* 11 (2):179–204.

Kitzinger, Celia. 1993. "'Psychology Constructs the Female': A Reappraisal." *Feminism & Psychology* 3 (2):189–193.

Klein, Marian van der, Rebecca Jo Plant, Nichole Sanders, and Lori R. Weintrob, eds. 2012. *Maternalism Reconsidered: Motherhood, Welfare, and Social Policies in the Twentieth Century.* New York: Berghahn.

Klein, Viola. 1946. *The Feminine Character: History of an Ideology.* London: Routledge. Reprint, 1971.

Klemesrud, Judy. 1977. "Keys to Success: A Study of 95 Men." *New York Times,* September 28, C1, C14.

Klerman, Gerald L., and Daniel J. Levinson. 1969. "Becoming the Director: Promotion as a Phase in Personal-Professional Development." *Psychiatry: Interpersonal and Biological Processes* 32 (4):411–427.

Kline, Wendy. 2010. *Bodies of Knowledge: Sexuality, Reproduction, and Women's Health in the Second Wave.* Chicago: University of Chicago Press.

Kluger, Richard. 1986. *The Paper: The Life and Death of the New York Herald Tribune*. New York: Knopf.

Knopf, Olga. 1932. *The Art of Being a Woman*. Boston: Little, Brown.

Kohlberg, Lawrence. 1969a. "Stage and Sequence: The Cognitive-Development Approach to Socialization." In *Handbook of Socialization Theory and Research*, edited by David A. Goslin, 347–480. Chicago: Rand McNally.

———. 1969b. *Stages in the Development of Moral Thought and Action*. New York: Holt, Rinehart & Winston.

———. 1976. "Moral Stages and Moralization: The Cognitive-Development Approach." In *Moral Development and Behavior: Theory, Research, and Social Issues*, edited by Thomas Lickona, 31–53. New York: Holt, Rinehart & Winston.

———. 1981. *The Meaning and Measurement of Moral Development*. Worcester, MA: Clark University Press.

———. 1982. "A Reply to Owen Flanagan and Some Comments on the Puka-Goodpaster Exchange." *Ethics* 92 (3):513–528.

Kohlberg, Lawrence, and Carol Gilligan. 1971. "The Adolescent as a Philosopher: The Discovery of the Self in a Postconventional World." *Daedalus* 100 (4):1054–1087.

———. 1977. "From Adolescence to Adulthood: The Rediscovery of Reality in a Postconventional World." In *Topics in Cognitive Development: Language and Operational Thought*, edited by Barbara Presseisen, David Goldstein, and Marilyn H. Appel, 125–136. New York: Plenum.

Kohlberg, Lawrence, and Richard Kramer. 1969. "Continuities and Discontinuities in Child and Adult Moral Development." *Human Development* 12 (2):93–120.

Kohli, Martin. 1986. "Gesellschaftszeit und Lebenszeit: Der Lebenslauf im Strukturwandel der Moderne." In *Die Moderne: Kontinuität und Zäsuren*, edited by Johannes Berger, 183–208. Göttingen: Schwartz.

Kohlstedt, Sally Gregory. 1995. "Women in the History of Science: An Ambiguous Place." *Osiris* 10:39–58.

Komarovsky, Mirra. 1953. *Women in the Modern World: Their Education and Their Dilemmas*. Boston: Little, Brown.

———. 1967. *Blue-Collar Marriage*. New York: Vintage.

Komesaroff, Paul A., Philipa Rothfield, and Jeanne Daly, eds. 1997. *Reinterpreting Menopause: Cultural and Philosophical Issues*. New York: Routledge.

Korinek, Valerie. 2000. *Roughing It in the Suburbs: Reading "Chatelaine" Magazine in the Fifties and Sixties*. Toronto: University of Toronto Press.

Koselleck, Reinhart. 2006. "Crisis." *Journal of the History of Ideas* 67 (2):357–400.

Koven, Seth, and Sonya Michel. 1990. "Womanly Duties: Maternalist Politics and the Origins of Welfare States in France, Germany, Great Britain, and the United States, 1880–1920." *American Historical Review* 95 (4):1076–1108.

———, eds. 1993. *Mothers of a New World: Maternalist Politics and the Origins of Welfare States*. New York: Routledge.

Kumar, Anuradha, Leila Hessini, and Ellen M. H. Mitchell. 2009. "Conceptualising Abortion Stigma." *Culture, Health & Society* 11 (6): 625–639.

Krier, Beth Ann. 1978. "Help for Adult Growing Pains: Psychiatrist's Advice: Relax." *Los Angeles Times*, July 5, I1.

Kroll, Gary. 2008. *America's Ocean Wilderness: A Cultural History of Twentieth-Century Exploration*. Lawrence: University Press of Kansas.

Kuhn, Thomas S. 1962. *The Structure of Scientific Revolutions*. London: University of Chicago Press. Reprint, 2012.

Kury, Patrick. 2012. *Der überforderte Mensch: Eine Wissensgeschichte vom Stress zum Burnout.* Frankfurt am Main: Campus.

Lachman, Margie E. 2001. *Handbook of Midlife Development.* New York: Wiley.

Lachman, Margie E., and Jacquelyn Boone James, eds. 1997. *Multiple Paths of Midlife Development.* Chicago: University of Chicago Press.

Ladd-Taylor, Molly. 1994. *Mother-Work: Women, Child Welfare, and the State, 1890–1930.* Urbana: University of Illinois Press.

Lague, Louise. 1977. "Written Advice Gets New Respectability." *Chicago Tribune,* August 30, A1, 8.

Lamb, Sharon. 2001. *The Secret Lives of Girls: What Good Girls Really Do—Sex Play, Aggression, and Their Guilt.* New York: Free Press.

Landers, James. 2010. *The Improbable First Century of "Cosmopolitan" Magazine.* Columbia and London: University of Missouri Press.

Langer, Marshall J. 1975. *How to Use Foreign Tax Havens.* New York: Practicing Law Institute.

Langholf, Volker. 1990. *Medical Theories in Hippocrates: Early Texts and the "Epidemics."* Berlin: De Gruyter.

Lasch, Christopher. 1976. "Planned Obsolescence." Review of *Passages,* by Gail Sheehy. *New York Review of Books,* October 28, 7, 10.

———. 1977. *Haven in a Heartless World: The Family Besieged.* New York: Basic Books.

———. 1979. *The Culture of Narcissism: American Life in an Age of Diminishing Expectations.* New York: Norton.

———. 1992. "Gilligan's Island." Review of *Meeting at the Crossroads,* by Lyn Mikel Brown and Carol Gilligan. *New Republic,* December 7, 34–39.

Laslett, Barbara, Sally Gregory Kohlstedt, Helen Longino, and Evelynn Hammonds, eds. 1996. *Gender and Scientific Authority.* Chicago: University of Chicago Press.

Latour, Bruno. 2005. *Reassembling the Social: An Introduction to Actor-Network-Theory.* Oxford: Oxford University Press.

Lauerman, Connie. 1984. "Doctor's Own Trauma Reveals Male Crisis." *Chicago Tribune,* September 14, E1.

Laughlin, Kathleen A. 2000. *Women's Work and Public Policy: A History of the Women's Bureau, U.S. Department of Labor, 1945–1970.* Boston: Northeastern University Press.

Laughlin, Kathleen A., and Jacqueline Castledine. 2012. *Breaking the Wave: Women, Their Organizations, and Feminism, 1945–1985.* New York: Routledge.

Laughlin, Kathleen A., Julie Gallagher, Dorothy Sue Cobble, Eileen Boris, Premilla Nadasen, Stephanie Gilmore, and Leandra Zarnow. 2010. "Is It Time to Jump Ship? Historians Rethink the Waves Metaphor." *Feminist Formations* 22 (1):76–135.

Lavietes, Stuart. 2003. "Elliott Jaques, 86, Scientist Who Coined 'Midlife Crisis,' Is Dead." *New York Times,* March 17, B7.

Lawrence, Josephine. 1956. *The Empty Nest.* New York: Harcourt, Brace.

Leaffer, Marshall. 2009. "American Copyright Law since 1945." In *A History of the Book in America,* vol. 5, *The Enduring Book: Print Culture in Postwar America,* edited by David Paul Nord, Joan S. Rubin, and Michael Schudson, 151–166. Chapel Hill: University of North Carolina Press.

Lee, Hermione. 1997. *Virginia Woolf.* London: Vintage.

Lehmann-Haupt, Christopher. 1973. "A Report on Prostitution." Review of *Hustling,* by Gail Sheehy. *New York Times,* August 10, 29.

Lemov, Rebecca. 2015. *Database of Dreams: The Lost Quest to Catalog Humanity.* New Haven, CT: Yale University Press.

"Lena Levine Dies; Psychiatrist, 61; Marriage Adviser Was Active in Planned Parenthood." 1965. *New York Times*, January 11, 45.

Leng, Kirsten. 2013. "An 'Elusive' Phenomenon: Feminism, Sexual Science, and the Female Sex Drive, 1880–1914." *Centaurus* 55 (2):131–152.

Leo, John. 1976. "The Gripes of Academe." *Time*, May 10, 66, 69.

———. 1981. "All About Men: Shere's Sequel." Review of *The Hite Report on Male Sexuality*, by Shere Hite. *Time*, June 15, 83–84.

———. 1991. "Toxic Feminism on the Big Screen." *U.S. News & World Report*, June 10, 20.

———. 1994. *Two Steps Ahead of the Thought Police*. New York: Simon & Schuster.

———. 2001. *Incorrect Thoughts: Notes on Our Wayward Culture*. New Brunswick, NJ: Transaction.

Lepore, Jill. 2014. *The Secret History of Wonder Woman*. New York: Knopf.

LeShan, Eda J. 1973. *The Wonderful Crisis of Middle Age: Some Personal Reflections*. New York: McKay.

"Letters." 1974. *New York*, March 11, 5.

"Letters from Readers." 1976. *Glamour*, June, 13, 16.

"Letters to the Editor." 1976a. *McCall's*, July, 10.

"Letters to the Editor." 1976b. *McCall's*, August, 12.

Levey, Jane F. 2000. "Spock, I Love Him." *Colby Quarterly* 36 (4): 273–294.

Levey, Robert. 1976. "Bumps on the Road of Life." *Boston Globe*, June 3, 45, 52.

Levin, Hillel. 1983. *Grand Delusions: The Cosmic Career of John De Lorean*. New York: Viking.

Levine, Adeline. 1977. Review of *Passages*, by Gail Sheehy. *Contemporary Psychology* 22 (4):284–285.

Levine, Lena. 1938. *The Doctor Talks with the Bride*. New York: Planned Parenthood Federation of America. Reprint, 1948.

Levine, Lena, and Beka Doherty. 1952. *The Menopause*. New York: Random House.

LeVine, Robert A., and Sarah LeVine. 1998. "Fertility and Maturity in Africa: Gusii Parents in Middle Adulthood." In *Welcome to Middle Age! (And Other Cultural Fictions)*, edited by Richard Shweder, 189–201. Chicago: University of Chicago Press.

Levinson, Daniel J. 1978a. "Becoming Your Own Man." *Esquire*, April 11, 85–88, 91, 93.

———. 1978b. "Growing Up with the Dream." *Psychology Today*, January, 20–31, 89.

———. 1978c. *The Seasons of a Man's Life*. New York: Knopf.

Levinson, Daniel J., Charlotte M. Darrow, Edward B. Klein, Maria H. Levinson, and Braxton McKee. 1974. "The Psychosocial Development of Men in Early Adulthood and the Mid-life Transition." In *Life History Research in Psychopathology*, vol. 3, edited by David F. Ricks, Alexander Thomas, and Merrill Roff, 243–258. Minneapolis: University of Minnesota Press.

Levinson, Daniel J., and Judy D. Levinson. 1996. *The Seasons of a Woman's Life*. New York: Knopf.

Lewenstein, Bruce V. 1992. "The Meaning of 'Public Understanding of Science' in the United States after World War II." *Public Understanding of Science* 1 (1):45–68.

———. 1995. "From Fax to Facts: Communication in the Cold Fusion Saga." *Social Studies of Science* 25:403–436.

Lewis, Jane. 1990. "Myrdal, Klein, Women's Two Roles and Postwar Feminism." In *British Feminism in the Twentieth Century*, edited by Harold L. Smith, 167–188. Aldershot: Elgar.

———. 2001. "The Decline of the Male Breadwinner Model: Implications for Work and Care." *Social Politics* 8 (2):152–169.

Lewis, Roselle M. 1984. "Guidance for Male 'Menopause' Crisis." *Los Angeles Times,* November 22, H19.

Lightman, Bernard. 2007. *Victorian Popularizers of Science: Designing Nature for New Audiences.* Chicago: University of Chicago Press.

Lindner, Rolf. 1996. *The Reportage of Urban Culture: Robert Park and the Chicago School.* Cambridge: Cambridge University Press.

Lingeman, Richard R. 1978. "Literary Cloning Scandal." *Nation,* May 6, 544–545.

Linstrum, Erik. 2016. *Ruling Minds: Psychology in the British Empire.* Cambridge, MA: Harvard University Press.

Lock, Margaret. 1990. *Encounters with Aging: Mythologies of Menopause in Japan and North America.* Berkeley: University of California Press.

———. 1998. "Deconstructing the Change: Female Maturation in Japan and North America." In *Welcome to Middle Age! (And Other Cultural Fictions),* edited by Richard Shweder, 45–74. Chicago: University of Chicago Press.

Long, Judy. 1999. *Telling Women's Lives: Subject, Narrator, Reader, Text.* New York: New York University Press.

Longcope, Kay. 1984. "Caryl Rivers: Everyday Optimist." *Boston Globe,* August 22, 61, 64.

Longino, Helen E. 2003. "Does *The Structure of Scientific Revolutions* Permit a Feminist Revolution in Science?" In *Thomas Kuhn,* edited by Thomas Nickles, 261–281. Cambridge: Cambridge University Press.

Lowenthal, Marjorie Fiske, and David A. Chiriboga. 1972. "Transition to the Empty Nest: Crisis, Challenge or Relief?" *Archives of General Psychiatry* 26:8–14.

Lowry, Edith B. 1919. *The Woman of Forty.* Chicago: Forbes.

Luker, Kristin. 1975. *Taking Chances: Abortion and the Decision Not to Contracept.* Berkeley: University of California Press.

———. 1984. *Abortion and the Politics of Motherhood.* Berkeley: University of California Press.

Lunbeck, Elizabeth. 1994. *The Psychiatric Persuasion: Knowledge, Gender, and Power in Modern America.* Princeton, NJ: Princeton University Press.

———. 2014. *The Americanization of Narcissism.* Cambridge, MA: Harvard University Press.

Lutkehaus, Nancy C. 2008. *Margaret Mead: The Making of an American Icon.* Princeton, NJ: Princeton University Press.

Lutz, Tom. 1991. *American Nervousness, 1903: An Anecdotal History.* Ithaca, NY: Cornell University Press.

Lykknes, Annette, Donald L. Opitz, and Brigitte Van Tiggelen, eds. 2012. *For Better or Worse? Collaborative Couples in the Sciences.* Basel: Springer.

Lynd, Robert S., and Helen Merrell Lynd. 1929. *Middletown: A Study in Modern American Culture.* New York: Harcourt Brace Jovanovich.

Lyon, E. Stina. 2007. "Viola Klein: Forgotten Émigré Intellectual, Public Sociologist and Advocate of Women." *Sociology* 41 (5):829–842.

Maas, Henry S. 1979. Review of *The Seasons of a Man's Life,* by Daniel J. Levinson. *Psychiatry* 42 (2):188–191.

Maas, Henry S., and Joseph A. Kuypers. 1974. *From Thirty to Seventy.* San Francisco: Jossey-Bass.

Maccoby, Eleanor. 1968. "The Development of Moral Values and Behavior in Childhood." In *Socialization and Society,* edited by John A. Clausen, 227–269. Boston: Little, Brown.

Maccoby, Eleanor E. 1958. "Effects upon Children of Their Mothers' Outside Employment." In *Work in the Lives of Married Women: Proceedings of a Conference on Womanpower,* edited by National Manpower Council, 150–172. New York: Columbia University Press.

Maccoby, Eleanor E., and Carol Nagy Jacklin. 1974. *The Psychology of Sex Differences.* Stanford, CA: Stanford University Press.

MacDermid, Shelley M., Gabriela Heilbrun, and Laura Gillespie DeHaan. 1997. "The Generativity of Employed Mothers in Multiple Roles: 1979 and 1991." In *Multiple Paths of Midlife Development,* edited by Margie E. Lachman and Jacquelyn Boone James, 207–240. Chicago: University of Chicago Press.

Macdonald, Myra. 1995. *Representing Women: Myths of Femininity in the Popular Media.* London: Edward Arnold.

Machung, Anne. 1989. "Talking Career, Thinking Job: Gender Differences in Career and Family Expectations of Berkeley Seniors." *Feminist Studies* 15 (1):35–58.

Mackenzie, Catherine. 1946. "First-Aid to Parents." Review of *Common Sense Book of Baby and Child Care,* by Benjamin Spock. *New York Times,* July 14, BR14.

Macko, Lia, and Kerry Rubin. 2004. *Midlife Crisis at 30: How the Stakes Have Changed for a New Generation.* New York: St. Martin's.

MacLeish, Roderick. 1976. "A Time to Every Purpose." Review of *Passages,* by Gail Sheehy. *Washington Post,* May 23, 1976, L7.

Macleod, David. 1983. *Building Character in the American Boy: The Boy Scouts, YMCA, and Their Forerunners, 1870–1920.* Madison, WI: University of Wisconsin Press.

Maheu, Marlene M., Myron L. Pulier, Frank H. Wilhelm, Joseph P. McMenamin, and Nancy E. Brown-Connolly. 2005. *The Mental Health Professional and the New Technologies: A Handbook for Practice Today.* Mahwah, NJ: Erlbaum.

Maier, Thomas. 1998. *Dr. Spock: An American Life.* New York: Harcourt Brace.

Mainardi, Patricia, and Kathie Sarachild. 1975. "*Ms.* Politics and Editing: An Interview." In *Feminist Revolution,* edited by Redstockings, 171–172. New Paltz, NY: Redstockings.

Maitzen, Rohan Amanda. 1998. *Gender, Genre, and Victorian Historical Writing.* New York: Garland.

Maksian, George. 1977. "ABC Trains Its Sights on Ike, Gail Sheehy." *Chicago Tribune,* March 10, A10.

Malich, Lisa. 2017. *Die Gefühle der Schwangeren: Eine Geschichte somatischer Emotionalität (1780–2010).* Bielefeld: Transcript.

Malkiel, Nancy Weiss. 2016. *"Keep the Damned Women Out": The Struggle for Coeducation.* Princeton, NJ: Princeton University Press.

Mandler, Peter. 2013. *Return from the Natives: How Margaret Mead Won the Second World War and Lost the Cold War.* New Haven, CT: Yale University Press.

Mann, Judy. 1983. "Woman's Way." *Washington Post,* December 21, B1.

Manuel, Frank E. 1971. "The Use and Abuse of Psychology in History." *Daedalus* 1 (4):187–213.

Markoutsas, Elaine. 1978. "Ann-Margret's Midlife Journey." *Chicago Tribune,* February 5, D1, D4.

Marks, Stephen R. 1977. "Multiple Roles and Role Strain: Some Notes on Human Energy, Time and Commitment." *American Sociological Review* 41:921–936.

Markus, Hazel Rose, Carol D. Ryff, Katherine B. Curhan, and Karen A. Palmersheim. 2004. "In Their Own Words: Well-being at Midlife among High School–Educated and College-Educated Adults." In *How Healthy Are We? A National Study of Well-being at Midlife,* edited by Orville G. Brim, 64–89. Chicago: University of Chicago Press.

Marland, Hilary. 2013. *Health and Girlhood in Britain, 1874–1920*. Basingstoke: Palgrave.

Marmor, Judd. 1974. *Psychiatry in Transition*. New York: Brunner/Mazel.

Marmot, Michael G., and Rebecca Fuhrer. 2004. "Socioeconomic Position and Health across Midlife." In *How Healthy Are We? A National Study of Well-being at Midlife*, edited by Orville G. Brim, 64–89. Chicago: University of Chicago Press.

Marshall, Andrew G. 2017. *It's Not a Midlife Crisis, It's an Opportunity*. London: Marshall Method.

Martin, Emily. 1989. *The Woman in the Body: A Cultural Analysis of Reproduction*. Milton Keynes: Open University Press.

Martschukat, Jürgen. 2011. "Men in Gray Flannel Suits: Troubling Masculinities in 1950s America." *Gender Forum* 32:8–27.

Marty, Martin E. 1978. "A People in Search of the Self." *Baltimore Sun*, April 16, K1.

Maslow, Abraham H. 1943. "A Theory of Human Motivation." *Psychological Review* 50 (4):370–396.

May, Elaine Tyler. 1988. *Homeward Bound: American Families in the Cold War Era*. New York: Basic Books. Reprint, 2008.

McCabe, Bruce. 1977. "Lit'ry Life." *Boston Globe*, March 5, 6.

McCain, Nina. 1977. "Fun Reading, College Style." *Boston Globe*, April 2, 1, 12.

McCarthy, Helen. 2016. "Social Science and Married Women's Employment in Post-War Britain." *Past & Present* 233 (1):269–305.

McClintock, Anne. 1995. *Imperial Leather: Race, Gender, and Sexuality in the Colonial Contest*. New York: Routledge.

McCracken, Ellen. 1993. *Decoding Women's Magazines: From "Mademoiselle" to "Ms."* New York: St. Martin's.

McDermott, Patrice. 1994. *Politics and Scholarship: Feminist Academic Journals and the Production of Knowledge*. Urbana: University of Illinois Press.

McKinney, Patty. [1981?]. "How to Survive Your Abortion: A Guide to Rebuilding Your Life" (pamphlet). Snowflake, AZ: Precious Feet People.

McLaren, Angus. 2007. *Impotence: A Cultural History*. Chicago: University of Chicago Press.

McLellan, Dennis. 1982. "Turning a Mid-life Crisis to Advantage." *Los Angeles Times*, February 4, C1.

Mead, Margaret. 1946. *Male and Female: A Study of the Sexes in a Changing World*. New York: Morrow. Reprint, 1975.

———. 1972. *Blackberry Winter: My Earlier Years*. New York: Morrow.

Mead, Shepherd. 1957. "How to Handle Women in Business." *Playboy*, January, 53–54.

Mellin, Maribeth. 1984. "Help in Fighting 'Superwoman Syndrome.'" *Los Angeles Times*, October 15, C1–C2.

Mellor, Felicity. 2003. "Between Fact and Fiction: Demarcating Science from Non-Science in Popular Physics Books." *Social Studies of Science* 33 (4):509–538.

Mercer, Ben. 2011. "The Paperback Revolution: Mass-Circulation Books and the Cultural Origins of 1968 in Western Europe." *Journal of the History of Ideas* 72:613–636.

Merritt, Deborah J. 1991. "Hypatia in the Patent Office: Women Inventors and the Law, 1865–1900." *American Journal of Legal History* 35 (3): 235–306.

Meyerowitz, Joanne. 1993. "Beyond the Feminine Mystique: A Reassessment of Postwar Mass Culture, 1946–1958." *Journal of American History* 79 (4):1455–1482.

———, ed. 1994. *Not June Cleaver: Women and Gender in Postwar America, 1945–1960*. Philadelphia: Temple University Press.

Michel, Sonya. 1999. *Children's Interests/Mother's Rights: The Shaping of America's Child Care Policy*. New Haven, CT: Yale University Press.

Milam, Erika L. 2013. "Dunking the Tarzanists: Elaine Morgan and the Aquatic Ape Theory." In *Outsider Scientists*, edited by Oren Harman and Michael R. Dietrich, 223–237. Chicago: University of Chicago Press.

Milbauer, Barbara. 1983. "What Does Woman Want from the Marketer?" *Madison Avenue*, May, 34, 38.

Milius, Peter. 1979. "EEOC: Job Bias at 'All Levels' of Sears." *Washington Post*, February 25, A1, A6.

Millar, Erica. 2017. *Happy Abortions: Our Bodies in the Era of Choice*. London: Zed.

Miller, Alice E. 1979. "A Descriptive Analysis of Health-Related Articles in the Six Leading Women's Magazines: Content Coverage and Readership Profile." PhD diss., Southern Illinois University at Carbondale.

Miller, Jean Baker, ed. 1973. *Psychoanalysis and Women*. Baltimore: Penguin.

———. 1976. *Toward a New Psychology of Women*. Boston: Beacon Press.

Miller, Laura. 2000. "The Best-Seller List as Marketing Tool and Historical Fiction." *Book History* 3:286–304.

Miller, Lois Mattox. 1939. "Changing Life Sensibly." *Independent Woman*, September, 297, 311.

Millett, Kate. 1970. *Sexual Politics: A Surprising Examination of Society's Most Arbitrary Folly*. New York: Doubleday.

Milliot, Jim. 2014. "Dutton Marks 150 Years of Publishing: The Penguin Random House Imprint Has a Storied History." *Publishers Weekly*, January 27, 2–3.

Mills, C. Wright. 1951. *White Collar: The American Middle Classes*. New York: Oxford University Press.

———. 1956. *The Power Elite*. New York: Oxford University Press.

Mills, Kay. 1988. *A Place in the News: From the Women's Pages to the Front Page*. New York: Columbia University Press. Reprint, 1990.

Mintz, Steven. 2015. *The Prime of Life: A History of Modern Adulthood*. Cambridge, MA: Harvard University Press.

Mirowski, Philip. 2002. *Machine Dreams: Economics Becomes a Cyborg Science*. New York: Cambridge University Press.

Mischel, Walter. 2014. *The Marshmallow Test*. Boston: Little, Brown.

Mischel, Walter, and Carol Gilligan. 1964. "Delay of Gratification, Motivation for the Prohibited Gratification, and Responses to Temptation." *Journal of Abnormal and Social Psychology* 69 (4):411–417.

Misciagno, Patricia S. 1997. *Rethinking Feminist Identification: The Case for De Facto Feminism*. New York: Praeger.

Mitchell, Juliet. 1974. *Psychoanalysis and Feminism: Freud, Reich, Laing and Women*. New York: Pantheon.

Mitgang, Herbert. 1977. "Publishing 'Fourth of July' in 1977." *New York Times*, July 8, 58.

Monks, John P. 1957. *College Men at War*. Boston: American Academy of Arts and Sciences.

Moore, Kelly. 2008. *Disrupting Science: Social Movements, American Scientists, and the Politics of the Military, 1945–1975*. Princeton, NJ: Princeton University Press.

Moran, Barbara. 1972. "Women's Rights Address Book." *Woman's Day*, October, 25, 32, 210–214.

Morantz-Sanchez, Regina Markell. 1985. *Sympathy and Science: Women Physicians in American Medicine*. Chapel Hill, NC: University of North Carolina Press. Reprint, 2000.

Moravcsik, Andrew. 2015. "Why I Put My Wife's Career First." *Atlantic*, October, 15–17.

Morawski, Jill G. 1994. *Practicing Feminisms, Reconstructing Psychology: Notes on a Liminal Science.* Ann Arbor: University of Michigan Press.

Morgan, Elaine. 1972a. "The Descent of Woman." *McCall's*, June, 103–110.

———. 1972b. *The Descent of Woman.* New York: Stein & Day.

Morgan, Robin, ed. 1970a. *Sisterhood Is Powerful: An Anthology of Writings from the Women's Movement.* New York: Random House.

———. 1970b. "The Women's Revolution." In *Sisterhood Is Powerful: An Anthology of Writings from the Women's Movement*, xiii–xl. New York: Random House.

Morris, Bailey. 1981a. "Cure Sought for Superwoman's Disease." *Boston Globe*, January 25, B6.

———. 1981b. "Working: A Plan Gone Awry?" *Boston Globe*, May 31, A5.

Mosher, Clelia Duel. 1901. "Normal Menstruation and Some of the Factors Modifying to It." *Johns Hopkins Hospital Bulletin* (May–June):127–173.

———. 1916. *Health and the Woman Movement.* New York: Young Women's Christian Associations National Board.

Moskowitz, Eva S. 1996. "'It's Good to Blow Your Top': Women's Magazines and a Discourse of Discontent, 1945–1965." *Journal of Women's History* 8 (3):66–98.

———. 2008. *In Therapy We Trust: America's Obsession with Self-Fulfillment.* Baltimore: Johns Hopkins University Press.

Mosse, George L. 1996. *The Image of Man: The Creation of Modern Masculinity.* New York, Oxford: Oxford University Press.

Moulton, Ruth. 1977. "The Fear of Female Power: A Cause of Sexual Dysfunction." *Journal of the American Academy of Psychoanalysis* 5 (4):499–519.

———. 1986. "Professional Success: A Conflict for Women." In *Psychoanalysis and Women: Contemporary Reappraisals*, edited by Judith L. Alpert, 161–181. Hillsdale, NJ: Analytic Press.

Müller, Kathrin Friederike. 2010. *Frauenzeitschriften aus der Sicht ihrer Leserinnen: Die Rezeption von Brigitte im Kontext von Biografie, Alltag und Doing Gender.* Bielefeld: Transcript.

Munk, William. 1895. *The Life of Sir Henry Halford.* London: Longmans, Green.

Murphy, Michelle. 2012. *Seizing the Means of Reproduction: Entanglements of Feminism, Health, and Technoscience.* Durham, NC: Duke University Press.

Murphy, Priscilla Coit. 2005. *What a Book Can Do: The Publication and Reception of "Silent Spring."* Amherst: University of Massachusetts Press.

Muson, Howard. 1977. "The Lessons of the Grant Study." *Psychology Today*, September, 42–49.

Myerson, Abraham. 1920. *The Nervous Housewife.* Boston: Little, Brown.

Myrdal, Alva, and Viola Klein. 1956. *Women's Two Roles: Home and Work.* London: Routledge & Kegan Paul.

Naffine, Ngaire. 2004. "Our Legal Lives as Men, Women and Persons." *Legal Studies* 24 (4): 621–642.

Nandy, Ashis. 1987. "Reconstructing Childhood: A Critique of the Ideology of Adulthood." In Nandy, *Traditions, Tyranny and Utopias: Essays in the Politics of Awareness*, 56–76. New Delhi: Oxford University Press.

Narr, Wolf-Dieter. 1980. "The Selling of Narcissism." *Dialectical Anthropology* 5 (1):63–73.

National Institute of Mental Health. 1969–72. *Mental Health Research Grant Awards.* Washington, DC: US Government Printing Office.

National Manpower Council. 1957. *Womanpower: A Statement.* New York: Columbia University Press.

———. 1958. *Work in the Lives of Married Women: Proceedings of a Conference on Woman-power*. New York: Columbia University Press.

Nelkin, Dorothy. 1987. *Selling Science: How the Press Covers Science and Technology*. New York: Freeman.

Neubeck, Gerhard, ed. 1969. *Extramarital Relations*. Englewood Cliffs, NJ: Prentice-Hall.

Neugarten, Bernice L. 1968a. "The Awareness of Middle Age." In *Middle Age and Aging: A Reader in Social Psychology*, edited by Bernice L. Neugarten, 93–98. Chicago: University of Chicago Press.

———, ed. 1968b. *Middle Age and Aging: A Reader in Social Psychology*. Chicago: University of Chicago Press.

Neugarten, Bernice L., and Nancy Datan. 1974. "The Middle Years." In *American Handbook of Psychiatry*, edited by Silvano Arieti, 592–608. New York: Basic Books.

———. 1996. "The Middle Years." In *The Meanings of Age: Selected Papers*, edited by Dail A. Neugarten, 135–159. Chicago: University of Chicago Press.

Neustadtl, Sara. 1986. "They Hear Different Voices." Review of *Women's Ways of Knowing*, by Mary Field Belenky, Blythe McVicker Clinchy, Nancy Rule Goldberger, and Jill Mattuck Tarule. *New York Times*, October 5, BR38.

Newman, Katherine. 1998. "Place and Race: Midlife Experience in Harlem." In *Welcome to Middle Age! (And Other Cultural Fictions)*, edited by Richard A. Shweder, 259–293. Chicago: University of Chicago Press.

Newson, John, and Elizabeth Newson. 1975. "Intersubjectivity and the Transmission of Culture: On the Social Origins of Symbolic Functioning." *Bulletin of the British Psychological Society* 28:437–446.

Newton, Peter M. 1978. Review of *The Seasons of a Man's Life*, by Daniel J. Levinson. *American Scientist*, September–October, 630.

———. 1994. "Daniel Levinson and His Theory of Adult Development: A Reminiscence and Some Clarifications." *Journal of Adult Development* 1 (3):135–147.

Nichols, Michael P. 1986. *Turning Forty in the '80s: Personal Crisis, Time for Change*. New York: Norton.

Nikolova, Milena, and Carol Graham. 2015. "Bentham or Aristotle in the Development Process? An Empirical Investigation of Capabilities and Subjective Well-being." *World Development* 68:163–179.

Nissley, Erin L. 2017. "Ahead of Her Time: Science-Minded Scranton Native Encountered Sexism, Success." http://thetimes-tribune.com/news/local-history-science-minded -scranton-native-finds-success-as-author-1.2169669 (accessed December 19, 2017).

Nobile, Philip. 1972. "What Is The New Impotence, and Who's Got It?" *Esquire*, October, 95–98, 218.

Noddings, Nel. 1984. *Caring: A Feminine Approach to Ethics and Moral Education*. Berkeley, CA: University of California Press.

Nolen, William A. 1968. *The Making of a Surgeon*. Nashville, TN: Mid-List.

———. 1972. *A Surgeon's World*. New York: Random House.

———. 1976. *Surgeon under the Knife*. New York: Coward, McCann & Geoghegan.

———. 1980. "What You Should Know about 'Male Menopause.'" *McCall's*, June, 84–88.

———. 1981. "Male Menopause: Myth or Mid-life Reality?" *Reader's Digest*, June, 181–183.

———. 1984. *Crisis Time! Love, Marriage, and the Male at Mid-life*. New York: Dodd, Mead.

Notman, Malkah T. 1982. "Midlife Concerns of Women: Implications of the Menopause." In *The Woman Patient: Concepts of Femininity and the Life Cycle*, edited by Carol C. Nadelson and Malkah T. Notman, 135–144. New York: Plenum.

Oakley, Ann. 1972. *Sex, Gender, and Society*. San Francisco: Harper & Row.

O'Brien, Patricia. 1976. "Dr. Spock for Adults." Review of *Passages*, by Gail Sheehy. *Ms.*, August, 112–113.

O'Neill, Nena, and George O'Neill. 1972. *Open Marriage: A New Life Style for Couples.* New York: M. Evans.

O'Rand, Angela M., and John C. Henretta. 1982. "Women at Middle Age: Developmental Transitions." *Annals of the American Academy of Political and Social Science* 464:58–64.

O'Reilly, Jane. 1971. "The Housewife's Moment of Truth." *Ms.*, December 20, 54–55, 57–59.

Oertzen, Christine von. 2007. *The Pleasure of a Surplus Income: Part-time Work, Gender Politics, and Social Change in West Germany, 1955–1969.* New York: Berghahn.

Oertzen, Christine von, Maria Rentetzi, and Elizabeth S. Watkins. 2013. "Special Issue: Beyond the Academy: Histories of Gender and Knowledge." *Centaurus* 55 (2).

Offen, Karen. 1987. "Sur l'origine des mots 'féminisme' et 'féministe.'" *Révue d'histoire moderne et contemporaine* 3:492–496.

———. 1988. "Defining Feminism: A Comparative Historical Approach." *Signs* 14 (1):119–157.

Offer, Daniel. 1969. *The Psychological World of the Teenager: A Study of Normal Adolescent Boys.* New York: Basic Books.

Offer, Daniel, and Judith Baskin Offer. 1975. *From Teenage to Young Manhood: A Psychological Study.* New York: Basic Books.

Offer, Daniel, and Melvin Sabshin. 1984. "Adolescence: Empirical Perspectives." In *Normality and the Life Cycle: Critical Integration*, edited by Daniel Offer and Melvin Sabshin. New York: Basic Books.

Oldenziel, Ruth. 1999. *Making Technology Masculine: Men, Women and Modern Machines in America, 1870–1945.* Amsterdam: Amsterdam University Press.

Ong, Walter. 1982. *Orality and Literacy: The Technologizing of the Word.* New York: Routledge. Reprint, 2012.

Onion, Rebecca. 2015. "Against Generations." http://aeon.co/magazine/psychology/we-need-to-ditch-generational-labels/ (accessed December 19, 2017).

Onosaka, Junko R. 2006. *Feminist Revolution in Literacy: Women's Bookstores in the United States.* New York: Routledge.

Oppenheimer, Valerie K. 1974. "The Life-Cycle Squeeze: The Interaction of Men's Occupational and Family Life Cycles." *Demography* 11:227–245.

———. 1976. "The Easterlin Hypothesis: Another Aspect of the Echo to Consider." *Population and Development Review* 2:433–457.

———. 1977. "The Sociology of Women's Economic Role in the Family." *American Sociological Review* 42:387–406.

Orme, Nicholas. 2001. *Medieval Children.* New Haven, CT: Yale University Press.

Osgerby, Bill. 2001. *Playboys in Paradise: Masculinity, Youth and Leisure-Style in Modern America.* Oxford: Berg.

Osherson, Samuel D. 1980. *Holding On or Letting Go: Men and Career Change at Midlife.* New York: Free Press.

Osipow, Samuel H. 1973. *Theories of Career Development.* New York: Appleton-Century-Crofts.

Oudshoorn, Nelly. 1994. *Beyond the Natural Body: An Archeology of Sex Hormones.* New York: Routledge.

Ouellette, Laurie. 1999. "Inventing the Cosmo Girl: Class Identity and Girl-Style American Dreams." *Media, Culture & Society* 21 (3):359–383.

Ozment, Steven. 2001. *Ancestors: The Loving Family in Old Europe*. Cambridge, MA: Harvard University Press.

Pace, Eric. 1972. "New Book Crop Is Full of Novels." *New York Times*, September 5, 44.

Paletschek, Sylvia. 2001. "Kinder—Küche—Kirche." In *Deutsche Erinnerungsorte*, edited by Étienne François and Hagen Schulze, 419–433. München: C. H. Beck.

Palm, Kerstin. 2011. "Altern in lebenswissenschaftlicher Perspektive: Das Beispiel 'männliche' Menopause." *Gegenworte* 25 (1):74–76.

Palmatier, Robert Allen. 1995. "Empty-Nest Syndrome." In Palmatier, *Speaking of Animals: A Dictionary of Animal Metaphors*, 136. Westport, CT: Greenwood.

Palmer, Rachel Lynn, and Sarah Koslow Greenberg. 1936. *Facts and Frauds in Woman's Hygiene: A Medical Guide against Misleading Claims and Dangerous Products*. New York: Sun Dial.

Pandora, Katherine. 1997. *Rebels within the Ranks: Psychologists' Critiques of Scientific Authority and Democratic Realities in New Deal America*. Cambridge: Cambridge University Press.

Park, Hyung Wook. 2016. *Old Age, New Science: Gerontologists and Their Biosocial Visions, 1900–1960*. Pittsburgh, PA: University of Pittsburgh Press.

Parker, Rebecca A., and Carolyn M. Aldwin. 1997. "Do Aspects of Gender Identity Change from Early to Middle Adulthood? Disentangling Age, Cohort, and Period Effects." In *Multiple Paths of Midlife Development*, edited by Margie E. Lachman and Jacquelyn Boone James, 67–108. Chicago: University of Chicago Press.

Parnes, Ohad, Ulrike Vedder, and Stefan Willer. 2008. *Das Konzept der Generation: Eine Wissenschafts- und Kulturgeschichte*. Frankfurt am Main: Suhrkamp.

"*Passages* II: Advice for the Demon-Worn." 1978. *Time*, August 14, 70.

Patterson, Michelle, and Lucy Sells. 1973. "Women Dropouts from Higher Education." In *Academic Women on the Move*, edited by Alice S. Rossi and Ann Calderwood, 79–91. New York: Russell Sage Foundation.

Payant, Katherine B. 1993. "Female Friendship in the Contemporary Bildungsroman." In *Communication and Women's Friendships: Parallels and Intersections in Literature and Life*, edited by Janet Doubler Ward and JoAnna Stephens Mink, 151–165. Bowling Green, OH: Bowling Green State University Popular Press.

Pearce, Diana. 1978. "The Feminization of Poverty: Women, Work, and Welfare." *Urban and Social Change Review* 11 (1&2):28–36.

Pearlin, Leonard I., and Joyce S. Johnson. 1977. "Marital Status, Life-Strains and Depression." *American Sociological Review* 42 (5):704–715.

Pecile, Jordan. 1978. "Times of Change." Review of *The Seasons of a Man's Life*, by Daniel J. Levinson. *Hartford Courant*, October 19, 30.

Perkin, Harold. 1996. *The Third Revolution: Professional Elites in the Modern World*. London: Routledge.

Pesmen, Curtis. 1984. *How a Man Ages: Growing Older: What to Expect and What You Can Do about It*. New York: Ballantine.

Piaget, Jean. 1980. *Adaptation and Intelligence: Organic Selection and Phenocopy*. Chicago: University of Chicago Press.

Pinkerton, Walter. 1971. "Believe It or Not: The 'New Journalism' Is Sometimes Less than Meets the Eye." *Wall Street Journal*, August 13, 1, 19.

Pitkin, Walter B. 1930. *The Psychology of Achievement*. New York: Simon & Schuster.

———. 1932. *Life Begins at Forty*. New York: McGraw-Hill.

———. 1937. *Careers after Forty*. New York: Whittlesey House.

Pitzulo, Carrie. 2011. *Bachelors and Bunnies: The Sexual Politics of "Playboy."* Chicago: University of Chicago Press.

Plant, Rebecca Jo. 2010. *Mom: The Transformation of Motherhood in Modern America.* Chicago: University of Chicago Press.

———. 2015. "Motherhood." In *Rethinking Therapeutic Culture*, edited by Timothy Aubry and Trysh Travis, 72–84. Chicago: University of Chicago Press.

Plate, Tom. 2007. *Confessions of an American Media Man: What They Don't Tell You at Journalism School.* Singapore: Marshall Cavendish Editions.

Pogrebin, Letty Cottin. 1975. *Getting Yours: How to Make the System Work for the Working Woman.* New York: McKay.

Poirot, Kristan. 2004. "Mediating a Movement, Authorizing Discourse: Kate Millett, *Sexual Politics*, and Feminism's Second Wave." *Women's Studies in Communication* 27 (2):204–235.

Pollock, Kristian. 1988. "On the Nature of Social Stress: Production of a Modern Mythology." *Social Science & Medicine* (26) 3:381–392.

Polsgrove, Carol. 2009. "Magazines and the Making of Authors." In *A History of the Book in America*, vol. 5, *The Enduring Book: Print Culture in Postwar America*, edited by David Paul Nord, Joan S. Rubin, and Michael Schudson, 256–268. Chapel Hill: University of North Carolina Press.

Pool, Gail. 2009. *Faint Praise: The Plight of Book Reviewing in America.* Columbia: University of Missouri Press.

Poovey, Mary. 1988. *Uneven Developments: The Ideological Work of Gender in Mid-Victorian England.* Chicago: University of Chicago Press.

Popper, Karl. 1963. *Conjectures and Refutations.* London: Routledge.

Pratt, Mary Louise. 1992. *Imperial Eyes: Travel Writing and Transculturation.* New York: Routledge.

Preciado, Beatriz. 2014. *Pornotopia: An Essay on Playboy's Architecture and Biopolitics.* Cambridge, MA: MIT Press.

Prescott, Heather Munro. 2002. "Using the Student Body." *Journal of the History of Medicine and Allied Sciences* 57 (1):3–38.

———. 2007. *Student Bodies: The Influence of Student Health Services in American Society and Medicine.* Ann Arbor: University of Michigan Press.

President's Commission on the Status of Women. 1963. *American Women: Report on the President's Commission on the Status of Women.* Washington, DC: Government Publications Office.

Prose, Francine. 1990. "Confident at 11, Confused at 16: Carol Gilligan Studies Girls Growing Up." *New York Times Magazine*, January 7, 23–25, 37–39, 45–46.

Pugh, Derek S., and David J. Hickson. 2016. "Elliott Jaques and the Glacier Investigations." In Pugh and Hickson, *Great Writers on Organizations*, 32–35. New York: Routledge.

"PW Hardcover Bestsellers." 1976a. *Publishers Weekly*, August 16, 130.

"PW Hardcover Bestsellers." 1976b. *Publishers Weekly*, December 13, 74.

"PW Paperback Bestsellers." 1978. *Publishers Weekly*, May 1, 90.

Pycior, Helena, Nancy G. Slack, and Pnina G. Abir-Am, eds. 1996. *Creative Couples in the Sciences.* New Brunswick, NJ: Rutgers University Press.

Quinn, Naomi. 1982. "'Commitment' in American Marriage: A Cultural Analysis." *American Ethnologist* 9 (4):775–798.

Rabinbach, Anson. 1992. *The Human Motor: Energy, Fatigue, and the Origins of Modernity.* Berkeley: University of California Press.

Rabkin, Judith G., and Elmer L. Struening. 1976. "Life Events, Stress, and Illness." *Science* 194:1013–1020.

Radler, Barry T. 2014. "The Midlife in the United States (MIDUS) Series: A National Longitudinal Study of Health and Well-being." *Open Health Data* 2 (1).

Radway, Janice. 1984. *Reading the Romance: Women, Patriarchy, and Popular Literature.* Chapel Hill: University of North Carolina Press.

———. 1997. *A Feeling for Books: The Book-of-the-Month Club, Literary Taste, and Middle-Class Desire.* Chapel Hill: University of North Carolina Press.

Rahe, Richard H., Merle Meyer, Michael Smith, George Kjaer, and Thomas H. Holmes. 1964. "Social Stress and Illness Onset." *Journal of Psychosomatic Research* 8:35–44.

Rains, Prudence Mors. 1971. *Becoming an Unwed Mother: A Sociological Account.* Chicago: Atherton.

Ramsden, Edmund. 2014. "Stress in the City: Mental Health, Urban Planning, and the Social Sciences in the Postwar United States." In *Stress, Shock, and Adaptation in the Twentieth Century*, edited by David Cantor and Edmund Ramsden, 291–319. Rochester, NY: University of Rochester Press.

Randall, Marilyn. 2001. *Pragmatic Plagiarism: Authorship, Profit, and Power.* Toronto: University of Toronto Press.

Ransom, Roger L., and Richard Sutch. 1986. "The Labor of Older Americans: Retirement of Men on and off the Job, 1870–1937." *Journal of Economic History* 46 (1):1–30.

Rapoport, Robert N. 1970. *Mid-career Development: Research Perspectives on a Developmental Community for Senior Administrators.* London: Tavistock.

Rauch, Jonathan. 2014. "The Real Roots of the Midlife Crisis." *Atlantic*, December, 88–95.

———. *The Happiness Curve: Why Life Gets Better after 50.* New York: St. Martin's.

Raymond, John. 1980. "Man's Life Stages Missed by the Bard." *Atlanta Constitution*, September 28, F1.

Reagan, Leslie. 1997. *When Abortion Was a Crime: Women, Medicine, and Law in the United States, 1867–1973.* Berkeley: University of California Press.

Reed, Charles A. L. 1901. *A Text-book of Gynecology.* New York: Appleton.

Reger, Jo. 2012. *Everywhere and Nowhere: Contemporary Feminism in the United States.* Oxford: Oxford University Press.

Reuben, David. 1969. *Everything You Always Wanted to Know about Sex (but Were Afraid to Ask).* New York: McKay.

Reverby, Susan M. 1987. *Ordered to Care: The Dilemma of American Nursing, 1850–1945.* Cambridge: Cambridge University Press.

"Review of *A Different Woman*, by Jane Howard." 1973. *Kirkus Reviews*, November 7.

Rhode, Deborah L. 2016. *Adultery: Infidelity and the Law.* Cambridge, MA: Harvard University Press.

———. 2017. *Women and Leadership.* Oxford: Oxford University Press.

Rhodes, Richard. 1978. "Passionate Explorations of Man's 'Passages.'" Review of *The Seasons of a Man's Life*, by Daniel J. Levinson, and *Coming of Middle Age*, by Arnold Mandell. *Chicago Tribune*, April 16, F7.

Richardson, Laurel Walum. 1977. *The Dynamics of Sex and Gender: A Sociological Perspective.* Chicago: Rand McNally.

———. 1979. Review of *The Seasons of a Man's Life*, by Daniel J. Levinson. *Journal of Marriage and the Family* 41 (4):915–916.

———. 1991. "Sharing Feminist Research with Popular Audiences." In *Beyond Method-*

ology: Feminist Scholarship as Lived Research, edited by Mary Margaret Fonow and Judith A. Cook, 284–296. Bloomington, IN: Indiana University Press.

Riesman, Daniel, with Nathan Glazer and Reuel Denney. 1950. *The Lonely Crowd*. New Haven, CT: Yale University Press.

Rivers, Caryl. 1983. "Crocodile Tears for the Working Woman." *Los Angeles Times*, May 30, B5.

Rivers, Caryl, Rosalind C. Barnett, and Grace K. Baruch. 1979. *Beyond Sugar and Spice: How Women Grow, Learn, and Thrive*. New York: Putnam.

Roazen, Paul. 1976. *Erik H. Erikson: The Power and Limits of a Vision*. New York: Free Press.

Robb, Christina. 1980. "Vive la Difference." *Boston Globe Magazine*, October 5, 11, 69–80.

———. 2007. *This Changes Everything: The Relational Revolution in Psychology*. New York: Farrar, Straus and Giroux.

Robinson, Leonard Wallace. 1974. "The New Journalism: A Panel Discussion with Harold Hayes, Gay Talese, Tom Wolfe and Professor L. W. Robinson." In *The Reporter as Artist: A Look at the New Journalism Controversy*, edited by Ronald Weber, 66–75. New York: Hastings House.

Rodgers, Daniel T. 2011. *Age of Fracture*. Cambridge, MA: Belknap.

Rose, Harold. 1980. Review of *The Seasons of a Man's Life*, by Daniel J. Levinson. *Adult Education Quarterly* 30 (4):245–246.

Rose, Nikolas. 1990. *Governing the Soul: The Shaping of the Private Self*. New York: Routledge.

———. 1998. *Inventing Our Selves: Psychology, Power, and Personhood*. New York: Cambridge University Press.

Rosen, Gerald M. 1978. "Suggestions for an Editorial Policy on the Review of Self-Help Treatment Books." *Behavior Therapy* 9 (5):960.

———. 2004. "Remembering the 1978 and 1990 Task Forces on Self-Help Therapies." *Journal of Clinical Psychology* 60 (1):111–113.

Rosen, Judith. 2013. "Harvard University Press Turns 100." *Publishers Weekly*, April 15, 4.

Rosen, R[ichard] D. 1980. "Epping: Plagiarize or Perish." *New Republic*, November 15, 13–14.

———. 1989. "Bullcrit: The Reading Disorder of the Literary Fast Lane." *New York Magazine*, February 6, 44–47.

Rosen, Ruth. 2000. *The World Split Open: How the Modern Women's Movement Changed America*. New York and London: Penguin.

Rosenberg, Charles E. 1962. "The Place of George M. Beard in Nineteenth-Century Psychiatry." *Bulletin of the History of Medicine* 36:245–259.

Rosenberg, Rosalind. 1982. *Beyond Separate Spheres: Intellectual Roots of Modern Feminism*. New Haven, CT: Yale University Press.

Rosenblum, Constance. 1979. "'Just Blame It on My Midlife Crisis.'" *Chicago Tribune*, January 14, K1.

Rosenfield, Sarah. 1980. "Sex Differences in Depression: Do Women Always Have Higher Rates?" *Journal of Health and Social Behavior* 21 (1):33–42.

Rosin, Hanna. 2012. *The End of Men: And the Rise of Women*. London: Penguin.

Rossi, Alice S. 1964. "Equality between the Sexes: An Immodest Proposal." *Daedalus* 93 (2):607–652.

———. 1980. "Life-Span Theories and Women's Lives." *Signs* 6 (1):4–32.

———, ed. 1994. *Sexuality across the Life Course*. Chicago: University of Chicago Press.

———, ed. 2001. *Caring and Doing for Others: Social Responsibility in the Domains of Family, Work, and Community*. Chicago: University of Chicago Press.

Rossiter, Margaret W. 1982–2012. *Women Scientists in America*. 3 vols. Vol. 1, *Struggles and*

Strategies to 1940 [1982]. Vol. 2, *Before Affirmative Action, 1940–1972* [1995]. Vol. 3, *Forging a New World since 1972* [2012]. Baltimore: Johns Hopkins University Press.

———. 1993. "The Matilda Effect in Science." *Social Studies of Science* 23 (2):325–341.

Rowold, Katharina. 2010. *The Educated Woman: Minds, Bodies, and Women's Higher Education in Britain, Germany, and Spain, 1865–1914*. New York: Routledge.

Rubin, Gayle. 1975. "The Traffic in Women: Notes on the 'Political Economy' of Sex," in *Toward an Anthropology of Women*, edited by Rayna R. Reiter, 157–210. New York: Monthly Review Press.

Rubin, Joan S. 1992. *The Making of Middlebrow Culture*. Chapel Hill: University of North Carolina Press.

Ruddick, Sara. 1980. "Maternal Thinking." *Feminist Studies* 6 (2):342–367.

———. 1989. *Maternal Thinking: Toward a Politics of Peace*. Boston: Beacon Press.

Ruddick, Sara, and Pamela Daniels, eds. 1977. *Working It Out: 23 Women Writers, Artists, Scientists, and Scholars Talk about Their Lives and Work*. New York: Pantheon.

Rupnow, Dirk, Veronika Lipphardt, Jens Thiel, and Christina Wessely, eds. 2008. *Pseudowissenschaft: Konzeptionen von Nichtwissenschaftlichkeit in der Wissenschaftsgeschichte*. Frankfurt am Main: Suhrkamp.

Rupp, Leila J. 2001. "Is Feminism the Province of Old (or Middle-Aged) Women?" *Journal of Women's History* 12 (4):164–173.

Russett, Cynthia Eagle. 1989. *Sexual Science: The Victorian Construction of Womanhood*. Cambridge, MA: Harvard University Press.

Rutherford, Alexandra. 2017. "'Making Better Use of U.S. Women': Psychology, Sex Roles, and Womanpower in Post-WWII America." *Journal of the History of the Behavioral Sciences* 53 (3):1–18.

Rutherford, Alexandra, Kelli Vaughn-Blount, and Laura C. Ball. 2010. "Responsible Opposition, Disruptive Voices: Science, Social Change, and the History of Feminist Psychology." *Psychology of Women Quarterly* 34 (4):460–473.

Ryback, David. 1976. "Crisis Can Conceal Opportunity." Review of *Passages*, by Gail Sheehy. *Atlanta Constitution*, July 18, 11C.

Ryder, Norman B. 1965. "The Cohort as a Concept in the Study of Social Change." *American Sociological Review* 30 (6):843–861.

Sabine, Gordon, and Patricia Sabine. 1983. *Books That Made the Difference: What People Told Us*. Hamden, CT: Library Professional Publications.

Salholz, Eloise. 1986. "Feminism's Identity Crisis." *Newsweek*, March 31, 58–59.

Sammon, Virginia. 1969. "Surviving the *Saturday Evening Post*." *Antioch Review* 29 (1):101–108.

Sanborn, Sara. 1976. "A Gesell for Adults." Review of *Passages*, by Gail Sheehy. *New York Times*, May 30, BR3–4.

Sandage, Scott A. 2005. *Born Losers: A History of Failure in America*. Cambridge, MA: Harvard University Press.

Sandberg, Sheryl. 2013. *Lean In: Women, Work, and the Will to Lead*. London: Allen. Reprint, 2015.

Sarachild, Kathie. 1970. "A Program for Feminist 'Consciousness Raising.'" *Notes from the Second Year*, 78–80.

Sarasin, Philipp. 2007. "Unternehmer seiner selbst." Review of *Geschichte der Gouvernementalität*, by Michel Foucault. *Deutsche Zeitschrift für Philosophie* 55 (3):473–493.

Sassen, Georgia. 1980. "Success Anxiety in Women: A Constructivist Interpretation of Its Sources and Its Significance." *Harvard Educational Review* 50 (1):13–25.

Saur, Michael. 2013. "Der weite Weg zum Glück: Interview mit George Vaillant." *Süddeutsche Zeitung Magazin*, March 28, 32–38.

Savage, Mike. 2010. *Identities and Social Change in Britain since 1940: The Politics of Method.* Oxford: Oxford University Press.

Scanlon, Jennifer. 1995. *Inarticulate Longings: The "Ladies' Home Journal," Gender, and the Promises of Consumer Culture.* New York: Routledge.

———. 2009. *Bad Girls Go Everywhere: The Life of Helen Gurley Brown.* New York: Oxford University Press.

Scarf, Maggie. 1972. "Husbands in Crisis." *McCall's*, June, 76–77, 120–125.

———. 1976a. *Body, Mind, Behavior.* Washington, DC: New Republic.

———. 1976b. "Time of Transition: The Male in the Mid-life Decade." In Scarf, *Body, Mind, Behavior*, 263–281. Washington, DC: New Republic.

———. 1978. "Rough Passages." Review of *Transformations*, by Roger Gould. *New York Times*, July 16, BR2.

Schäfer, Daniel. 2015. *Old Age and Disease in Early Modern Medicine.* New York: Routledge.

Schiebinger, Londa. 1999. *Has Feminism Changed Science?* Cambridge, MA: Harvard University Press. Reprint, 2003.

Schmidt, Susanne. 2018. "The Anti-Feminist Reconstruction of the Midlife Crisis: Popular Psychology, Journalism and Social Science in 1970s America." *Gender & History* 30 (1):153–176.

Schnädelbach, Sandra. 2017. "Entscheidende Gefühle: Rechtsgefühl und juristische Emotionalität in der deutschsprachigen Jurisprudenz, 1870–1930." PhD diss., Freie Universität Berlin.

Schoen, Johanna. 2015. *Abortion after Roe.* Chapel Hill: University of North Carolina Press.

Schudson, Michael. 1978. *Discovering the News.* New York: Basic Books.

Schwandt, Hannes. 2015. "Why So Many of Us Experience a Midlife Crisis." https://hbr .org/2015/04/why-so-many-of-us-experience-a-midlife-crisis (accessed December 19, 2017).

Scott, James F. 1898. *The Sexual Instinct: Its Use and Dangers as Affecting Heredity and Morals.* New York: Treat.

Scott, Joan W. 1983. "Women in History: The Modern Period." *Past & Present* 101:141–157.

———. 1989. "French Feminists and the Rights of 'Man': Olympe de Gouges's Declarations." *History Workshop* 28 (1):1–21.

———. 1996. *Only Paradoxes to Offer: French Feminists and the Rights of Man.* Cambridge, MA: Harvard University Press.

Secord, Anne. 1994. "Science in the Pub: Artisan Botanists in Early Nineteenth-Century Lancashire." *History of Science* 32:269–315.

Secord, James A. 2000. *Victorian Sensation: The Extraordinary Publication, Reception, and Secret Authorship of Vestiges of the Natural History of Creation.* Chicago: University of Chicago Press.

———. 2004. "Knowledge in Transit." *Isis* 95 (4):654–672.

See, Carolyn. 1996. "Days of the Lives of Women." Review of *Seasons of a Woman's Life*, by Daniel J. Levinson. *Washington Post*, February 2, B2A.

Segrave, Kerry. 2001. *Age Discrimination by Employers.* Jefferson, NC: McFarland.

Sejersted, Francis. 2011. *The Age of Social Democracy: Norway and Sweden in the Twentieth Century.* Princeton, NJ: Princeton University Press.

Self, Robert. 2012. *All in the Family: The Realignment of American Democracy since the 1960s.* New York: Farrar, Straus & Giroux.

Sengoopta, Chandak. 2000. "The Modern Ovary: Constructions, Meanings, Uses." *History of Science* 38:425–88.

———. 2006. *The Most Secret Quintessence of Life: Sex, Glands, and Hormones, 1850–1950*. Chicago: University of Chicago Press.

Senn, Milton J. E., ed. 1950. *Symposium on the Healthy Personality: Transactions of Special Meetings of Conference on Infancy and Childhood*. New York: Macy Foundation.

Setiya, Kieran. 2014. "The Midlife Crisis." *Philosophers' Imprint* 14 (31):1–18.

———. 2017. *Midlife: A Philosophical Guide*. Princeton, NJ: Princeton University Press.

Shaevitz, Marjorie Hansen. 1984. *The Superwoman Syndrome*. New York: Warner.

Sharp, Daryl. 1988. *The Survival Papers: Anatomy of a Midlife Crisis*. Toronto: Inner City Books.

Shaughnessy, Joan M. 1988. "Gilligan's Travels." *Law and Inequality* 7 (1):1–27.

Shaw, Katherine. 1990. "*Reader's Digest*." In *American Mass Market Magazines*, edited by Alan Nourie and Barbara Nourie, 425–431. Westport, CT: Greenwood.

Sheehy, Gail. 1968a. "Nanas in the Park." *New York*, June 3, 18–21.

———. 1968b. "Powwow in Middle Village." *New York*, August 19, 32–35.

———. 1968c. "The Tunnel Inspector and the Belle of the Bar Car." *New York*, April 29, 20–26.

———. 1969a. "Bachelor Mothers: Missing Elements in New York Families, Part I." *New York*, January 13, 20–26.

———. 1969b. "Childless by Choice: Missing Elements in New York Families, Part II." *New York*, January 20, 35–41.

———. 1970a. "A City Kind of Love: A Report on the State of the Art in New York City, 1970." *New York*, February 16, 28–34.

———. 1970b. "The Great St. Valentine's Day Uprising." *New York*, February 16, 46–52.

———. 1970c. "Lovesounds of a Wife." *McCall's*, August, 90–102.

———. 1970d. "The Men of Women's Liberation Have Learned Not to Laugh." *New York*, May 18, 28–35.

———. 1971a. "Divorced Mothers as a Political Force." *New York*, May 10, 10.

———. 1971b. "Divorced Mothers as a Political Force." In *The Future of the Family*, edited by Louise Kapp Howe, 55–57. New York: Simon & Schuster. Reprint, 1972.

———. 1971c. "Nice Girls Don't Get into Trouble." *New York*, February 15, 26–30.

———. 1971d. *Panthermania: The Clash of Black against Black in One American City*. New York: Harper & Row.

———. 1971e. "Teach Me Tonight." *New York*, May 17, 8–9.

———. 1972a. "The Fighting Women of Ireland." *New York*, March 13, 45–55.

———. 1972b. "The Landlords of Hell's Bedroom." *New York*, November 20, 67–80.

———. 1972c. "The Secret of Grey Gardens." *New York*, January 10, 24–29.

———. 1973a. *Hustling: Prostitution in Our Wide Open Society*. New York: Delacorte.

———. 1973b. "Why Can't a Woman Be More like Margaret Mead?" *New York*, August 13, 39–47.

———. 1974a. "Catch-30: And Other Predictable Crises of Growing Up Adult." *New York*, February 18, 30–51.

———. 1974b. "Why Mid Life Is Crisis Time for Couples." *New York*, April 29, 31–35.

———. 1976a. "The Age 40 Crucible." *Wharton Magazine*, Fall, 31–35.

———. 1976b. "The Crisis Couples Face at 40." *McCall's*, May, 107, 155–162.

———. 1976c. "A Crisis Every Woman Must Face." *Family Circle*, July, 52–56.

———. 1976d. "Impasse: A Stinging Look at One Couple's Marriage, Plus Crucial Questions for the Two of You." *Bride's*, December, 62, 88–92.

———. 1976e. "No Pure Ideas." *Time*, June 28, 6.

———. 1976f. *Passages: Predictable Crises of Adult Life*. New York: Dutton.

———. 1976g. "Why Do Men Marry? For Love, for Money, for Safety, for Freedom or All of the Above?" *Glamour*, April, 70, 72–74.

———. 1976h. "You Are in Good Company." *Sky*, October, 13–15, 55–62.

———. 1977a. "The Crisis Couples Face at Forty." *Reader's Digest*, March, 73–76.

———. 1977b. "A Fistful of Dollars: Featuring the Good, the Bad, and the Ugly." *Rolling Stone*, July 14, 47–59.

———. 1978. "What Do Men Want?" *New York Times*, BR4.

———. 1980. "Women and Leadership: Gloria Steinem." *New York Times*, January 31, C2.

———. 1984. "Culture of Survivalism." Review of *The Minimal Self*, by Christopher Lasch. *Vogue*, November, 266–267.

———. 1986. "The Passage of Corazón Aquino." *Parade Magazine*, June 8, 4–9.

———. 1988. *Character: America's Search for Leadership*. New York: Morrow.

———. 1989. "The Blooming of Margaret Thatcher." *Vanity Fair*, June, 102–112, 164–174.

———. 1990. *The Man Who Changed the World: The Lives of Mikhail S. Gorbachev*. New York: HarperCollins.

———. 1991. "The Silent Passage: Menopause." *Vanity Fair*, October, 222–227, 252–263.

———. 1992. *The Silent Passage: Menopause*. New York: Random House.

———. 1996. *New Passages: Mapping Your Life across Time*. New York: Random House.

———. 1998. *Understanding Men's Passages: Discovering the New Map of Men's Lives*. New York: Random House.

———. 2006. *Sex and the Seasoned Woman: Pursuing the Passionate Life*. New York: Random House.

———. 2010. *Passages in Caregiving*. New York: Morrow.

———. 2014. *Daring: My Passages*. New York: Morrow.

Shenk, Joshua Wolf. 2009. "What Makes Us Happy?" *Atlantic*, June, 36–41, 44, 46–48, 50–53.

Shepherd, Glen R. 1952. "Doctor's Notebook: Menopause Causes Baseless Fears." *Washington Post*, March 9, S10.

Sherfey, Mary Jane. 1972. *The Nature and Evolution of Female Sexuality*. New York: Random House.

Shergold, Peter R. 1982. *Working-Class Life: The "American Standard" in Comparative Perspective, 1899–1913*. Pittsburgh, PA: University of Pittsburgh Press.

Sherman, Geraldine. 1995. "The Joy of 'Middlescence' and Other Passages in Time." *Globe and Mail*, July 1, C20.

Sherwood, Margaret. 1949. "You Can Have Glamour after Forty." *Independent Woman*, June, 183–184.

Shinn, Terry, and Richard Whitley, eds. 1985. *Expository Science: Forms and Functions of Popularisation*. Dordrecht: Reidel.

Showalter, Elaine. 1985. *The Female Malady: Women, Madness, and English Culture, 1830–1980*. New York: Pantheon.

———. 1998. "Changing Places: This Time, Gail Sheehy Examines the Problems Men Face." *New York Times*, June 7, BR38.

Shweder, Richard A., ed. 1998. *Welcome to Middle Age! (And Other Cultural Fictions)*. Chicago: University of Chicago Press.

Sidel, Ruth. 1978. *Urban Survival: The World of Working-Class Women*. Lincoln: University of Nebraska Press.

Sieber, Sam D. 1974. "Toward a Theory of Role Accumulation." *American Sociological Review* 39 (4):567–578.

Siegel, Reva B. 2008. "The Right's Reasons: Constitutional Conflict and the Spread of Woman-Protective Antiabortion Argument." *Duke Law Journal* 57:1641–1692.

Sifford, Darrell. 1985. "How to Cope with Midlife Crisis: An Interview with William Nolen." *South China Morning Post*, May 27, 41.

Silverman, Chloe. 2012. *Understanding Autism: Parents, Doctors, and the History of a Disorder*. Princeton, NJ: Princeton University Press.

Simmons, Dana. 2016. "Impostor Syndrome: A Reparative History." *Engaging Science, Technology, and Society* 2:106–127.

Simpson, Elizabeth L. 1974. "Moral Development Research: A Case Study of Scientific Cultural Bias." *Human Development* 17:81–106.

Skinner, Quentin. 1969. "Meaning and Understanding in the History of Ideas." *History and Theory* 8(1):3–53.

Skae, Francis. 1865. "Climacteric Insanity." *Edinburgh Medical Journal* 10:703–716.

Skopek, Jeffrey M. 2011. "Principles, Exemplars, and Uses of History in Early 20th Century Genetics." *Studies in History and Philosophy of Biological and Biomedical Sciences* 42:210–225.

Slater, Philip E. 1963. "On Social Regression." *American Sociological Review* 28:339–364.

———. 1974. *Earthwalk*. Garden City, NY: Anchor Press/Doubleday.

Slaughter, Anne-Marie. 2015. *Unfinished Business: Women, Men, Work, Family*. New York: Random House.

Smith, Cecil. 1976. "TV Review: A Meeting of the Minds on KCET." *Los Angeles Times*, July 29, F16.

Smith, David. 1973. "Forty Hear Reporter Discuss Investigation of Prostitution." *Columbia Spectator*, March 30, 3.

Smith, Lynn. 1983. "Psychologists Analyze Their Needs: Group Probes Personal Pitfalls of Fame, Fortune, Power, Alcohol." *Los Angeles Times*, September 6, C1, C6, C8.

Smith, Tony. 1976. "Social Violence and Conservative Social Psychology: The Case of Erik Erikson." *Journal of Peace Research* 13 (1):1–13.

Smith-Rosenberg, Carroll. 1985. "Puberty to Menopause: The Cycle of Femininity in Nineteenth-Century America [1973]." In Smith-Rosenberg, *Disorderly Conduct: Visions of Gender in Victorian America*, 182–196. New York: Oxford University Press.

Soddy, Kenneth. 1967. *Men in Middle Life*. London: Tavistock.

Solomon, Barbara Miller. 1985. *In the Company of Educated Women: A History of Women and Higher Education in America*. New Haven, CT: Yale University Press.

Sommers, Tish. 1974. "The Compounding Impact of Age on Sex: Another Dimension of the Double Standard." *Civil Rights Digest* 7 (1):2–9.

Sontag, Susan. 1972. "The Double Standard of Aging." *Saturday Review*, September 23, 29–38.

"Special Issue on Men: As Sons, as Lovers, at Work, in Bed, or . . . Not at All." 1975. *Ms.*, October.

Spencer, Anna Garlin. 1913. *Woman's Share in Social Culture*. New York: Kennerley.

Spock, Benjamin. 1946. *The Common Sense Book of Baby and Child Care*. New York: Duell, Sloan & Pearce.

Srole, Leo, Thomas S. Langner, Stanley T. Michael, Marvin K. Opler, and Thomas A. C. Rennie. 1962. *Mental Health in the Metropolis: The Midtown Manhattan Study*. New York: McGraw-Hill.

Stack, Carol B. 1975. *All Our Kin: Strategies for Survival in a Black Community*. New York: Harper & Row.

Stearns, Peter N. 1980. "Old Women: Some Historical Observations." *Journal of Family History* 5:44–57.

Steinem, Gloria. 1970. "'Women's Liberation' Aims to Free Men, Too." *Washington Post*, June 7, 192.

———. 2015. *My Life on the Road*. New York: Random House.

Steptoe, Andrew, Angus Deaton, and Arthur Stone. 2014. "Subjective Wellbeing, Health, and Ageing." *Lancet* 385 (9968):640–648.

Stern, Richard. 1974. "For Hal Scharlatt (1935–1974)." *New York Review of Books*, February 21, 388.

Sternbergh, Adam. 2006. "Up with Grups: The Ascendant Breed of Grown-Ups Who Are Redefining Adulthood." *New York*, April 3, 26–34.

Steward, James B. 2011. "Top Aide To a C.E.O.: Her Husband." *New York Times*, Nov. 5, B11.

Stockham, Alice B. 1887. *Tokology: A Book for Every Woman*. Chicago: Sanitary Publishing. Original edition, 1883.

Stolberg, Michael. 2007a. "Das männliche Klimakterium: Zur Vorgeschichte eines modernen Konzepts (1500–1900)." In *Männlichkeit und Gesundheit im historischen Wandel ca. 1800—ca. 2000*, edited by Martin Dinges, 105–121. Stuttgart: Steiner.

———. 2007b. "From the 'Climacteric Disease' to the 'Male Climacteric': The Historical Origins of a Modern Concept." *Maturitas* 58:111–116.

Stoler, Ann Laura. 1995. *Race and the Education of Desire: Foucault's "History of Sexuality" and the Colonial Order of Things*. Durham, NC: Duke University Press.

Stoll, Clarice Stasz. 1973a. Review of *Speed Is of the Essence*, by Gail Sheehy. *Journal of Contemporary Ethnography* 2:121–122.

———. 1973b. Review of "Cleaning Up Hell's Bedroom" and "The Landlords of Hell's Bedroom," by Gail Sheehy. *Journal of Contemporary Ethnography* 2:114–115.

Stoltzfus, Emilie. 2003. *Citizen, Mother, Worker: Debating Public Responsibility for Child Care after the Second World War*. Chapel Hill: University of North Carolina Press.

Stone, Abraham, and Lena Levine. 1956. *The Premarital Consultation: A Manual for Physicians*. New York: Grune & Stratton.

Stone, Alison. 2004. "Essentialism and Anti-Essentialism in Feminist Philosophy." *Journal of Moral Philosophy* 1 (2):135–153.

Stone, Arthur A., Joseph E. Schwartz, Joan E. Broderick, and Angus Deaton. 2010. "A Snapshot of the Age Distribution of Psychological Well-being in the United States." *Proceedings of the National Academy of Sciences* 107 (22):9985–9990.

"Student and Teacher of Human Ways: Anthropologist Margaret Mead, America's Best-Known Woman Scientist, Gives Modern America Some Tips for Improvement." 1959. *Life*, September 14, 143–148.

Surkis, Judith. 2014. "Of Scandals and Supplements: Relating Intellectual and Cultural History." In *Rethinking Modern European Intellectual History*, edited by Darrin M. McMahon and Samuel Moyn, 94–111. Oxford: Oxford University Press.

Swidler, Ann. 1980. "Love and Adulthood in American Culture." In *Themes of Work and Love in Adulthood*, edited by Neil J. Smelser and Erik H. Erikson, 120–147. Cambridge, MA: Harvard University Press.

———. 2001. *Talk of Love: How Culture Matters*. Chicago: University of Chicago Press.

Swinth, Kirsten. 2018. *Feminism's Forgotten Fights: The Unfinished Struggle for Work and Family*. Cambridge, MA: Harvard University Press.

Symonds, Alexandra. 1974. "The Liberated Woman: Healthy and Neurotic." *American Journal of Psychoanalysis* 34 (3):177–183.

Tager-Flusberg, Helen, Simon Baron-Cohen, and Donald J. Cohen, eds. 1993. *Understanding Other Minds: Perspectives from Autism*. Oxford: Oxford University Press.

Tarde, Gabriel. 1969. "Opinion and Conversation [1898]." In *Gabriel Tarde on Communication and Social Influence: Selected Papers*, edited by Terry N. Clark, 297–318. Chicago: University of Chicago Press.

Tarrant, Shira. 2009. *When Sex Became Gender*. New York: Routledge.

Tavris, Carol. 1982. "Women and Men and Morality." *New York Times*, May 2, BR14.

———. 1992. *The Mismeasure of Woman: Why Women Are Not the Better Sex, the Inferior Sex, or the Opposite Sex*. New York: Simon & Schuster.

———. 1995. "Forward to Middlescence." *New York Times*, June 25, BR15.

Taylor, Charles. 1989. *Sources of the Self: The Making of the Modern Identity*. Cambridge, MA: Harvard University Press.

Taylor, Jill McLean, Carol Gilligan, and Amy M. Sullivan. 1996. *Between Voice and Silence: Women and Girls, Race and Relationship*. Cambridge, MA: Harvard University Press.

Taylor, Walter C. 1871. *A Physician's Counsels to Woman, in Health and Disease*. Springfield, MA: Holland.

Tebbel, John William. 1981. *A History of Book Publishing in The United States*, vol. 4, *The Great Change, 1940–1980*. New York: Bowker.

Thane, Pat, ed. 2005. *The Long History of Old Age*. London: Thames & Hudson.

Theorell, Tores. 1976. "Selected Illnesses and Somatic Factors in Relation to Two Psychosocial Stress Indices: A Prospective Study on Middle-Aged Construction Building Workers." *Journal of Psychosomatic Research* 20:7–20.

Théré, Christine. 2015. "Life Change and Change of Life: Asymmetrical Attitudes towards the Sexes in Medical Discourse in France (1770–1836)." *Clio* 42:53–77.

Thoits, Peggy A. 1983. "Multiple Identities and Psychological Well-being." *American Sociological Review* 48 (2):147–187.

Thom, Mary. 1997. *Inside "Ms.": 25 Years of the Magazine and the Feminist Movement*. New York: Holt.

Thomson, Irene Taviss. 2000. *In Conflict No Longer: Self and Society in Contemporary America*. New York: Rowman & Littlefield.

———. 2005. "The Theory That Won't Die: From Mass Society to the Decline of Social Capital." *Sociological Forum* 20 (3):421–448

"Three Sticky Subjects: Kids, Oil, and Middle Age." 1978. *Esquire*, April 11, 6.

Tiedeman, David V., and Robert P. O'Hara. 1963. *Career Development: Choice and Adjustment*. New York: College Entrance Examination Board.

Tiefer, Leonore. 1986. "In Pursuit of the Perfect Penis: The Medicalization of Male Sexuality." *American Behavioral Scientist* 29:579–599.

Tilley, Helen. 2011. *Africa as a Living Laboratory: Empire, Development, and the Problem of Scientific Knowledge, 1870–1950*. Chicago: University of Chicago Press.

Tilt, Edward John. 1851a. "On the Management of Women at, and after the Cessation of, Menstruation." *Provincial Medicine and Surgery Journal* 15:281–287, 342–344, 401–404, 545–548.

———. 1851b. *On the Preservation of the Health of Women at the Critical Period of Life*. London: Churchill.

———. 1851c. "On the Right Management of Women, at First Menstruation, and during the Persistence of that Function." *Provincial Medicine and Surgery Journal* 15 (8):206–210.

————. 1851d. "On the Right Management of Young Women before the First Appearance of Menstruation." *Provincial Medicine and Surgery Journal* 15 (6):148–150.

————. 1857. *The Change of Life in Health and Disease: A Practical Treatise on the Nervous and Other Affections Incidental to Women at the Decline of Life*. London: John Churchill. Reprint, 1870.

Toffler, Alvin. 1970. *Future Shock*. New York: Random House.

Tomasello, Michael. 2009. *Why We Cooperate*. Cambridge, MA: MIT Press.

Topham, Jonathan R. 2009. "Rethinking the History of Science Popularization/Popular Science." In *Popularizing Science and Technology in the European Periphery, 1800–2000*, edited by Faidra Papanelopoulou, Agustí Nieto-Galan, and Enrique Perdiguer, 1–20. Surrey: Ashgate.

Traister, Bruce. 2000. "Academic Viagra: The Rise of American Masculinity Studies." *American Quarterly* 52 (2):274–304.

Trent, Sarah. 1934. *Women over Forty*. New York: Macaulay.

Trentmann, Frank. 2008. *Free Trade Nation: Commerce, Consumption, and Civil Society in Modern Britain*. Oxford: Oxford University Press.

Tunc, Tanfer Emin. 2010. "Talking Sex: Deciphering Dialogues of American Female Sexuality in the Mosher Survey, 1892–1920." *Journal of Women's History* 22 (1):130–153.

Twemlow, Stuart W. 2005. "Elliott Jaques on the Life and Behavior of Living Organisms." *International Journal of Applied Psychoanalytic Studies* 2:389–395.

Tyrer, Louise, Betty Friedan, Charlayne Hunter-Gault, Cora Weiss, Mary Tyler Moore, Eliza Collins, Grace Mirabella, and Lorraine Davis. 1983. "Women Now: The Open Doors: *Vogue's* Eighth Annual American Woman Symposium." *Vogue*, June, 188–195, 254–255.

United States Census Bureau. 1957. "Women Past Thirty-five in the Labor Force: 1947 to 1956." *Current Population Reports* P-50 (75).

————. 1986. *Money Income and Poverty Status of Families and Persons in the United States: 1985*. Washington, DC: GPO.

United States Cong. S. Subcomm. on the Constitution of the S. Comm. on the Judiciary. 1981. *Constitutional Amendments relating to Abortion: Hearings on S.J. Res. 18, S.J. Res. 19, and S.J. Res. 110*, 97th Cong.

United States Department of Labor. 1956. *Handbook on Women Workers*. Bulletin of the Women's Bureau no. 261.

————. 1960. *Handbook on Women Workers*. Bulletin of the Women's Bureau no. 275.

————. 1991. *The Glass Ceiling Initiative: A Report*. Washington, DC.

University Grants Committee. 1964. *University Appointments Boards: A Report by the Rt. Hon. the Lord Heyworth*. London: Her Majesty's Stationery Office.

Vaidhyanathan, Siva. 2003. *Copyrights and Copywrongs: The Rise of Intellectual Property and How It Threatens Creativity*. New York: New York University Press.

Vaillant, George E. 1977a. *Adaptation to Life*. Boston: Little, Brown.

————. 1977b. "The Climb to Maturity: How the Best and the Brightest Came of Age." *Psychology Today*, September, 34–41, 107–110.

————. 1985. "Loss as a Metaphor for Attachment." *American Journal of Psychoanalysis* 45 (1):59–67.

————. 1986. *Empirical Studies of Ego Mechanisms of Defense*. Washington, DC: American Psychiatric Press.

————. 1992. *Ego Mechanisms of Defense: A Guide for Clinicians and Researchers*. Washington, DC: American Psychiatric Press.

———. 1993. *The Wisdom of the Ego*. Cambridge, MA: Harvard University Press.

———. 2002. *Aging Well: Surprising Guideposts to a Happier Life from the Landmark Harvard Study of Adult Development*. Boston: Little, Brown.

———. 2012. *Triumphs of Experience: The Men of the Harvard Grant Study*. Cambridge, MA: Belknap.

Vaillant, George E., and Charles C. McArthur. 1972. "Natural History of Male Psychologic Health, I: The Adult Life Cycle from 18–50." *Seminars in Psychiatry* 4 (4):415–427.

Vandewater, Elizabeth A., and Abigail J. Stewart. 1997. "Women's Career Commitment Patterns and Personality Development." In *Multiple Paths of Midlife Development*, edited by Margie E. Lachman and Jacquelyn Boone James, 375–410. Chicago: University of Chicago Press.

Verbrugge, Lois M. 1982. "Women's Social Roles and Health." In *Women: A Developmental Perspective*, edited by Phyllis W. Berman and Estelle R. Ramey, 49–78. Bethesda, MD: National Institutes of Health.

Verheyen, Nina. 2014. "Age(ing) with Feeling." In Ute Frevert et al., *Emotional Lexicons: Continuity and Change in the Vocabulary of Feeling, 1700–2000*. Oxford: Oxford University Press.

Vicedo, Marga. 2013. *The Nature and Nurture of Love: From Imprinting to Attachment in Cold War America*. Chicago: University of Chicago Press.

Voss, Kimberly Wilmot, and Lance Speere. 2007. "A Women's Page Pioneer: Marie Anderson and Her Influence at the *Miami Herald* and Beyond." *Florida Historical Quarterly* 85 (4):398–421.

Wachowiak, Dale. 1977. "Counseling Inside/Out." Review of *Passages*, by Gail Sheehy. *Personnel & Guidance Journal* 55 (7):376.

Waggoner, Walter H. 1973. "Times Sq. Bookstores Sue City and Landlords for 'Harassment.'" *New York Times*, January 20, 38.

Wahl-Jorgensen, Karin. 2001. "Letters to the Editor as a Forum for Public Deliberation: Modes of Publicity and Democratic Debate." *Critical Studies in Media Communication* 18 (3):303–320.

———. 2007. *Journalists and the Public: Newsroom Culture, Letters to the Editor, and Democracy*. New York: Hampton Press.

Waite, Linda J., and Mark Nielsen. 2001. "The Rise of the Dual-Earner Family, 1963–1997." In *Working Families*, edited by Rosanna Hertz and Nancy L. Marshall, 23–41. Berkeley: University of California Press.

Walker, Lawrence. 1984. "Sex Differences in the Development of Moral Reasoning: A Critical Review." *Child Development* 55 (3):677–691.

Walker, Nancy A. 2000. *Shaping Our Mothers' World: American Women's Magazines*. Jackson: University Press of Mississippi.

Wallace, R., and D. Wallace. 1990. "Origins of Public Health Collapse in New York City: The Dynamics of Planned Shrinkage, Contagious Urban Decay and Social Disintegration." *Bulletin of the New York Academy of Medicine* 66:391–434.

"Washington Best Sellers." 1984. *Washington Post*, January 29, BW12.

Watkins, Elizabeth Siegel. 2007a. *The Estrogen Elixir: A History of Hormone Replacement Theory in America*. Baltimore: Johns Hopkins University Press.

———. 2007b. "The Medicalisation of Male Menopause in America." *Social History of Medicine* 20 (2):369–388.

———. 2008. "Medicine, Masculinity, and the Disappearance of Male Menopause in the 1950s." *Social History of Medicine* 21 (2):329–344.

Watlington, Dennis. 2006. *Chasing America: Notes from a Rock 'n' Soul Integrationist*. New York: Macmillan.

Weber, Ronald, ed. 1974. *The Reporter as Artist: A Look at the New Journalism Controversy*. New York: Hastings House.

Weed, Elizabeth, and Naomi Schor, eds. *The Essential Difference*. Bloomington: Indiana University Press.

Wegman, Myron E. 1946. Review of *Common Sense Book of Baby and Child Care*, by Benjamin Spock. *American Journal of Public Health* 36 (11):1329.

Weidman, Nadine. 2016. "Between the Counterculture and the Corporation: Abraham Maslow and Humanistic Psychology in the 1960s." In *Groovy Science: Knowledge, Innovation, and American Counterculture*, edited by David Kaiser and W. Patrick McCray, 109–141. Chicago: University of Chicago Press.

Weingarten, Marc. 2005. *The Gang That Wouldn't Write Straight*. New York: Three Rivers Press.

Weinstein, Fred, and Gerald Platt. 1975. "The Coming Crisis in Psychohistory." *Journal of Modern History* 47:202–228.

Weisman, Abner I. 1951. *Women's Change of Life*. New York: Renbayle House.

Weiss, Alexander, James E. King, Miho Inoue-Murayama, Tetsuro Matsuzawa, and Andrew J. Oswald. 2012. "Evidence for a Midlife Crisis in Great Apes Consistent with the U-Shape in Human Well-being." *Proceedings of the National Academy of Sciences of the United States of America (PNAS)* 109 (49):19949–19952.

Weiss, Jessica. 2000. *To Have and to Hold: Marriage, the Baby Boom, and Social Change*. Chicago: University of Chicago Press.

Weiss, Nancy Pottishman. 1977. "Mother, the Invention of Necessity: Dr. Benjamin Spock's *Baby and Child Care*." *American Quarterly* 29 (5):519–546.

Weissman, Myrna. 1979. "The Myth of Involutional Melancholia." *JAMA* 242 (8):742–744.

Weisstein, Naomi. 1968. *Kinder, Küche, Kirche as Scientific Law: Psychology Constructs the Female*. Boston: New England Free Press.

———. 1970. "Kinder, Küche, Kirche as Scientific Law: Psychology Constructs the Female [1968]." In *Sisterhood Is Powerful: An Anthology of Writings from the Women's Liberation Movement*, edited by Robin Morgan, 205–219. New York: Vintage.

———. 1989. "The Early Years of the Women's Liberation Movement in Chicago." *Phoebe: An Interdisciplinary Journal of Feminist Scholarship, Theory and Aesthetics* 1 (1):3–20.

Wessely, Christina. 2014. *Welteis: Eine wahre Geschichte*. Berlin: Matthes & Seitz.

West, Charles. 1858. *Lectures on the Diseases of Women*. Philadelphia: Blanchard & Lea.

Wethington, Elaine. 2000. "Expecting Stress: Americans and the 'Midlife Crisis.'" *Motivation and Emotion* 24:85–103.

Wethington, Elaine, Ronald C. Kessler, and Joy E. Pixley. 2004. "Turning Points in Adulthood." In *How Healthy Are We? A National Study of Well-being at Midlife*, edited by Orville G. Brim, 586–613. Chicago: University of Chicago Press.

Wheeler, Helen Rippier. 1997. *Women and Aging: A Guide to the Literature*. Boulder, CO: Lynne Rienner.

Whelehan, Imelda. 2005. *The Feminist Bestseller: From "Sex and the Single Girl" to "Sex and the City."* New York: Palgrave Macmillan.

Whitbourne, Susan Krauss. 1986. *The Me I Know: A Study of Adult Identity*. New York: Springer.

———. 2010. *The Search for Fulfillment: Revolutionary New Research That Reveals the Secret to Long-term Happiness*. New York: Ballantine.

———. 2012. "The Top 10 Myths about the Midlife Crisis: It's Time to Demystify the Midlife Crisis." psychologytoday.com/blog/fulfillment-any-age/201207/the-top-10 -myths-about-the-midlife-crisis (accessed December 19, 2017).

White, Cynthia L. 1970. *Women's Magazines, 1693–1968*. London: Michael Joseph.

Whitt, Jan. 2008. *Women in American Journalism: A New History*. Urbana: University of Illinois Press.

Whyte, William H. 1956. *The Organization Man*. New York: Simon & Schuster.

Wiel, Lucy van de. 2014a. "For Whom the Clock Ticks: Reproductive Ageing and Egg Freezing in Dutch and British News Media." *Studies in the Maternal* 6 (1):1–28.

———. 2014b. "The Time of the Change: Menopause's Medicalization and the Gender Politics of Aging." *International Journal of Feminist Approaches to Bioethics* 1:74–89.

———. 2015. "Frozen in Anticipation: Eggs for Later." *Women's Studies International Forum* 53:119–128.

Wilbush, Joel. 1980. "Tilt, E. J., and *The Change of Life* (1857)—The Only Work on the Subject in the English Language." *Maturitas* 2 (4):259–267.

———. 1981. "What's in a Name? Some Linguistic Aspects of the Climacteric." *Maturitas* 3:1–9.

Willer, Stefan, Sigrid Weigel, and Bernhard Jussen. 2013. *Erbe: Übertragungskonzepte zwischen Natur und Kultur*. Berlin: Suhrkamp.

Williams, Bernard. 1981. "Moral Luck." In Williams, *Moral Luck: Philosophical Papers, 1973–1980*, 20–39. Cambridge: Cambridge University Press.

Williams, Bernard, and Thomas Nagel. 1976. "Moral Luck." *Proceedings of the Aristotelian Society* 50:115–151.

Williams, Whiting. 1920. *What's on the Worker's Mind*. New York: Scribner's.

Willis, Ellen. 1975. "The Conservatism of *Ms.*" In *Feminist Revolution*, edited by Redstockings, 170–171. New Paltz, NY: Redstockings.

Wilson, Elizabeth. 1985. *Adorned in Dreams: Fashion and Modernity*. London: Virago.

Wilson, Robert A. 1966. *Feminine Forever*. New York: Evans.

Wilson, Robert A., and Thelma A. Wilson. 1963. "The Fate of the Nontreated Postmenopausal Woman: A Plea for the Maintenance of Adequate Estrogen from Puberty to the Grave." *Journal of the American Geriatrics Society* 11:347–362.

Wilson, Sloan. 1955. *The Man in the Gray Flannel Suit*. New York: Simon & Schuster.

Wind, Eddy de. 1968. "The Confrontation with Death." *International Journal of Psychoanalysis* 49 (2–3):302–305.

Wing, Lorna. 1974. *Children Apart: Autistic Children and Their Families*. London: National Society for Autistic Children.

Wing, Lorna, and Judith Gould. 1979. "Severe Impairments of Social Interaction and Associated Abnormalities in Children: Epidemiology and Classification." *Journal of Autism and Developmental Disorders* 9:11–29.

Winnicott, Donald W. 1965. *The Maturational Processes and the Facilitating Environment: Studies in the Theory of Emotional Development*. London: Hogarth.

———. 1971. *Playing and Reality*. New York: Basic Books.

———. 1988. "The Ordinary Devoted Mother [1966]." In *Babies and Their Mothers*, 1–14. London: Free Association.

Witmer, Helen. 1950. Introduction to *Symposium on the Healthy Personality: Transactions of Special Meetings of Conference on Infancy and Childhood*, edited by Milton J. E. Senn, 13–14. New York: Josiah Macy, Jr. Foundation.

Wolfe, Linda. 1972. "A Time of Change." *New York*, June 5, 68–69.

Wolfe, Tom. 1970. "Radical Chic: That Party at Lenny's." *New York*, June 8, 25–56.

———. 1976. "The 'Me' Decade and the Third Great Awakening." *New York*, August 23, 26–40.

———. 2008. "A City Built of Clay." *New York*, July 6, 16–21, 84.

Wolff, Cynthia Griffin. 1979. "Erikson's 'Inner Space' Reconsidered." *Massachusetts Review* 20 (2):355–368.

"Women Needn't Worry." 1953. Review of *The Menopause*, by Lena Levine and Beka Doherty. *Psychiatric Quarterly* 27 (1):170–171.

"Women's Lib and Me! (Our Readers Speak Out)." 1970. *Ladies' Home Journal*, 69, 74.

Woods, William Leon, Lucien Brouha, and Carl Coleman Seltzer. 1943. *Selection of Officer Candidates*. Cambridge, MA: Harvard University Press.

Worell, Judith. 1978. "Sex Roles and Psychological Well-being: Perspectives on Methodology." *Journal of Consulting and Clinical Psychology* 46:777–791.

———. 1988. "Single Mothers." *Women & Therapy* 7 (4):3–14.

———. 2000. "Feminism in Psychology: Revolution or Evolution?" *Annals of the American Academy of Political and Social Science* 571:183–196.

Work in America: Report of a Special Task Force to the Secretary of Health, Education, and Welfare. 1973. Cambridge, MA: MIT Press.

Wright, J. Patrick. 1979. *On a Clear Day You Can See General Motors: John Z. De Lorean's Look inside the Automotive Giant*. Grosse Pointe, MI: Wright.

Wylie, Philip. 1942. *Generation of Vipers*. New York: Rinehart.

———. 1963. "The Career Woman." *Playboy*, January, 117–118, 154–156.

Yankelovich, Daniel. 1981. *New Rules: Searching for Self-Fulfillment in a World Turned Upside Down*. New York: Random House.

Yankelovich, Skelly and White, Inc. 1978. *The 1978 Consumer Research Study on Reading and Book Purchasing: A Study Inquiring into the Nature of Reading and Book Buying Habits of the American Public*. New York: Book Industry Study Group.

Young, Iris Marion. 1998. "Polity and Group Difference: A Critique of the Ideal of Universal Citizenship." In *The Citizenship Debates: A Reader*, edited by Gershon Shafir, 263–290. Minneapolis, MN: University of Minnesota Press.

Zaretsky, Natasha. 2007. *No Direction Home: The American Family and the Fear of National Decline, 1968–1980*. Chapel Hill: University of North Carolina Press.

Zeisler, Andi. 2016. *We Were Feminists Once: From Riot Grrrl to CoverGirl®, the Buying and Selling of a Political Movement*. New York: PublicAffairs.

Zola, Irving Kenneth. 1972. "Medicine as an Institution of Social Control." *Sociological Review* 20 (4):487–504.

Zuckerman, Mary Ellen. 1998. *A History of Popular Women's Magazines in the United States, 1792–1995*. Westport, CT: Greenwood.

Zunz, Olivier. 1990. *Making America Corporate, 1870–1920*. Chicago: University of Chicago Press.

Index

Lightning Source UK Ltd.
Milton Keynes UK
UKHW041834130320
360318UK00002B/3

9 780226 637143